MW00643354

THREADS AND TRACES

The publisher gratefully acknowledges the generous support of the Ahmanson Foundation Humanities Endowment Fund of the University of California Press Foundation.

The publication of the present book was made possible by the contribution of the Italian Ministry of Foreign Affairs.

THREADS AND TRACES

TRUE FALSE FICTIVE

Carlo Ginzburg

Translated by Anne C. Tedeschi and John Tedeschi

UNIVERSITY OF CALIFORNIA PRESS

Berkeley   Los Angeles   London

University of California Press, one of the most distinguished
university presses in the United States, enriches lives around
the world by advancing scholarship in the humanities, social
sciences, and natural sciences. Its activities are supported by
the UC Press Foundation and by philanthropic contributions from individuals and institutions. For more
information, visit www.ucpress.edu.

University of California Press
Berkeley and Los Angeles, California

University of California Press, Ltd.
London, England

© 2012 by The Regents of the University of California

Library of Congress Cataloging-in-Publication Data

Ginzburg, Carlo.
    [Filo e le tracce. English]
    Threads and traces : true, false, fictive / Carlo Ginzburg ;
translated by Anne C. Tedeschi and John Tedeschi. —1
        p.   cm.
    Includes bibliographical references and index.
    ISBN 978-0-520-25961-4 (cloth : alk. paper)
    1. Historiography—Philosophy.   2. Literature and
history.   3. History—Errors, inventions, etc.
4. Truth.   5. Collective memory.   I. Title.
    D16.8.G536513   2012
    907.2—dc23

                                            2011020079

Manufactured in the United States of America

20   19   18   17   16   15   14   13   12
10   9   8   7   6   5   4   3   2   1

In keeping with a commitment to support environmentally
responsible and sustainable printing practices, UC Press has
printed this book on Rolland Enviro100, a 100 percent
postconsumer fiber paper that is FSC certified, deinked,
processed chlorine-free, and manufactured with renewable
biogas energy. It is acid-free and EcoLogo certified.

CONTENTS

ILLUSTRATIONS

Introduction

1. The Greeks tell us that Theseus received a thread as a gift from Ariadne. With that thread he found his bearings in the labyrinth, located the Minotaur, and slew him. The myth says nothing about the traces that Theseus left as he made his way through the labyrinth.

What holds together the chapters of this book dedicated to some highly heterogeneous topics is the relation between the thread—the thread of narration, which helps us to orient ourselves in the labyrinth of reality—and the traces.[1] I have been a historian for some time: using such traces, I seek to narrate true stories (which at times have falsehoods as their object). Today it seems to me that none of the terms of that definition (*narrate, traces, stories, true, false*) can be taken for granted. When I began to learn my craft, toward the end of the 1950s, the prevailing attitude in the guild of historians was completely different. Writing narrative history was not considered a matter for serious reflection. I remember one exception to this rule: Arsenio Frugoni, who, as I understood later, returned now and then in his seminars in Pisa to the topic of the subjective nature of the narrative sources, which he had discussed a few years earlier in his *Arnaldo da Brescia*.[2] Frugoni suggested to me—I was in my second year at the University of Pisa—that I prepare a colloquium on the school of the *Annales*, so I began to read Marc Bloch. In his *Métier d'historien* I ran into a page which many years later, though I was not fully aware of it, helped me to reflect on traces of evidence.[3] But in those days historians did not speak of traces and the trail they leave.

2. I refer to that distant background to explain to myself the unreasonable euphoria I felt when I wrote the first sentences of my first book.[4] It seemed to me that the documents on which I was working (inquisitorial trials) opened a broad range of narrative possibilities. The tendency to experiment in that direction, which also sprang from my family background, found both encouragement and limits in the sources. But I was persuaded (and still am today) that between testimonies, both narrative and nonnarrative, and the reality to which they bear witness there exists a relationship that needs to be analyzed from time to time. The possibility that someone could radically put in doubt that relation did not even enter my mind.

All this is part of the prehistory of the present book. In the second half of the 1960s the climate began to change. Some time later it was announced with great fanfare that historians write. I remember at first remaining indifferent to the hyperconstructionist (and, in fact, skeptical) implications of that revelation. It shows up in a passage of my essay "Spie" (1979), which considers the connection between deciphering traces and narration without mentioning any eventual skeptical objections.[5] The turning point came for me only when, thanks to an essay of Arnaldo Momigliano's, I realized the moral and political (as well as cognitive) implications of the thesis that basically canceled the distinction between historical and fictional narrations. The afterword that I wrote (1984) for the Italian translation of Natalie Davis's *The Return of Martin Guerre* (see chapter 4) registers that somewhat belated awareness.

Those pages might be the place to begin reading the present book since they outline a program of study and its polemical objective. Or, more precisely, its inverse, the *pars destruens* came first, as is perhaps always the case. Against the tendency of postmodern skepticism to blur the borders between fictional and historical narrations, in the name of the constructive element they share, I proposed a view of the relation between the two as a competition for the representation of reality. But rather than trench warfare, I hypothesized a conflict made up of challenges and reciprocal, hybrid borrowings. If this was how things stood, one could not combat neoskepticism by going back to old certitudes. We have to learn from the enemy in order to oppose it more efficaciously.

These are the hypotheses which, in the course of twenty years, have oriented the studies included in this volume.[6] Only gradually did I discern the significance of the challenge in Bertolt Brecht's "bad new things" (see chapter 1) or the choice of terrain on which to challenge it. Today the postmodernists seem less strident and less confident: the winds of fashion may already be blowing from another quarter, but it does not matter. The difficulties ensuing from that discussion and the attempts to resolve them remain.

3. The skeptical attack on the scholarly nature of historical narrations has emphasized their subjectivity, which allegedly likens them to fictional narratives. Historical narratives speak to us less about reality than they do about whoever has constructed them. It is useless to object that a constructive element is present to some extent even in the so-called hard sciences: they, too, have been the object of similar criticism.[7] Let us talk instead about historiography. We know that historiography has a subjective component, but the radical conclusions which the skeptics have drawn from that fact did not consider a fundamental shift about which Marc Bloch spoke in his posthumous methodological reflections: "Today [1942–1943], even in the most spontaneous and voluntary testimonies, what the text tells us no longer constitutes the primary object of our attention." The *Mémoires* of Saint-Simon or the lives of early medieval saints interest us not so much for their allusions to actual facts, which are often invented, as for the light they throw on the mentality of the writers of those texts. "Despite our inevitable subordination to the past," Bloch continues, "we have freed ourselves at least to the extent that, eternally condemned to know only by means of its 'tracks,' we are nevertheless successful in knowing far more of the past than the past itself had thought it good to tell us. . . . Properly speaking, it is a glorious victory of mind over its material."[8] In another passage in *Métier d'historien* Bloch responds to the doubts of those who lament the impossibility of ascertaining what happened in single historical events—for example, the circumstances in which the gunshots were fired that ignited the revolution of 1848 in Paris. Bloch observes that such skepticism does not touch on what lay behind the event but rather on mentalities, technology, society, and economics: "What is most profound in history may also be the most certain."[9] Against the positivist skepticism that cast doubt on the believability of one document or another, Bloch offered, on the one hand, involuntary testimonies, and on the other, the possibility of isolating within voluntary testimonies an involuntary, hence deeper, core.

Against the radically antipositivist skepticism which attacks the reliability of texts as such, one can use a line of argument that is in some way analogous to Bloch's. By digging into the texts, against the intentions of whoever produced them, uncontrolled voices can be made to emerge: for example, those of the women or men who, in witchcraft trials, eluded the stereotypes suggested by the judges. In medieval romances we can trace involuntary historical testimonies relating to habits and customs, isolating fragments of truth within the fiction. This is a discovery that today seems to us almost banal, but toward the mid–seventeenth century, in Paris, when it was explicitly formulated for the first time (chapter 5), it had a paradoxical ring to it. This was a research strategy not too different from the one Bloch describes concerning the lives of early medieval saints. In the long run, the gap opened up by this simultaneously detached and participatory attitude toward the literature of the past had unpredictable results. Three centuries later, we find the great scholar Erich Auerbach taking a similar path in his analysis of Voltaire and Stendhal when he read the *Lettres philosophiques* and *Le Rouge et le Noir* not as historical documents but as texts impregnated with history. Interpretation is infinite, even though its contents are not unlimited: Auerbach's interpretations can be read in a different perspective, following the intentions and the perspective of their author, by making use of the traces that he himself left more or less involuntarily (chapters 7 and 10). Fiction, fed by history, becomes material for historical reflection or else for fiction, and so on. This unpredictable intermingling can come together in a knot, or in a name (chapter 9).

Reading historical testimonies against the grain, as Walter Benjamin suggested—that is, against the intentions of the person or persons producing them (even if those intentions must of course be taken into account)—means supposing that every text includes uncontrolled elements.[10] The same can be said of literary texts that strive to present an autonomous reality. Something opaque insinuates itself into them as well, much like the perceptions that sight registers without understanding them, as does the impassible eye of the camera. This is a theme that Siegfried Kracauer acquired from Proust, who in turn was reworking a passage of Saint-Simon (chapter 13). These opaque zones are some of the traces which a text—any text—leaves behind. I have found them when I sought to reflect on my own studies in two experiments suggested by temporal distance (and, in one case, spatial distance as well: chapters 14 and 15).

4. To draw up an inventory of the forms taken on by fiction in the service of truth would obviously be impossible. The human and intellectual generosity that inspired Montaigne to write his essay on Brazilian cannibals had ab-

sorbed something from the mannerist taste for the grotesque and bizarre (chapter 3). The thin narrative thread of the *Voyage du jeune Anacharsis en Grèce* enabled Jean-Jacques Barthélemy to organize an enormous mass of antiquarian data, making them accessible, in the span of a century, to a vast public scattered throughout Europe (chapter 8). Montaigne is considered an exception; Barthélemy, at most an anomaly. But both men refer back to a choice that shaped, without my being aware of it at first, much of the physiognomy of the present book. Given that it is an area infested with commonplaces and generalities, the relation between historical narration and fictional narration had to be confronted in the most concrete manner possible, through a series of examples. Chapter 6, which seeks to reconstruct "not the exception but the rule," falls within this viewpoint, but, to be accurate, it treats an exception. In retrospect, I realized that most of the topics discussed were not illustrations or examples referring to a preexistent norm, but rather *cases:* stories (or histories) in miniature which, according to the definition of André Jolles, pose a question without furnishing the answer, thus signaling an unsolved difficulty.[11] When I began to work on documents which speak of a Jew who was the only surviving witness to the extermination of his community, I thought that cases like this one showed just how unsustainable the position was of the skeptics who, de facto, equated fictional narration and historical narration. If an account is based on a single document, how is it possible to avoid questioning its authenticity (chapter 12)? At almost the same time, I found myself asking the very same question about a text from the fifth century, a letter of Bishop Severus of Minorca (chapter 2) recounting an early case of Christian-Jewish conflict. Here the *unus testis*, the only surviving witness, is a document, not an individual, as also occurs in medieval legal writings which reflect on the characteristics of a community (*universitas*) through the fictional case of a unique survivor.[12]

5. From the thicket of relations between fiction and truth we have seen a third term emerge: the false, the nonauthentic—the pretense that advertises itself as true.[13] Naturally, after Marc Bloch (*Les rois thaumaturges*) and Georges Lefebvre (*La grande peur de 1789*), no one will think it useless to study false legends, false events, or false documents, but it is indispensable to take a preliminary stand, on each occasion, about their falsity or authenticity. On this point I have nothing to add regarding the infamous anti-Semitic *Protocols*

of the Elders of Zion (chapter II). I have limited my efforts to a parallel reading of the fabricated *Protocols* and their principal source, the imaginary dialogue of Maurice Joly. From this comparison sprout not only many very bad old things but also some "bad new things," unpleasant truths which merit reflection.

Historians, Aristotle tells us (*Poetics* 51b), speak of what has been (of the true, of the real world); and poets, of what might have been (of the possible). But, of course, truth is a point of arrival, not a point of departure. The historian's craft (and, in a different way, the poet's) involves something that is part of everyone's life: untangling the strands of the true, the false, and the fictional which are the substance of our being in the world.

Bologna, December 2005

CHAPTER 1

Description and Citation

FOR ARNALDO MOMIGLIANO

1. Today, for some people, words such as *truth* and *reality* have become impossible to utter unless they are set off by quotation marks, written out or mimed.[1] This ritual gesture, common in American academic circles even before becoming a fairly standard practice, was meant to exorcise the specter of a thoughtless positivism: the attitude of those who hold that reality is knowable directly without intermediaries. Behind this often encountered polemic one usually comes across a skeptical position, variously argued. Moral, political, and intellectual objections have been formulated against it, even by me. But to simply keep ourselves virtuously aloof from the exaggerations of the positivists and the skeptics would serve no purpose. Walter Benjamin recalls a Brechtian maxim: "Don't start from the good old things but the bad new ones."[2] Skeptics and deconstructionists almost always react to real questions in a dramatically inadequate way. Elsewhere I have argued against their responses, but here I would like to consider some of their basic assumptions.[3]

2. A false statement, a true statement, and an invented statement do not present any differences among themselves, from a formal point of view. When Emile Benveniste studied the tenses of the French verb he did not hesitate to use examples taken from both romances and histories.[4] In a short novel entitled *Pontius Pilate* Roger Caillois astutely explored the implications of this analogy.[5] It is nighttime: the next morning Jesus will be tried. Pilate has not yet decided on the sentence. To persuade him to choose condemnation, someone predicts a long series of events that would follow the death of Jesus: some

are important, others are insignificant—but, as the reader grasps, all are true. The next day Pilate decides to absolve the accused. The disciples repudiate Jesus; the history of the world takes a different path. The affinity between fiction and history brings to mind those paintings by Magritte which without a break portray a landscape and its reflection in a broken mirror.

To say that a historical narrative resembles a fictional one is obvious enough. More interesting is to ask ourselves why we perceive as real the events recounted in a work of history. Usually it is a result produced by both textual and extratextual elements. I shall focus on the latter and attempt to show some procedures, associated with literary conventions, with which both ancient and modern historians have attempted to communicate that "effect of reality" which they considered an essential part of the task they had set for themselves.[6]

3. We can begin with a fragment from the *Universal History* of Polybius (34: 4, 4), quoted by Strabo. To demonstrate Homer's truthfulness, Polybius writes: "The object of history is truth, as when in the catalogue of ships the poet describes the features of the several localities, calling one city 'rocky,' another 'frontier-placed,' another 'with wealth of doves,' or 'hard by the sea.' But the object of picturesque detail is vividness, as when he introduces men fighting; and that of mythological allusion is to give pleasure or rouse wonder." In opposing history to myth, Homer stands squarely on the side of history and of truth: the purpose *(telos)* to which his poetry tends is in fact "vividness" *(enargeian)*.

In some manuscripts we find *energeian* rather than *enargeian*, but the context makes us think that the second is the more convincing reading.[7] A similar confusion occurs in the manuscript tradition of a passage of Aristotle's *Rhetoric* (1411 b, 33–34), echoed in much later texts and coming down to our own day.[8] In actual fact, the two words have nothing in common: *energeia* signifies "act, activity, energy"; *enargeia*, "clarity, vividness."[9] The importance of the first term in Aristotelian terminology, decisive for the European intellectual lexicon, explains why *energeia* has survived in so many languages: it suffices to think of "energia," "energy," "énergie," and so forth. *Enargeia* instead died out. But it is possible to reconstruct its meaning: more precisely, the constellation of meanings that revolve about it.[10]

In the Homeric poems, often seen as supreme examples of *enargeia*, the word does not appear.[11] We find *enargés*, associated with the "manifest presence" of the gods (*Iliad*, 20: 131; *Odyssey*, 16: 161), and a connected adjective, *argos*, which signifies "white, brilliant"—like a goose, like an ox—or "rapid." According to Pierre Chantraine, "we must suppose at its origin a notion that expresses both the blinding whiteness of lightning and velocity."[12] *Enargés* can be translated, depending on the context, as "clear" or "tangible." Like *enargeia*, it is a word that can be connected to a sphere of immediate experience, as another fragment from Polybius suggests (20: 12, 8): "To see an operation with one's eyes is not like merely hearing a description of it. It is, indeed, quite another thing; and the confidence which such vivid experience gives is always greatly advantageous. . . ."[13] This passage, as well as Homer's cited above, concerns historical knowledge. In both, *enargeia* is considered a guarantee of truth.

The ancient historian had to communicate the truth regarding that of which he was speaking by using *enargeia* to move and convince his readers: a technical term which, according to the author of the treatise *On the Sublime* (15: 2), marked the aim of the orators, which was different from that of the poets, who attempted to enthrall their public. The Latin rhetorical tradition repeatedly tried to find terms equivalent to *enargeia*. Quintilian (*Institutio Oratoria*, 4: 2, 63) proposed *evidentia in narratione*. "Palpability, as far as I understand the term, is no doubt a great virtue, when a truth requires not merely to be told, but to some extent obtruded, still it may be included under lucidity."[14] In another passage (6: 2, 32), Quintilian noted that Cicero had used, as synonyms for *enargeia*, *illustratio* and *evidentia*, "*illumination* and *actuality*, which makes us seem not so much to narrate as to exhibit the actual scene, while our emotions will be no less actively stirred than if we were present at the actual occurrence."[15] In effect, for Cicero, "*inlustris . . . oratio*" indicated "the part of the speech that places, in a matter of speaking, the fact before the eyes."[16] The anonymous author of the *Rhetorica ad Herennium* used similar words to define *demonstratio*: "It is ocular demonstration when an event is so described in words that the business seems to be enacted and the subject to pass vividly before our eyes."[17]

Demonstratio. The terminology corresponding to this word in the European languages—*dimostrazione, demonstration, démonstration,* and so forth—conceals under a Euclidean veil a rhetorical nucleus. *Demonstratio* designated the orator's gesture that indicated an invisible object, rendering it almost palpable—*enargés*—to the listener, thanks to the almost magical power of the words themselves.[18] Similarly, the historian succeeded in communicating to readers his own experience—direct, as a witness, or indirect—placing an invisible reality before their eyes. *Enargeia* was a means to communicate the *autopsia*—in other words, immediate vision—by virtue of style.[19]

4. Even Demetrius, the author of the famous treatise *On Style* (long erroneously identified with Demetrius of Phalerum), dedicated a relatively long section to *enargeia*, describing it as a stylistic effect that ensues from a description which contains nothing superfluous. After citing a Homeric simile (*Iliad*, 21: 257), he observed: "We shall treat first of vividness, which arises from an exact narration overlooking no detail and cutting out nothing."[20] Further on, however, we run into a broader definition, which identifies as examples of "vividness" even the cacophony and the onomatopoeic words used by Homer. We seem to have veered away from the discussion of historical method from which we began, but only apparently so. The definition of *enargeia* as an accumulation of particulars casts an unexpected light on the claim, recurring among Greek historians, that they have recorded every event, or at least all the significant ones.[21] In a society in which archives were rare and oral culture still dominated, Homer offered historians a model that was both stylistic and cognitive.

In chapter 1 of *Mimesis*, Erich Auerbach juxtaposed two different types of narration: Homer's analytical richness and the Bible's synthetic concision. The importance of the Homeric narrative style for the birth in Greece of a new way to represent the human body on the one hand, and of history as a literary genre on the other, has been underlined by E. H. Gombrich and Hermann Strasburger.[22] The latter, one of the scholars who has most profitably discussed the theoretical implications of *enargeia*, has noted that the term assumed a more technical significance in the Hellenistic age, when historians such as Duris of Samos and his disciple Philarchus created a new type of historiography, inspired by the tragic poets and aspiring to mimetic effects.[23]

5. Thus far we have portrayed *enargeia* as a notion bordering historiography and rhetoric, but painting needs to be added to this semantic sphere. Here is a metaphor taken from Plato's dialogue the *Statesman*: "And our discussion might be compared to a picture of some living being which had been fairly drawn in outline, but had not yet attained the life and clearness which is given by the blending of colours."[24]

These implications of *enargeia* emerge fully, at a distance of many centuries, in a passage from the *Images* of Philostratus the Younger, a famous collection of descriptions (*ekphraseis*) of artworks, presumably imaginary. We read the following passage in an account of a painting representing the shield of Pyrrhus, inspired by one of the shields of Achilles in the *Iliad*, the model for this literary genre: "And if you should also notice the herd of cattle which press forward to their pasture followed by the herdsmen, you might not, indeed, marvel at the colour, although the whole scene is made of gold and tin, but the fact that you can almost hear the cows lowing in the painting and that the river along the banks of which are the cows seems to be making a splashing sound,—is not that the height of vividness [*enargeia*]?"[25]

This rhetorical query could be compared to an orator's gesturing: a *demonstratio* intended to present an invisible object, made vivid and almost tangible by the power of the *ekphrasis*. At this point we can grasp why Plutarch, in his treatise *De gloria athenensium* ("On the Fame of the Athenians") (347a), compared a painting by Euphranor representing the battle of Mantinea to Thucydides' description of that same battle. Plutarch praised the pictorial vivacity [*graphiké enargeia*] of Thucydides; then he clarified the theoretical implications of the comparison:

> Simonides, however, calls painting inarticulate poetry and poetry articulate painting: for the actions which painters portray as taking place at the moment literature narrates and records after they have taken place. Even though artists with colour and design, and writers with words and phrases, represent the same subjects, they differ in the material and the manner of their imitation; and yet the underlying end and aim of both is one and the same; the most effective historian is he who, by a vivid representation of emotions and characters, makes his narration like a painting. Assuredly Thucydides is always striving for this vividness in his writing, since it is his desire to make the reader a spectator, as it were, and to produce vividly in the minds of those who peruse his narrative the emotions of amazement and consternation which were experienced by those who beheld them.[26]

6. Some of the leading authorities on Greek and Roman history have recognized in the *ekphrasis*, along with Plutarch, the purpose of historical narration. The *ekphrasis*, writes Hermann Strasburger, was a concept embracing an extensive sphere containing pathos-ridden battle scenes, the Athens plague about which Thucydides spoke, and geographic and ethnographic

descriptions *(ekphraseis tou topou).*[27] If *enargeia* was the purpose of the *ekphrasis*, truth was the result of *enargeia.*[28] We can imagine a sequence of this type: historical narration—description—vividness—truth. The difference between our concept of history and that of the ancients could be summed up as follows: for the Greeks and Romans historical truth was based on *evidentia* (the Latin equivalent of *enargeia* proposed by Quintilian); for us, on evidence.[29]

This is not an oversimplification. In a passage of the *Institutio Oratoria* (4: 2, 64–65) Quintilian observed that there were those who protested against the use of *evidentia in narratione:* "Some, however, regard this quality as actually being injurious at times, on the ground that in certain cases it is desirable to obscure the truth. The contention is, however, absurd. For he who desires to obscure the situation will state what is false in lieu of the truth, but must still strive to secure an appearance of palpability for the facts which he narrates."[30]

This fair-minded description of the comportment of lawyers could have been extended to historians, given the intimate relationship between history and rhetoric. The definitive criterion of truth did not correspond to the reactions of the public. And yet truth was considered above all a question of persuasion, linked only marginally to an objective weighing of the facts.

7. For historians who, from the sixteenth century on, considered themselves heirs of Herodotus, Thucydides, and Livy, this was an obvious conclusion. The breach emerged later. Only in the second half of the seventeenth century did one begin to analyze systematically the differences between primary and secondary sources. In his famous essay "Ancient History and the Antiquarian," Arnaldo Momigliano demonstrated that this decisive contribution to the historical method came from antiquarians who used nonliterary evidence to reconstruct facts connected to religion, to political or administrative institutions, to the economy—spheres not touched upon by historians tendentiously oriented toward political and military history and toward the present. In the face of the corrosive criticism, sometimes taken to paradoxical limits, which skeptics like La Mothe Le Vayer directed against Greek and Roman historians, antiquarians objected that medals, coins, statues, and inscriptions offered a mass of much more solid documentary material, and more reliable, as well, compared to literary sources polluted by errors, superstitions, or lies.

Modern historical writing came into being from the convergence—actually realized for the first time in the work of Edward Gibbon—between two different intellectual traditions: Voltaire's type of *histoire philosophique* and antiquarian research.[31]

8. But the trajectory vigorously argued by Momigliano should be moved up by a century. In the mid–sixteenth century both the crisis of the skeptics and its dissipation as a consequence of antiquarian labors were lucidly formulated by a philologist and antiquarian of exceptional qualities, Francesco Robortello of Udine. He is known today especially for a pioneering work on the emendation of ancient texts (1557), which has received the attention it deserves.[32] The few solid pages written on Robortello's *De historica facultate disputatio* (1548) have instead met a different fate. Its success in the sixteenth century, exemplified by its posthumous inclusion in the first collection of writings on the historical method (*Artis historicae penus*, 1579), was often followed, in times closer to our own, by befuddled and superficial readings.[33]

Robortello was fully cognizant of the originality of these pages. He was little more than thirty years old, teaching at the University of Pisa and a friend of the great philologist Pier Vettori. In his usual aggressive tone, Robortello declared in his dedication to Lelio Torelli (the philologist and jurist who a few years later would publish for the first time the famous Florentine manuscript of the *Pandects*) that he had tried to accomplish something totally new: to bring to light the art and method hidden in historical writing.

The purpose of the historian, Robortello begins, is narration, although immediately afterward he clarifies this: the historian is the one who "narrates and explains." This is followed by still another elucidation: the historian explains "the actions carried out by men themselves" (*quas ipsi homines gerunt*). The historian does not invent, but explains (*non est effictor rerum, sed explanator*). History is different from poetry, and, perhaps, in suggesting examples of what is just and unjust, it is superior to philosophy. The importance of this last statement emerges a few pages later when Robortello cites the critique, which he considered unpublished, attributed to Sextus Empiricus, "a Greek author who has expounded all the ideas of the Pyrrhonists." This is followed by a long quotation, translated into Latin but with a sprinkling of Greek words and phrases, from the treatise *Adversus mathematicos* (1: 252–260), a key and, in a sense, unique source on Greek skepticism.

Robortello was justifiably proud to have drawn attention to the novelty of this quotation. At that particular moment Sextus Empiricus was still primarily just a name. He would make his grand entrance in European philosophy in 1562 when Henri Estienne translated his *Outlines of Pyrrhonism* into Latin.[34] It has been said that before that, Sextus had only one modern reader, Gian Francesco Pico, author of an *Examen vanitatis doctrinae gentium* ("Examination of the Vacuity of Pagan Philosophy"), a harsh critique written in the name of the intransigent Christianity of Savonarola, of whom he was a follower. This vast work, based on the still-unpublished writings of Sextus, contained pages used by Robortello almost thirty years later.[35] But Robortello may not have seen them: even if he had, in any case, he used the Greek text, probably MS. Laur. 85, 11, dated 1465, which includes two works by Sextus: the *Outlines of Pyrrhonism* and the *Adversus mathematicos*.[36]

The second part of the latter work deals with the grammarians, some of whom—the celebrated Dionysius, surnamed Thrax, among them—had maintained that grammar has a historical component.[37] Sextus Empiricus objected that history lacks method: it is not a *techné* (in Latin, *ars*) but a simple accumulation of facts, irrelevant, doubtful, or mythical. Against this, Robortello attempted to demonstrate the existence of an *ars historica*: a polemical expression which inspired the title of an anthology such as the *Artis historicae penus*, conceived as a response, though too polemical, to the spread of skepticism about historiography.[38]

Robortello begins his argument by affirming that the methodological element in history is identifiable with rhetoric. In fact, he concedes, the ancients, as Cicero reminds us (*De oratore* 2), wrote annals totally lacking in method, free of rhetorical preoccupations. But if we invent (*effingantur*) speeches and actions that are probable and appropriate, as Thucydides did, we can see clearly that rhetoric is the mother of history.

Robortello's position has been identified with this response, which in itself had nothing especially original about it.[39] It has not been noted that the insistence on the capacity to invent (*effingere*) speeches contradicted the previous statement about the historian who does not invent but, rather, explains (*non est effictor rerum, sed explanator*). Above all, it has not been noticed that immediately thereafter, Robortello takes a different approach.

The historian deals with actions, both public and private: and thus necessarily with the names of the persons involved in them. This, Robortello states, is the particular element ("what Alcibiades did or experienced") which Aristotle had identified in history, setting it against the universality of poetry. Behind this statement are Robortello's labors on two books appearing that very year—1548: the commentary to the *Poetics* of Aristotle, and an erudite piece, *De nominibus Romanorum (On Roman Names)*. The name, that *datum* which is the backbone of the annalistic genre, brings along with it a reflection on the nature of historical narration. In the praise which Aristotle lavishes on Homer for having initiated his narrations in the middle of things (*in media res*), Robortello reads an implicit invitation to historians to follow, instead, a chronological sequence, to recount "a long series of years." Even if, Robortello muses, the hypothesis of a new cyclical beginning suggested by certain philosophers was true, historians must resolve to recount history commencing with those crude, rough beginnings of the human species that have been described by the poets: "But if the historian has to dedicate himself to this long progression of years, clearly his competence must embrace all of antiquity: all that which concerns customs, the means of supporting oneself, the foundation of cities, the migrations of people."

Thus, for Robortello history is synonymous with antiquarianism, although quite different from that congeries of trivial facts ridiculed by Sextus Empiricus. And he goes on to say:

> Let Thucydides set an example for us, who in the sixth book explains in a detailed and truthful manner the antiquity of the cities and peoples in all of Sicily. And since to know these antiquities the remains of old buildings, the inscriptions cut into marble, gold, bronze, and silver are extremely useful, he must take these into account. And once again Thucydides (is there perchance need to seek out any other authority than that of such an illustrious historian?) establishes [*probat*], on the basis of an inscription cut into a marble in the Acropolis as a warning to posterity, something that many had forgotten: Hippias the Athenian was a tyrant, and had fathered five sons.[40]

With a sure eye Robortello had selected a page in Thucydides (6: 54–55) which made his case: an argument which transformed a fragment of an inscription into evidence. He had accepted an invitation to broaden the framework of the research. Since history is a component of rhetoric, it has to embrace everything that rhetoric encompasses: political systems, the election of magistrates, the operation of courts, the military art. History must describe "rivers, lakes, swamps, mountains, plains, the sites of cities"—an allusion to Lucian, who is specifically mentioned at the end of the piece: "The best author of history must possess two things principally: political intelligence and expressive ability."[41]

These were not abstract admonitions on Robortello's part. (During his activity as antiquarian and philologist he emended a series of passages in Livy on the basis of inscriptions—a chapter in his long, corrosive controversy with Carlo Sigonio.)[42] Instead, he quietly dropped the grandiose project, outlined in the *Disputatio*, to combine political history and antiquarianism.

9. Robortello's writings teemed with ideas and contradictions. He defended history from the accusation made by Sextus Empiricus that it lacked method because of its relationship to rhetoric: but what Robortello meant by the term *rhetoric* was not clear. Earlier he had identified it with fictional speeches in Thucydides, later with the interpretation—it, too, using Thucydides as an example—of nonliterary evidence from an antiquarian perspective. These two meanings for rhetoric were not necessarily incompatible: in Aristotle's *Rhetoric* evidence had great importance.[43] But Robortello seemed to hesitate on this point. After having rejected annals, following Cicero, for their stylistic crudeness, Robortello resurrected them under the table as the chronological framework for antiquarian history which had its origins in the distant past. This rehabilitation of annals, cautiously proposed, found an unforeseen opportunity for development in the Paduan environment, already the scene of the Robortello–Sigonio controversy.

According to a traditional definition, annals were a sort of intermediate genre between history and antiquarianism.[44] The grammarian Verrius Flaccus, quoted by Aulus Gellius (*Noctes Atticae*, 5: 18), affirmed: "Some think that history differs from annals in this particular, that while each is a narrative of events, yet history is properly an account of events in which the narrator took part."[45] This distinction (about which Flaccus actually nurtured some doubts) was resurrected some centuries later in the great encyclopedic work by Isidore of Seville (*Etymologiae*, 1, 44): "The difference between history and annals resides in the fact that history concerns periods which we have been able to see, while annals deal with years which our age has not known."[46] Naturally history was considered a much more complex genre than annals. As Gellius wrote, resting on the authority of Sempronius Asellio, history revealed not only what had taken place but also with what intention and for what reason [*quo consilio quaque ratione*] it had taken place.

These definitions must be kept in mind when weighing the controversial implications of the thesis advanced by Sperone Speroni (1500–1588) in his unfinished *Dialogo della Istoria*, a writing on which he was hard at work up to the time of his death.[47] The dialogue, in two parts, consists of a discussion, which is imagined to have taken place in Rome among the scholar Paolo Manuzio, son of the famous Venetian printer Aldus; Silvio Antoniano, secretary of the College of Cardinals from 1568; and the Paduan philosopher Girolamo Zabarella.[48] In the first part Zabarella describes an unpublished "booklet" by Pietro Pomponazzi on history. (No copies of it are known today.) It was not "a complete and separate work, as are others published by the same author, but rather a commentary."[49] Pomponazzi had given the "booklet" to be copied to one of his students, who at the time was twenty-one or twenty-two years old. The latter, still living in Padua, "now more than eighty-six years of age," had given his own copy to Zabarella. The student, naturally, was Speroni himself, and Pomponazzi's "booklet" would have been written in 1520 or 1521.[50]

The thesis of Peretto, as Pomponazzi was familiarly called, was simple. Repudiating the contemptuous view that went back to Cicero, Peretto argued that annals, although crude stylistically, were of greater value than history, being the very foundation of it. In the penultimate draft of part 1 of the *Dialogo della Istoria*, Speroni gave ample attention, using Zabarella's own words, to his old teacher's reasoning. Although "annals can be found in the world only in pieces, like the statues of citizens, and the arches and temples of the city," Zabarella observed, "[i]f you know them well and reason about them so as to be able to teach them, it would appear as if nothing has been lost." The tales narrated in annals "are in the judgment of my booklet the most faithful, and most useful and most honored . . . that the human hand can record. I say the hand, and not industriousness, or intelligence, to indicate how simple and pure and clear and open their facts are, that it is almost as if first they were written, before being uttered or thought about."[51]

Simple, pure, clear, open: through Zabarella, his spokesman, Speroni expressed unqualified hostility toward rhetoric and its flourishes. In another writing, the *Dialogo secondo Virgilio*, Speroni attributed similar dissatisfaction to the Aristotelian philosopher Pietro Trapolino (Trapolin). After saying that "the *Aeneid* by its very nature is history, but has much that is poetry about it," Trapolin further clarified that "the *Decades* of Livy are certainly history in spite of the many orations they contain to puff them up, which smack too much of rhetoric and its causes."[52] In this dig against the city's glory by the Paduan Speroni, using the words of his fellow citizen Trapolino, teacher and later colleague of Pomponazzi, the thesis of the superiority of annals expounded in the latter's "booklet" is once again visible.[53]

But other passages in Speroni reveal a more conciliatory attitude.[54] In the *Dialogo della Istoria*, Silvio Antoniano intervenes in the discussion on the correctness of including fictitious speech in a work of history, and proposes a compromise solution. We need to allow the good historian "for the pleasure of the reader, to embellish the truth, just as in the construction of palaces the marble is decorated with carvings and the interiors with paintings; and these two exertions are not the work of the builder, but of the painter and the sculptor."[55] Fictitious speech in the mouths of the leaders of armies or of conspiracies is acceptable as ornamentation, but on one condition: that it be indicated as direct discourse. If, instead, the historian "offers it in his own name with a roundabout narration, it makes it seem that he is affirming as something he experienced, as if it were part of history, what he does not know, not having been present, and those who had been present having had something else to do other than string together words, in order to attribute them to the writer."[56]

When Speroni was comparing the speeches of historians to the paintings which adorned palaces, he may have been thinking of the frescoes executed twenty years earlier by Paolo Veronese for the Villa Barbaro built at Maser by Andrea Palladio. Gazing upon the images created by Veronese, which for an instant deceive the spectator's eye with their splendid, subtle clarity, Speroni might have evoked the *enargeia*, the vividness of ancient rhetoric (figure 1). But where historical works were concerned, Speroni's patience with ornamentation had definite limits. A lasting deception, an indirect speech passed off as authentic, would have violated the responsibility of the historian toward truth.

These rigid views corresponded to some broached by Pomponazzi in his memorable discussion with the Greek humanist Janus Lascaris, which we can read in another of Speroni's writings, *Dialogo delle lingue*.[57] This was noted by Paolo Manuzio, one of the interlocutors in the *Dialogo della Istoria*: "Peretto was very fond . . . of the truth simply presented, without concern for the latinity of the language: and therefore he always read the text of his Aristotle in ancient translations, paying little notice to the elegant versions of the

FIGURE 1. Paolo Veronese, frescoes of Villa Barbaro: child opening door.

teachers of the two languages, who imitated Cicero; and thus this may be how his apparent affection for annals came about. . . ."[58]

And, turning to Zabarella, he concluded: "Subtly you compare the truth of the annals to the premises of syllogism and to the principles of the sciences, and to the truth of particular histories, which are dependent on annals, to syllogistic conclusions. . . ."[59]

The provocative originality of the glorification of annals as the kernel of historiography was grasped by Alvise Mocenigo, Speroni's intimate friend who was copying the penultimate version of the *Dialogo della Istoria*. "I am fully aware," Mocenigo commented, "that the history which serves all functions is none other than the annal; that the others are for the glory of their writers for the use of their readers; and without them we would proceed quite blindly in our deliberations, because through them, as in other things, the best principle comes from experience, which is founded on the annal, which treasures its memory, and serves as guide for the consideration of the future."[60]

In an ambience which had experienced Robortello's teaching and writings, Pomponazzi's ideas on history were accepted with less difficulty. Only the discovery of the lost "booklet" would permit us to reintroduce those ideas in their original context. But why did Speroni resurrect them almost seventy years later?

The answer probably lies in the presence among the interlocutors of the *Dialogo della Istoria* of Silvio Antoniano, from 1568 secretary of the College of Cardinals and vice-rector of the University of Rome, "La Sapienza." In the moment when the aged Speroni was proclaiming, through Pomponazzi's "booklet," the superiority of annals over histories, Antoniano was receiving from Caesar Baronius the text of the first volume of the just-completed *Annales Ecclesiastici* so that he could give his approval before its publication (1588). It could not have been by chance. Speroni was rehabilitating the themes and the terms of the old battle fought by Pomponazzi for the truth of things against verbal embellishment, and he was restating them in a completely different context, putting them in the service of the *Ecclesiastical Annals*, that great and learned anti-Protestant undertaking, conceived in the circles of the Oratory of San Filippo Neri, with which both Baronius and Antoniano were in close contact.[61]

10. Annals and history, as we have seen, were traditionally looked upon as very different literary genres. The former, oriented toward the reconstruction of remote events, were considered more closely related to erudition than to rhetoric. Initially, Baronius had conceived writing a *Historia ecclesiastica controversa*: a title that presumably presupposed a very different type of work than what was eventually produced.[62] The decision to orient himself toward the annal was certainly dictated by the desire to counter with facts the Protestant historiography of the Centuriators of Magdeburg. But this choice was then justified on religious, not just controversialist, grounds. In the general introduction to the first tome of the *Annales Ecclesiastici*, published in 1588, Baronius declared that he had wanted to avoid the pagan custom (actually not just pagan)

of introducing long fictional passages, intertwined with rhetorical flourishes. Rather, he had preferred to obey Christ's injunction: "Let what you say be simply 'yes' or 'no'; anything more than this comes from evil" (Matt. 5:37).[63]

Tension between religion and rhetoric, and attempts to bridge it, have occurred frequently in Christian history. Think, for example, of the famous letter in which St. Jerome tells of having dreamed of Jesus in the guise of a judge condemning him to be flogged, reproaching him for being more Ciceronian than Christian.[64] In the case of Baronius, the exclusion of fictional speech, imposed by the genre of annals, was in accord with antirhetorical views based on lean, unadorned discourse inspired (or at least looked upon with favor) by St. Philip Neri, the founder of the Congregation of the Oratory. The search for truth, to Baronius, seemed incompatible with polished and stylistically homogeneous speech. He used to say that he avoided commentaries as much as possible, relying on the words he found in the sources themselves, even if rough and inelegant, "quamvis horridula et incomposita."[65] The brusque stylistic dissonance created by the insertion of terms taken from documents dating to late antiquity or the Middle Ages was emphasized typographically by the notes. What he had written, Baronius declared, was based not on the chatter of the ignorant (*indoctas fabulas*), but on the most reliable witnesses, easily recognizable in the margins of his pages, without having to look up a long list of authors.[66]

11. The marginal notes, referenced in the text of the *Annales Ecclesiastici* by a lowercase letter, indicate the beginning of the citation, introduced by verbs such as *inquit, ait, tradit, dicit, scribit,* and so forth. The end of the citation is generally marked by a square parenthesis (]). The use of typographical marks in the left-hand margin of the page (") to indicate quotations had been in use for more than half a century.[67] The employment of marginal notes is supposed to have come later.[68]

Citations, as well as notes and the linguistic-typographical marks that accompany them, can be considered as equivalents of *enargeia* since they are procedures intended to communicate an effect of authenticity. Naturally, these were conventional signs: for Sperone Speroni, we recall, direct discourse (presumably preceded by quotation marks) announced fictional speech. But the similarity of the functions highlights the difference among the tools. *Enargeia* was connected to a culture based on oral communication and hand gestures; the marginal citations, the cross-references to the text, and the bracketed parentheses, to a culture dominated by printing. *Enargeia* attempted to communicate the illusion of the proximity of the past; the citations emphasized that the past is approachable only in an indirect, mediated manner.

12. In 1636 a treatise entitled *Dell'arte historica* appeared in Rome. Its author, the Jesuit Agostino Mascardi, argued, against Speroni, that the search for causes pertained to philosophers, not historians.[69] Mascardi's approach was primarily rhetorical and stylistic. Astutely he analyzed the stylistic processes that had been used by both ancient and modern historians, among which was *enargeia*, which he italianized as *enargia*, and distinct from *energeia*, thereby disagreeing with Julius Caesar Scaliger.[70] This attention to the language of historians was accompanied by a lack of interest in the sources, with a notable exception. Mascardi noted that ancient Greece was without "the archives which right up to today we find among us and that in every nation are considered venerable and sacrosanct for preserving writings, especially public documents." But historians should not deceive themselves, even where archives exist: "Princes conduct . . . their affairs with such great secrecy that to penetrate their inner workings is of greater difficulty than even to decipher the riddle of the Sphinx."[71] In some rather lively writing, Mascardi, author of a work on the conspiracy of Gianluigi Fieschi, observed that the doings of sovereigns leave either no trace or distorted and misleading ones in the reports of their ambassadors.[72] For Mascardi history was essentially political history. He utters nary a word about Baronius's *Annales Ecclesiastici*, a European best seller which had become the target of ferocious attacks. About antiquarian research, Mascardi spoke with obvious complacency in a passage that alluded, without naming it, to the *Museo cartaceo* of Cassiano dal Pozzo: "The relics of the arches of Constantine and Septimius in Rome, the last relics of the voracity of time and the pride of the barbarians, the two columns of Trajan and Antoninus, entirely figured in bas-relief, contain records that are so beautiful, that antiquarians have copied many things from them, to enrich their very learned books: many military costumes, many weapons of war, many adornments of triumphs, and much else have been taken from these books of marble and transferred to paper books to teach us all. But I have not proposed memorials of this kind as subjects for the art of history which I am writing."[73]

13. That which Mascardi's "art of history" had ignored exacted its revenge. Thanks especially to ecclesiastical history and to antiquarianism, "evidence"

won out over *enargeia (evidentia in narratione)*. Even if they are not at all in-compatible, no historian today can imagine using the latter as a surrogate for the former.

But a subtle devaluation of historiography as a consequence of antiquarian-ism had begun earlier, as demonstrated by a celebrated writing of Manuel Chrysoloras, the learned Greek who moved to Italy c. 1395. In 1411, after having traveled to Rome, he wrote a long letter to Manuel Paleologus, the Byzantine emperor, in which he contrasted Rome, first pagan and then Christian, with the new Rome, Constantinople.[74] Of ancient Rome, Chrysoloras described the majestic ruins, including "the trophies and arches, built to recall the triumphs with their solemn processions, sculpted with the very images of war, of the prisoners, of the booty, of the sieges."

This was followed by an *ekphrasis* focusing especially on the Arch of Constantine:

> And it is still possible to see in them the sacrificial victims, the altars, the votive gifts, the naval battles, the clashes between infantry and cavalry and we can say every type of battle, of war machines and arms, and the vanquished rulers whether Medes or Persians, Iberians or Celts or Assyrians, all in their proper vestments, the enslaved populace, the generals who celebrate their triumphs over them. . . . And it is possible to know all this from how they are represented, as if they dealt with a living reality, so that every single detail becomes perfectly com-prehensible thanks to the inscriptions that are engraved there, to the point that we can see clearly what arms and what vestments were in use in ancient times, what distinctive signs identified the offices, how their formations were drawn up, the battles. . . .

Assemblies, spectacles, celebrations, occupations were represented "ac-cording to the usages of the various peoples." "For having represented them," Chrysoloras concluded:

> it is thought that Herodotus and other writers of history have done us a great service when they describe these things. But in these works it is possible to see everything, just as if we were really living in those times and among those people, so that they form a history that defines everything simply. In fact, it is not a his-torical work *[historian]* but I would prefer to say almost the direct vision *[autop-sian]* and manifestation *[parousian]* of everything that existed anywhere at that time.[75]

From the written word to the immediate evocation which brings forth life itself: the sequence *ekphrasis–autopsia–parousia* underlined the *enargeia* of

Chrysoloras's epistle. Much more unusual was the juxtaposition between Herodotus and the statuary of the Arch of Constantine, followed by the recognition of the superiority of the latter over the former.[76] The *ekphrasis*, so frequently used as a tool in the service of historiography, in the present case affirmed what historians had ignored or treated inadequately. But in Chrysoloras's letter the evocation that almost brought the past into the present was followed by the recognition of the inescapable transience of pagan authority. Conquerors and vanquished experienced the same fate; "everything is reduced to dust."[77]

The subject was not new; what was new was the distrust in the possibility of being able, with the help of rhetoric, to evoke the past as an accomplished fact. Its place was taken by an awareness that our understanding of the past inevitably was uncertain, discontinuous, lacunar, based only on fragments and ruins.

CHAPTER 2

The Conversion of the Jews of Minorca (A.D. 417–418)

1. This is an experiment *in corpore nobilissimo*. Peter Brown's *The Cult of the Saints* is a splendid book, full of learning, imagination, and grace. Even the perplexities I am about to express will reveal my profound intellectual debt to this work.

At the end of chapter 5 (*"Praesentia"*) Brown illustrates the "ideal 'clean' power associated with the relics of the saints" with an episode which followed the arrival of the relics of St. Stephen in Minorca in 417. The peaceful coexistence of Jews and Christians in the town of Mahon came brusquely to an end. Tensions emerged; the Jews gathered up stones and clubs and barricaded themselves in the synagogue. After a number of clashes, the Christians razed the synagogue to the ground. Then they urged the Jews to convert. Their efforts were largely successful, although Theodore, the *defensor civitatis*, who was the most prominent member of the Jewish community, for some time stubbornly opposed the joint pressure exerted on him by Christians and converted Jews. In a public debate on religious matters he almost prevailed over the bishop himself. Finally, Theodore gave up. Then the last Jewish resistance, which had included a number of women, collapsed. "Through becoming Christians," Brown writes, "[the Jews] maintained their full social status within their own community, though now subject to the higher *patrocinium* of Saint Stephen, and seated beside the Christian bishop as Christian *patroni*. Thus, far from being eradicated, the 'unclean' power of the established Jewish families has been 'washed clean' by being integrated into the Christian community under Saint Stephen."[1]

Brown does not deny that "violence and fear of yet greater violence played a decisive role" in these events. But his final comments emphasize the integration of Jews and Christians in a single community, not the human cost paid for it. He prepares for this conclusion by the use of negative analogies such as "it was something marginally more decent than a mere *pogrom*," or "his [i.e., Stephen's] arrival on the island was not seen as an occasion to purge the island of Jews."[2] Deliberate anachronisms such as *pogrom* and "purge" do not seem particularly illuminating in a case like this, which is among the earliest known occurrences of Jewish-Christian tensions. Even more perplexing is the opposition between "clean" and "unclean" power, which plays a crucial role in Brown's presentation of the Minorcan events. "The reader must bear with me," Brown says, "if, in describing a thoroughly dirty business . . . I limit myself to the perspective of Bishop Severus, our only source, and speak of the *patrocinium* of Saint Stephen as 'clean' power." The problem of method raised here is obviously of great import. But this slightly ambiguous passage could be wrongly interpreted by some readers to mean that such categories as "clean" and "unclean" derive from the evidence itself. On the contrary, they are "etic," not "emic" categories—to employ the terminology of the linguist K. L. Pike, and inspired implicitly by Mary Douglas's *Purity and Danger*, and not by Severus's long letter about the Minorcan events.[3] This is a perfectly legitimate choice, of course, although somebody could object to the idea of lumping together pagans and Jews under the category of "unclean" power, in light of the much later hostile association between Jews and filth.[4]

These remarks on Brown's historical approach to the Minorcan events are bound to remain inconclusive if they are not supplemented by an analysis of the primary evidence on which Brown relies: the letter written by Severus, bishop of Minorca, in 418. This statement is not as obvious as it should be. "History of historiography without historiography," as Arnaldo Momigliano put it ironically, has become more and more fashionable in recent times.[5] That there was a radical disjunction between historical narratives and the research on which it relies had already been suggested by Benedetto Croce as early as 1895.[6] Roughly a century later, in a largely different intellectual climate, this approach to historiography has become popular for reasons I will not try to explain here.

Its limitations (not to mention dangers) are immediately obvious, as in the case with which I am dealing, based on a single piece of evidence.[7] Doubts about the authenticity of Severus's letter have been raised in the past, as

Gabriel Seguí Vidal has shown in his critical edition of 1937.[8] More recently, on several occasions, Bernhard Blumenkranz has authoritatively argued that the letter is a seventh-century forgery (even if the announced detailed demonstration has not as yet appeared).[9] Brown mentions neither Seguí Vidal's edition nor Blumenkranz's criticism. He quotes the letter of Severus from one of the two nearly identical texts reproduced in Migne's *Patrologia Latina*. Both are based, with a few minor corrections, on the *editio princeps* provided by Caesar Baronius in his *Annales ecclesiastici* (1588). To evaluate Brown's approach to the Minorcan events, an examination of Severus's letter seems unavoidable.[10]

I should say straight off that Brown was absolutely correct in his tacit acceptance of the letter's authenticity. Recently discovered evidence has proved this beyond any reasonable doubt. But a quick recapitulation of the discussions concerning the authenticity of the document will I hope shed additional light on the events it purports to describe.

2. In his edition of Severus's letter Seguí Vidal observed that the style of the document was perfectly compatible with an early fifth-century date.[11] Nearly twenty years later, in an essay written with J. N. Hillgarth, Seguí Vidal introduced two additional arguments: (a) the identification of a pseudo-Augustinian treatise, *Altercatio Ecclesiae contra Synagogam*, with the *commonitorium* mentioned by Severus in his letter; (b) some archeological excavations suggesting the existence of a large paleo-Christian basilica in Minorca.[12] The irrelevance of the second argument in a discussion concerning the date of Severus's letter—which in any case is probably earlier than the basilica—has been rightly emphasized by José Vives (who, on the other hand, accepted the identification of the *commonitorium* with the *Altercatio*).[13] The first argument was effectively rejected by Blumenkranz, who demonstrated that the *Altercatio* is a later (probably tenth-century) text.[14] Moreover, he claimed that the letter ascribed to Severus (or Pseudo-Severus, as he says) reflects the preoccupations of a later period: the fact that Bishop Severus was nearly vanquished by Theodore, for instance, would suggest the risks involved in public religious confrontations with the Jews. Blumenkranz added to this a rather vague linguistic argument: the words "Theodorus in Christum credidit," shouted by the Christians and misunderstood by the Jews as "Theodore crede in Christum," seems to imply a homophony between the Spanish "cree" (imperative) and "cree" (indicative) which would be incompatible with an early fifth-century date.[15]

Fifth or seventh century? Lellia Cracco Ruggini rightly rejected Blumen-kranz's late date, but she gave a disproportionate importance to a more than doubtful argument—the archeological evidence mentioned by Seguí and Hill-garth.[16] On the other hand, the unfounded skepticism of Díaz y Díaz about an early date contained some valuable suggestions.[17] He noted that all the manuscripts (nine) used by Seguí Vidal for his critical edition include, be-sides the Severus letter, the so-called *Liber de miraculis sancti Stephani pro-tomartyris*, which describes the miracles produced by the relics of St. Stephen in an African town, Uzalis.[18] Both texts begin with the same biblical quota-tion (Tob. 2:7); the second cites the first, affirming (*Patrologia Latina* 41:83) that the saint's relics were brought to Uzalis with a letter, written by Bishop Severus of Minorca, which was to be read aloud from the pulpit: it proclaimed the extraordinary feats already performed by these relics in converting the Jews of Minorca. Díaz y Díaz suggests two alternative possibilities: (a) that the allusion to the letter of Severus in the *Liber de miraculis*, which is the only external proof of the early date of the letter, is an interpolation; (b) that the letter itself is a fake constructed on the basis of the allusion in the *Liber*.[19]

These clever conjectures have been disproved by J. Divjak's discovery of letters to and from Augustine. They include two written from the Balearic Is-lands by Consentius (known independently to be a correspondent of Augus-tine).[20] In one of them (12*) Consentius mentions the letter of Severus on the conversion of the Jews, even claiming that he had some responsibility in its wording.[21] It has been remarked, however, that the plain, straightforward style of Severus is very different from that of Consentius.[22]

3. So much for the date and authenticity of Severus's letter. All remaining doubts concerning these two issues stem, in my opinion, from a hypercritical attitude.[23] Other problems, however, are far from settled. Two recent essays insist on analyzing the letter as an autonomous document, related to a more or less isolated event.[24] This approach is certainly not without merit, but I will try to suggest the possibilities offered by a different method, based on more extensive documentation, encompassing a longer time frame—an approach implying the construction (and reconstruction) of a different historical object.

The connections between the letter of Severus and the *Liber de Miraculis Sancti Stephani* have already been pointed out by Díaz y Díaz. Both texts are related to the same person: Paulus Orosius, the author of the *Historiarum Adversus Paganos libri VII*, the first universal history written from a Christian perspective. Elements in Orosius's life explain his involvement with the two texts. Having left his birthplace, Braga, formerly a Spanish and then a Portuguese town, Orosius had come to Africa to meet Augustine and become his pupil. Augustine trusted him to the point that he sent him to Jerusalem (415) to challenge Pelagius and his ideas.[25] Orosius took part in the Council of Diospolis, which turned out to be a success for Pelagius. During the synod the relics of St. Stephen, Gamaliel, and Nicodemus were found at Caphar-Gamala, near Jerusalem, by a priest named Lucianus, who had been led there by a series of nocturnal visions. He was asked by Avitus, a priest from Braga, to dictate to him the circumstances of his extraordinary discovery. Lucianus spoke Greek, a language with which Avitus was familiar. Having prepared a Latin translation of Lucianus's report, known to us as *De revelatione corporis sancti Stephani*, Avitus entrusted it, with some relics of St. Stephen, to his fellow citizen Orosius, who was supposed to bring them to Palchonius, bishop of Braga.[26] In 416 Orosius left Jerusalem with his precious objects and, after a halt in Africa, proceeded to Minorca, hoping to reach Spain. Events turned out differently. In his letter, written at the beginning of 418,[27] Severus speaks of a priest coming from Jerusalem who, unable to get to Spain, altered course and returned to Africa, leaving behind in Minorca, "by divine inspiration," fragments of St. Stephen's body. For quite some time this anonymous priest has long been identified with Orosius. What convinced him to give up his original quest—whether winter storms, Vandal ships, or both—we do not know. In any case, I think we can trust the passage from the *Liber de miraculis sancti Stephani* mentioning Severus's letter. The unnamed individual who brought it to Uzalis, along with additional fragments from that apparently inexhaustible treasure—the relics of St. Stephen—can be safely identified with Orosius. His *Historiae adversus paganos*, probably written in the same year (418), shows that, as did his teacher Augustine, Orosius rejected the apocalyptic view in which Severus, at the end of the letter, placed the conversion of Minorca's Jews.[28]

4. Orosius could be regarded mistakenly as the protagonist in this story. In fact, he played only the role of intermediary, although admittedly an important one. The principal figure is Stephen. The arrival of his relics in Africa triggered a series of miracles, duly recorded some years later in the *Liber de Miraculis Sancti Stephani Protomartyris*, written under the impulse of Evodius, bishop of Uzalis. Since his youth Evodius had been one of Augustine's closest

followers.[29] In the past Augustine had been openly skeptical toward miracles. The discovery in Milan in 386 of the relics of two unknown martyrs, Gervasius and Protasius, which were immediately exploited by Ambrose as a symbolic weapon in his struggle with Arians, had left Augustine unmoved.[30] In his treatise *De vera religione* (389–391), the latter explained that, after the spread of the Christian faith, miracles had become impossible: otherwise, people would have craved only for visible things.[31] The title of book 22, chapter 8, of the *City of God*, written in 425, reads like a retraction of the aforementioned passage, as well as a turning point in the history of the cult of saints: "De miraculis, quae ut mundus in Christum crederet facta sunt et fieri mundo credente non desinunt" ("On miracles, which were done that the world might believe in Christ, and are still performed even though the world believes in Him"). The cult of the martyrs' relics was widespread in Africa: the Council of Carthage (398) had tried to exert some control over it, ordering the destruction of all superstitious or illicit altars.[32] But the change in Augustine's attitude was specifically related, as Victor Saxer has shown, to the wave of miracles connected to the shrine of St. Stephen in Uzalis.[33] Why was St. Stephen so important? He had been, of course, the protomartyr; his passion had reflected the passion of Christ. Other elements will become immediately evident as we focus on the momentous discovery of his relics. Let us now go back to 415.

5. The discovery of the relics of St. Stephen occurred at the right time and in the right place—a notion expressed by Victor Saxer, an eminent scholar whom nobody will suspect of militant anticlericalism.[34] The event enhanced the prestige of a person who clearly had played a major role in it: John II, bishop of Jerusalem. In a recent essay Michael van Esbroeck has argued that some cults actively supported by John II—St. Stephen's being the most prominent— implied a coherent religious policy, consciously addressed toward Jewish-Christian groups.[35] This is a valuable suggestion: but the polemical, even aggressive implications of the event were disregarded by van Esbroeck. The discovery of the tombs of Gamaliel and Nicodemus, suggesting a continuity between Old and New Testaments, was more than counterbalanced by the discovery of the relics of St. Stephen, the protomartyr, the first man who "fought for the Lord against the Jews" (*primum adversus Judaeos dominica bella bellavit*).[36] These words, included in both versions of the *De revelatione corporis Sancti Stephani*, are eloquent enough.[37] Religious contiguity went hand in hand with religious competition. As Marcel Simon has shown in his important

book, the Christians' claim to being "the true Israel" had ambivalent, potentially tragic overtones.[38]

These tensions lurk behind the discovery of St. Stephen's relics. Even scholars who have emphasized the perfect timing of this event have, as far as I know, disregarded the following matter: on 20 October 415 the emperor deprived Gamaliel II, patriarch of Jerusalem, of his traditional title of *praefectus honorarius*. Significantly, Jewish proselytism, in the form of the construction of new synagogues and the circumcision of Christians and Gentiles, was the reason mentioned for the suppression of this dignity.[39] The patriarch was the highest spiritual and political authority for the Jews of Palestine and the Diaspora; Origen regarded him as a kind of monarch of the Jews.

The suppression of the *praefectura honoraria* led, a few years later, to the disappearance of the patriarchate.[40] The weakened position of the Jews under Christian emperors was made evident, less than two months later, by another symbolic blow: the sudden reemergence of the relics of St. Stephen, announced by the visions of Lucianus at the beginning of December 415.

6. Retrospectively, it seems obvious that the relics were bound to reappear sooner or later. To explain this, we need to take another step backward—to the well-known sermons against Judaizing Christians delivered by St. John Chrysostom in Antioch in 385–386.[41] Marcel Simon in a major essay has examined the underlying complex religious reality.[42] Both Jews and Christians, for instance, fervently worshipped the relics of the seven Maccabees and their mother, which were thought to be preserved in a synagogue in Antioch. Around 380 this edifice was seized and transformed into a Christian church. This act, which was far from being exceptional,[43] demonstrates the ambivalent implications of the formula *verus Israel.* The desire to emphasize the continuity between Old and New Testaments inspired the inclusion of the Maccabees in Antioch's religious calendar, as well as the violent seizure of the holy place where their relics were preserved.[44]

The cult of the Maccabee brothers and their mother was not limited to Antioch. In 388, as we learn from a letter of St. Ambrose, at Callinicon, on the left bank of the Euphrates, heretics attacked some monks who, "following an ancient tradition," were chanting psalms as they made their way to a sanctuary of the Maccabees. For some unknown reason, even in this case the local synagogue was destroyed by these monks, encouraged to do so by the bishop (*auctore episcopo*).[45] Such a widespread cult, shared by Jews and Christians, undoubtedly had deep roots. The precedent of 2 Macc. 7 has been detected behind the description of Blandina, the Christian martyr put to death at Lyon in A.D. 177.[46] It has been suggested that the very notion of *martyrium* ultimately derives from the story of the seven Jewish brothers and their mother, tortured and killed for their refusal to eat pork.[47]

We have already mentioned the attempts to Christianize the cult of these Jewish protomartyrs. The new balance of power, which had emerged between the end of the fourth and the beginning of the fifth centuries, led to the discovery of the relics of the Christian protomartyr, who according to the tradition had been killed by the Jews. The veneration of Stephen was thus raised up against the veneration of the Maccabees.[48] In Minorca, as Severus stated in his letter, the tensions generated by the arrival of the relics of St. Stephen unleashed actual hostilities: "the Jews exhorted one another by recalling the examples of the age of the Maccabees, ready to die in order to defend the Law."[49]

7. Up to this point I have dealt with a hagiographic stereotype, tied to a name: "Stephen." It might be possible to go beyond this and try to disentangle, on the basis of Acts 6–8, the historical Stephen and his attitude toward Jewish tradition.[50] Although I lack the competence to do this, the evidence I have collected shows, in my opinion, that a highly ambivalent attitude toward Jews played a crucial role in the emergence of the cult of the Christian saints. The religious violence occurring on Minorca is just one episode in a much longer story in which St. Stephen, or at least his relics, inevitably performed an anti-Jewish function.[51]

The role played by St. Stephen is so obvious that Peter Brown, in his work from which this discussion began, did not even mention it. This silence seems significant because it is connected to a larger tendency on his part to underplay tensions, divisions, opposition of all kinds—social, cultural, and religious. In an autobiographical fragment Brown remarked (with a touch of self-criticism) that British functionalist anthropology has had "a tendency to isolate the holy man ... from the world of shared values in which he operated as an exemplar."[52] Brown preferred, instead, to focus on elements shared by an entire community. I agree totally with the objections, raised in the first chapter of *The Cult of Saints*, to the more or less openly paternalistic spirit with which the religious history of illiterate groups has been studied. Much more debatable is

Brown's tacit progression from this type of criticism to a rejection of what he defines as a "two-tier model"—in other words, any approach that presupposes the existence of cultural and religious dichotomies.

The Cult of the Saints is an indispensable book. But it is difficult to accept how it deals (or fails to deal) with the Jewish-Christian dichotomy.[53]

CHAPTER 3

Montaigne, Cannibals, and Grottoes

1. There are figures from the past that time seems to bring closer and closer to us. Montaigne is one such figure. We are irresistibly attracted by his openness toward distant cultures, by his curiosity about the multiplicity and diversity of human life, by the conspiratorial and pitiless dialogue he carries on with himself. These apparently contradictory traits make him seem familiar, but it is a deceptive impression: in the end, Montaigne eludes us. We must try to approach him on his own terms, not ours.

This does not mean interpreting Montaigne through Montaigne himself—a highly questionable, and ultimately fruitless, approach. Let's follow a different track by attempting to read the essay "On Cannibals," starting with the contextual elements that can be found, directly or indirectly, in the text itself. This will be an erratic path which at times will appear to be echoing the digressions so dear to Montaigne. I want to try to show how these contexts served to mold the text: as both constraints and challenges.

2. The first context, both literal and metaphorical, is provided, of course, by the *Essais*, the volume in which "On Cannibals" is included. A relationship between parts and the whole exists for all of Montaigne's essays (and for all his books): but in this case there is a special significance. This is understood at once from the words in which the author presents his work to the reader. "Had my intention been to court the world's favor," Montaigne writes, "I should have trimmed myself more bravely, and stood before it in a studied attitude. I desire to be seen in my simple, natural, and everyday dress, without

artifice or constraint, for it is myself I portray." But this decision to represent his "faults to the life" and his "native form" had to come to terms, as Montaigne explains subsequently, with his "respect for the public." In presenting to the reader the result of such a compromise—his book—Montaigne expresses a nostalgic longing for "those nations who are said to be still living in the sweet freedom of Nature's first laws." If he had been living among those people, he concludes, "I assure you that I should have been quite prepared to give a full-length, and quite naked, portrait of myself."[1]

On the very threshold of the *Essais* we meet the Brazilian savages who will reappear in "On Cannibals." Their nakedness points at two crucial, and closely related, themes: on the one hand, the opposition between *coustume* and *nature*; on the other, the author's intention to speak of himself in the most direct, immediate, and truest way possible. Allusions to naked savages and naked truth have nothing surprising about them. But their convergence implies an intermediate link tied to one of Montaigne's boldest assumptions: the identification of tradition (*coustume*) with artificiality. Clothing, as he explains in the essay "On the Custom of Dressing" (1:36), demonstrates that we have departed from the law of nature, from that "general polity of the world, where there can be nothing counterfeit."[2] Nakedness was "the original custom of mankind"—words that clarify the already noted allusion to the Golden Age's lack of constraints: the "sweet freedom of Nature's first laws."[3] We find anticipated, in a concise form, some of the crucial ideas which will be developed in the *Essais*.[4]

But how widespread at that time was the association between the Golden Age, nakedness, and freedom from the constraints of civilization? Here another possible context emerges. These three motifs converge in a famous passage of the *Aminta*, the pastoral poem by Torquato Tasso, whom Montaigne regarded as "one of the most judicious and inventive of Italian poets, who was more highly trained in the manner of pure and ancient poetry than any other that had lived for a long time."[5] The chorus which closes the first act of the *Aminta* is a nostalgic evocation of the Golden Age and its naked nymphs: an age in which erotic pleasure was not constrained by honor, "that vaine and ydle name."[6] It should be added that Pierre de Brach, councillor of the Parlement of Bordeaux and author of the first translation of the *Aminta* into French (1584), was a friend of Montaigne's.[7] But the possibility that Montaigne, who knew Italian very well, echoed Tasso's verses in his address to the reader must be absolutely rejected. The first edition of Montaigne's *Essais* (which already included the address to the reader) appeared in the summer of 1580, a few months after the publication of the first edition of the *Aminta*.[8] In the second edition of the *Essais* (1582) Montaigne added a moving reference to his meeting with Tasso at the Sant'Anna hospital in Ferrara, where the poet was confined for insanity.[9]

Montaigne could not possibly have read the *Aminta*, for chronological reasons; Tasso could not have read the *Essais* for reasons both chronological and linguistic (his French was very poor). The analogies between the two texts must be related to a widespread motif. This can be proven by a page of *La métamorphose d'Ovide figurée*, a French poetical adaptation of Ovid's *Metamorphoses*, published in Lyons in 1557. The etcher, Bernard Salomon, known as "le petit Salomon," depicted the Golden Age as the triumph of free love and nakedness: at that time, the caption reads, people lived "sans loy, force ou contrainte/On meintenoit la foy, le droit, l'honneur" ("without law, force or constraint/faith, right, honor were preserved") (figure 2).[10]

The tone is less aggressive, but we are not very far from either Tasso's denunciation of honor or from Montaigne's lament for the "sweet freedom of Nature's first laws."[11] But *La métamorphose d'Ovide figurée* suggests Montaigne to us on a different level as well. The representation of the Golden Age is framed by "grotesques"—decorations which had become fashionable at the end of the fifteenth century, after the discovery of the frescoes which decorated the grottoes of the Domus Aurea.[12] In an often quoted passage, Montaigne compared his own essays specifically to "grotesques, that is to say, fantastic paintings whose only charm lies in their variety and extravagance. And what are these essays but grotesques and monstrous bodies, pieced together of different members, without any definite shape, without any order, coherence, or proportion, except they be accidental."[13]

The illustrations of *La métamorphose d'Ovide figurée* contributed to the diffusion of this kind of decoration throughout France. A series of mid-sixteenth-century frescoes in the castle of Villeneuve-Lebrun, near the Puy-de-Dôme, was actually based on Bernard Salomon's etchings.[14] We do not know whether Montaigne was familiar with these illustrations; but they may provide a visual parallel to, and context for, the passage we have just read.

The comparison of his own work to the "grotesques" had a twofold significance, both negative and positive. On the one hand, Montaigne was suggesting what his *Essais* lacked: they were "without any definite shape, without any order, coherence, or proportion, except they be accidental." On the other,

L'aage d'Or.

L'aage premier d'une innocente sainte
A ces viuans aporta ce bon heur,
Que franchement sans loy, force, ou contreinte
On meintenoit la foy, le droit, l'honneur.
L'amour n'estoit suget au blasonneur,
Ains pouuoit on de s'amie estre aymé,
Hanté, baisé, sans creindre deshonneur:
Dont à bon droit l'aage d'Or fut nommé.

a 4

FIGURE 2. Bernard Salomon, engraving for *La métamorphose d'Ovide figurée* (Lyons, 1557).

he indicated what they were: "fantastic paintings," "monstrous bodies." In Montaigne's tongue-in-cheek self-denigrating judgment we recognize the accompanying narcissism that his readers know so well: "whose only charm lies in their variety and extravagance." As Jean Ceárd has shown, words such as *variety, strangeness,* and *monster* had a positive connotation for Montaigne.[15] But there is something to add to their aesthetic implications.

3. Montaigne had a true passion for poetry. It has been supposed, on the basis of his *Journal de voyage en Italie,* that he was less interested in the visual arts. Certainly, we will not find in the *Journal* comments on the Sistine ceiling or Leonardo's *Last Supper.* But this proves only that Montaigne (who, by the way, did not record everything he saw) did not have a nineteenth- or twentieth-century guidebook in his pocket. In fact, the passages of his *Journal* dedicated to the villas of Pratolino, Castello, Bagnaia, and Caprarola display a definite interest in gardens, fountains, and grottoes.[16] Montaigne avoided technical terms in his descriptions, which should not surprise us if we recall the ironical reference in his *Essais* to architects preening themselves "with big words like Pilasters, Architraves, Cornices, Corinthians, Doric and such," all of which referred to "the paltry parts of my kitchen door."[17]

The art historian André Chastel wrote that this passage indicates first of all that Montaigne was more conversant with such ancient authors as Seneca and Cicero than with Vitruvius.[18] Such a conclusion seems to me far from evident. Montaigne was presumably familiar with the vivid description of the first, uncivilized stage of human society contained in the *De architectura* of Vitruvius. Besides the original Latin text, reprinted many times, Montaigne could have known the French translation of 1547 by Jean Martin, itself based on an earlier Italian version by Cesare Cesariano (Como, 1521). In commenting on the passage in Vitruvius on the invention of fire, Cesariano identified the harsh beginning of human society with the Golden Age (*aurea aetas*) and compared those early humans to the inhabitants of the recently discovered lands of southern Asia, whom Spanish and Portuguese travelers had found still lived in caves (figure 3).[19]

In his essay on cannibals Montaigne described the Brazilian savages as being both primitive and similar to the people of the Golden Age. It is impossible to say whether he took these ideas from the commentaries on Vitruvius. But that is not the point. Montaigne's ironical remark on contemporary

ÁVREA AETAS QVÆ PRISCOR. HOMINVM VITA: HVMANI/
TATIS Q INITIVM: &PROPTER IGNEM SERMONV PROCRE/
ATIO AC ARCHITECTVRÆ PRINCIPV FVISSE DICITVR ‹

óuento .i. cógregatione de homini aut p respecto de supplicatione a Dio in le Ecclesie : aut p caufa de Iudicii quando
iftrati fono ogregati : aut se p qualche altro respecto in uno loco la multitudine ouene : & dicif a ouenio qd proprie eft
or Virg. in primo æneidos: conueniunt quibus aut odiú crudele tyrani : aut metus acererat. Salu . poftq unú in locú oés
: Cóuento anchora fignifica coniunctione: Iuue .faty . 6 . Cóuentú tamé & pactú & fponfalia noftra tépeftate paras: di
ientus in iudiciú uocatus ab aliquo . Vnde cóuenticula : quale quafi fep fe piglia in mala parte : hoc eft p il cóuento &
atione de feditiofi & fcelerati. Concilio fi e una multitudine de populo congregata per respecto di confultare : & tanto
› fapienti & diuini: quanto piu fe ouenено al bene cómune : p che omne bonú quáto cómunius : tanto diuinius : a Cócil
iliabulú locus in quo ocihú ogregat Feftus. Cóuicto fi e deriuato a uictus : qd plane fignificat omne id qd ad cibú p
ct : quare frequenter hec duo cóiungimus uictú & ueftitú: Victo anchora fignifica una generatione di uita quáto a li coft
le dicemo : Conuicto : fi e una cómune congregatione coadunata a uiuere in una focietate como faria le pfone de una
ápia : uel de qualche magna religione : o uero hofpitali : quale nó tanto manzano & beueno de cópagnia : ma anche ufa
lemi coftumi : Dice aduncha Vitruuio la inuentione dil foco hauer cógregato ad uiuere & habitare infema & ufare li me
umi feu lege p li mortali: qualiprimo ne le filue difperfi & con le fere uagauano : & quefto nó effere fta difficile lo demo
ndo da la natura ihomo qual e animal fociabile nó como li altri aiali pni i terra effere al pafto abiecto: Ma erecto a otépl
abile magnificétia del Cœlo & Stelle ql cofa áchora Ouidio ha dicto primo metamor . Pronaor quó fpectent aialia cætera

FIGURE 3. Vitruvius, *De architectura* (Como, 1521).

architectural jargon does not imply a disregard for architecture. His *Journal de voyage en Italie* proves just the opposite.

Here is how he describes the Medici villa at Pratolino, near Florence:

> There is . . . a grotto, consisting of several cells, which is the finest we ever saw. It is formed, and all crusted over, with a certain material, which they told us was brought from some particular mountain; the wood-work is all ingeniously fastened together with invisible nails. Here you see various musical instruments, which perform a variety of pieces, by the agency of the water; which also, by a hidden machinery, gives motion to several statues, single and in groups, opens doors, and gives apparent animation to the figures of various animals, that seem to jump into the water, to drink, to swim about, and so on. . . . The beauty and richness of this place cannot be conveyed by any description, however detailed.[20]

The fountain, built by the architect Bernardo Buontalenti, has been destroyed. We may be able to figure out what Montaigne saw by looking at another grotto, also built by Buontalenti and still extant in the Boboli Gardens in Florence.

The construction of the facade of the grotto, begun by Giorgio Vasari, was taken over by Buontalenti in 1583—that is, two years after Montaigne's voyage to Italy—and finished in 1593. The two *Prigioni* by Michelangelo (today replaced by copies) were installed in the grotto in 1585.[21] The fashion for grottoes had started in Italy some decades earlier. In 1543, Claudio Tolomei, in his description of the grottoes built in his Roman villa by *messer* Agapito Bellomo, mentioned "the ingenious artifice of making fountains, which has been recently discovered and now has been widely practiced in Rome. By combining art with nature, it has become impossible to discern which is which. Sometimes it looks like a natural artifice, sometimes like an artificial nature: in this way nowadays they have learned to make fountains which look as if they had been made by nature, not by chance but through a masterful artifice. . . ."[22]

Tolomei's praise for devices characterized by "natural artifice" and "artificial nature" immediately makes us think of Montaigne's enthusiasm for the Pratolino grotto.[23] This convergence inspired by a common taste was analyzed brilliantly many years ago by Ernst Kris.[24] Studying the casts made from nature by two late-sixteenth-century sculptors—the German Werner Jamnitzer and the Frenchman Bernard Palissy—Kris demonstrated that this practice was related to a widespread form of extreme naturalism, which he labeled "*style*

FIGURE 4. Giulio Romano, Palazzo del Te, Mantua.

rustique." Among the prominent examples of this style he mentioned the
Tuscan gardens and grottoes so warmly appreciated by Montaigne.[25]

More recent research has shown that this "rustic style" had been preco-
ciously transmitted to France by Sebastiano Serlio, the celebrated architect
and theorist. In the fourth volume of his influential treatise, *Libro di architettura,* published in 1537, Serlio identified the Tuscan order (which had been
mentioned only briefly by Vitruvius) with the rustic order, and he cited as an
example of this combination *(mistura)* the extremely beautiful Palazzo del
Te, the country residence of the Gonzaga family, not far from Mantua, constructed a few years earlier by Giulio Romano.[26] Serlio particularly praised
Giulio Romano's use of both rough and polished stone in the facade of the
palace, making it seem "part work of nature and part artifice" (figure 4).[27]

A few years later Serlio found a new patron in Francis I and left Italy
for France forever. In 1551 he published in Lyons a book almost entirely

dedicated to the rustic order: *Libro estraordinario, nel quale si dimostrano trenta porte di opera rustica mista con diversi ordini* ("Extraordinary Book, in Which Are Displayed Thirty Doors in the Rustic Style Mixed with Several Others").[28] In the introduction Serlio apologized to the (presumably Italian) followers of Vitruvius, from whom he had departed "not much," suggesting that his transgressions had been dictated by the desire to satisfy French taste ("having regard for the country where I find myself").[29] Probably Serlio's excuse contained a kernel of truth. His physical distance from the imposing heritage of Roman architecture could have had a liberating effect on him. In any case, through both his buildings at Fontainebleau (most of them now destroyed) and his treatise on architecture Serlio contributed to the spread of a style which developed some of Giulio Romano's boldest ideas. A work such as Bernard Palissy's *Architecture et Ordonnance de la grotte rustique de Monseigneur le duc de Montmorency connestable de France* (1563) attests to Serlio's dramatic impact on French architecture. In order to convey to his readers the monstrosity (*monstruosité*) of a grotto he had built, Palissy listed innumerable details which associated a close combination of nature and the pursuit of bizarre effects: terra-cotta statues whose worn aspect simulated the effects of time; columns made of seashells; columns sculpted in the form of rocks eroded by the wind; or rusticated columns to make one think they had been repeatedly struck by a hammer; and so forth.[30]

Montaigne's enthusiasm for Pratolino, Bagnaia, and Caprarola, as recorded in his *Journal de voyage en Italie*, was clearly related to a pervasive taste which may shed some light on both the structure and style of his *Essais*. It is a lead worth pursuing.

4. Antoine Compagnon has suggested that Montaigne, in writing his essays, had an ancient model in mind: the *Noctes Atticae* (the *Attic Nights*), written by the grammarian Aulus Gellius c. 150 B.C. The work consists of a series of arbitrarily arranged chapters, each of which focuses on a word, a motto, an anecdote, or at times a general topic. Compagnon has emphasized that the structural resemblance between the two works is reinforced by a series of other analogies such as the rejection of learning, the frequent use of titles related only vaguely to the content of the essays, and the huge number of quotations from a heterogeneous collection of books.[31] The hypothesis is certainly convincing. But why was Montaigne, who repeatedly quoted from Gellius, so struck by his work? And in what vein did he read it?

An answer to these questions can be found in a passage from Gellius's introduction to the *Noctes Atticae*. After having listed a series of elegant, sometimes pretentious titles by famous scholars, he explains how he came to choose the title for his book: "But I, bearing in mind my limitations, gave my work offhand, without premeditation, and indeed almost in a rustic fashion (*subrustice*), the title *Attic Nights*, derived merely from the time and place of my winter vigils; I thus fall as far short of all other writers in the dignity even of my title, as I do in care and elegance of style."[32]

The key word in the passage, *subrustice*, "almost in a rustic fashion," obviously did not imply a literal reference to peasants. The use of the rustic order by Giulio Romano in the Palazzo del Te, the Gonzagas' splendid country home, was equally metaphorical (figure 4). What was being suggested in both cases was a deliberate, highly controlled lack of stylistic refinement. We can easily imagine how Gellius's tongue-in-cheek modesty, as well as his dismissal of rhetorical elegance in the name of a different rhetoric—one based on simplicity and disorder—must have appealed to Montaigne, writing from the tower of his provincial castle.[33] The capricious structure of Gellius's chapters and the large number of heterogeneous quotations with which they are encrusted were made-to-order to seduce such a reader as Montaigne, himself inclined to violate the classical laws of symmetry.

In a similar spirit, in the introduction to the *Libro estraordinario*, Serlio proudly trumpeted his own licentiousness, which had induced him to push to an extreme Giulio Romano's experiments by inserting ancient fragments in a mixture of different styles. These included even a previously unheard of "bestial order" (*ordine bestiale*): addressing himself "to those bizarre persons who are fond of novelties," Serlio stated that he had wanted "to break and spoil (*rompere e guastare*) the beautiful shape of this Doric door" (figure 5).[34] A similar desire for transgression, even if less brutal, is discernible in Serlio's praise of grotesques: they, too, favored "licentiousness," the free play of decorative elements, legitimized by examples from ancient Rome which Giovanni da Udine had not only imitated but even surpassed in the Vatican loggias.[35]

Rejection of symmetry, inflation of details, violation of classical norms: Serlio would have approved the loose structure as well as the uneven stylistic texture of Montaigne's essays. The abrupt juxtapositions may be compared to the alternate use of polished and rough stone in Giulio Romano's Palazzo del Te, representing respectively, as Serlio remarked, "works of art" and "works of nature."[36] In the essay on cannibals Montaigne cites as authorities a writing

FIGURE 5. Sebastiano Serlio, *Libro estraordinario* (Lyons, 1551).

doubtfully attributed to Aristotle (*De mirabilis auditis*) and another to a "plain, simple fellow." But the latter is judged to be more trustworthy, because he had lived for ten or twelve years in the New World: "This tale of Aristotle's relates no more closely to our new lands than Plato's. This man who stayed with me was a plain, simple fellow, and men of this sort are likely to give true testimony."[37]

Readers of the first edition of the *Essais* (Bordeaux, 1580) were confronted with a text in which each essay was printed as a single, unbroken typographical unit.[38] By splitting the sequence into two different paragraphs, modern publishers have attenuated the original harsh tone, but without making it disappear entirely.

5. "Une marqueterie mal jointe," an inlay badly joined: this definition which Montaigne gave to his own writings (like the one previously analyzed about the grotesques) reveals, in addition to his customary teasing tone, a remarkable literary self-awareness. Montaigne was referring to the uneven stylistic texture of the *Essais,* an unevenness exacerbated by his compulsive habit of inserting additions (*allongeails*) of various lengths in subsequent editions.[39] Some years after the death of Montaigne, another famous reader, Galileo Galilei, penned a similar phrase in the margin of his interfoliated copy of the *Gerusalemme Liberata.* Tasso's narrative, he observed, resembles "more inlaid wood or intarsia than an oil painting. For, since an intarsia is a composite of little varicolored pieces of wood, which one can never combine and unite so fluidly that the contours would not remain clear cut and the colors sharply distinct in their variety, the figures are of necessity stiff, crude and without conformation and relief." As an example of a narrative comparable to an oil painting, "soft, round, forceful and rich in relief," Galileo mentioned Ariosto's *Orlando Furioso.*[40]

The analogy between Montaigne's rather indulgent self-representation and Galileo's hostile judgment of Tasso seems to suggest once again the existence of a larger common framework. In a famous paper, Panofsky used Galileo's text to demonstrate Tasso's connection to the Mannerist culture of a Salviati or Bronzino. Panofsky's definition can be extended to Montaigne as well. I am well aware that this assertion is not new. In the last few decades Montaigne has been repeatedly described as a typical representative of Mannerism.[41] But the category of Mannerism, itself quite debatable, has become more and more vague. It would be prudent to use it in a strictly nominalist

perspective: as a twentieth-century intellectual construction whose historical pertinence needs to be systematically checked. All the elements in the
structure which we have seen emerge piece by piece—Tasso, the Pratolino
grotto, Serlio, the facade of the Palazzo del Te, the intarsia as a stylistic metaphor, again Tasso—have been independently connected to Mannerism. But
the tortuous course we have traveled thus far seems to me more important
than our point of arrival.

6. "When I begin reading the *Furioso*," Galileo wrote, "I see opening up before
me a regal gallery adorned with a hundred ancient statues by the most re-
nowned sculptors." Tasso's *Gerusalemme*, instead, gave him the impression

> of entering the study of some little man with a taste for the curious who has taken
> delight in fitting it out with things that have something strange about them, ei-
> ther because of age or because of rarity or for some other reason, but are, as a mat-
> ter of fact, nothing but bric-a-brac, such as a petrified crayfish; a dried-up chame-
> leon; a fly and a spider embedded in a piece of amber; some of those little clay
> figures which are said to be found in the ancient tombs of Egypt; and, as far as
> painting is concerned[,] little sketches by Baccio Bandinelli and Parmigianino,
> and other similar trifles.[42]

"Here Galileo," Panofsky remarks, "portrays to a nicety, and with evident
gusto, one of those jumbled *Kunst- und Wunderkammern* so typical of the Mannerist age."[43] In such a *Wunderkammer* we can easily imagine a cast of an in-
sect from Palissy's workshop, as well as "the beds . . . ropes . . . wooden swords
and bracelets . . . and large canes open at one end" used by the Brazilian natives as musical instruments in their dances: objects collected by Montaigne,
who (as we learn from his essay on cannibals) had them in his house.[44]

Aesthetic taste can act as a filter, with both moral and cognitive implications.[45] Montaigne's effort to understand the Brazilian natives was fed by his
attraction for the bizarre, the distant, the exotic, for works of art which imitated nature and for people close to the state of nature. In the essay on cannibals Montaigne shed light on the moral and intellectual implications of the
Wunderkammer.[46]

7. Collecting is an activity that aims at completeness—a principle that tendentiously ignores hierarchies religious, ethnic, cultural. We are struck by
this conclusion as we leaf through *Les vrais pourtraits et vies des hommes illustres grecz, latin et payens recueilliz de leurs tableaux, livres, medailles antiques*

et modernes ("The True Portraits and Lives of Famous Greek, Latin and Pagan Men, Collected from Their Pictures, Books, Medals, Both Ancient and Modern"), a large, richly illustrated in-folio volume published in Paris in 1584. Its author, the Franciscan André Thevet, was known especially as a cosmographer. His account of the French expedition to Brazil (*Les singularitez de la France antarctique*, 1557) had been attacked as fallacious by the Huguenot Jean de Léry. Montaigne, in speaking of the New World, dismissed "what the cosmographers may say," and perhaps agreed with Léry's attacks against Thevet.[47] But the latter's volume, *Les vrais pourtraits*, must have aroused Montaigne's curiosity. Thevet had been working on this huge work for many years, attempting to create an accurate portrait for each individual, which he had then passed on to the engraver "pour graver et representer au naif l'air et le pourtrait des personnages que ie propose."[48] The living were excluded. The portraits and the accompanying lives were arranged according to categories: popes, bishops, warriors, poets, and so forth. The cosmographer Thevet had searched well beyond Europe's borders, including in his book even (as the title itself announced) "pagan" personages who were neither Greek nor Latin. The eighth book, on the subject of "emperors and kings," included Julius Caesar; Ferguz, first king of Scotland; Saladin; Tamerlane; Mahomet II; Tomombey, the last sultan of Egypt; Atabalipa, king of Peru; and Motzume, king of Mexico. In this colorful company we also find Nacolabsou, king of the Promontory of Cannibals (figure 6).[49]

The French anthropologist Alfred Métraux, in his monograph on the Tupinamba religion, made extensive use of Thevet and praised his curiosity, the fruit of his capacity to be astonished.[50] To be sure, Thevet is not comparable to Montaigne for originality and intelligence. Both, however, shared an antihierarchical attitude which permitted Thevet to include the names of the rulers mentioned above. In this version, the series enjoyed long life. In 1657 the English translation of Plutarch's *Lives of the Noble Grecians and Romans*, based on Amyot's French version, was reprinted with an appendix entitled "The Lives of Twenty Eminent Persons, of Ancient and Latter Times." This consisted of a selection from Thevet's *Pourtraits*, including Atabalipa, king of Peru (figure 7).[51]

This medley was an essential component of Thevet's project. The *Vrais pourtraits et vies des hommes illustres* was modeled on the *Elogia virorum bellica virtute illustrium* and on the *Elogia virorum litteris illustrium*, two in-folio volumes published in Basel in 1577. They were a product of the museum that

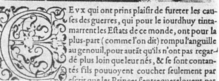

Evx qui ont prins plaisir de fureter les causes des guerres, qui pour le iourdhuy tinta-
marrent les Estats de ce monde, ont pour la
plus-part (comme l'on dit) rompu l'anguille
au genouil, pour autāt qu'ils n'ont pas regar-
dé plus loin que leur nés, & se sont contan-
tés fils pouuoyent coucher seulement par
ofrit que les Princes s'entreguerelovent par

FIGURE 6. Nacolabsou, king
of the Promontory of Cannibals
(from André Thevet, *Les vrais
pourtraits et vies des hommes illustres*
(Paris, 1584).

Es hommes plus nobles, riches & pui
fans de la terre Perusienne furent les Iuga
peuples felons, belliqueux & subtils aupol
sible issus d'vn peuple Tiguicata, prenant l
nom d'vne ville, située aupres d'vn lac, en l

FIGURE 7. Atabalipa, king of
Peru (from André Thevet, *Les
vrais pourtraits et vies des hommes
illustres* (Paris, 1584).

their author, Paolo Giovio, had built at his villa near Como. His collection of portraits of famous men (kings, generals, scholars), housed in the Museo Gioviano and subsequently dispersed, had been inspired by a classical model: the seven hundred portraits of illustrious men described by Varro, the great Roman erudite, in one of his lost works, the *Imagines* or *Hebdomades*.[52] In his historical writings Giovio paid careful attention to the Ottoman Empire, and in general to events transpiring outside Europe.[53] His *Elogia virorum bellica virtute illustrium* included African and Asian kings, but none from the Americas (figure 8).

The Museo Gioviano possessed a portrait of Hernán Cortés and an emerald in the shape of a heart, which the explorer had donated.[54] Among the objects of New World provenance in Thevet's own cabinet of curiosities could be found the famous Aztec manuscript the *Codex Mendoza*, now at Oxford. It had been transcribed for Charles V, stolen from a Spanish galleon by a French pirate who donated it to Thevet, who, in turn, sold it to Richard Hakluyt.[55] The portraits of the American kings included in *Les vrais pourtraits et vies des hommes illustres* had been inspired by the *Codex Mendoza*.[56]

8. The taste for the exotic and the passion of the collector obviously inspired Montaigne to include, in the essay on cannibals, the translation of two Brazilian songs which he warmly praised.[57] Montaigne has been seen occasionally as the founder of anthropology, as the first who tried to avoid the ethnocentric distortions involved when we approach what has been referred to as "the Other."[58] But by seeing him thus we impose our words on Montaigne. Instead, we could learn from him, using his own language.

Montaigne can also be considered an antiquarian, even though sui generis.[59] This statement is almost paradoxical, since *antiquarian* for more than two centuries has been synonymous with *pedant*: Montaigne hated pedantry. But a passage in the *Journal de voyage en Italie* might make us think that the label was justified. During his visit to the Vatican Library, Montaigne saw a Virgil manuscript which he thought he could date, on the basis of its elongated narrow characters, to the age of Constantine. Lacking in the manuscript were the four autobiographical verses ("Ille ego qui quondam...") which had often been printed in the *Aeneid*. This convinced Montaigne that he was justified in assuming those lines to be apocryphal.[60]

Montaigne was right on this last point.[61] His earlier hypothesis on the date was less accurate. The manuscript which he saw at the Vatican was

Hordæ, quæ à Iaxarte ad Volgam amnem, & vltra id flumen vſq; ad Moſcam ſedes habent. Hordas enim agmina Tartarorum vocant, quæ incertis ſemper ſedibus per immenſas ſolitudines vſque ad Imaum montem euagantur, Amaxobij ab antiquis vocati, quòd in curribus centone protectis aduerſus frigora vitam degant. Harum Hordarum maximè potentes & bellicoſæ Caſsania, Sciabania, Nogaiaque Moſcouitis commercio familiares Tamerlani paruerunt. Nam reliquæ remotiores à magno Cane Cathaino, qui in ora Oceani regioneque Sinarum potentiſsimus regnat, imperia accipiunt. Sublatis itaque ſignis Tamerlanes, eam multitudinem tranando Volgam traduxit, curſus rapiditate & multitudine aquarum poſt Nilum & Iſtrum fluuiorum ampliſsimū. Sed is diductus in ſeptem cornua quibus in mare Caſpium turbidus & lenior erumpit, commodiorem tranſi

FIGURE 8. Paolo Giovio, *Elogia virorum bellica virtute illustrium* (Basel, 1577).

FIGURE 9. From the *Vergilius Romanus* (Vat. lat. 3867).

identified long ago with the so-called *Vergilius Romanus* (Vat. lat. 3867) (figure 9).[62] After decades of debate, scholars now tend to date the manuscript toward the end of the fifth century A.D., a century and a half after the approximate date suggested by Montaigne.[63] This scarcely diminishes the originality of his observations. Half a century before, the French antiquarian Claude Bellièvre had also examined the *Vergilius Romanus*, noticing the elongated form of its letters as well as an orthographic detail ("Vergilius" instead of "Virgilius") which had already been pointed out by Angelo Poliziano in his *Miscellanea*.[64] But Montaigne had never read Poliziano's philological writings. He was not a philologist; moreover, he could not have been a paleographer; paleography, in the modern sense of the word, emerged only in the late seventeenth century. But his attention to a detail such as the form of the letters in a manuscript was part of a boundless curiosity for the concrete, the specific, the singular. This was the attitude with which, as he said in his essay on education, an imaginary pupil should have been inculcated: "Let an honest curiosity be instilled in him, so that he may inquire into everything; if there is anything remarkable in his neighborhood let him go to see it, whether it is a building, a fountain, a man, the site of an ancient battle, or a place visited by Caesar or Charlemagne."[65]

These were the topics dealt with by antiquarians, and systematically ignored by historians.[66] "A man," could have been, for instance, the "simple and ignorant fellow," returned from the New World, who kindled Montaigne's curiosity. Ethnography emerged when the antiquarian's curiosity and methodology were transferred from people remote in time, as were the Greeks and Romans, to people remote in space. Montaigne's role in this crucial intellectual turning point remains to be explored.[67]

9. The gaze of the antiquarian permitted Montaigne to look at Brazilian natives as belonging to a distinct and different civilization, although the word *civilization* did not exist as yet.[68] He refused to label their poetry barbarian ("... a fiction that by no means savours of barbarity"; "... there is nothing barbarous in this idea").[69] In general, Montaigne said, "I do not believe, from what I have been told about this people, that there is anything barbarous or savage about them, except that we call barbarous anything that is contrary to our own habits."[70] But a few pages later, this purely relative meaning of *barbarous* acquired a negative connotation. Given that we, civilized people, are more cruel than cannibals, we are the true barbarians: "I consider it more barbarous to eat a man alive than to eat him dead.... We are justified therefore in calling these people barbarians by reference to the laws of reason, but not in comparison with ourselves, who surpass them in every kind of barbarity."[71]

A third meaning, but a positive one this time, as applied to the word *barbarian*, had prepared the way for this sudden shift in perspective. Brazilian natives could be called "barbarians" or "savages" because they were still close to nature and its laws: "These people are wild in the same way as we say that fruits are wild, when nature has produced them by herself and in her ordinary way; whereas, in fact, it is those we have artificially modified, and removed from the common order, that we ought to call wild. In the former, the true, most useful, and natural virtues and properties are alive and vigorous; in the latter we have bastardized them, and adapted them only to the gratification of our corrupt taste."[72]

Three different meanings. Each one implies distance between *us* and *them*: "... there is an amazing difference between their characters and ours."[73] Distance and diversity, as we have seen, were definitely appealing to Montaigne, on both an aesthetic and an intellectual level, so he tried to make sense of the life and customs of those strange populations. Then, with a sudden shift of perspective he looked at us, civilized people, through the eyes of the Brazilian natives who had been brought to Rouen, where they stood before the king of France. What they saw, and what he saw through their eyes, made no sense at all. At the end of his essay, he recorded their astonishment when confronted with our society. Even though his words have been quoted innumerable times, they are still painful and hard to read:

> [They said] that they had noticed among us some men gorged to the full with things of every sort while their other halves were beggars at their doors, emaciated with hunger and poverty. They found it strange that these poverty-stricken halves should suffer such injustice, and that they did not take the others by the throat or set fire to their houses.[74]

CHAPTER 4

Proofs and Possibilities

Postscript to Natalie Zemon Davis, The Return of Martin Guerre

1. Extraordinary, almost prodigious, is how this sixteenth-century story re-lated by Natalie Zemon Davis appeared to contemporaries. The first to pre-sent it in this light was the judge Jean de Coras, who had actually investigated and narrated it. Montaigne alluded to it in his essay "Des boyteux," ("Of the Lame"): "Il me souvient . . . qu'il me sembla avoire rendu l'imposture de celuy qu'il jugea coulpable si merveilleuse et excedant de si loing nostre connois-ance, et la sienne qui estoit juge, que je trouvay beaucoup de hardiesse en l'arrest qui l'avoit condamné à estre pendu."[1] It is a telling judgment introducing the celebrated pages on the "sorcieres de mon voisinage" ("the witches of my neigh-borhood"), who had been accused of crimes which Montaigne thought even more unlikely and unproven. Montaigne implicitly links the temerity of the judges who condemn them to death to Coras's: "Après tout, c'est mettre ses conjectures à bien haut pris que d'en faire cuire un homme tout vif."[2] Sobriety, a sense of proper limits—these themes, dear to Montaigne, constitute the guiding thread of the essay. Just before the sudden mention of Coras they had inspired in him these beautiful words: "On me faict hayr les choses vray-semblables quand on me le plante pour infallibles. J'ayme ces mots, qui amolis-sent et moderent la temerité de nos propositions: *A l'avanture, Aucunement, Quelque, On dict, Je pense,* et semblables."[3]

With a sense of discomfort which would have met with Montaigne's approval, Natalie Zemon Davis writes that in the film about Martin Guerre, in which she participated, she sensed the absence of all those "'perhapses,' the 'may-have-beens,' to which the historian has recourse when the evidence is inadequate or perplexing." We would be misinterpreting these words if we saw them only as a consequence of a cautious attitude nurtured through a lifetime of working in archives and libraries. On the contrary, Davis says, it was precisely in the course of the filming, seeing Roger Planchon experimenting with different intonations for the dialogue of the judge [Coras], "that I had my own historical laboratory, generating not proofs, but historical possibilities."[4]

The expression "historical laboratory" is, naturally, used metaphorically. If a laboratory is a place where scientific experiments take place, the historian, by definition, is a researcher for whom such experiments, in the strict sense of the term, are excluded. To reproduce a revolution, an upheaval, a religious movement is impossible, not only in actuality, but even in principle, for a discipline that studies temporally irreversible phenomena *as such*.[5] This characteristic does not pertain just to history; we have only to think of astrophysics and paleontology. The impossibility of falling back on actual experiments has not prevented each of these disciplines from working out its own scientific criteria, based, in the common consciousness, on the notion of proof.[6]

The fact that this notion was elaborated initially in the legal sphere has been dismissed freely by contemporary historians. Until not so long ago the controversy against *histoire événementielle* waged in the name of constructing more substantial phenomena—economies, societies, cultures—had created an apparently unbridgeable chasm between historical and juridical research. The latter, in fact, was often seen as the destructive model of the moralistic diatribes coming from an older political historiography. But in the last few years the rediscovery of the event (an actual decisive battle, such as the one at Bouvines studied by Georges Duby)[7] as the ideal terrain to analyze the interconnection of deeply rooted historical tendencies has implicitly opened up to discussion questions thought to have been settled. Moreover, and more specifically, the attempt—of which Davis's book is an example—to discern the concreteness of social processes through the reconstruction of the lives of men and women of modest birth has once again brought out the partial contiguity between the viewpoint of the historian and that of the judge. This is so if only because the richest sources for research of this type are documents produced by lay and ecclesiastical courts. In these situations the historian has the impression that he is conducting his investigations through an intermediary—an inquisitor or a judge. Trial records, either directly accessible or, as in the case of Davis, indirectly, are comparable to the firsthand documentation collected by an anthropologist in his field notes, and bequeathed to future historians. These are precious sources even if, inevitably, insufficient: an infinity of questions that the historian asks himself—and that he would ask the actual defendants and witnesses if he were able—were not asked, nor could they have been, by those judges and inquisitors of the past. It is not just a question of cultural distance, but of different objectives. The awkward professional juxtaposition between the historians and anthropologists of today and the judges and inquisitors of the past is hindered at some point by the difference of their methods and objectives. However, this does not diminish the partial overlapping that exists between the two points of view. We are reminded of this vividly the moment that historians and judges find themselves physically working together in the same society and with the same phenomena.[8] A classic problem, one that might seem to have been resolved for good—that of the relationship between historical inquiry and judicial inquiry—reveals unexpected theoretical and political implications.

Unfortunately, the records of the trial celebrated at Toulouse against Arnaud du Tilh, bigamist and impostor, have been lost. Davis had to content herself with literary reconstructions such as the *Arrest memorable* of the judge Jean de Coras and Guillaume Le Sueur's *Admiranda historia*. In her punctilious reading of these texts, bountiful as they are, we detect her regret (fully shared by the reader) for the lost judicial source. We can scarcely imagine what a mine of involuntary data (data not sought by the judges) the trial records would have offered to a scholar like Davis. But she also asked herself a series of questions for which, four centuries earlier, even Jean de Coras and his colleagues from the Parlement of Toulouse had sought answers. How had Arnaud du Tilh succeeded in impersonating so convincingly the part of Martin Guerre, the real husband? Had the two men struck up an earlier understanding? And to what extent had Bertrande, the wife, been the impostor's accomplice? To be sure, if Davis had limited herself to these questions, the narrative would have remained at the level of the anecdotal. But it is significant that, along with the continuity of the questions, there is a corresponding continuity of answers. On the whole Davis accepts the reconstruction of events achieved by the sixteenth-century judges, with one significant exception. The Parlement of Toulouse judged Bertrande to be innocent and the son born from her second husband legitimate, because the child was conceived while she was convinced that Arnaud was her true husband—juridically a very delicate point on which Coras dwelt with learned arguments in his *Arrest memorable.* But according to Davis, Bertrande had grasped almost at once that the alleged Martin Guerre was actually a stranger, and not her husband: if she accepted him on these terms, it was from choice and not because she was the innocent victim of deception.

This conclusion is based on conjecture. Bertrande's thoughts and feelings are unfortunately unavailable but, given the evidence, seem quite obvious to us. Davis takes issue with those historians who tend to portray peasants (especially the women) of this period as persons virtually without any freedom of choice. They argue at this point that this is an exceptional case and not typical, stressing the ambiguity between statistical representation (real or imagined) and historical representation. Actually, the argument should be turned on its head: it is precisely the exceptional nature of the Martin Guerre case that sheds some light on a normality that is difficult to document. Inversely, similar situations help in some way to fill out the lacunae in the story which Davis has set out to reconstruct: "When I could not find my individual man or woman . . . then I did my best through other sources from the period and place to discover the world they would have seen and the reactions they might have had. What I offer you here is in part my invention, but held tightly in check by the voices of the past."[9]

The term "invention" is deliberately provocative, but somewhat deceiving. Davis's research (and the narration) are not based on the juxtaposition between "true" and "invented," but on the integration, always scrupulously noted, of "reality" and "possibility." From this stems the frequent use in her book of expressions like "perhaps," "should have," "one may presume," "certainly"—which in the language of the historian usually signifies "quite probably"—and so forth. At this point the divergent perspectives of the judge and the historian seem clear. For the former, the margin of uncertainty had a purely negative significance and might have resulted in a *non liquet*, or, in modern terms, a dismissal for lack of evidence. For the latter, it sparked further investigation, to link the specific case to the context, here understood as the realm of historically determined possibilities. The biographies of Davis's personages resemble, from time to time, the biographies of other "men and women of the same time and place," reconstructed wisely and patiently through the use of notarial, judicial, and literary sources. "True," "probably," "proofs," and "possibilities" are interwoven, while at the same time remaining rigorously distinct.

We have spoken about "narration" in connection with Davis's book. The notion that all books of history, including works based on statistics, graphs, and charts, have an intrinsically narrative component is rejected by many—wrongly, in my opinion. All, however, are willing to acknowledge that some books of history, among which is undoubtedly *The Return of Martin Guerre*, have a richer narrative physiognomy than others. The story of Martin Guerre, so dramatic, so full of sensational events, obviously lent itself to such an expository choice. The fact that it has been recounted successively by jurists, novelists, historians, and cinema directors makes it a useful case study for reflection on a problem that is widely debated today—the connection between the narrative in general and historical narrative.

The oldest accounts of the event—the *Admiranda historia* of Le Sueur and the *Arrest memorable* of Jean de Coras—have something dissimilar about them, as Davis notes, although both were written by professional jurists. Common to them is the insistence that the case of the false husband is an unheard-of novelty. But whereas the *Admiranda historia* takes its inspiration from the then-popular genre of histories of prodigious events, the *Arrest memorable* offers unusual features. In its alternation between narrative and learned annotations, it has the structure of a legal work. In his dedication to Jean de Monluc, bishop of Valence, in the first edition of his work, Coras modestly underlines its literary limitations: "the tale is brief, I admit, poorly developed, roughly polished, written in a style that is excessively rustic." Instead, he lauds the subject: "an affair, so beautiful, so appealing and so monstrously strange."[10] Almost contemporaneously, the opening sonnet addressed to the reader in the French translation of Le Sueur's *Historia* (*Histoire admirable d'un faux et supposé mary*) emphatically declared that the case exceeded "the prodigious histories" of Christian or pagan writers, "the fables of the ancient poets" (citing Ovid's *Metamorphoses* shortly afterward), the "monstrous depictions," the guiles of Plautus, of Terence or the "new comics," and "the strangest cases of the tragedians."[11] The analogy with the mix-up of characters in classical comedy was unremarkable: Coras himself had compared the occurrence of the false Martin Guerre with the *Amphitrion* of Plautus. Le Sueur, instead, had spoken of "tragedy" on two occasions. Coras followed his example in the section added in 1565 to the new edition of the *Arrest*, expanded to 111 notes from 100. The introduction of the term "tragedy" was followed by a comment: "It was truly a tragedy for that genteel rustic (*gentil rustre*), since his end was sad and miserable. Because no one knows the difference between tragedy and comedy." This last statement was promptly contradicted by an apparent digression in which Coras, following Cicero's formula, contrasts comedy, which "describes and represents in a low and humble style the private happenings of men, such as the love and seduction of young girls," to tragedy, in which "in lofty and grave style the customs, adversities and lives full of misfortunes of captains, dukes, kings and princes are told."[12] But the affinity between a stylistic hierarchy and a social hierarchy which inspired this traditional juxtaposition was implicitly rejected by Coras, who merely accepted the equivalence (still familiar to us) between comedy and a happy ending on the one hand, and tragedy and a sad ending on the other. What persuaded him to reject the traditional doctrine (with which he was certainly familiar, although claiming not to know it) was the exceptional nature of the event, and especially of its protagonist, Arnaud du Tilh, nicknamed Pansette, "that genteel rustic." Davis provides a subtle analysis of that ambivalent fascination exercised on Coras by his hero (whom, in his capacity of judge, he had helped to send to the gallows). We may add that this ambivalence may be underlined precisely by that highly contradictory expression *gentil rustre*, an oxymoron which Coras repeats twice.[13] Is a peasant capable of "refinement," an attribute by definition tied to social privilege? And how should this contradictory marvel be described? With the "high and grave" style of tragedy, as would seem to be required by the adjective (*gentil*), or with the "low and humble" ones of comedy, suitable to the noun *rustre*? At some point even Le Sueur had felt the need to allow the personages in his story more prestige, observing, apropos the precocious marriage of Martin Guerre with the ten-year-old Bertrande, that the wish for posterity is common "not only to great lords, but also to plebeians (*mechaniques*)."[14] In an impetuous moment Coras actually manages to say that, faced by "the happy event of such an extraordinary memory" exhibited by Arnaud du Tilh during the trial, the judges had been on the point of comparing him to "Scipio, Cyrus, Theodectes, Mithridates, Themistocles, Cineas, Metrodorus or Lucullus"—in other words, to those "captains, dukes, kings and princes" who are the heroes of tragedies. But Arnaud's "miserable end," Coras adds, almost as if awakening from a trance, would have obfuscated the splendor of such personages.[15] The humble life and ignominious death on the gallows of Arnaud du Tilh, nicknamed Pansette, in the end kept him from being seen as a tragic figure in the traditional sense: but in another sense, the one transmitted to us by Coras, he can be considered tragic precisely because of that death. In Arnaud, in this peasant impostor, who appeared to him as if enveloped in a demonic halo, Coras implicitly recognized, straining the confines of classical doctrine based on the separation of styles, a certain dignity that drew its origins from the common human condition—a theme that was central in the thought of his contemporary and critic Montaigne. As Natalie Davis has shrewdly observed, the judge in some way had succeeded in identifying himself with his victim. How much the probable adherence of both to the reformed faith contributed to this, it is difficult to say. But while writing the *Arrest memorable*, Coras did not suspect that he himself was destined to a "miserable end": hanging—the same end he had inflicted on Arnaud.

The classical doctrine of the separation of literary styles and its transgression by Christianity is the dominant theme in Erich Auerbach's great work on the representation of reality in western European literature. Analyzing passages from historians of antiquity (Tacitus, Ammianus Marcellinus) and of the Middle Ages (Gregory of Tours) along with writings of poets, dramatists, and novelists, Auerbach suggested an approach that has not been pursued further. It would be worthwhile to attempt to do so and show how more or less extraordinary facts taken from chronicles and books of travel to distant parts contributed to the birth of the novel and—through this significant intermediary—also to modern historical writing. Jean de Coras's recognition of a tragic dimension in the Arnaud du Tilh affair would then find a suitable place among the examples of the weakening of a rigidly hierarchical vision under the pressure of diversity—social, cultural, or natural, depending on the case.[16]

2. In the last few years the narrative component in historical writing has been, as we have mentioned, the subject of lively discussion among philosophers and students of method, and, more recently, among some leading historians.[17] But their failure to communicate among themselves prevented them thus far from achieving satisfactory results. Philosophers have studied single historiographical propositions that are usually detached from the context, ignoring the preparatory research that had rendered them possible.[18] In turn, historians have asked themselves if in recent years there has been a return to narrative history, disregarding the cognitive implications of the various types of narration.[19] The very page from Coras which we have just discussed reminds us that the adoption of a stylistic codex determines certain aspects of reality and not others, emphasizes certain connections and not others, establishes certain hierarchies and not others. That all this seems to be connected to the changing relations in the course of two and a half millennia between historical narration and other types of narration—from the epic poem, to the novel, to

film—seems obvious. To analyze these relationships historically—composed, in turn, of exchanges, hybridization, juxtapositions, one-way influences— would be much more useful than proposing abstract theoretical formulations, which are often implicitly or explicitly normative.

One example may suffice. The first masterpiece of the bourgeois novel is entitled *The Life and Strange Surprizing Adventures of Robinson Crusoe of York, Mariner*. In the preface its author, Daniel Defoe, stresses the truthfulness of the story, as opposed to "history," a "fiction": "The story is told with modesty, with seriousness. . . . The Editor believes the thing to be a just history of fact; neither is there any appearance of fiction in it. . . ."[20] Henry Fielding, instead, entitled his most famous book *The History of Tom Jones, a Foundling*, explaining that he had preferred "history," a "life," or "an apology for a life" following the example of historians: but which ones? "We intend in it rather to pursue the method of those writers, who profess to disclose the revolutions of countries, than to imitate the painful and voluminous historian, who, to preserve the regularity of his series, thinks himself obliged to fill up as much paper with the detail of months and years in which nothing remarkable happened, as he employs upon those notable eras when the greatest scenes have been transacted on the human stage."[21]

Fielding's model is Edward Hyde, first earl of Clarendon, the author of *History of the Rebellion*. From him he learned to condense or expand the time of the narration, breaking with the uniform time frames of the chronicle and the epic that seemed set by an invisible metronome.[22] This perception is so important to Fielding that it persuaded him to entitle each of the books into which *Tom Jones* is divided, beginning with the fourth, with a temporal reference, which until the tenth becomes progressively, convulsively more brief: a year, six months, three weeks, three days, two days, twelve hours, about twelve hours. Two Irishmen, Laurence Sterne[23] and James Joyce, will later reveal the consequences of taking this expansion of narrative time in relation to the actual calendar to extremes: and we get an entire novel dedicated to the description of a single, interminable day in Dublin. Thus, at the birth of this remarkable narrative upheaval, we find the history of the first great revolution of the modern era.

In the last few decades historians have discussed at length the rhythms of history; but, significantly, they have said little or nothing about the rhythms of historical narration. If I am not mistaken, an inquiry into the possible repercussions of the narrative model inaugurated by Fielding on twentieth-century historiography is yet to be done. What is clear, instead, is the dependence—not limited to the treatment of the temporal flow—of the English novel, which arose in opposition to the "Gothic" current, on older or contemporary historiography. In the prestige that envelops the latter, such writers as Defoe and Fielding sought legitimacy for a literary genre that at first was still socially discredited. We recall Defoe's concise declaration about Robinson Crusoe's adventures as "a true history of facts" without "semblance of falsehood." In a more elaborate way Fielding asserts that he had wanted to avoid the term "novel," which, in fact, would have been an appropriate definition for *Tom Jones*, so as not to fall into the disrepute which afflicts "all historical writers who do not draw their materials from records." Instead, *Tom Jones*, Fielding concludes, truly deserves the epithet of "history" (which appears in the title): all the characters are well documented because they step out "of the vast and authentic doomsday-book of nature."[24] Brilliantly fusing the mention of the land register ordered by William the Conqueror with the traditional image of "book of Nature," Fielding claimed historical truth for his work by comparing it to archival research. You could call historians those who occupied themselves with "public happenings," as well as those, like himself, who restricted themselves to "scenes from private life."[25] For Edward Gibbon, instead, even if pronounced in the sphere of hyperbolic praise ("that exquisite picture of human manners will outlive the palace of the Escurial and the Imperial Eagle of the House of Austria"), *Tom Jones* remained, in spite of its title, a "Romance."[26]

But with the growing prestige of the novel the situation changed. Though they continued to compare themselves to historians, novelists began to shed their position of inferiority little by little. Balzac's falsely modest declaration (in reality haughty) in the introduction of his *Comédie humaine*, "French society would be the real author, I should only be the secretary," acquired all its piquancy from that which followed shortly after: "I might perhaps succeed in writing the history which so many historians have neglected: that of manners. By patience and perseverance I might produce for France in the nineteenth century the book which we must all regret that Rome, Athens, Tyre, Memphis, Persia and India have not bequeathed to us...."[27] Balzac hurled this grand challenge at historians while claiming a field of research which basically they had left untouched: "...I attach to common, daily facts, hidden or patent to the eye, to the acts of individual lives, and to their cause and principles, the importance which historians have hitherto ascribed to the events of the public life of nations."[28]

Balzac wrote these words in 1842. Roughly a decade earlier, Giambattista Bazzoni, in the introduction to his *Falco della Rupe, o la guerra di Rupo*, had expressed himself in similar terms:

> The historical novel is a great lens applied to a detail of an immense painting [sketched by historians, populated by great personages; in this way] so that what had been barely visible receives its natural dimensions; lightly outlined contours become a regular and perfect design, or, better yet, a composition in which every object receives its true color. No longer the usual kings, dukes, magistrates, but common folk, women, children make their appearance; we see in action vices, domestic virtues, and the influence of public institutions on private habits, on the needs and happiness of life, which ultimately is what should interest the universality of mankind.[29]

The starting point for Bazzoni quite obviously was *I promessi sposi (The Betrothed)*. But more time had to pass before Manzoni would decide to publish those pages from *Del romanzo storico e, in genere, de' componimenti misti di storia e d'invenzione (On the Historical Novel)* in which the entire question was carefully discussed. He attributed to an imaginary speaker the idea of the historical novel, a form not only different from but even superior to current historical writing:

> The aim of your work was to put before me, in a new and special form, a richer, more varied, more complete history than that found in works which more commonly go by this name, as if by *antonomasia*. The history we expect from you is not a chronological account of mere political and military events or, occasionally, some other kind of extraordinary happening, but a more general representation of the human condition, in a time and place naturally more circumscribed than that in which works of history, in the more usual sense of the word, ordinarily unfold. In a way, there is the same difference between the usual sort of history and your own as between a geographic map that simply indicates the presence of mountain chains, rivers, cities, towns, and major roads of a vast region, and a topographic map, where all of this (and whatever else might be shown in a more restricted area) is presented in greater detail and, indeed, where even minor elevations and less noteworthy particulars—ditches, channels, villages, isolated homes, paths—are clearly marked. Customs, opinions, whether they are generally accepted or peculiar to certain social classes; the private consequences of public events that are more properly called historical, or of the laws, or will of the powerful, however these are expressed—in short, all that a given society in a given time could claim as most characteristic of every way of life and of their interactions—this is what you sought to reveal at least as far as you managed, through long hard research to discover in yourself.

For the imaginary interlocutor the presence of invented elements in this program was contradictory. It does not matter here how Manzoni responded to this and other objections concerning the historical novel. What should be acknowledged, instead, is that he ended up opposing to the historical novel a "possible" history, even if it already had been expressed by many works "whose goal is to reveal not so much the political course of a society at a given time as its way of life from any number of points of view." These were vague words which receded immediately before the scarcely veiled recognition that history "still falls short of its goal, still fails to exploit what its subject matter, re-searched and viewed from a broader and more philosophic perspective, has to offer. . . ." From this stemmed the appeal to the future historian to "search every document from that period that you can find. Even treat as documents writings whose authors never, in their wildest imaginations, dreamt they were writing in support of history."[30]

When Balzac argued for juxtaposing the importance of the private lives of individuals with the public life of nations, he was thinking of *Lys dans la vallée*: "The unknown battle which goes on in a valley of the Indre between Mme. Mortsauf and her passion is perhaps as great as the most famous battles. . . ."[31] And when Manzoni's imaginary interlocutor spoke of "the private consequences of public events that are more properly called histori-cal, or of the laws, or will of the powerful, however these are expressed," he was naturally alluding to *I promessi sposi*. But in the considerations of a gen-eral character voiced by both Balzac and Manzoni, in hindsight it is impos-sible not to rediscover the anticipation of the most obvious characteristics of the historical research of the last few decades—from the polemic against the limitations of history that is exclusively political and military, to the promo-tion of history of the mentality of individuals and social groups, right up to, in the case of Manzoni, a theorization of microhistory and the systematic use of new documentary sources. This is a result, as we have said, of an anachronistic reading conducted with the benefit of hindsight, but nevertheless not wholly arbitrary. It took a century for historians to accept the challenge issued by the great nineteenth-century novelists, from Balzac to Manzoni, from Stendhal to Tolstoy, delving into fields of endeavor they had previously ignored, assisted by more subtle and complex explanatory models than the traditional ones. The growing predilection of historians for themes (and, in part, for expository devices) previously reserved for novelists—a phenomenon inappropriately de-fined as "the rebirth of narrative history"—is nothing more than another chapter in the long challenge on the terrain of the knowledge of reality. Compared with Fielding's time, the pendulum is now oscillating in the opposite direction.

Until not so long ago the great majority of historians saw a definite incompatibility between the emphasis on the scientific character of historiography (tendentiously assimilated into the historical sciences) and recognition of its literary dimension. Today, this awareness is more and more often extended also to works of anthropology or sociology without allowing this to necessarily imply a negative judgment by those who advance it. What is usually emphasized, however, is not the cognitive nucleus one finds in fictional narratives—novels, for example—but rather the fictional nucleus in narratives with scholarly pretensions, beginning with the historical. The convergence between the two types of narration should be sought—to make a long story short—in the sphere of art, and not science. Hayden White, for example, has studied the works of Michelet, Ranke, Tocqueville, and Burckhardt as examples of "historical imagination."[32] And François Hartog, independently of White and probably inspired instead by the writings of Michel de Certeau, examined book 4 of Herodotus on the Scythians as an autonomous discussion, complete in itself as the description of an imaginary world. In both cases the analysis does not go into the pretense to truth in the historical narratives. To be sure, Hartog does not reject in principle the legitimacy of a comparison of the descriptions of Herodotus with, for example, the results of the archeological excavations in the area north of the Black Sea, or of the research on the folklore of those distant descendants of the Scythians, the Ossetians.

But this chance comparison with the Ossetian documentation, collected by Russian folklorists at the end of the nineteenth century, prompted Hartog to conclude that Herodotus, in an essential point, "attenuated and misunderstood" the "alterity," or otherness, of Scythian divination.[33] How can we not conclude that an *Essai sur la représentation de l'autre* (the subtitle of Hartog's book) necessarily implied a less episodic comparison between the text of Herodotus and other documentary series? Similarly, White declared that he had wanted to limit his own research to the "artistic" elements in the "realistic" historiography of the nineteenth century (Michelet, Ranke, Tocqueville, and so forth, using a notion of "realism" taken specifically from Erich Auerbach [*Mimesis*] and E. H. Gombrich [*Art and Illusion*]).[34] But these two great books, even in their diversity (which White quite properly underlines), are founded on the conviction that it is possible to decide, after a verification of the historical or natural reality, whether a novel or a painting is more or less adequate, from the point of view of the representation, than another novel or another painting. The refusal, basically relativistic, to descend to this level makes the categories of "realism" used by White a formula without substance.[35] An analysis of the claims to truth within historical narratives as such would have involved discussing the concrete problems, connected to the sources and to research techniques, which individual historians had set for themselves in their work. If, like White, we ignore these elements, historiography takes the form of a pure and simple ideological document.

This is Arnaldo Momigliano's criticism of White's most recent work (which could be extended, with a certain difference, also to Hartog). Momigliano disapprovingly recalls certain elementary truths: on the one hand, that the historian works with sources, known or to be discovered; on the other, that ideology contributes to prime research, but then must be kept at a distance.[36] But this final prescription oversimplifies the problem. Momigliano himself has demonstrated better than anyone else that the principle of reality and ideology, philological analysis and projection into the past of present-day problems, intertwine, each conditioning the other, in *every* phase of the historical endeavor—from the identification of the objective and the selection of the documents to the research methods and the weighing of the evidence, and even to the literary presentation. The unilateral reduction of this highly complicated interweaving of so many parts to an action immune from the contentiousness of the historical imagination, as proposed by White and Hartog, in the final analysis appears unproductive. It is precisely thanks to the discord raised by the principle of reality (or whatever we want to call it) that historians, from the time of Herodotus, have ended up, in spite of everything, appropriating extensively from "the other," at times in a rather ordinary mode, at others by profoundly modifying the cognitive schemes from which they had set out. The "pathology of representation," in Gombrich's words, does not exhaust the possibilities. If it had not been possible to correct our actual imaginings, expectations, and ideologies on the basis of the responses, frequently unpleasant, emanating from the outside world, the species *Homo sapiens* would have perished long ago. Among the intellectual devices that permitted us to adapt to our surroundings (both natural and social), transforming them along the way, historiography must also be included.

3. Today the insistence on the narrative dimension of historiography (of every type, even if not in equal measure) is accompanied, as we have seen, by relativistic positions which tend to erase de facto all distinctions between "fiction" and "history," between narratives of the fantastic and narratives with pretense to truth. Against these tendencies, it should be emphasized instead that a greater awareness of the narrative dimension does not imply a weakening of the cognitive possibilities offered by historiography, but rather, to the contrary, their intensification. This will have to be the starting point of a sweeping critique of the language of historiography, which has been barely suggested up to now.

Thanks to Momigliano we know that antiquarian research contributed decisively to the birth of modern historiography.[37] But it was Edward Gibbon himself, the person whom Momigliano named as the symbol of the fusion between antiquarianism and the philosophy of history, who attacked in a brief exercise in self-criticism an aspect of chapter 31 of his *History of the Decline and Fall of the Roman Empire*. He was addressing himself to the conditions of Britannia in the first half of the fifth century—specifically, to the modifying influence exercised by narrative schemes on the presentation of research findings: "I owe it to myself and to historic truth to declare, that some *circumstances* in this paragraph are founded only on conjecture and analogy. The stubbornness of our language has sometimes forced me to deviate from the *conditional* into the *indicative* mood."[38] For his part, Manzoni, in a page from his *On the Historical Novel*, suggested a different solution. After having contrasted geographical to topographical maps as images, respectively, of traditional historiography and the historical novel, understood as "a new and special historical form . . . , richer, more varied, more complete," Manzoni complicated the metaphor by inviting us to distinguish, within the map, what was indisputable from what was speculative. The proposal was not in itself new: similar practices had been used for quite some time among philologists and antiquarians. But the extension to narrative history was certainly unusual, as demonstrated by the aforementioned passage from Gibbon. In Manzoni's words:

> It might not be out of place to mention that history sometimes also uses the verisimilar, and can do so harmlessly if it uses it properly and presents it as such, thereby distinguishing it from the real. . . . It is a characteristic of man's impoverished state that he can know only something of what has been, even in his own

little world; and it is an aspect of his nobility and his power that he can conjecture beyond what he can actually know. When history turns to the verisimilar, it does nothing other than favor or promote this tendency. It stops narrating momentarily and uses, instead, inductive reasoning, because ordinary narrative is not the best instrument for this, and in adjusting to a different situation, it adopts a new purpose. In fact, all that is needed to clarify the relationship between fact and verisimilar is that the two appear distinct. History acts almost like someone who, when drawing a city map, adds in a distinctive color the streets, plazas, and buildings planned for the future and who, while distinguishing the potential from the actual, lets us see the logic of the whole. History, at such moments, I would say, abandons narrative, but only in order to produce a better narrative. As much when it conjectures as when it narrates, history points to the real; there lies its unity.[39]

The integration of the lacunae achieved (and immediately after denounced) by Gibbon might be compared to a pictorial restoration understood as drastic overpainting; while the systematic indication of Manzoni's historiographical conjectures might be likened to an instance of restoration in which the lacunae are identified by means of fine lines. In every sense this sort of solution was ahead of its time. Manzoni's text remained without echo. We do not even find a trace of it in the essay "Immaginazione, aneddotica e storiografica," in which Benedetto Croce perceptively discussed examples of fallacious narrative integrations dictated by the "combinatory imagination."[40] Croce, for that matter, significantly reduced the significance of his observations by applying them exclusively to the anecdotal, closely related to the historical novel: historiography, in the strict and highest sense of the term, in his opinion, was immune from risks of this type. As we have seen, a historian like Gibbon was not of this opinion.

Arsenio Frugoni construed the implications of Croce's essay in a much more radical sense.[41] In his *Arnaldo da Brescia* he bitterly censured the "philological-combinatory method"—in other words, the obstinate, ingenuous faith of scholars in the providential, complemental aspect of testimonies from the past. This belief had created an image of Arnaldo that was fictitious and unreliable, which Frugoni demolished, reading each of the sources internally, holding it to the light, to reveal its singular uniqueness. From the writings of St. Bernard, of Otto of Freising, of Gerhoh of Reichersberg, and of similar figures emerged other portraits of Arnaldo da Brescia, drawn from many visual perspectives. But this effort at "restoration" was accompanied by the attempt to reconstruct, within the limits of the possible, the personality of the "true" Arnaldo: "Our portrait will emerge like one of those fragments of ancient sculpture, created from vigorous suggestive strokes (do I delude myself?) free of the adulterations of later accretions."[42]

Frugoni's *Arnaldo*, published in 1954, has been discussed only by specialists. But it is obvious that it was not intended only for students of medieval heresy or of twelfth-century religious movements. Today, many decades after the book appeared, we can read it as an anticipatory work, which may have suffered from a certain timidity in bringing the initial critical intention to its conclusion. With the benefit of hindsight, it now seems clear that its target was not solely the philological-combinatory method but traditional historical narration, often helplessly inclined to integrate (with an adverb, a preposition, an adjective, or an indicative, rather than a conditional, verb) the lacunae in the documentation, transforming a mere torso into a complete statue.

Pietro Zerbi, a careful reviewer, was disturbed to recognize in Frugoni's book a tendency toward "historiographical agnosticism," moderated only feebly by the "aspirations of a true historical mentality, which feels itself mortified when it only perceives dust, even if it is gold dust."[43] This is not a baseless concern: the excessive weight given to narrative sources, as in the case of Frugoni (and also, from totally different cultural presuppositions, in Hartog), contains the inception of an idealistic dissolution of history into the history of historiography. But in principle the criticism of evidence so shrewdly suggested by Frugoni not only does not exclude but rather furthers the integration of different documentary categories with an awareness that was unknown to the old combinatory method. There is still much to do in this direction.

4. In the very act of proposing to introduce conjecture, identified as such, in historical narration, Manzoni reiterated, in somewhat contorted fashion, that "history . . . abandons the telling of the tale, in order to draw nigh, in the only way possible, to that which is the purpose of the narration." In Manzoni's eyes there was an obvious incompatibility between conjecture and the historical account, understood as the exposition of positive truths. Today, instead, the interweaving of truth and possibility, together with the discussion of opposed research hypotheses, alternating with pages of historical reconstruction, no longer disconcerts us. Our sensitivity as readers has undergone a change thanks to M. I. Rostovzeff and Marc Bloch, but also thanks

to Marcel Proust and Robert Musil. It is not only the category of historical narration that has been transformed, but narration *itself*. The relationship between the narrator and reality becomes more uncertain, more problematic.

Historians, however, sometimes hesitate to admit this. And at this point we are better able to understand why Natalie Davis was able to call the screening room of the film about Martin Guerre an actual "historical laboratory." The succession of scenes in which Roger Planchon tried to enunciate with different intonations a single utterance of the judge Coras transformed in one swoop (Gibbon would have said) the indicative of the historical narrative into a conditional. Viewers of Federico Fellini's film 8 1/2 (historians or not) have lived an experience in some ways similar to a scene in which various aspiring actresses follow one after the other on a theater stage to impersonate the same personage, uttering wearily or clumsily the same words before the protagonist-director. In Fellini's film the effect of this "dis-realization" is accentuated by the fact that the spectator has already seen the "real" person which the aspiring "actresses" are endeavoring to impersonate—a "real" personage who, herself, is a film personality. This dizzying game of mirrors reminds us of a well-known fact—namely, that the intertwining between reality and fiction, between truth and possibility, is at the heart of the artistic creations in this century. Natalie Davis has reminded us of the benefits that historians can draw from this for their work.

Terms such as "fiction" and "possibility" must not deceive us. More than ever the question of evidence remains the nub of historical research: but its status inevitably is modified the moment different themes are confronted in respect to the past, with the assistance of documentation which is itself diverse.[44] Davis's attempt to work around the lacunae with archival materials contiguous in space and time to that which has been lost or never materialized is only one of the many possible solutions. But extendable to what point? It would be worthwhile to discuss this. Invention is one solution we can instantly reject, not only because it would contradict what has been said, but also because it would be absurd, since some of the most celebrated nineteenth-century novelists have disparaged the recourse to invention, attributing it ironically to historians themselves. "Cette invention est ce qu'il y a de plus facile et de plus vulgaire dans le travail de l'esprit, ce qui exige le moins de réflexion, et même le moins d'imagination," Manzoni wrote in his *Lettre à M. Chauvet*, claiming for poetry inquiry into the world of the passions from which history, instead, was excluded. This is the same history which, "fortunately," is accustomed to conjecture, as we read in the famous words from *I promessi sposi*.[45] "I often think it odd that it [history] should be so dull," reflected one of Jane Austen's characters, "for a great deal of it must be invention."[46] "To represent and illustrate the past, the actions of men, is the task of either writer [novelist or historian]," wrote Henry James at the end of the nineteenth century, "and the only difference I can see is, in proportion as he succeeds, to the honor of the novelist, consisting as it does in his having more difficulty in collecting his evidence, which is so far from being purely literary."[47] One could go on.

For the novelists of more than a century earlier, instead, the prestige of historiography was based on an image of absolute veracity in which recourse to conjecture played no part at all. In contrasting historians who occupied themselves with "public transactions" to others, such as himself, who limited themselves to "scenes of private life," Fielding was pointing out reluctantly the position of greater credibility of the former, based on "public records, with the concurrent testimony of many authors": on the consensual testimony, in other words, of archival and narrative sources.[48] This contrasting of historians to novelists now seems very remote to us. Today historians claim the right to concern themselves with the public acts of Trajan, Antoninus Pius, Nero, or Caligula (the examples cited by Fielding) but also with scenes from the private life of Arnaud du Tilh, nicknamed Pansette, of Martin Guerre and of his wife, Bertrande. By adroitly uniting erudition and imagination, proofs and possibilities, Natalie Davis has shown that we can write even the history of men and women like them.

CHAPTER 5

Paris, 1647

A Dialogue on Fiction and History

1. Some years ago Marcel Detienne discussed with some irony Moses Finley's attempt to identify historical elements in Homeric poems.[1] The elimination of the mystical element when writing history, Detienne suggested, is a penchant typical of historians: it seems worthwhile to examine this idea critically from its most distant roots.[2] Let us look first at an important occurrence, but from a perspective very different from Detienne's.

2. The dialogue *De la lecture des vieux romans (On Reading Old Romances)*, by Jean Chapelain, written sometime between the end of 1646 and early 1647, long remained unpublished; it appeared posthumously eighty years later.[3] At the time Chapelain was working on *La Pucelle ou la France delivrée*, an ambitious poem which, after an initial success, was attacked savagely and became totally discredited.[4] To us today, the rest of Chapelain's literary activity—his critical essays and vast correspondence—seems much more significant.[5] The dialogue *De la lecture des vieux romans* has enjoyed many editions: 1728 (the first), 1870, 1936, 1971, 1999.[6] But much remains to be said about it.

The piece is dedicated to Paul de Gondi, at the time the vicar of the archbishop of Paris, later celebrated as the cardinal of Retz.[7] In addition to Chapelain, two younger men of letters take part in the discussion: the scholarly Gilles Ménage and the historian and poet Jean-François Sarasin.[8] Chapelain recounts that the two men took him by surprise while he was reading a medieval romance, *Lancelot du Lac*. (We learn from the catalogue of Chapelain's library that he possessed two printed editions of this work).[9] The two friends reacted differently. Sarasin had observed that *Lancelot* was "the source for all the romances that in the last four or five centuries have enjoyed great success in every European court." Ménage, enamored of the ancients, had expressed his astonishment at seeing a person of Chapelain's taste praising a book disdained even by partisans of the modern. Chapelain had replied by saying that he began to read *Lancelot* to collect materials for a book on the origins of French, an idea that Ménage himself had suggested.[10] In *Lancelot*, Chapelain said, he had found words and expressions which showed how the French language passed from crude beginnings to the refinements of that day. Ménage had nothing to say against this projected study. But when Chapelain suggested that he had started to appreciate *Lancelot*, Ménage could not restrain himself: "How can you dare to praise this horrid carcass, despised even by the ignorant and by commoners? I hope you are not thinking to discover in this barbaric writer another Homer or Livy?"

Naturally, this was a rhetorical question. But to this double, paradoxical comparison, Chapelain reacted unexpectedly. From the literary point of view Homer and the author of *Lancelot* were wholly dissimilar: the first noble and sublime, the second vulgar and low. But the subject matter in their works was alike: both had written "invented narratives" (*fables*).[11] Aristotle would have judged *Lancelot* favorably, just as he had done with the poems of Homer: the way magic was used in the former was not too different from the intervention of the gods in the latter.

All this is in accord with the writings of seventeenth-century erudites who opened the way for Mabillon and Montfaucon, laying the premises for the discovery of the Middle Ages—what Chapelain called "modern antiquity."[12] (The dialogue *De la lecture des vieux romans* is a precocious forerunner—in some sense an eccentric one—of the *querelle* between the ancients and the moderns).[13] *Lancelot's* author, Chapelain tells us, was "a barbarian, who was praised by barbarians . . . even if he was not wholly barbarous." In this attempt to soften his judgment, which was accompanied by the awareness that a romance like *Lancelot* conformed, after all, to Aristotle's maxims, it may be possible to recognize retrospectively the origins of a profound transformation in taste. But in the case of Chapelain the discovery of the Middle Ages was tied to history rather than to literature. The most original part of his dialogue begins here.

Ménage contemptuously asks if the author of *Lancelot* should be compared to Livy. Chapelain replies, "To compare *Lancelot* and Livy would be absurd, just as it would be absurd to compare Virgil and Livy, the false and the true. And yet I dare to declare that, even if *Lancelot*, since it is based on imaginary events, cannot be compared to Livy as an example of a true narrative *(par la vérité de l'histoire)*, on another level it can, as a true reflection of manners and customs *(par la vérité des mœurs et des coutumes)*. On this level both authors provide us with perfect accounts: each one, whether Livy or the author of the *Lancelot*, about the age of which he wrote."[14]

Ménage is bewildered. Chapelain tries to explain his statement in general terms. A writer who invents a story, an imaginary account which has human beings as its protagonists, has to depict people based on the usages and customs of the age in which they lived; otherwise they would not be credible.[15] Chapelain is alluding implicitly to the famous passage in the *Poetics* (1451b) in which Aristotle states that "a poet's object is not to tell what actually happened but what could and would happen either probably or inevitably." But separating himself from the tradition, Chapelain identifies in poetic verisimilitude an element that is historical, not logical or psychological.[16] *Lancelot*, he says, "since it was written in the dark days of our modern antiquity, inspired only by the book of nature, gives a faithful image, if not of that which really happened between the kings and knights of the time, at least of that which we suppose happened, on the basis of similar customs that still exist, or of documents from which it emerges that similar customs had flourished in the past."

Chapelain then concluded: *Lancelot* provides us with "a veritable representation *[une représentation naïve]* as well as, in a certain sense *[pour ainsi dire]*, a sure and exact history of the customs that prevailed in the courts of the day *[une histoire certaine et exacte des mœurs qui régnaient dans les cours d'alors]*."[17]

3. The idea that one could draw historical facts from literary writings was not new. Similar attempts can be found even among classical historians. Thucydides, for example, tried to reconstruct the dimensions of ancient Greek vessels from Homer's ship catalogue in the *Iliad*. But when Chapelain proposed reading *Lancelot* more as a historical document than a literary monument, he was undoubtedly thinking of the work of antiquarians.[18] Etienne Pasquier, in his *Recherches de la France*, first published in 1560 and then revised

and reprinted many times, included a section on the medieval origins of French poetry. In a similar vein, Claude Fauchet had compiled a *Recueil de l'origine de la langue et poésie françoise, ryme et romans*, in which he recorded the names and the writings of 127 French poets who lived before 1300.[19] Even more obvious is the connection to another of Fauchet's works, *Origine des dignitez et magistrats de la France*, in which passages from the *Roman de la Rose* or from romances of Chrétien de Troyes were used to clarify such official positions as *maire du Palais, sénéschal*, and the *grand maistre*.[20]

At the end of the dialogue Chapelain mentioned a still-unpublished treatise by Chantereau Le Fèvre in which the "great antiquarian" had repeatedly cited *Lancelot* as an authority on medieval usages and customs. Actually, in the *Traité des fiefs et de leur origine*, published seventeen years later by Chantereau Le Fèvre's son, a single, but significant, reference to *Lancelot* appears. To clarify the precise meaning of *meffaire* (the severing of the feudal pact between vassal and lord, on the part of the latter), Chantereau Le Fèvre used a passage from *Lancelot*, explaining that its author (undoubtedly a monk) had tried to describe, by means of an invented plot and imaginary names, "the customs and way of life *[les mœurs et la manière de vivre]* of the knights of the time."[21] In an unpublished writing which mirrors Chapelain's dialogue, Sarasin compared reading *Lancelot* to antiquarianism: "The old tapestries, paintings and sculptures that have been passed down to us by our ancestors resemble those old romances which (as Chapelain said) give us a faithful image of the usages and customs of those times."[22]

In his own dialogue Chapelain had developed the same analogy but in another direction. From fictional narratives we can extract more fleeting, but more precious, evidence, *precisely because* they are fictional narratives: "Physicians diagnose the corrupt humors of their patients on the basis of their dreams; similarly, we can analyze the usages and customs of the past through the fantasies portrayed in these writings."

To isolate history from poetry, truth from imagination, reality from mere possibility means reformulating implicitly the distinctions traced by Aristotle in his *Poetics*. But to dub the anonymous author of *Lancelot* "the historian of the customs of his day," asked Ménage, recalling Chapelain's judgment—is that not perchance the highest praise possible? Especially because, he continued, you claim that his work "constitutes a completion of existing chronicles. They tell us merely that a prince was born or that a prince died; they record the most important events of their reigns, and it all ends there. Through a book like *Lancelot*, instead, we become the intimate friends of these people, even to the point of grasping the very essence of their souls."[23]

4. Chapelain had begun his defense of *Lancelot* by comparing it provocatively, as far as its veracity was concerned, to the most famous medieval chronicles: those of Saxo Grammaticus, Jean Froissart, and Enguerrand de Monstrelet. But then he had raised the bar, arguing for the superiority of the history of manners, *histoire des mœurs*, over the superficiality of the chronicles, although he prudently acknowledged that each complemented the other. Today these assertions seem highly original,[24] but they appeared that way even to contemporaries. To propose a more profound sort of history on the basis of a romance like *Lancelot*, Ménage observed, was the height of paradox: it signified "presenting as worthy of trust a writer whose narratives were, by your own admission, wholly invented [*fabuleuses*]."[25] To comprehend the meaning of these words we must make a digression, or perhaps only an apparent one.

5. The rediscovery of ancient skepticism, which Pierre Bayle equated with the birth of modern philosophy, went through various phases which, in large part, were tied to the publication of the works of Sextus Empiricus. The first Latin translation of his *Outlines of Pyrrhonism*, edited by Henri Estienne (1562), was followed by a reprinting that included the treatise *Adversus mathematicos* in the Latin version by Gentian Hervet (1569). In 1621 these two Latin translations were republished in four European cities, in a large in-folio volume, together with the original Greek text.[26]

The writings of Sextus Empiricus, our principal source for ancient skepticism, sparked a discussion on "historic Pyrrhonism,"—in other words, on historical knowledge and its limits—that persisted for a century and a half. This was a formula, both polemical and generic, that caused the texts from which the discussion had initiated to be forgotten.[27] Among these were the pages that at mid–sixteenth century had attracted Francesco Robortello's attention: *Adversus mathematicos* (1:248–269).[28] Here Sextus Empiricus was arguing with a number of grammarians—Tauriscus, Asclepiades of Myrleia, Dyonisius (Thrax)—who had broken up grammar into various components, including a historical segment.[29] Asclepiades, for example, maintained that the historical component of grammar should be subdivided into three categories: "History can be either true or false or 'as-if-it-was-true': true history is that which has as its subject things that really happened; false history is that which deals with fiction and myth 'as-if-it-was-true,' the kind we meet in plays and in pantomimes."[30]

Sextus objected: true history is the sum of numberless facts large and small and thus (unlike medicine or music) lacks method and is not a *techné* (in Latin, *ars*). False history—namely, myth and history as-if-it-was-true, such as plays and pantomimes—deals in facts that have not taken place: impossible in the first instance, possible (but purely hypothetical) in the second. But "since . . . there is no art that has as its subject false and nonexistent things, and since those myths and fictions are false on which the historical component of grammar dwells especially, we shall have to conclude that any art that concerns itself with the historical part of grammar cannot exist."[31]

There were some who objected, however, that even if the subject matter of history is without method, the judgment formulated on that matter is not, because it is based on a criterion which permits the distinction to be made between what is true and what is false. Sextus responded sharply to this objection: first of all, grammarians do not provide a criterion to distinguish the true from the false; second, no facts adduced by them are true, as the various myths about the death of Ulysses demonstrate.

6. True history, false history, history as-if-it-was-true: a threefold target, one more complex than what we usually associate with the seventeenth-century rediscovery of Sextus Empiricus. Today the expression "historic Pyrrhonism" promptly recalls for us the *Du peu de certitude qu'il y a dans l'histoire* (1668), by La Mothe Le Vayer—the learned skeptic to whom the education of the crown prince had been assigned.[32] The kind of history about which La Mothe Le Vayer, by now in his seventies, expressed his uncertainty was naturally that history claiming to be true. But this was just one stage in a much more complex intellectual journey, as is testified by *Jugement sur les anciens et principaux historiens grecs et latins, dont il nous reste quelques ouvrages*, which La Mothe Le Vayer had published twenty years earlier (1646).[33] Bayle's opinion that it was a mere compilation, although competently done, has weighed heavily over this work.[34] The negative judgment is undeserved.

The letter of dedication to Cardinal Mazarin turns on the relationship between history and poetry. One might think, La Mothe Le Vayer writes, that such poems as those of Lucan and Silius Italicus, if judged by their content, could be defined as histories. But poetry "cannot do without fiction [*fable*]," while history "is worthy of note only for the truth it expresses [*ver-ité*], and considers falsehood a mortal enemy." It would be absurd to confuse things that are so different. But a survey of ancient historians, La Mothe Le Vayer concludes, will meet with scant success among "the infinite number of persons who prefer imaginary accounts [*contes fabuleux*] to true narratives [*narrations véritables*], and the history of romances to the entire history of the Romans [*et l'histoire des Romans à toute celle des Romains*]."[35]

Reading these pages, it is impossible not to think of Chapelain's dialogue, *De la lecture des vieux romans*. It undoubtedly was prompted by La Mothe Le Vayer's just-published *Jugement*, but it took the form of a discussion, not a polemical reaction.[36] In the course of the *Jugement* the contrast between *fable* and *histoire* expressed by La Mothe Le Vayer in his dedication to Cardinal Mazarin reappears in guises that bit by bit assume more complex and nuanced forms, beginning with the first chapter, on Herodotus. From antiquity the work of Herodotus as a historian had been treated as *fabula*, as falsehood—an accusation rejected by Henri Estienne (Stephanus), the first editor of Sextus Empiricus, who in his *Apologia pro Herodoto* had championed the veracity of Herodotus on the basis of the accounts provided by travelers to the New World.[37] La Mothe Le Vayer's defense, instead, turned on an argument in Herodotus: "We cannot say either that he mixed up indifferently truth and falsehood without distinguishing between them, or that he was a liar, although he often reiterated the lies of others, something which is admitted by even the most rigorous historical norms. It is precisely these norms, in fact, which oblige us to include the rumors that abound and the various opinions of men, as Herodotus observes most opportunely in his *Polimnia* apropos the Argives in a forewarning that serves for the entire work."[38] In effect, Herodotus had asserted in no uncertain terms his own distance from the subject matter under discussion: "For myself, though it be my business to set down that which is told me, to believe it is none at all of my business; let that saying hold good for the whole of my history" (7:152).[39]

La Mothe Le Vayer extends this claim to historiography in general. No one demonstrates this better than Polybius, who has been reproached unfairly for being more philosopher than historian.[40] A strong affinity exists between history and philosophy: history can be defined as "philosophy full of examples."[41] Polybius observes, at the close of book 6 of his *Histories*, continues La Mothe Le Vayer:

that the superstition condemned by all peoples was considered a virtue by the Romans. Even if it was possible to establish a state composed only of wise and virtuous men, we have to recognize that these imaginary opinions [opinions fabuleuses] about the gods and the underworld would be totally useless. But since there are no states in which the people are different than those we can observe, inclined toward all sorts of unlawful and malicious acts, we must make use, to keep them in check, of the imaginary fears provoked by our religion and of the terrors of the other world, so opportunely introduced by the ancients, and which today only fearless persons who have lost use of their reason could contradict.[42]

Taking his cue from a famous page in the *Histories* of Polybius (6: 6, 6–15), La Mothe Le Vayer was restating the thesis so dear to learned libertines of the origin and political function of religion.[43] Feeling protected by the fact that he was quoting another writer, La Mothe Le Vayer could speak tranquilly of the "imaginary fears stirred up by our religion [craintes imaginaires qu'imprime nostre religion]." The objective reader [deniaisé] immediately understood that here it was not just the religion of the Romans that was being discussed. Today, as then, the populace had to be controlled through the terror of a nonexistent hell. Today, as then, this truth was understood only by the privileged few. Polybius was one of them. It is impossible to present him as a man "devoted to the religion of his day"; Isaac Casaubon's attempt to defend him at all costs was in vain, La Mothe Le Vayer comments with irony.[44]

The historian-philosopher who writes about the beliefs of the people without sharing them takes on the semblance of the learned libertine. Conversely, the erudite libertine who looks upon the beliefs of the populace from afar, without accepting them, recognizes himself in the historian: in Herodotus, and, even more, in Polybius. Thereby La Mothe Le Vayer was in fact rejecting the accusation which Sextus Empiricus had directed at history: that it was not an art. History is indeed an art which, contrary to what Sextus Empiricus sustained, can very well have "as its subject false and nonexistent things"—in other words, myths and the fictional. For La Mothe Le Vayer one of the assignments of history is to expose that which is false.[45]

7. And yet, the most fiery pages of the *Jugement* are reserved not for Thucydides or Polybius but for an entirely different type of historian: Diodorus Siculus. There were those who criticized his *History* as vacuous and inconsistent, but La Mothe Le Vayer wholeheartedly disagreed: "I would be disposed to journey

to the tip of the world, so to speak," he wrote forcibly, "if I thought I could find there such a great treasure," the lost books of Diodorus:[46]

> As far as that which concerns the fictions *[les fables]* and the excellent mythology contained in the first five books of Diodorus, not only do I not condemn them but, instead, I believe that they are the most precious that have been left to us by antiquity. Apart from the fact that what is fictional can be recounted seriously *[on peut conter des fables serieusement]*, and that if they were wholly useless, we would also have to reject, together with Plato's *Timaeus*, quite a few other famous works, we can say that they [the first books of Diodorus] introduce us to the complete theology of the idolaters. And if it was permissible to call a profane thing by a sacred name, I would dare to define the five books of which I am speaking the Bible of paganism. First of all, they introduce us to pagan beliefs about eternity and the creation of the world. Then they describe the birth of the first humans in accord with natural intelligence. . . .[47]

The last sentence clarifies what preceded it. It pays implicit homage to Giulio Cesare Vanini, burned by order of the Parlement at Toulouse in 1619 as a heretic, atheist, and blasphemer.[48] In his *De admirandis Naturae arcanis* (1616) Vanini affirmed that the first men had been born from the soil warmed by the sun, just as in the account of Diodorus (1: 10), and that mice emerged from the mud of the Nile.[49] The first books of Diodorus's history can be read in a way that helps us to put the Bible into perspective: in a sense, as an anti-Bible. But La Mothe Le Vayer recognizes that Diodorus "can be censured for the great superstition he exhibits in his writings," just as with Livy among Latin historians.[50]

Thus, in this case, not Diodorus but his readers, and principally La Mothe Le Vayer, are responsible for the critical distance from the subject matter treated. For the French writer, what fed into history was not just what was fictional but even fictional history, to use once more the categories of the Alexandrine grammarians revived polemically by Sextus Empiricus. The fictions (*fables*) reported, and shared, by Diodorus could have become the subject matter of history.[51] Chapelain, who took for granted Livy's veracity, extended the discussion in La Mothe Le Vayer's *Jugement* to the fictions (*fables*) of Homer and of *Lancelot*: both could become the stuff of history.

8. What we call critical detachment often can have unforeseen consequences. But at its roots we invariably find a sense of superiority: social, intellectual, religious. (The most famous instance is that of the preeminence claimed by

Christianity over Judaism, to which we owe the idea of historical perspective.)[52] La Mothe Le Vayer and the erudite libertines looked down with scorn on the populace imprisoned by the fictions of religion[53]—a populace which had to be kept ignorant about the attacks leveled against those fictions: if the fear of hell should vanish, the latent violence in society would explode, destroying it.[54] To this sense of detached superiority we owe the comparison between pagan myths and the biblical accounts proposed by La Mothe Le Vayer in his *Cinq dialogues faits à l'imitation des anciens*.[55] There was a strong temptation to see religions as a sequence of errors. But the demystification could open the way for attempts at understanding the error from within, from the viewpoint of those who had been its protagonists (or, if you will, its victims).[56]

Chapelain's dialogue *De la lecture des vieux romans* illustrates this transition. He did not share the erudite impiety of the libertines: his sense of superiority when confronting "modern antiquity" was rooted in taste. In a society dominated by swift changes in fashion, the literary production of what would come to be called the Middle Ages seemed ever more remote.[57] Shortly after, the culture promoted by Louis XIV and his court would widen this gulf still further. "Who is there delighting in reading Guillaume de Loris or Jean de Meun," asked Valentin Conrart in 1665, the first secretary of the Académie, "unless he is moved by a curiosity similar to what might have been felt by the Romans who in the age of Augustus read verses by the brothers Salius which they would not have been able to understand?"[58] But this antiquarian curiosity was nothing new. Fifty years before the advent of the new Augustus, the erudite Claude Fauchet had written: "Any writer, even the worst, can be useful under certain circumstances, if only as a witness of his own time [*au moins pour le témoignage de son temps*]."[59]

Even the worst, or perhaps precisely the worst: the distance from the dominant taste facilitated the reading of medieval literary texts from a documentary perspective. But Chapelain went a step further by transforming the distance into emotive proximity. Ménage understood this. Toward the conclusion of *De la lecture des vieux romans* he seems to be accepting the point of view of his interlocutor: "Through a book like *Lancelot* . . . we become the intimate friends of these people, even to the point of grasping the very essence of their souls."[60]

9. This unambiguous assertion brings us back to a well-known fact: the imperceptible impulse we feel when we come to a fictional work. A famous

passage comes to mind in which Coleridge, setting out from an extreme case (the description of supernatural events), attempts to define the effects of poetry in general. It is a question, he wrote, of transferring from our inner nature "a semblance of truth sufficient to procure for these shadows of imagination that willing suspension of disbelief for the moment, which constitutes poetic faith."[61]

Poetic faith gives form to shadows, endows them with an appearance of truth; it causes us to suffer "and all for nothing! for Hecuba!"[62] Historical faith functioned (or functions) totally differently.[63] It allows us to overcome incredulity, nourished by the recurring objections of skepticism, relating to an invisible past, through a series of opportune operations—marks scratched on paper or on parchment; coins; fragments of statues corroded by time; and so forth.[64] Not only this: it permits us, as Chapelain showed, to build the truth on fiction (fables) and true history on the fictitious.

CHAPTER 6

The Europeans Discover (or Rediscover) the Shamans

1. In *La historia del mondo nuovo*, a book published in Venice in 1565 which was reprinted and translated many times, the Milanese Girolamo Benzoni described what he had seen in the course of a series of voyages, extending over fourteen years, to the "islands and seas newly discovered" beyond the ocean. On the island of Hispaniola, he recounted:

> Just as in the other provinces of these new lands, there are certain small trees, shaped like reeds, which produce a leaf resembling that of the walnut, but larger, held in the highest esteem by the inhabitants and greatly prized by the slaves whom the Spaniards brought from Ethiopia. When these leaves are in season, they gather them and tying them in bundles where they make their fires they hang them until the time they are quite dry, and when they are ready to use them they take a leaf from their ears of corn, and placing one of these other leaves inside it, they roll them together into a tube, then they light it at one end and insert the other in their mouths, inhale so that the smoke enters their mouths, in their throat and in their heads, and they tolerate it as much as possible, bearing it because it gives them pleasure, and they fill themselves with this cruel smoke to the point that they leave their senses; and there are some who inhale it so much, that they fall to the ground as if they were dead, and here they lie the greater part of the day or night stupefied. . . . See what a pestilential and evil poison of the devil this is. It has happened to me often, traveling through the province of Guatimalla and Nicaraqua, to enter the house of some Indian who had taken this herb which in the Mexican language is called tobacco. . . .[1]

In the footsteps of the Russian formalists, especially those of Viktor Sklovskij (1893–1984), we have learned to search for estrangement in the expression of the savage, of the child, or even of an animal: beings outside the conventions of civilized life, who react with a bewildered or indifferent gaze, thus indirectly communicating their insensibility.[2] Here we find ourselves in a situation that is paradoxically reversed: the alien is the Milanese Girolamo Benzoni; the persons performing under his very eyes the senseless act of lighting up a cigarette and smoking it are the Indian savages—opposites of ourselves, the dwellers in the civilized world. In Girolamo Benzoni's flight ("instantly sensing the acute stench of this truly diabolical and fetid smoke, I was forced to escape with great haste and proceed elsewhere") we are tempted to see the symbolic anticipation of a centuries-old historical phenomenon: the retreat of nonsmokers in the face of the advance, which now has perhaps reached its extreme limit, of the army of smokers.

The account by our Milanese traveler is but one of countless testimonials of the Europeans' encounter with the bewildering novelties found beyond the seas: animals, plants, customs. Today it is fashionable to examine these documents by means of a generalized category: that of the confrontation with the Other—a term which has something of the metaphysical about it but which appropriately underlines the intimate connection, in these reactions, between natural otherness and cultural otherness. Girolamo Benzoni's invective against the effects of tobacco ("See what a pestilential and evil poison of the devil this is") is immediately followed by a description of how the plant was used by native doctors for healing purposes. The patient, "intoxicated" by smoke, "upon returning to his senses recounted a thousand things, of having been to the council of the gods, experiencing exalted visions"; then the doctors "turned him around . . . three or four times, and with their hands rubbed his body, devoting much attention to the face, holding a bone or a stone in the mouth; and these things are believed by women to be sacred, considering that they are good, helping with childbirth. . . ."[3] Clearly, in the eyes of the Milanese traveler, the native doctors were simply warlocks; and the effects of the tobacco they administered, merely diabolical hallucinations.

The attribution of these negative qualities to tobacco can also be found, even if mingled with contrary considerations, in a book written some years later by a physician of Seville, Nicolas Monardes: *Primera y secunda y tercera partes de la historia medicinal.*[4] On the one hand we find praise for the "great healing qualities" of tobacco, only recently introduced in the gardens and orchards of Spain, in the cure of every type of malady: asthma; chest, stomach, and uterine pains; and on the other, scandalized descriptions of the uses which the *Indios* made of this miraculous plant in their religious ceremonies. The priests, Monardes wrote, before divining the future, became stupefied with the tobacco smoke to the point of collapsing on the ground as if dead. Then, after they were revived, they responded to the questions which had been put to them, interpreting "in their own way, or by following the inspiration of the Devil," the fantasies and illusions they had experienced in their cataleptic states. But it was not only priests who became "inebriated" *(emborracharse)* with tobacco smoke: the natives used to do the same to draw, from the images that entered their minds, pleasure or signs about the future. "The Devil, who is a deceiver and knows the powers of the plant," Monardes comments, "has taught the *Indios* the virtues of tobacco, and he tricks them through the imagining and fantasizing induced by it."

For Monardes, then, one of the characteristics of tobacco is the power to cause "imaginings and fantasies" which physicians in antiquity had attributed to the root of the black nightshade, to anise, and to horseradish.[5] But in Monardes's book the greatest attention is concentrated on two substances endowed with hallucinatory properties and widely consumed in the East Indies: *bangue* and *anphion*, identifiable, respectively, with marijuana and opium. For *bangue* (or *Cannabis indica*, as it was called by European botanists) Monardes cites the discussion dedicated to this plant by the Portuguese physician Garcia da Orta, author of a work in dialogue form on the grasses and aromas of the East Indies; but he adds details and explanations based on direct observation.[6] Garcia de Orta spoke generically about the spread of *bangue* and of opium; Monardes stated that the latter substance was the choice of the poor, whereas the wealthy preferred *bangue*, which was tastier and had a better aroma. A few years earlier a physician of Burgos, Cristóbal Acosta, in his *Tractado de las drogas y medicinas de las Indias Orientales*, had sketched a sort of typology of *bangue* users: some took it to forget their fatigue and to achieve restful sleep; others, to induce pleasurable dreams and illusions; still others, to become intoxicated, or for its aphrodisiac effects (about which Monardes, instead, was silent); and the great lords and military leaders, to forget their worries.[7] The entire corpus of evidence emphasizes the reliance on these stupefying substances by the inhabitants of the East Indies: five grains of opium, observed an astonished Monardes, suffices to kill one of us; sixty grains gives the *Indios* health and repose.

Repose, *descanso*: the barbarians of the West Indies (it is still Monardes writing) make use of tobacco to dispel fatigue; those of the East Indies use opium, an extremely common substance there which is sold in the shops.[8] In Peru, Girolamo Benzoni related, natives "carry in their mouths an herb called coca, and they use it to sustain themselves so they will be able to walk an entire day without eating or drinking: and this herb is their principal trading object. . . ."[9] The significance of this becomes clearer if we examine the evidence over the course of many centuries. The transoceanic journeys of discovery came upon such widespread and intense dissemination of inebriating and stupefying substances as to be compared by Le Roy Ladurie in a famous essay to the microbic unification of the globe.[10] In fact, in the span of a few centuries tobacco, opium, marijuana, and derivatives from coca penetrated (by various means and to different degrees) the cultures of the colonizers; wine and liquors, even more rapidly, spread among the colonized societies.

Since I have broached a serious problem which often is treated lightly, a possible misunderstanding needs to be dispelled at once. It is sometimes argued that since all intoxicating and stupefying substances are, as "drugs," potentially harmful, it is inevitable—if we do not want to succumb to a general sort of prohibitionism—that we should legalize their sale, without exceptions of any sort. In my opinion this is an artificial conclusion, based on a false premise. Many, perhaps most, human societies have used or still use, in differing ways and circumstances, substances which offer those who adopt them temporary access to an extraordinary set of experiences. Temporary escape from history (partial or total) is an unavoidable ingredient in human history. But the degree of control which each culture—naturally in addition to the individuals who compose them—exercises over these substances varies greatly, and is only in part explainable by a pharmacological analysis of their effects. On each occasion a cultural component, a filter, also intervenes, although how it functions largely eludes us. Why, one may ask, have alcoholic beverages with which, for better or worse, European societies have learned to live in the course of a few millennia (in the case of wine) or only a few centuries (with distilled liquors) had such a destructive effect in just a few decades on the native cultures of North America?

This is an obvious example. I mention it here because it permits me to introduce an extraordinary passage from a report which the French Jesuit Paul de Brebeuf sent in 1636 to the provincial of his order to inform him of events occurring that year in the Quebec mission. One of the members had explained to the natives (the report naturally calls them "*sauvages*" [savages]) that their high mortality rate was caused by the wines and liquors, which they did not know how to consume in moderation. "Why do you not write to your great King," one of the natives asked, "to prohibit the transporting of these beverages which are killing us?" "The French," the Jesuit answered, "need them to help them stand the sea voyages and the freezing temperatures of these places." "Well, then," the other said, "arrange that they be the only ones to drink them." At this point, a second native stood up: "No, it is not these beverages which kill us, it is your writings. As soon as you started to describe our country, our rivers, our lands, our forests, we all began to die, in a way that was not happening before you came."

Paul de Brebeuf and his fellow missionaries had reacted to these words with hearty laughter.[11] Today, three and a half centuries later, we can admire the clearheadedness of the anonymous native and agree with his assessment. The geographical writings of the Jesuits opened the way to the European colonial conquests: they were a first step.[12] The immoderate consumption of the alcoholic beverages brought by the Europeans was only an aspect of the disintegration of native culture caused by colonization.

Even the use of intoxicating and numbing substances by the colonizers had undoubtedly been conditioned by cultural filters. But how these filters worked is not so obvious. An imaginary sixteenth-century gambler who might have tried to foresee, on the basis of the reactions of travelers, missionaries, and botanists, which of these substances popular outside Europe would have been the first to arrive in the old continent, presumably would have pointed to *bangue,* to opium, and to coca. In the contemporary documentation they are mentioned in a neutral, objective tone, without any suggestion of moral or religious disapproval. Tobacco, instead—even in the writings of the Seville physician Monardes, who insisted on its extraordinary medicinal properties—is associated unequivocally with vice, sin, or even the Devil. But in spite of these condemnations, or perhaps partly because of them, what took root in Europe was precisely the use of that "pestiferous and evil" tobacco.[13]

2. Why did these intoxicating substances provoke such different reactions among sixteenth-century European travelers? A reply to this question has to be cautious and provisional, since marijuana (otherwise known as *bangue*), opium, and coca have not received the kind of serious, critical bibliographical attention evident in Jerome E. Brooks's massive *Tobacco.*[14] Presumably the conjectures which follow will have to be corrected in the light of more systematic future research.

We can begin with a few pages from a celebrated work: the *Historia general y natural de las Indias*, by Gonzalo Fernández de Oviedo (1535). The second chapter of book 5 is dedicated to the use of tobacco on the island of Hispaniola. From the outset we detect a tone of strong moral reproach: "The *Indios* of this island, in addition to other vices, had a terrible one [*muy malo*]: that of inhaling smoke, which they call tobacco, for the purpose of losing their senses."[15] This is followed by a description which agrees on many points with that of Girolamo Benzoni, who undoubtedly knew Oviedo's work when he wrote his own a few decades later.[16] The *Indios*, Oviedo observes, cultivate the plant, believing that its use "is not only healthy but holy" (*no tan solamente les era cosa sana, pero muy sancta cosa*). Sometimes they resort to it to alleviate their physical pain; and even an occasional Christian does the same. The *negro* slaves use it to ease their fatigue at the end of a hard day's labor. Nonetheless, these factual observations are followed, in the concluding paragraph, by a condemnation:

> In this regard it seems appropriate to recall a vicious and evil habit practiced, to-gether with other criminal offenses, by the inhabitants of Thrace, according to what Abulensis writes on Eusebius, *De observatione temporum* [3:168]. He states that these people, both men and women, follow the custom of gathering around the fire to eat, trying to become drunk, or feigning it; and since they are without wine, they take the seeds of certain plants which grow in those parts and roast them in the embers. The fragrance given off by these seeds intoxicates those pres-ent, even in the absence of wine. In my opinion, all this resembles the tobacco which is taken by the *Indios*.[17]

Abulensis is the Spanish theologian Alonso de Madrigal, better known as Alonso Tostado, bishop of Ávila. In his commentary, published in Sala-manca in 1506, to Eusebius's ecclesiastical *History*, he speaks, apropos a pas-sage in Solinus's wide-ranging *Polyhistor*, of the Thracians' custom of gather-ing around the fire to inebriate themselves by inhaling the smoke of roasted seeds.[18] But Tostado's allusion to the absence of wine among the Thracians can be traced to one of Solinus's sources, the geographer Pomponius Mela. The latter, in the first century of the Christian era, wrote a work, *De orbis situ*, which recounts, in the chapter on Thrace (2:2), the ceremony which we have just described.[19]

The story does not end here, because Pomponius Mela, in turn, had ap-plied to the Thracians Herodotus's account (4:73–75) of a Scythian custom. But more about that later. Where has this digression taken us? It has al-lowed us to reconstruct the cultural filter which enabled Oviedo, among others, to become acclimated to the natural and cultural peculiarities of the North American continent. Thanks to Pomponius Mela and to Solinus, the intoxicating herb smoked by the *Indios* could be identified with one used by the Thracians, which, although not fully described, had similar inebriating effects. An obvious element contributed to making this connection: the drunkenness caused by alcoholic beverages, primarily wine, constituted for a Latin cosmographer of the first century A.D., as for a French or Italian traveler of fourteen or fifteen centuries later, the implicit model by which to describe and evaluate behavior provoked by any sort of inebriating substance. Pomponius Mela observed that Thracians, who did not know wine, entered a happy state resembling drunkenness by inhaling smoke exuded by the roasted seeds of an unidentified plant. The Jesuit François du Creux wrote in 1664 in his history of Canada that the inhabitants of those lands always traveled equipped with *petun*—tobacco—and with "a rather longish tube" (a sort of pipe) to be able to enter into a state of inebriation "resembling that which is caused by wine."[20] Quite possibly this learned cleric, ready to compare the nomadism of the Canadian natives with that of the Scythians,[21] was familiar with the passage in Pomponius Mela. But the perception of tobacco as an alternative to wine goes far beyond an occasional erudite citation. It permeates the vocabulary of travelers and missionaries. "We find people who delight in drinking this smoke," wrote Girolamo Benzoni apropos the natives of Hispaniola. The Canadian savages "usent aussi du petun [tobacco] et en boivent la fumée," we read in a report written a half century later by the Jesuit Pierre Biard.[22]

Many European observers noted that tobacco was used by North American natives on ritual occasions. It is Biard who underscores that among the savages of New France any sort of ceremony—from decision making, to treaties, to public receptions—involved the use of *petun*: "They seat themselves in a circle around a fire, passing the pipe from hand to hand, and in this way they consume many hours together very pleasurably."[23] The recognition of a ritual dimension in the use of tobacco, even if not an actually religious one, is discernible also in those words of Oviedo: for the natives of Hispaniola it is "not only healthy but holy." We have already mentioned the use made of it by priests on the same island. All this suggests that tobacco, as an instrument for private pleasure and public rituals, appeared to the eyes of European observers as a kind of symbolically reversed wine: a sort of sacred substance, but used by natives in ceremonies that they, the Europeans, considered idolatrous. This explains the difference between the relaxed attitude in regard to opium, *bangue*, and coca—inebriating substances which the colonizers associated, correctly or not, with a sort of purely private consumption—and the open hostility they showed toward tobacco.[24] It was an aversion destined to give way in the face of the aggressive offensive launched by tobacco producers.[25]

In the early sixteenth century, we recall, Oviedo had deduced, through the texts of Pomponius Mela and Solinus on the Thracians, that it was tobacco the *Indios* smoked. At mid–seventeenth century the trajectory became reversed, and a highly cultivated scholar, Isaac Vossius, interpreted the passage in Pomponius Mela as an allusion to tobacco. Ivy, arbutus, and cyclamen can induce inebriation: but what other plant, "praeter [besides] nicotianam," can stupefy by its very smoke?[26]

This rhetorical question made it clear that tobacco was already known in antiquity: it was a thesis cropping up often from the sixteenth century on.[27] In 1724 the Jesuit Joseph-François Lafitau discussed the question fully in a work entitled *Mœurs des sauvages amériquains, comparées aux mœurs des premiers temps*.[28] As for the Greeks and Romans, Lafitau reached, perhaps reluctantly, a negative conclusion. But a passage from Maximus of Tyre on the Scythians,[29] along with those by Pomponius Mela and Solinus on the Thracians, seemed to him to offer solid (even if not definitive) proof that those barbaric peoples used tobacco. It was one more clue to add to numerous others that testified, according to Lafitau, to the European origins of the first inhabitants of the American continent.[30] But the demonstration of the antiquity of tobacco use led to high praise of its virtues—significant because it was couched in definitely non-Eurocentric terms which overturned the previous negative connotations. That which in Europe served for simple pleasurable consumption, in America (according to Lafitau) was used by the natives as a sacred herb "with countless religious applications" (*à plusieurs usages de religion*). In addition to the power ascribed to it of "extinguishing the flame of concupiscence and the rebellion of the flesh, [tobacco serves] to enlighten the soul, to purify it, to prepare it for ecstatic dreams and visions; it works to summon the spirits, forcing them to communicate with men and accommodate the needs of the people who pay them homage; it serves to heal all the infirmities of soul and body. . . ."[31]

3. Ecstatic dreams and visions; communing with spirits: we are approaching the subject of this chapter, "The Europeans Discover (or Rediscover) the Sha-

mans." What has been said thus far appears to constitute only a series of digressions, imposed by the fleeting nature of our subject.

In the years when the Jesuit Lafitau was publishing the results of his grandiose and daring work on the customs of the American continent, Russian penetration into Central Asia and the Far East was proceeding apace. Descriptions of those remote lands and the nomadic peoples who inhabited them began to reach the West.[32] In 1698, a merchant of Lübeck, Adam Brand, the secretary of a mission that had been sent to China by Peter the Great, produced a report, quickly translated into various European languages, which for the first time considered the Tungusic term *shaman* as synonymous with *priest* or *magus*.[33] Brand was echoed some years later (1704) by the Dutch merchant E. Isbrants Ides, who had guided the original mission.[34] Not long after, a captain in the dragoons, Johann Bernhard Müller, previously in the service of the Swedish monarchy and then a prisoner of war of the Russians, inserted in a report on the Ostiacks and their customs an analytical description (though probably not based on direct observation) of a shamanistic session replete with cataleptic fits and divination.[35] Toward mid–eighteenth century large tomes began to appear written by scholars who had participated in actual scientific expeditions to Siberia, such as one, spanning almost a decade, involving Johann Georg Gmelin, professor of chemistry and botany at Tübingen; there were other works—by the physician Daniel Gottlieb Messerschmidt, by the philologist Müller, and by a botanist, Johann Amman. In a prolix, three-volume relation of his travels Gmelin reported on his encounters with shamans in Siberia, a few of whom revealed their tricks to him.[36] Although there is no doubt that Gmelin considered these persons crude charlatans, he faithfully transcribed their chants.[37] Even their ecstatic moments filled him with curiosity: in his great Latin work on Siberian flora he noted that the Buryats used the juniper berry to awaken their "praestigiatores" (shamans) from swoons, and that the inhabitants of Kamchatka used stinging nettle, supposedly ideal for inducing visions, in their idolatrous cults.[38]

In just a few decades this research assured Siberian shamans a prominent place in the developing field of comparative religion.[39] A small work by Christoph Meiners, a Göttingen professor, is a significant example of this progress: *Grundriß der Geschichte aller Religionen* (Lemgo, 1785). The title is deceptive. The book is a pioneering effort in phenomenology, not in the history of religion. The decision to center the narration "on the natural succession of the most important constituent elements [*nach der natürlichen Folge ihrer*

wichtigsten Bestandtheile]," rather than on a chronological-geographical sequence, took in en bloc all religions, whether revealed or not, with obvious
deistic implications. Shamans were assigned a special niche in the chapter
dedicated—a significant juxtaposition—to *jongleurs* (literally "conjurers") and
priests.[40] But then the thematic subdivisions caused shamans to reappear in
the furthest imaginable places: for example, at the end of the bibliographical
notes of the chapter on sacrifice (including human sacrifices), which begin
with the Pentateuch, continue with Greek and Roman writers, and conclude
with a contemporary traveler, Johann Gottlieb Georgi, who wrote a description of Siberia.[41]

Ten years earlier Christoph Meiners had published a comprehensive essay, "On the Mysteries of the Ancients, and in Particular on the Eleusian
Secrets," preceded by an introduction of a comparative nature, in which[42] he
distinguished mysteries celebrated by priests from mysteries tied to oral or
written doctrines: in neither of the two cases could the phenomenon be considered universal. It was unknown to the Samojedi, to the dwellers of Kamchatka, to the Tartar hordes (about whom Meiners referred the reader to
Gmelin), to Californians, to Eskimos, Laps, and Greenlanders. For all these
peoples, Meiners observed, one cannot speak of a common religion or of national gods, and neither of priests in a strict sense, but only of "charlatans
and diviners" (*Quacksalber und Wahrsager*).[43] Consequently, shamans, even if
only evoked and not named directly, entered the religious history of humanity consigned to its poorest and most elementary stage.

4. Thus, thanks to the eastern expansion of the Russian empire, Europeans
discovered—or better, rediscovered—the shamans. It seems useful to stress
the "rediscovery" aspect for two reasons. First of all, between the sixteenth and
seventeenth centuries, scholars such as Caspar Peucer and John Scheffer had
collected and transmitted data on the magicians of Lapland, who were closely
related (as Meiners had perceptively discerned) to the Siberian shamans.[44]
Second, as I have tried to illustrate exhaustively elsewhere, an ancient shamanistic nucleus was included in the well-established stereotype of the witches'
Sabbath.[45]

Learning and rediscovering are complicated operations: perceptions and
cultural schemes become intertwined and in turn modify one another. For
the Seville physician Monardes, the priests of the *Indios* who begin to divine
the future as they come out of the cataleptic fits induced by tobacco smoke

were inspired by the Devil. A great scholar like Vossius thought he had recognized Pomponius Mela's Thracians as tobacco smokers. Vossius certainly was mistaken (and Lafitau also), but was absolutely correct to connect the passage in Pomponius Mela to the description of a Scythian rite in Herodotus:[46]

> After the burial the Scythians cleanse themselves as I will show: they anoint and wash their heads; as for their bodies, they set up three poles leaning together to a point and cover these over with woollen mats; then in the place so enclosed to the best of their power, they make a pit in the centre beneath the poles and the mats and throw red-hot stones into it. They have hemp growing in their country, very like flax, save that the hemp is by much the thicker and taller. This grows both of itself and also by their sowing, and of it the Thracians even make garments which are very like linen. . . . The Scythians then take the seed of this hemp and, creeping under these mats, they throw it on the red-hot stones; and, being so thrown, it smolders and sends forth so much steam that no Greek vapor-bath could surpass it. The Scythians howl in their delight at the vapor-bath. This serves them instead of bathing, for they never wash their bodies with water. (4:73–75)[47]

The more or less identical texts from Maximus of Tyre, Pomponius Mela, and Solinus, the first referring to the Scythians and the latter two to the Thracians, originate from this page in Herodotus—an important source for our investigation. To the best of my knowledge, the first step toward its correct identification was taken by an antiquarian-naturalist Engelbert Kaempfer (1651–1716).[48] The tables which accompany his observations accumulated during many years of travel—*Amoenitatum Exoticarum politico-physico-medicarum fasciculi V*—give an idea of Kaempfer's boundless curiosity: we pass from a cuneiform inscription copied from the ruins of Persepolis to a remarkably accurate description of the points used by Japanese acupuncturists to cure colic diarrhea.[49] One of these notations ("Kheif seu Keif, sive inebriantia Persarum et Indorum") discusses the properties and effects of tobacco, opium, and cannabis, or *bangue*, which Kaempfer identifies as the plant which by its smoke inebriated Scythians and Thracians.[50]

These remarks seem to have passed unnoticed. At the end of the eighteenth century another and no less extraordinary personage, Count Jan Potocki—author of *Manuscrit trouvé à Saragosse*, a novel which achieved international renown thanks to a partial edition by Roger Caillois—independently reached similar conclusions.[51] In a remarkable book published in St. Petersburg in 1802, the *Histoire primitive des peuples de la Russie*, Potocki accurately identified some of the customs of the nomadic peoples of Central Asia mentioned in

book 4 of Herodotus. In the Scythian seers he recognized at once "the shamans of Siberia."[52] He had not traced to the Tartars the custom of becoming
drugged with the smoke of roasted hemp seeds; but he observed that hashish,
which was very common in Cairo (where he spent some time in 1790), gives an
intoxication differing from that caused by opium or fermented liquor, because
it "tient davantage de la folie."[53]

These intuitions also passed unnoticed. In an essay presented in 1811 and
then revised for publication in 1828, Barthold Georg Niebuhr with great
finesse outlined the earliest history of the Scythians, Geti, and Sarmatians,
reaching conclusions substantially similar to Potocki's, but without mentioning him, doubtless because he did not know his work. In the funerary ceremony
described by Herodotus (4:73–75), Niebuhr unequivocally saw a shamanistic
ritual, giving further credence to his hypothesis (still discussed today) of a
Mongolian origin for a segment of the Scythian population.[54]

It is no accident that Potocki and Niebuhr agreed on this point. In the
course on Slavic literature that Adam Mickiewicz gave at the Collège de France
in 1842–1843, he stated that Potocki had been "the first among historians of
modern Europe to recognize the importance of oral tradition. Niebuhr que-
ried peasants and old women in the Roman markets about the story of Romulus and Remus. Long before him, Potocki had sought out information about
the Scythians in the tents of the Tartars." And he concluded: Potocki traveled, he examined places, he spoke with people—things that no antiquarian
had done before him.[55]

Mickiewicz was exaggerating. One only needs to think about the journeys undertaken toward the end of the seventeenth century by the antiquarian and naturalist Kaempfer. But Mickiewicz was certainly correct to emphasize the importance of such a method, only resurrected in the last few
decades by students of ethnohistory. Karl Meuli pursued this approach in an
essay published in 1935 (*Scythica*) which in a certain sense rediscovered, perhaps for the last time, the shamanistic connotations of the Scythian funerary
rite described by Herodotus. I say "in a certain sense rediscovered" because in
the thick notes to *Scythica* there is no mention of Kaempfer and Potocki, who,
to a greater and lesser measure, had anticipated its basic thesis; however, the
name of Niebuhr appears.[56] This does not detract in any way from the originality of Meuli's excellent essay, which, for the first time, analyzed in depth
both the shamanistic elements in Scythian culture and their reception on
the part of Greek colonists residing on the banks of the Black Sea.[57]

The results of an archeological dig dating from a few years earlier in the Altai Mountains of Central Asia had already provided, unknown to Meuli, an unforeseeable confirmation of the findings of his essay. In a place called Pazyryk, tombs had been discovered, dating to two or three centuries before Christ, which had preserved, buried under the ice, a horse transformed to resemble a reindeer (today exhibited at the Hermitage); a drum of the kind used by shamans; and seeds of *Cannabis sativa,* some of which were preserved in a leather flask, others roasted among the pebbles in a small bronze bowl.[58]

5. This is how the advancement of knowledge always seems to occur: in stages rather than in a continuum; through false starts, corrections, forgotten facts, rediscoveries; and thanks to filters and schemas which contemporaneously blind and open our eyes. In this sense the attempts at interpretation which I have tried to reconstruct, perhaps too minutely, could be considered almost banal—not the exception but the rule.

CHAPTER 7

Tolerance and Commerce

Auerbach Reads Voltaire

FOR ADRIANO SOFRI

1. In the sixth of Voltaire's *Lettres philosophiques* (1734, but written a few years earlier) we come upon a famous page:

> Enter the London Stock Exchange, that more respectable place than many a court; you will see the deputies of all nations gathered there for the service of mankind. There the Jew, the Mohammedan and the Christian deal together as if they were of the same religion, and apply the name of infidel only to those who go bankrupt; there the Presbyterian trusts the Anabaptist, and the Anglican accepts the Quaker's promise. On leaving these peaceful and free assemblies, some go to the synagogue, others go to drink; one goes to have himself baptized in a great basin in the name of the Father, through the Son, to the Holy Ghost; another has his son's foreskin cut off and Hebrew words mumbled over him which he does not understand; others go to their church to await the inspiration of God, their hats on their heads, and all are content.[1]

Erich Auerbach dealt at length with this text in his great book (*Mimesis*, 1946). His analysis opened with a word of caution: Voltaire's "description of the London exchange was not really written for a realistic purpose." This is not an obvious statement, just as the notion of realism was not obvious to Auerbach.[2] Among the many variants of realism studied in *Mimesis* we find the modern form exemplified by the novels of Balzac and Stendhal, in which individual events and experiences are interwoven with impersonal historical forces.[3] One such force is international commerce, mentioned by Voltaire in his passage on the London Stock Exchange. Auerbach preferred, instead, to emphasize the intentionally deforming characteristics of a description which, by taking the details of the religious ceremonies out of their respective contexts, makes something absurd and comical out of them. This is, Auerbach observes, "the searchlight device" (Scheinwerfertechnik), typical of propaganda: "Especially in times of excited passions, the public is again and again taken in by such tricks, and everybody knows more than enough examples from the very recent past. . . . Whenever a specific form of life or a social group has run its course or has only lost favor and support, every injustice which the propagandists perpetrate against it is half consciously felt to be what it actually is, yet people welcome it with sadistic delight."[4]

This implicit allusion to Nazism crops up again immediately afterward in a bitter and ironic observation: "[Gottfried] Keller was fortunate in that he could not imagine an important change in government which would not entail an expansion of freedom." Mimesis, Auerbach wrote retrospectively, "is a book written in total awareness by a resolute man, in a determinate situation, at the beginning of the forties at Istanbul."[5] With these words Auerbach was reiterating his own adherence to the critical considerations which he had worked out in reflecting on Vico's Scienza Nuova.[6]

More than fifty years have passed since the publication of Mimesis. The voice of Voltaire on the page discussed by Auerbach rings out today more powerfully than ever. But to really understand it we need to apply a twofold, bifocal perspective, taking into consideration both Voltaire and his most astute reader.

2. The wordplay over infidèle, together with Voltaire's treatment of the London Stock Exchange, could have been inspired by that famous tribute to Amsterdam's intellectual and religious liberty contained in the final chapter of Spinoza's Tractatus theologico-politicus (1670): "Take, for example, the city of Amsterdam, that to its great advantage and the admiration of all people enjoys the fruits of this freedom. In this flourishing state, in this city without equals, men of all backgrounds and of all sects cohabit in the greatest harmony, and before entrusting their property to someone want to know only if he be rich or poor, or if he is accustomed to act in good or bad faith [num bona fide, an dolo solitus sit agere]."[7] The last few words, in the anonymous French translation of the Tractatus published in 1678, which circulated with three different title pages, closely echo the original Latin: "S'il est homme de bonne foy ou accoûtumé à tromper."[8]

In Spinoza's writings, the word fides has, depending on the context, different meanings, religious and not: credulity, prejudice, piety, loyalty, and so forth.[9] The transition from the religious to the political sphere is explicit in the final chapter of the *Tractatus theologico-politicus:* "Finally, if we take into account the fact that the devotion of a man toward the State, like the one toward God, can be known only through actions *[Quod si denique ad hoc etiam attendamus, quod fides uniuscujusque erga rempublicam, sicuti erga Deum, ex solis operibus cognosci potest].*"[10] In these words we hear the echo of one of Spinoza's favorite writers. In his *Discorsi sopra la prima Deca di Tito Livio,* Machiavelli had argued that a well-ordered republic requires a religious anchor, a civic religion comparable to that of ancient Rome.[11] But to Spinoza, in his praise of Amsterdam and its liberties, *fides*—more precisely, the juridical notion of "bona fides"— meant commercial trustworthiness.[12] Thus, he appears to have paved the way for Voltaire's quip about bankruptcy as a form of faithlessness. It reappears, transformed into a solemn declaration, on American banknotes: "In God we trust."[13]

The comparison between the praise of Amsterdam and the description of the London Stock Exchange reinforces the hypothesis, already formulated but on a wholly different basis, that Voltaire might have known Spinoza's *Tractatus theologico-politicus* before publishing the *Lettres philosophiques.*[14] However, the tone of the two passages differs. For Spinoza, Amsterdam was the living demonstration that freedom of thought is not dangerous politically—in fact, contributes to general happiness through commercial prosperity. For his part, Voltaire, more than a half century later, imparted the idea that in London, commercial prosperity had made religious differences wholly irrelevant. In the historical battle between reason and religious intolerance, for him, England was a model:

> Come then! Is it only in England
> That mortals dare to think?

> Quoi, N'est-ce donc qu'en Angleterre
> Que les mortels osent penser?

These verses, which distorted the meaning of a passage from Horace (*Ep.* I, 2, 40, *ad Lollium*), transforming the "being wise" into "thinking," are parts of a poem which Voltaire had written at the death of the actress Adrienne Lecouvreur. A half century later, Kant chose the same words of Horace, in the same deformed interpretation, for his famous definition of the Enlightenment: "Sapere aude!"[15]

3. To express his sense of the irrelevance of religious differences Voltaire resorted to estrangement *(straniamento)*, a literary process which transformed something familiar—an object, a behavior, an institution—into something strange, senseless, ridiculous. Viktor Sklovskij, who was the first to identify and analyze this literary device, noted that the *philosophes* had used it frequently. In the *Lettres philosophiques* we encounter it everywhere. This is how Voltaire describes, in the first letter, his meeting with an unnamed Quaker: "There was more courtesy in the open and humane physiognomy of his countenance than there is in the fashion of dragging one leg after another and of carrying in one's hand what is intended to cover one's head."[16]

With laborious, deliberately clumsy circumlocution, Voltaire invites the reader to share the Quaker's scorn for social conventions. A little later this scorn is extended to religious rites. "We are Christians," he says, "and we try to be good Christians; but we do not hold that Christianity consists of sprinkling some cold water on one's head, mixed with a little salt."[17]

After baptism comes war. Relying on the same literary process of estrangement, the Quaker describes, and condemns, military conscription: "Our God, who has ordered us to love our enemies and to suffer without complaining, certainly does not want us to traverse the seas to go and slit the throats of our brethren simply because some assassins dressed in red and sporting caps two feet tall are enrolling their citizens making noise beating two little sticks on some tightly stretched donkey skin."[18]

The literary process used by Voltaire builds on a long tradition going back to Marcus Aurelius.[19] In his *Meditations* he spoke of the band worn by Roman senators: "This garment with its purple border is nothing but sheep's wool impregnated by fish blood." Voltaire similarly looked askance at social customs, reducing persons and events to their essential components. Soldiers are only "assassins dressed in red and sporting caps two feet tall"; instead of evoking a solemn rolling of drums, they make "noise beating two little sticks on some tightly stretched donkey skin." Even the most obvious gestures become strange, opaque, absurd, as if they were observed through the eyes of an outsider, of a savage, or of an ignorant *philosophe*, as Voltaire defined himself in a later writing.

But Voltaire's model was English. In one of his *Notebooks* from the period of his London exile (1726–1728), he slipped in a comparison which anticipated the nub of the sixth philosophical letter: "England is meeting of all religions, as the Royal exchange is the rendezvous of all foreigners." In another passage Voltaire penned, in his uncertain English, a more elaborate version of the same idea:

> Where there is not liberty of conscience, there is seldom liberty of trade, the same tyranny encroaching upon the commerce as upon Religion. In the Common-wealths and other free contrys one may see in a see port, as many relligions as shipps. The same god is there differently worship'd by jews, mahometans, hea-thens, catholiques, quackers, anabaptistes, which write strenuously one against another, but deal together freely and with trust and peace; like good players who after having humour'd their parts and fought one against another upon the stage, spend the rest of their time in drinking together.[20]

The title attached to this passage, *A Tale of a Tub*, has been called mis-leading by the modern editor of Voltaire's *Notebooks*.[21] Actually, the title tells us how the technique of estrangement was used in the evolution of the *Lettres philosophiques*. In *A Tale of a Tub* (1704) Jonathan Swift related, among many digressions, the story of three sons who fight over their father's inheritance: a parable symbolizing the conflicts among the Church of Rome, the Church of England, and the Protestant dissenters. Even though he sharply castigated both Catholics and enthusiasts, Swift openly stated that the points of agree-ment among Christians were more important than their differences.[22] In his *Notebooks* Voltaire went back to the source of Swift's parable, to the story of the three rings which an elderly father leaves to his sons: but he expanded the original reference to Christians, Jews, and Muslims to include pagans. In the final version, set in the London Stock Exchange rather than a seaport, the pagans disappear and the deistic message becomes more attenuated. But Voltaire's debt to Swift is greater still. *A Tale of a Tub* announced the immi-nent publication of other writings by its anonymous author, among which was "A Voyage into England, by a Person of Quality in Terra Australis incog-nita, Translated from the Original"—an idea that reappeared in reverse form in *Gulliver's Travels* (1726). Without the *Travels* Voltaire would never have be-come what he was.[23] We can imagine the enthusiasm with which he read the inventory of objects in Gulliver's pockets scrupulously recorded by two tiny inhabitants of Lilliput. Among these items we find: "A great silver chain, with a wonderful kind of engine at the bottom. We directed him to draw out what-ever was at the end of that chain; which appeared to be a globe, half silver, and half of some transparent metal; for on the transparent side we saw certain strange figures circularly drawn. . . . He put this engine to our ears, which made an incessant noise like that of a watermill. And we conjectured it is either some unknown animal, or the god that he worships. . . ."[24]

Swift transforms an object of everyday life into something sacred; Voltaire transforms a sacred event into something ordinary: "Celui-ci va se faire baptiser *dans une grande cuve* [this person goes to have himself baptized *in a great basin*]."[25] In both cases we see the same strategy of turning the familiar into the unusual. The astonishment of the stranger destroys the aura generated by custom or reverence. No aura, instead, envelops the commercial transactions executed in the London Stock Exchange: their rationality is obvious.

In that section of the *Lettres philosophiques* dealing with Swift ("Vingt-deuxième lettre: Sur M. Pope et quelques autres poètes fameux"), *Gulliver's Travels* is not mentioned. But in the expanded edition, published in 1756, Voltaire inserted a long passage on *A Tale of a Tub*, identifying its sources in the story of the three rings and in Fontenelle. He concluded: "Thus, almost everything is imitation. The idea of the *Lettres persanes* is taken from *l'Espion turc*. Boiardo imitated Pulci, Ariosto imitated Boiardo. The most original minds borrow from each other. . . . It is with books as with the fire in our hearths; we go to a neighbor to get the embers and light it when we return home, pass it on to others, and it belongs to everyone."[26] A splendid masked confession.

4. Auerbach probably had not read Sklovskij's essay on estrangement.[27] But the latter's ideas, transmitted by Sergej Tret'jakov, had a decisive influence on the work of Brecht, whom Auerbach certainly knew well. Brecht's *Verfremdung-Effekt*, so profoundly linked to the Enlightenment tradition, recalls intimately the "searchlight device" used by Voltaire.[28] Auerbach accentuates only the risks in that technique, not its critical potential—a surprisingly unilateral opinion. To be sure, artistic or literary procedures are only instruments, which can be used for different or even opposed purposes. A weapon (and even estrangement is a weapon) can be used to kill a child or to prevent a child from being killed. But if we examine from close up the function of estrangement in the writings of Voltaire, we notice something more complicated which sheds greater light on the description of the London Stock Exchange and, indirectly, on how Auerbach read it.

The publication of the *Lettres philosophiques* (1734) coincided with the editing of the *Traité de métaphysique*, revised until the year 1738.[29] In this unfinished work, not destined for the public and printed only after his death,

Voltaire explored in depth the destructive effects of the unfriendly look he had cast on English society. In the introduction ("Doubts over man"), he wrote: "Few people have a broad view of what a man is. Peasants of one part of Europe have no other idea of our species except of a two-legged animal with gnarled skin, mumbling a few words, tilling the land, paying, without knowing why, certain tribute to another animal whom they call *king*, selling their produce as dearly as they can, and coming together certain days of the year to sing prayers in a language they do not understand."[30]

Voltaire dared to publish this passage only thirty years later, in a more developed form, in the pseudonymous *Philosophie de l'histoire*, later reprinted as the introduction to the *Essai sur les mœurs*.[31] In the new version the unsympathetic description of French society was attributed, certainly more plausibly, to Voltaire himself. In the *Traité de métaphysique*, instead, the point of view of the peasants introduced in rapid succession the equally one-sided positions of a king, a young Parisian, a young Turk, a priest, and a philosopher. To transcend these limited attitudes, Voltaire imagined a being descended from space: an invention, reminiscent of Swift, later brought back in *Micromégas*.[32] Having set out to search for man, the traveler sees "monkeys, elephants, negroes who all seem to have some glimmer of imperfect reason." Based on these experiences he declares: "Man is a black animal with wool on his head, who walks on two feet, almost as straight as a monkey, but not as strong as other animals of his size, with a few more ideas than they, and with greater facility expressing them; he is subjected to all the same necessities, he is born, lives and dies just like them."[33]

The innocence of the traveler who has come from space on the one hand leads him to fall into ridiculous generalization but on the other, because of an ambivalence dear to Voltaire, allows him to perceive an emphatic truth: human beings are animals. Little by little the traveler discovers that those beings belong to different species, each one of independent origin and holding a precise place in the grand hierarchy of the cosmos: "Finally, I see men who seem superior to negroes, just like negroes are superior to monkeys, and monkeys are superior to ostriches and to other animals of the same species."[34]

To underline the diversity among the human species Voltaire compares them to different types of trees. Twenty years later, this analogy was resurrected and further developed in the *Essai sur les mœurs* (chap. 114). Once again blacks were prominent in Voltaire's thought:

The mucous membrane of negroes, which is black, and is the cause of their color, proves in an obvious manner that in every human species, as in plants, there is a differentiating principle.

To this principle nature has subordinated the different degrees of spirit (*génie*) and those national characteristics which one sees change so rarely. That is the reason why negroes are the slaves of other men. They are bought on the African coasts like animals, and the mass of these blacks, transplanted into our American colonies, serve a very small number of Europeans.[35]

Voltaire thought that human history had developed within the hierarchy made up of the various human species—today we would say of races. Even if the words *racism* and *racist* did not exist then, to ask ourselves (as we have done so often) whether Voltaire was or was not a racist seems absolutely proper.[36] It seems useful, however, to begin by distinguishing between racism broadly construed and racism in a narrow sense. The former holds that (a) the human races exist and (b) the human races are arranged in a hierarchical scale. The latter, racism in a narrow sense, besides subscribing to (a) and (b), sustains that (c) the hierarchy between the races cannot be modified either by education or by culture. Voltaire, who was undoubtedly a racist in the broad sense, never fully adhered to racism in the narrow sense, but he came very close to it whenever he had to speak of blacks. "The vast majority of negroes, and all the kaffirs, are thrust deeply in the same stupidity," he wrote in the *Philosophie de l'histoire*. A few years later, in 1775, he added: "And they will rot there for a long time."[37]

5. Voltaire's attitude about race, and more specifically about blacks, was largely shared by the *philosophes*.[38] But a personal circumstance may have contributed to exacerbate it. From his youth he had invested large sums in a company which traded with the "Indies," deeply involved in the slave trade.[39] Voltaire, who, as we know, had a great aptitude for business, was certainly aware of this. And, in any case, the commerce in slaves was an important element in that economic system whose praises he sang in the short poem *Le mondain* (followed by the *Défense du mondain ou l'apologie du luxe*, 1736):

Le superflu, chose très nécessaire,
A réuni l'un et l'autre hémisphère.
Voyez-vous pas ces agiles vaisseaux.
Qui du Texel, de Londres, de Bordeaux,

S'en vont chercher, par un heureux échange,
Des nouveaux biens, nés aux sources du Gange,
Tandis qu'au loin, vainqueurs des musulmans,
Nos vins de France enivrent les sultans.[40]

The frivolous tone of this rococo poem stands out against the gravity of its content. One of the wares which had contributed to join the two hemispheres was the "black animals" sold as slaves. Luxury stimulates progress, Bernard Mandeville had explained in his *The Fable of the Bees*.[41] But his paradoxical assumption that private vices generate public virtues only applied to the European states. That earthly paradise evoked by Voltaire in the euphoric conclusion of his *Mondain* ("The earthly paradise is where I am") was the fruit of the systematic sacking of the world.

6. The eighteenth-century origin of later racist ideologies, although often remote, is unquestioned. I do not accept, however, the connection Auerbach suggests between Voltaire and Nazi propaganda. To be sure, we cannot exclude that Auerbach may have felt himself personally offended by Voltaire's sarcastic comment on Jewish rites. Nazi persecution had turned Auerbach into a Jew and an exile.[42]

Marvell's verse quoted in *Mimesis* ("Had we world enough and time . . .") refers ironically to the historical and geographical limitations which had conditioned the book's genesis. The irony concealed another, one even more bitter: Marvell goes on assuring his reluctant lover that she may resist him, if she so desires, "till the conversion of the Jews."[43] But the impatience, as well as admiration, which Auerbach felt toward Voltaire had broader implications.

Near the beginning of his exile in Istanbul, Auerbach wrote letters to Walter Benjamin, with whom he was obviously on friendly terms. In one of them, dated 3 January 1937, Auerbach related his first Turkish impressions: "The result [of the politics of Kemal Atatürk] is a nationalism fanatically hostile to tradition; a rejection of the entire Muslim cultural inheritance; the construction of an imaginary relationship with an earlier Turkish identity; and technological modernization in a European sense. . . . The result is an extreme nationalism, accompanied by the simultaneous destruction of the national historical character. This situation, which in countries such as Germany, Italy, and even Russia (?) is not visible to all, here is fully evident."

Auerbach followed this with a prediction: "For me it becomes ever clearer that the present international situation is nothing other than the cunning of providence, intended to bring us by a tortuous and bloody path toward an internationalism of trivialities and a cultural Esperanto. A suspicion of the kind had already come to me in Germany and in Italy, seeing the terrible dishonesty in the slogan of 'blood and native soil'; but only here did the evidence of such a turn seem almost certain."[44]

The nationalist dictatorships (the term "Russia," even if followed by a question mark, is symptomatic) were thus a stage in a historical process which would end up erasing all specific traits, including the national, arriving at the affirmation of one undifferentiated civilization on a world stage. This paradoxical trajectory suggested to Auerbach the expression "the cunning of providence"—a phrase inspired by a saying of Croce's, which combined Vico's providence with Hegel's cunning of reason.[45] Auerbach did not doubt that this process would signal a great loss culturally. The same concern reemerges, after the end of World War II, in the essay "Philologie und Weltliteratur" (1952).[46] The cold war, which had separated the world into two opposed but profoundly similar models, tended to produce a standardization, a uniformity, a loss of diversity which debilitated all individual and national traditions.

The evident continuity between the 1937 letter to Benjamin and the 1952 essay sheds light on a chronologically intermediate text: the chapter in *Mimesis* which analyzes Voltaire's passage on the London Stock Exchange. There Auerbach found an anticipation of a culturally homogeneous mass society, regulated by the rational laws of the market. In spite of their enormous differences, the Enlightenment and Nazism seemed to him as stages in a long-drawn-out historical process which would reduce individual aspects (religious or other types) to various and unimportant elements before canceling them out altogether.

A similar thesis had been suggested by Max Horkheimer and Theodor Adorno in their *Dialectic of Enlightenment* (1947, but written in 1944). Auerbach's sketchy notes in his letter to Benjamin cannot be compared to the well-developed comprehensive discussion of Adorno and Horkheimer in their "philosophical fragments." But it is not difficult to imagine a dialogue on the ambivalence of the Enlightenment between exiles in Istanbul and Santa Monica in the early 1940s.

7. This ambivalence stands out at the very outset, in the introduction to the *Dialectic of the Enlightenment*. "The critique of enlightenment" [in the first essay], write the two authors, "is intended to prepare a positive concept of enlightenment which liberates it from its entanglement in blind domination."[47] In the course of the book this positive notion of enlightenment, through dialectical contortion, reveals itself to be based on denial: "Not the good but the bad is the subject matter of theory. . . . Its element is freedom, its theme oppression. Where language grows apologetic, it is already corrupted. . . . There is only one expression for truth: the thought which repudiates injustice."

It is Voltaire, who has incarnated this thought, to whom the two writers forlornly turn: "You have trumpeted the scandal of tyranny eloquently, tearfully, sarcastically, thunderously; but the good that power has brought about—on that you have kept silent."[48] But as we know, the author of the *Treatise on Tolerance* shared with the great majority of his contemporaries a number of attitudes, especially on the question of the human races, which promoted injustice rather than denied it. There is no point in repeating the commonplace on the historical limits of a movement preeminently male, white, and European born. But that the Enlightenment is dead is not at all certain. The intellectual biography of Voltaire, the very symbol of the Enlightenment, reveals the wealth and complexity of the contradictions pointed out by Horkheimer and Adorno.

8. For Voltaire the Lisbon earthquake of 1755 marked an epochal turning point. The destruction of an entire city and the death of countless innocents compelled him to confront the problem of evil. In the *Poème sur le désastre de Lisbonne ou examen de cet axiome: Tout est bien*, written shortly after the event, Voltaire looked upon the entire world as an endless chain of horrors:

> Animal, human elements, everything is at war.
> It has to be admitted, evil is over the land:
> Its secret principle is not known at all.

> Éléments, animaux, humain, tout est en guerre.
> il le faut avouer, le mal est sur la terre:
> Son principe secret ne nous est point connu.

Voltaire looked for this "secret principle" in the work of Bayle, who had reflected in depth, but uselessly, on the question of evil. Even Bayle did not have an answer. Voltaire rejected Pope's maxim "All is well" and his own past philosophy: "Wise men mislead me, and God alone is correct [*Les sages me trompaient, et Dieu seul a raison*]."

To be sure, Voltaire was not a great poet. But his uninspired verses on the Lisbon earthquake express a real involvement in the tragedy, one more intellectual than emotional.[49] In the preface (1756) and especially in the *postscriptum*, Voltaire expressed himself more cautiously: "Unfortunately, it is always necessary to take note that the objections which an author directs at himself have to be distinguished from his response to the objections."[50] But his mental bent had changed profoundly. A passage from an earlier writing shows to what extent he had felt "betrayed": "As for the injustice and cruelty which we blame on God, I answer first of all that, even supposing that a moral evil exists (which to me seems like an illusion), this evil is just as unexplainable in a system based on matter as in one based on a God."

Cruelty and injustice are in fact purely human concepts: "We have no other notions of justice except those we have concocted ourselves, of an action useful to society, in conformity to the laws which we have ourselves established for the common good; but since this idea is connected only to relations among men it cannot have any analogy with God. In this sense, to say God is just or unjust is just as absurd as to say he is blue or square. It is thus senseless to reproach God because flies are eaten by spiders. . . ."[51]

This passage can be read in the *Traité de metaphysique*. When Voltaire wrote it he was forty, healthy, happy, wholly consumed by his romantic idyll with Madame du Châtelet. Evil for him simply did not exist. Old age, as Voltaire himself recognized in the *Poème sur le désastre de Lisbonne*, had contributed to his intellectual conversion.

> In a less lugubrious tone I could be seen in the past
> Singing of sweet pleasures the seductive laws;
> Of other times, of other customs: instructed by old age,
> I share the weakness of the humans who have been led astray, I seek a light
>   in a dark night,
> I know only to suffer, and not to grumble.

> Sur un ton moins lugubre on me vit autrefois
> Chanter des doux plaisirs les séduisantes lois;
> D'autres temps, d'autres mœurs: instruit par la vieillesse, des humains égarés
>   partageant la faiblesse,
> Dans une épaisse nuit cherchant à m'éclairer
> Je ne sais que souffrir, et non pas murmurer.[52]

Here Voltaire was alluding to two small works he wrote immediately after the *Traité de metaphysique*: *Le mondain* (mentioned above) and his apologia,
La défense du mondain. In the *Défense*, Voltaire quarreled with an imaginary
critic of *Le mondain*, reminding him that the luxury in which he lived was made
possible by global commerce. Silver was one of the items thus traded:

> This refined silver, embossed, ribbed,
> Transformed into plates, vases, saucers,
> Was extracted from the depths of the earth
> In the Potosi, in the heart of the New World.

> Cet argent fin, ciselé, godronné,
> En plats, en vase, en soucoupe tourné,
> Fut arraché dans la terre profonde
> Dans le Potose, au sein d'un Nouveau Monde.[53]

And freed from care, Voltaire concluded: "The entire universe has labored
for you. *[Tout l'univers a travaillé pour vous]*." No human agent appeared in
these youthful verses. The years passed. In the *Essai sur les mœurs* (chap. 148)
Voltaire spoke of the mines in Peru less impersonally, and with a greater sense
of anguish, alluding to "Negroes, purchased in Africa and transported to Peru
like animals condemned to human servitude,"[54] to be thrown in with the natives already laboring in the mines.

This passage might be dated to the early months of 1756, when Voltaire was
penning his final additions to the *Essai sur les mœurs* and to the *Poème sur le
désastre de Lisbonne*.[55] An addition to the 1761 printing of the *Essai sur les
mœurs* (chap. 152) is further testimony to this change of heart. We see emerging
a much more compassionate attitude toward the slaves and their sufferings:[56]

> In 1757 in French San Domingo the population totaled about thirty thousand,
> plus a hundred thousand negro and mulatto slaves who worked in the sugar refin-
> eries and plantations of indigo and cocoa, cutting short their lives to satisfy our
> newly acquired appetites and necessities unknown to our forebears. We go to
> purchase those negroes on the Guinea coast, on the Gold coast, on the Ivory coast.
> Thirty years ago one could purchase a good-looking negro for fifty *livres*, more or
> less a fifth of what one pays for a fat cow. . . . We tell them that they are men like
> us, redeemed by the blood of a God who died for them, and then we make them
> work like beasts of burden, but feed them less well; if they try to flee, we cut off a
> limb; we force them to turn by the strength of their arms the shafts of the sugar
> mills, after we have fitted them out with a wooden leg. After all this we dare to
> talk of human rights! . . . This commerce does not enrich a state; on the contrary,
> it destroys human lives, causes shipwrecks, and without doubt is not a true good;

but since men have created new necessities for themselves; France purchases at great cost from abroad the superfluous converted to a necessity.[57]

The final words echo a verse in *Le mondain* written almost forty years earlier: "the superfluous, a very necessary thing. . . ." Voltaire was quoting himself consciously and perhaps not without a touch of irony. As a younger man he had euphorically embraced the world just as it was; growing older, he had ended up accepting pain and suffering as part of the human condition. But as La Rochefoucauld wrote, "we are all strong enough to bear the sufferings of others."[58] Slavery was the answer to new desires, to new needs: it was, in the final analysis, Voltaire seemed to suggest, a cruel but inevitable consequence of progress.

9. The 1755 Lisbon earthquake had an even more profound effect on Voltaire. The rejection of necessity (including the necessity of evil) brought him, not always coherently, to eliminate the idea of the great chain of being which had been argued eloquently by Pope in his *Essay on Man*.[59] "There probably is an immense divide between man and beast, between man and superior substances," Voltaire wrote in a note to the *Poème sur le désastre de Lisbonne*.[60] But even this feeble anthropocentrism would collapse in the end.

"I would trade the forty-nine guests I had for dinner to have had you instead," Voltaire wrote to d'Alembert on 18 October 1760. The latter replied jokingly, comparing the meals at Ferney to the London Stock Exchange as Voltaire had described it: the Jesuit, the Jansenist, the Catholic, the Socinian, the Quaker, and the encyclopedist met to embrace and laugh together.[61] But some participated in these repasts not to eat but to be eaten. Some years later (1763) Voltaire chose to give them a voice in the *Dialogue du chapon et de la poularde*.[62] In a few apparently lighthearted pages, a pullet and a capon confide in one another: they have been neutered. The more worldly capon informs the more ingenuous pullet what awaits them: they will be killed, cooked, and eaten. The sous-chef arrives; the pullet and the capon say their farewells.

Animal dialogues are a genre dating back to Greek and Roman antiquity. Generally these writings have didactic purposes: the humanized voices of animals impart a moral lesson to humans. Voltaire began from this tradition but elaborated on it, once again using the doctrine of estrangement. The dialogue format allowed him to dispense with the external observer. He was not

obliged to make this choice. In the *Galimatias dramatique*, written in 1757 and
published in 1765, a Jesuit, a Jansenist, a Quaker, an Anglican, a Lutheran, a
Puritan, and a Muslim strike up a theological discussion which recalls the
description of the London Stock Exchange. The role of the distant and reasonable observer is entrusted not to the narrator but to a Chinese, who has
the last word: these Europeans are all mad and should be locked up in an
asylum.[63] In the *Dialogue du chapon et de la poularde*, instead, the estrangement is assigned to the voice of the two protagonists.

But *protagonists* is the wrong word. The two animals are victims: they do
not act but suffer.[64] To the capon who asks her why she is so sad, the pullet
replies by describing in minute detail the cruel operation to which she had
been subjected: "An accursed servant took me over her knees, stuck a long
needle in my rectum, seized my womb, twirled it around the needle, ripped it
out and gave it to her cat to eat."[65]

Can the desire to be nourished with delicious foods justify such terrible
mutilation? Voltaire forces the reader to ponder this question. A custom (the
consumption of poultry), which most of us consider commonplace, is suddenly
made abhorrent; the intellectual disjunction creates the premise for an unexpected emotional identification. The capon, while accusing human beings,
observes that certain enlightened spirits have prohibited the consumption of
animal flesh: Indian Brahmins, Pythagoras, and the neo-Platonic philosopher Porphyry. Porphyry's *De abstinentia* was translated into French with
the title *Traité . . . touchant l'abstinence de la chair des animaux* (1747). Voltaire
owned a copy and marked up a number of pages.[66] But even more important
and closer to the spirit of the *Dialogue du chapon et de la poularde* is a previously unidentified source: *The Fable of the Bees*, by Bernard Mandeville.
One of the notes, designated by the letter "P," includes a fable which inspired Voltaire's *Le Marseillois et le lion* (1768).[67] Commenting on the fable,
Mandeville alluded to the practice of castrating animals to render the flesh
more tender, and in emotional tones described the killing of a steer: ". . . as
soon as the wide wound is made, and the jugular is cut asunder, what mortal can without compassion hear the painful bellowings intercepted by his
blood?"

In his youth Mandeville had received a medical degree and had practiced
for a few years. In this period he wrote a short work, *De brutorum operationibus* (1690), in which he argued, following Descartes, that, since animals lack
souls, they are machines. The conclusion of note "P" in *The Fable of the Bees*

reads like a true recantation: "When a creature has given such convincing and undeniable proofs of the terrors upon him, and the pains and agonies he feels, is there a follower of Descartes so inur'd to blood, as not to refute, by his commiseration, the philosophy of that vain reasoner?"[68]

Voltaire's capon echoes Mandeville: "In effect, my dear pullet, would it not be an affront to the divine to affirm that we have senses that do not feel, and a brain that does not think? This fantasy, worthy of a madman by the name of Descartes, might it not be the height of the ridiculous and a useless justification of the barbaric?"[69]

The *Dialogue du chapon et de la poularde*, more than an exhortation to vegetarianism, seems a reflection on the possibility of expanding the limits of toleration to the point of including animals (or at least some of them).[70] Thus, even more striking is Voltaire's attack, through the mouth of the pullet, against Jews. Resurrecting one of his favorite themes, although without recourse, as elsewhere, to distorted biblical allusions, Voltaire accuses Jews of cannibalism: "It is proper that the representatives of such a perverse species should devour one another, and that the earth should be purged of that race."[71]

Words like *species* and *race* suggest a certain distance between the pullet and Voltaire, who usually speaks of Jews as a "people."[72] Even innocent victims, Voltaire seems to be suggesting ironically, are not free of prejudices. The capon defines men as "those animals who are bipeds like us and are very inferior to us because they lack feathers." The capon and the pullet share the prejudices of their persecutors—something that renders them at once both ridiculous and familiar. At the end of the dialogue the capon, who has spoken scornfully of Christians for their cruel alimentary customs, dies uttering the words of Jesus: "Agh! I am being seized by the neck. Let us forgive our enemies."[73]

Certainly, the allusion is free of blasphemous intentions. The suffering servant, taken as a model by Jesus, is compared to an innocent lamb being led to slaughter (Isa. 53:7).[74] For the vast majority of people, the sufferings of animals appear insignificant compared to the sufferings of humans. But many cultures make reference to animals to express condemnation of the killing of innocent human beings.

10. In 1772 Voltaire wrote a "diatribe" with the title *Il faut prendre un parti ou le principe d'action*. He was seventy-eight years old at the time. Once more he

was returning to questions over which he had reflected obsessively all his long life: God, evil, toleration. Voltaire spoke of the Eternal Being, of the eternal laws of nature to which every living being is subject. He described the world as a scene of mutual extinction: "All animals massacre one another reciprocally, impelled by an irresistible impulse. There is no animal that does not have his particular prey, and who, to capture it, does not recur to something resembling the cunning and the fury with which the hateful spider attracts and devours the innocent fly. A herd of sheep at pasture devours in an hour more insects than there are humans who inhabit the earth." This slaughter, Voltaire noted, is part of nature's plan: "These victims die only after nature has provided to replace them. Everything is born again for the murder."[75]

This passage made an unforgettable impression on a contemporary reader, the Marquis de Sade. In his celebrated pamphlet *Français, encore un effort si vous voulez être républicains*, Sade argued that assassination is perfectly normal behavior, since in the natural world it exists everywhere.[76] Voltaire had reached a different conclusion. He used words dictated by compassion such as *victims* and *assassination* and gave them greater emphasis by condemning the carnivorous customs of humans: "What can there be more abominable than to continually nourish oneself from cadavers?"[77]

From the sufferings of animals Voltaire passed to the sufferings of human beings. Evil exists: wars, diseases, earthquakes prove it. The principle "All is well" is absurd. Is the Supreme Being thus responsible for evil? In *Il faut prendre un parti* this is discussed by an atheist, a Manichean, a pagan, a Jew, a Turk, a theist, and a citizen. How each of the various interlocutors presents himself reveals Voltaire's attitudes toward them. For the arguments of the atheist he feels respect, but it is the theist who speaks for him, who explains that evil results from the distance between the creator and his creatures—an unsatisfactory argument, as Voltaire himself concedes. The theist ridicules all religions and criticizes the Jews especially: "The kaffirs, the Hottentots, the negroes of Guinea are much more reasonable and honest than Jews. You [Jews] have surpassed all people with your shameless fables, with your bad behavior, your barbarisms; for all this you bear the punishment, it is your destiny."

The Turk, instead, is praised for his tolerance: "Above all, continue to be tolerant: it is the true way to please the Being of Beings, who is the Father of the Turks and of the Russians, of the Chinese and of the Japanese, of the blacks, of the red and yellow skins, of nature in its entirety."[78]

The brusque passage from intolerance (toward Jews) to tolerance (toward all others, at least in theory) reveals a profound incoherence in the thought of Voltaire. His God may have been indifferent to skin color; Voltaire himself often was not. In general, he was not a rigorous thinker. But this inability to live up to the universal principles of the Enlightenment was not Voltaire's problem alone. The Enlightenment, as has often been said, is an unfinished affair. At the conclusion of *Il faut prendre un parti* the citizen looks forward to tolerance, expanding its parameters to include (even if facetiously) the animal realm: "In all the discussions which will take place, it is explicitly forbidden to call someone a dog, even in a paroxysm of anger, unless that is we treat dogs as humans, when they steal our dinners, or bite us, and so forth."[79]

In the tolerant society described in *Il faut prendre un parti* women are not even mentioned. It may be that this omission, just like the attitude toward slaves, has to be attributed to the historical limitations of the Enlightenment, and as such should be distinguished from its ideal legacy. We can ask ourselves if this legacy can be realized, if its realization is even desirable. As we have seen, Auerbach responded affirmatively to the first question, negatively to the second.

11. The reopening of the New York Stock Exchange a few days after the attack on the Twin Towers of the World Trade Center demonstrated (Adriano Sofri pointed this out to me) how extraordinarily contemporary was Voltaire's discussion of the London Stock Exchange. The rationality and universality of the financial markets have been contrasted to the sectarian fanaticism of the religious fundamentalists—something Voltaire would have applauded enthusiastically.

Auerbach obviously would have reacted differently. He was accustomed to gaze into the distance and from a distance. In the bloody events which take place under our very eyes he would have discerned a stage in the tortuous journey destined by means of upheavals of every sort to impose a culturally homogeneous society over the entire world. In his eyes, intolerance (similar to the one of which he was victim) and tolerance both played a part, from opposite directions, in achieving the same result. Auerbach might also have shared the concerns of those who, from a cosmic perspective, consider that the decline of biological and cultural diversity may threaten over time the capacity of the human species to adapt. The physicist Freeman Dyson articulated this preoccupation in one of the most intense chapters, "Slaughter and Clones," in his autobiography.[80] Some decades later Dolly was "born."

CHAPTER 8

Anacharsis Interrogates the Natives

A New Reading of an Old Best Seller

1. "Every Thursday evening he wrote a long letter to his mother in red ink and sealed it with three wafers; then he skimmed his history notebooks or read an old volume of the philosopher *Anacharsis* that happened to be in the study hall."[1] From the very first page of Flaubert's *Madame Bovary*, Charles, the future husband of the protagonist, is presented as mediocre and ridiculous. (His heroic dimensions will emerge only at the end of the novel.) Every slight detail that concerns him, including the mention of "the old volume" of the philosopher *Anacharsis* read at boarding school at Rouen, has something awkward and stuffy about it. Flaubert imagines the story of *Madame Bovary* commencing about the year 1835. At that date the *Voyage du jeune Anacharsis en Grèce*, by Jean-Jacques Barthélemy, first published in 1788, was still a best seller. In the span of a century it enjoyed about eighty editions, if we count the anthologies and the adaptations for young people. It was translated into English, Spanish, German, Italian, Danish, Dutch, modern Greek, and even Armenian. By way of this extremely long book, generations of readers, young and old, learned about the history and antiquities of Greece. "The old volume" of *Anacharsis*, read by Charles Bovary in the long evenings at school, was frayed from use. But for Flaubert it was also a relic from the past: testimony to a taste and a world gone forever.[2]

Enormous success was followed by oblivion. Today we can permit ourselves to contemplate the *Voyage* with equanimity. "It is a book which can be freed from the dust covering it," wrote V.-L. Saulnier.[3] The contrary may be true. What interests us today in the *Voyage du jeune Anacharsis* is its improbability.

2. Jean-Jacques Barthélemy was born in 1716 at Aubagne in Provence in a family of well-to-do merchants.[4] He studied in the seminary but probably never seriously considered an ecclesiastical career; he always remained the *abbé*. A number of learned contributions brought him to the notice of antiquarians. In 1753 he became the secretary of the Cabinet des Médailles. The following year he relinquished his position and left for Rome in the entourage of Étienne-François de Stainville, subsequently duke of Choiseul, who had been appointed the French ambassador.

In Rome, where he spent three years, Barthélemy found a stimulating intellectual atmosphere. He met Johann Joachim Winckelmann and corresponded with him; became involved in the discussions provoked by the archeological discoveries at Herculaneum; and began a piece of research, which he would publish a few years later, on the Nilotic mosaic of Palestrina.[5] In this period he began to reflect on a new project, one far removed from his usual erudite form of research.[6] In his autobiographical reminiscences published a half century later, he described it in this way:

> I was in Italy and in the cities I visited I was more interested in their ancient splendor than in their contemporary state. I spontaneously went back to the century in which they disputed among themselves the glory of cultivating the sciences and the arts, and I thought that to report an extended journey in that country at the time of Leo X, would put before our eyes one of the most useful and interesting spectacles for the history of the human spirit. A summary description should suffice to give the idea of it. A Frenchman crosses the Alps: in Pavia he meets Gerolamo Cardano. . . . In Parma he sees Correggio frescoing the cupola of the cathedral; in Mantua, Count Baldassar Castiglione. . . . In Ferrara he sees Ariosto. . . . In Florence, Machiavelli and the historians Guicciardini and Paolo Giovio. . . . in Rome, Michelangelo who is building St. Peter's dome, and Raphael decorating the Vatican galleries. . . . In Naples he finds Talesio [*sic*], whom Bacon defines as the first to restore philosophy, working to reconstruct the system of Parmenides; he finds Giordano Bruno, whom nature seems to have chosen as its interpreter. . . .[7]

Page after page Barthélemy spoke of this project, left unfinished. The concept undoubtedly had been inspired by the *Essai sur les mœurs* (1760)—more specifically, from the chapter in which Voltaire contrasts the ephemeral hostilities among the Italian cities with the intellectual advances achieved in the sixteenth century.[8] Barthélemy took this one step further and hypothesized that artistic and intellectual progress had been produced by the "tendency to emulation by the various states" into which Italy was divided—a thesis that would be taken up by J.C.L. Simonde de Sismondi and Jacob Burckhardt.[9] With Jules Michelet and Burckhardt, Barthélemy viewed in "this stupendous revolution [cette étonnante revolution] a first, decisive step toward the modern world: "Because, after all, the century of Leo X was the harbinger of those which followed, and many of the geniuses who distinguished themselves in various countries in the seventeenth and eighteenth centuries owe much of their glory to what Italy had produced in earlier centuries."[10]

The project was to take the form of a travel journal written by a Frenchman, a transparent alter ego of the writer. This narrative invention, vaguely inspired by Fénelon's Aventures de Télémaque, tied the presentation to a relatively circumscribed period of time.[11] The imaginary French traveler, as we seem to gather from Barthélemy's rather confused sketch, participated in the decoration of the Vatican Stanze worked on by Raphael between 1511 and 1514, and on the construction of the dome of St. Peter, which Michelangelo began in 1550; he saw Correggio, who was frescoing the ceiling of the Parma cathedral in 1526, and met Giordano Bruno in Naples about a half century later. All these events were compatible with the life of a person who was relatively long-lived. But Barthélemy did not hesitate to take liberties with the narrative constraints he had imposed on himself. Among Ariosto's contemporaries, he included Petrarch, who had lived a century and a half earlier, and Tasso, born eleven years later. The former was there because his works were read and commented upon in the sixteenth century, and the latter because he had been inspired by Ariosto: "In this same way," Barthélemy commented, "we call the Nile both the source and the mouth."[12] This panorama of Italian sixteenth-century artistic and intellectual life would evoke, in a condensed form, a much longer historical process. Through the description of his failed project Barthélemy may have influenced the synchronic presentation of the Italian Renaissance proposed by Burckhardt in his famous Civilization of the Renaissance in Italy.

Barthélemy abandoned his project because he began to realize that his knowledge of the Italian Cinquecento was inadequate. So he transposed a similar narrative device to a historical period with which his erudite researches had made him more familiar: the Greece of the fourth century B.C. I have imagined, we read in the preface to the first edition of the Voyage, that a Scythian named Anacharsis journeys to Greece and observes the usages and customs of the people, participating in their celebrations and meeting many famous persons: "I have written a travel account, rather than a history; because in a travel account everything can be used, even the most minor circumstances which are not proper for a historian to mention [qu'on y permet des détails interdits à l'historien].[13]

3. A historical novel stuffed with erudition, an undigested miscellany inspired by François Fénelon's *Aventures de Télémaque*: these are the images that today are vaguely associated with the *Voyage du jeune Anacharsis*. But the passage just quoted sheds light on a more complicated experiment. For Barthélemy the tenuous romantic mechanism set in motion by the imaginary Scythian traveler was a means, not an end.[14] But what were the "minor circumstances which are not proper for a historian to mention," recovered by the artifice of the narrative? A glance at the *Voyage* provides a preliminary answer. In the third edition (1791), the first volume recapitulates the political and military history of Greece. The six following volumes take a totally different form. The exposition swarms with footnotes (twenty thousand, Barthélemy proudly proclaimed).[15] Take a chapter at random, the twenty-fifth: "Of the Homes and the Meals of Athenians" (*Des maisons et des repas des Atheniens*). The reader finds himself before a minute description of a symposium in which the notes reference passages from Greek and, less often, Latin authors. Rarely, some modern writer may also be cited, such as Isaac Casaubon (for his commentary on Athenaeus) and Jacob Spon.[16] The chapters of the *Voyage* on religious ceremonies, on holidays, on the various places visited by Anacharsis are similarly constructed.[17]

These were the subjects traditionally treated by antiquarians.[18] In his memoirs Barthélemy asserted that he had made use especially of the great collection of Greek antiquities edited by Johann Frederik Gronovius: twelve folio volumes which contain, among other writings, treatises by Ubbo Emmius, Nicholas Cragius, and Johannes Meursius.[19] Barthélemy was especially influenced by Meursius, whose work was organized thematically. To overcome the lacunae left by his predecessors Barthélemy meticulously scrutinized every sort of text, including recently published inscriptions. Scores of minute tesserae, based on a myriad of citations, were joined to form an enormous mosaic: the *Voyage du jeune Anacharsis*.

4. It would take some thirty years to complete the work. In a letter to his friend Madame du Deffand written on 18 February 1771, Barthélemy alluded

bitterly to his decision, taken long before, in 1755, to follow the duke de Choiseul to Rome, and to leave his position at the Cabinet des Médailles. From that
time, he recounted, his obligations to the duke and to the duchess de Choiseul
(to whom he was, respectively, protégé and gentleman-in-waiting, perhaps even
lover) had prevented him from pursuing his true vocation, that of the scholar.[20]
A few months later, in December 1771, Louis XV, bowing to pressure from
Madame du Barry, exiled the powerful duke de Choiseul to his estate at Chanteloup, near Amboise. Not long afterward, Barthélemy, too, lost his position
(and a large part of his stipend) as secretary general of the Swiss Guards.[21]
After some hesitation he decided to follow the duke and duchess into their
rural exile: and for four years he resided with them in the isolated and tran-
quil surroundings of Chanteloup.

For the duke and duchess and their small court, Barthélemy, some time
before, had written a mock-heroic poem entitled *La Chanteloupée, ou la guerre
des puces contre Mme L.[ouise] D.[duchesse] d.[e] Ch.[oiseul]*.[22] It would be published, with some embarrassment, only after his death. In year six of the Republic a writing like this, testimony of the frivolity of the Ancien Régime, did
not seem to merit being included among Barthélemy's works. But the description of the home of Dinias, a wealthy Athenian, included in the aforementioned chapter 25 of the *Voyage*, evokes a not too dissimilar situation. Anacharsis asks the wife of Dinias, Lysistrata, permission to visit her residence:

> Her dressing table was first to catch my attention. I noticed silver basins and
> pitchers, mirrors made of various materials, hair pins, curling irons (a), ribbons
> of many sizes to bind them, nets to catch them (b), yellow powders to dye them
> blonde (c), many sorts of bracelets and ear rings, boxes of rouge and of white
> make-up, and of black vapors to tinge the eyelashes; and whatever was needed to
> keep teeth polished (d). I was examining these objects carefully, and Dinias could
> not understand how they could be a novelty for a Scythian.[23]

The footnotes, set off by letters of the alphabet inside parentheses, cited
Lucian, Homer, Hesychius, and even a gloss to Theocritus: all passages used
to construct a description of an Athenian boudoir of the fourth century B.C.
which reads like a passage of rococo antiquarianism. Neither ancient nor
eighteenth-century historians would have admitted the possibility of discussing details of this kind: frivolous, irrelevant, and thus prohibited (*interdits*). But for Barthélemy the antiquarian it was obvious, instead, to dwell on
aspects of what we would call today the material life, so prominent in the
Voyage du jeune Anacharsis. The quizzical gaze of the ignorant traveler, the

barbarian Anacharsis, propels us toward the informed view of the antiquarian Barthélemy. The ingenuous division on which the fiction hinges clears the way for the critical disjunction.

5. The *Voyage* is neither a systematic antiquarian treatise nor a historical narrative. Barthélemy followed a third way, combining fiction and erudition. This choice must have been dictated in part by the surroundings in which he passed much of his life: an aristocratic ambience open to intellectual curiosities of every type, dominated by the prepossessing figure of Marie Anne de Vichy-Chamrond, marquise du Deffand, an intimate friend of both the duchess de Choiseul and the abbé Barthélemy, with whom they corresponded almost daily.[24] In 1771, when Barthélemy unexpectedly unburdened himself in a letter to her concerning his relations with the duke and duchess de Choiseul (together with the request to destroy it which went unheeded), Madame du Deffand was seventy-four years old. Full of vitality, highly intelligent, she had been blind for more than two decades. She judged people and books with utter independence. She considered "detestable" *Les Scythes*, the drama by Voltaire (with whom she probably had an affair in her youth, and with whom she continued to correspond).[25] When she was seventy-eight she was reading Jacques Necker's *Sur la législation et le commerce des grains*.[26] At eighty-one she wrote to Barthélemy, who had advised her to read William Robertson's *History of America*: "I am delivering a recantation on Robertson's *America*. Of all the things I care nothing about, it is the most pleasurable, the one that is best written, almost interesting."[27]

In Madame du Deffand's letters we frequently encounter similar thoughts. To the duchess de Choiseul she wrote: "I no longer know what to read. I cannot stand books on philosophy and ethics, histories appear to me to be long and boring romances about events which are not always true and, which, even if they were, often would not be more interesting. All that remains then is conversation, and I am content with this, because I do not have a choice; once in a while it is of good quality, but rarely."[28]

Madame du Deffand had just read, or better, perused the twelve volumes of the *Cléopatre* by Gauthier de Costes (La Calprenède), published in the mid–seventeenth century. But in this interminable and, as she herself admitted, boring novel, she had found a few "absolutely beautiful" passages: the conversation between Agrippa and Artaman, the "moving" description of a battle between gladiators.[29] The duchess de Choiseul and the abbé Barthélemy, respectively forty and nineteen years younger than Madame du Deffand, had tastes that differed completely from hers where romances and books of history were concerned. The duchess de Choiseul, who found La Calprenède unbearable, wrote to Madame du Deffand, contrasting to the despotic authority of Catherine of Russia, so highly praised by Voltaire, the humble but genuine glory ("the kind that sets the heart and the imagination ablaze") earned by the Marquis Carlo Ginori, the man who had laid the foundations for Livorno's prosperity: "They speak to us of Catherine, and the Marquis Ginori is unknown!"[30] Madame du Deffand, who was not interested in the history of Roman and Carthaginian navigation and was bored reading Robertson, was chided by Barthélemy: what she lacked, he said, was that solid knowledge of antiquity gained by reading Greek and Latin writers.

> The exploits of those people [Romans and Carthaginians] are peaceful but exciting: and excitement attracts attention and interest. We are talking, it is true, of a tranquil interest: so much the better, because according to M. de Bucq happiness is nothing other than a calm interest. To witness the Romans and Carthaginians, the Spanish and the Portuguese crossing the seas to discover new lands seems to me preferable to seeing the factions of Guelfs and Ghibellines or of the Red Rose [House of Lancaster] and the White Rose [House of York] who put everything to the torch to conquer people who would have gladly done without them.[31]

The contrast between the passions and the interests, in both a psychological and economic sense, which emerged at the end of the seventeenth century had become, in the course of the eighteenth, a fundamental theme in political philosophy.[32] Barthélemy's words show that the same contrast had materialized, even if not so openly, in the historiographical domain. The polemical allusion to the War of the Roses probably concerned the *Histoire de la rivalité de la France et de l'Angleterre*, by Gabriel Henri Gaillard (1771), a book which Madame du Deffand had greatly liked.[33] Gaillard spoke of wars and internecine conflicts to argue that the European states wanted peace: "Europe is civilized, Europe believes itself to be enlightened, and yet it makes war! We have rushed to applaud the Europe of the Enlightenment, but Europe is still barbaric!"[34] Barthélemy agreed, but Gaillard's *Histoire* left him unmoved. Historians were beginning to learn to speak about peaceful activities, about the commerce which had achieved for Europe supremacy over the rest of the world: but it was a genre making slow progress.[35] To describe the peaceful occupations of the men and women who lived in Greece in the fourth century B.C., Barthélemy took his inspiration not from historians but from antiquarians, true as well as false.

6. In 1789 the *Monthly Review* discussed the *Voyage du jeune Anacharsis.* The assessment, which was basically favorable, closed with a poisonous insinuation: could Barthélemy have taken his cue from the *Athenian Letters?*[36] It was an exceedingly cryptic allusion. Under this title there had appeared in Cambridge in 1741 an edition of apocryphal correspondence, virtually a private printing consisting of only twelve copies and lacking the author's name.[37] In this collection a Persian spy by the name of Cleander and his correspondents exchanged detailed information about Greece in the age of Pericles, Egypt, and Persia. Cleander described his meetings with Herodotus, with Socrates, with Aspasia; he discussed the theater and philosophy and religion; he juxtaposed the political liberty and commercial vitality of Athens to the despotism of the Persians—a transparent allusion to the contrast between contemporary England and France.[38]

The *Athenian Letters* were presented as the English translation, commissioned by the British consul in Tunis, of a Spanish version, prepared by a "learned Jew," of the original written in "an ancient Persian tongue" and discovered in the library at Fez. The authenticity of the letters was emphasized in the footnotes: in one of them the veracity of a recently published Greek inscription (the *Marmor Sandvicense*) was proved, paradoxically, by fictitious statements of Cleander, the Persian spy.[39] A letter to Isaac Newton and Robert Boyle describing future scientific progress in the form of a prophetic vision was denounced as a forgery and thus relegated to an appendix—a final flourish which ironically reiterated the general authenticity of the *Athenian Letters.*[40] Each piece of correspondence was accompanied by a capital initial, the only clue offered deliberately by the authors of this erudite game, whose identity was revealed only when the *Athenian Letters* were reprinted in an edition of about one hundred copies in 1781.[41] The new preface was tinged with melancholy: almost all the authors in the interim had died. "When a certain period of time has elapsed," wrote one of the survivors, "the truth can be revealed; the illusion vanishes, the masquerade is over."[42] Some of the participants had occupied public positions: Charles Yorke, who with his brother Philip had authored the greater part of the collection, had been lord chancellor; William Heberden, who in one of the letters portrayed a meeting with Hippocrates, had become a famous physician.[43] All had been students at Cambridge; almost all had been members of Corpus Christi College. The group, about a dozen persons, included antiquarians such as Daniel Wray and Thomas Birch, who had thought up the initiative; a philologist, Samuel Salter; a writer on religious questions, Henry Coventry. A notable presence was that of Catherine Talbot, who would become the author of essays which were reprinted often: she was perhaps the first European woman to produce a historical work, even if in this case it was fictional history.[44]

In a letter to the *Monthly Review* Barthélemy, while acknowledging the similarity in structure between the *Athenian Letters* and the *Voyage*, unequivocally rejected the accusation of plagiarism.[45] To demonstrate his own originality, he affirmed that at one point, during his Roman sojourn, he had considered writing a book based on the experiences of a French traveler in the Italy of Leo X; later, he had decided instead to take advantage of his own antiquarian experiences, transforming the French traveler into the Scythian Anacharsis. There may have been some truth to these allegations (later repeated in his memoirs); not so credible, instead, was his assertion that he had learned of the existence of the English collection only after he had published the *Voyage*. Horace Walpole, who had a long association with Barthélemy, was well acquainted with many of the authors of the *Athenian Letters*.[46] And one of the imaginary characters in the *Voyage*, Arsame, minister to the king of Persia—in whom contemporary readers, starting with Walpole, recognized a transparent homage to the duke de Choiseul—resembled too closely, even in the name, the satrap Orsames, one of the interlocutors in the *Athenian Letters*.[47]

7. In the *Voyage du jeune Anacharsis* every detail is scrupulously, punctiliously documented; in the *Athenian Letters* the invented documents serve to support the genuine ones. In both cases the amalgam of authenticity and fiction attempts to substitute the limitations of the existing historiography. But how to recount the daily life, "the minute circumstances, which a historian is not permitted to report"? Here the dependence of Barthélemy's *Voyage* on the *Athenian Letters* is obvious: Cleander, the Persian spy, is the obvious model for Anacharsis the Scythian. Twenty-five years before Voltaire's *Essai sur les mœurs*, the *Athenian Letters* expressed the need for a type of historiography which did not yet exist: "These letters by our agents, which portray from life

the activities of Greeks and Persians, provide us with a better idea of their customs than what can be offered by severe antiquarians, with their elaborate and formal treatises."[48]

But even Cleander was not an original invention. Today the *Athenian Letters* immediately call to mind the *Lettres Persanes*. But the model for the *Athenian Letters*, mentioned explicitly in the introduction to the 1781 reprinting, was not Montesquieu, but rather the work which had inspired his *Lettres: L'esploratore turco*, by Gian Paolo Marana (1681), whose translations and adaptations in French and English had been disseminated throughout Europe (*L'espion turc; L'espion du grand seigneur dans les cours des princes chrétiens; The Turkish Spy*).[49]

The narrative artifice is identical, the results totally different. Montesquieu's corrosive viewpoint, here and there anticipated by the libertine Marana (for example, in the description of the Eucharist), observes without understanding them the surrounding social customs, thereby unveiling their absurdity and arbitrariness.[50] In the *Athenian Letters* and in the *Voyage du jeune Anacharsis* the foreigner (the spy, the traveler) seeks information on the simplest customs without harboring any hostile intention. In one case the purpose is to make the present time, which we take for granted, less familiar.[51] In the other, the purpose is that of familiarizing us with a past the everyday form of which eludes us: an apparently banal operation, which in fact presupposed a deep fissure within the historiographical tradition born in Greece.

8. Herodotus (8:26) recounts that Xerxes, king of Persia, after the battle of Thermopylae, asked a group of Arcadian deserters what was occupying the Greeks. Learning that they were celebrating the Olympic games, he inquired what the prize might be. An olive wreath, they replied.

Xerxes' questions, which no Greek would have dreamed of asking, irreparably revealed his barbarism and his disassociation from a world in which valor, not wealth, constituted the highest honor. The crown of laurel bestowed on the winner of the games ended up by symbolizing the relationship of reciprocal exclusion between Greeks and barbarians. In a dialogue by Lucian of Samosata, a Scythian who had come to Greece broke into wild laughter when he learned that young people were vying against one another for a crown of wild olive or pine branches. The name of the Scythian was Anacharsis.[52]

His alter ego, the protagonist of Barthélemy's voyage, was equally ignorant of the rules governing the games in Greek society. The questions posed by this barbarian brought to light everything that historians, both ancient and modern, had taken for granted and thus had not bothered to mention.

9. During the long gestation of the *Voyage du jeune Anacharsis*, a work of a wholly different kind appeared, one destined to much more lasting fame: *The History of the Decline and Fall of the Roman Empire*. Its author, Edward Gibbon, had imbibed that antiquarian culture which had produced Barthélemy, that of the Académie des Inscriptions.[53] But other elements had played a role in the education of Gibbon, principally the ideas of the *philosophes*, which were totally foreign to the abbé Barthélemy.[54] Gibbon has been called the founder of modern historiography for having understood how to combine antiquarianism and *histoire philosophique*.[55] The road taken, infinitely more modestly, by the abbé Barthélemy assumed the merging of antiquarianism and romanticized history: in the long run, a losing strategy.

The nineteenth century viewed Barthélemy's Greece as a vast panorama.[56] The success of the *Voyage du jeune Anacharsis* was like a bonfire enduring one hundred years, now forever extinguished. And yet it may be only fair to view this by-now-illegible book as a pioneering effort of historical ethnography, and to view in the Scythian Anacharsis, besides a descendant of the Anglo-Persian spy Cleander, an involuntary forerunner of anthropologists and inquisitors closer to our times.[57]

CHAPTER 9

Following the Tracks of Israël Bertuccio

1. In Eric Hobsbawm's autobiography, *Interesting Times*, the chapter entitled "Among the Historians" opens with a question regarding how history had changed in the course of his lifetime. The answer paints a picture filled with light and shadow. It begins with the long battle between innovators (Hobsbawm calls them "modernizers") and traditionalists which began c. 1890 and climaxed in the mid–twentieth century. For a while the innovators called themselves "social historians," a vague expression with which Hobsbawm does not fully identify. Their target was "the traditional bias of conventional historians in favour of kings, ministers, battles and treaties, i.e. top-level decision-makers both political and military."[1] Hobsbawm explains how the innovators achieved an ever more authoritative standing on the international scene: ". . . around 1970 it seemed reasonable to suppose that the struggle for the modernization of historiography that had begun in the 1890s had been won."[2] But during the 1970s the panorama suddenly changed, and it is clear that for Hobsbawm this was not progress. To illustrate this transformation he cites, on one hand, Braudel's *The Mediterranean* (1949), and on the other, "the brilliant *tour de force* of 'thick description,'" *Deep Play: Notes on the Balinese Cock-Fight*, by Clifford Geertz (1973), a great book and a brief essay which symbolize, respectively, the study of "structure" and of "culture." "There was a shift away," Hobsbawm continued, "from historical models or 'the large *why* questions,' a shift from 'the analytical to the descriptive mode,' from economic and social structure to culture, from recovering fact to recovering feeling, from telescope to microscope—as in the enormously influential

little monograph on the world-view of one sixteenth-century eccentric Friulian miller by the young Italian historian Carlo Ginzburg."[3] In a note Hobsbawm observed that *I benandanti*, the earlier (and, in his opinion, "more interesting") of my books, which he promptly reviewed in the *Times Literary Supplement*, "curiously . . . had not then attracted attention."[4]

Almost forty years have passed. This no longer young historian recalls that generous review with gratitude, and, before that, the strong impression made on him by Hobsbawm's writings.[5] But today Hobsbawm sees in my work an example of that regrettable historiographical turning point which has endangered the positive effects of the innovators. I do not entirely recognize myself in this characterization. For example, I think that I have always kept my distance from description, pure and simple, but this is beside the point. What interests me are Hobsbawm's observations on the state of historical writing today, and what they imply. According to him, historiography's cognitive ambitions have been weakened by the new directions of the social movements that emerged in the '60s: "More history than ever is today being revised or invented by people who do not want the real past, but only a past that suits their purpose. Today is the great age of historical mythology." The desire to be recognized coming from women, from ethnic or gender minorities, and from still others has run up against the pretense of history to formulate potentially universal discourse. What has been undermined is "the belief that historians' investigations, by means of generally accepted rules of logic and evidence, distinguish between fact and fiction, between what can be established and what cannot, what is the case and what we would like to be so."[6]

I share fully Hobsbawm's concern on this last point: much of what I have written in the last twenty years deals precisely with this topic.[7] About his earlier remarks, there would be much to say. Even his liquidation of postmodernism as a fashion that has only marginally touched history seems to have been reached too hastily.[8] Generally, it seems to me that we must distinguish between questions and answers: it is a lesson that I learned from someone who has been important for Hobsbawm as well. Antonio Gramsci's prison notebooks grow out of the awareness that Fascism had won out because it had been able to give ready answers, albeit reactionary ones, to questions which were not reactionary.[9] This observation has profound implications, even for the work of historians. It is one thing to reject decadent or irrelevant responses on the intellectual level; it is quite another to reject the questions which generated them.

In December 2004, *Le Monde Diplomatique*, under the title "Manifeste pour l'histoire," published the text of a lecture Hobsbawm had given a month earlier at a conference on Marxist historiography organized by the British Academy. The French version contained a passage (one which did not appear in the original text) in which Hobsbawm once again observed that contemporary historical writing had passed from a quantitative to a qualitative perspective, from macrohistory to microhistory, from analysis of structures to narratives, from the history of society to the history of culture.[10] In this series of antitheses I find that I am always on the wrong side. But when Hobsbawm writes that the greatest immediate political danger for historiography is "anti-universalism"—namely, the conviction that "my truth" is as worthy as yours, independent of the evidence proffered—then I am in complete agreement.

One can wage this battle using different tactics. In the case analyzed in this chapter, I have tried to oppose, using a microscopic scale, the postmodernist tendency to abolish the distinction between history and fiction. In other words, I have met my adversary on his own terrain, starting out from his own questions; but I have arrived at totally different answers.

2. "'Has not Israël Bertuccio got more character than all those noble Venetians?' said our rebellious plebeian to himself *[notre plébeien revolté]*."

The speaker is Julien Sorel, the protagonist of *The Red and the Black*. Stendhal wrote his novel in a mad frenzy between 1828 and 1830, completing the correction of the proofs just after the July Revolution. The sentence I have just quoted is from one of the most extraordinary chapters in the book. Julien Sorel accompanies Matilde de la Môle to a ball of high Parisian society. The narration, in the third person, is continually interrupted by the private thoughts of the characters.[11] The reader views the ball especially through the eyes of Julien, the peasants' son who regards with hate and contempt the high society to which he does not belong and which he dreams of destroying. He mentally compares Venetian nobility, which goes back to A.D. 700, to Parisian aristocracy, which is much newer, and concludes to himself: "Well, in spite of all those noble Venetians whom birth makes so great, it is Israël Bertuccio whom one remembers."

Who is this Israël Bertuccio with whom Julien Sorel, "rebellious plebeian," identifies himself? Stendhal himself clarifies the matter: "It happened that Julien had seen the day before *Marino Faliero*, a tragedy by Casimir Delavigne."[12] It is a seemingly factual reference, but, as we shall see, misleading.

Delavigne's *Marino Faliero* was performed in Paris at the theater of Porte Saint-Martin on 30 May 1829.[13] The play had been preceded, on the seventh of the month, by a parody, a vaudeville of Varner and Bayard entitled *Marino Faliero à Paris*, interspersed with popular songs that went: "Machine! Ce qui domine/C'est cela; Machine/Le siècle est là."[14] Even in Delavigne's tragedy references to the present were not lacking, but there were also many pertaining to a future that the Parisian public of 1829 must have imagined to be imminent. The speech of the old doge Marin Falier to the conspirators presages a society in which "only work will produce wealth, talent will give power and virtue will bestow nobility"—in other words, a bourgeois society.[15] The majority of the plotters is made up of fishermen, artisans, and gondoliers led by Israël Bertuccio, who is described as "un homme du peuple . . . un patron de galère."[16] There is a scene in which the gondolier Pietro lays his hand familiarly on the doge's shoulder and, when the latter reacts indignantly, exclaims, astonished, "Among equals!" This may have inspired Julien Sorel to reflect: "A conspiracy annihilates all titles conferred by social caprice."[17] But here Delavigne's Bertuccio, who reproaches the gondolier Pietro, reaffirming the authority of the doge, is a colorless character, just as Delavigne's play *Marino Faliero* is a pale imitation of the original, Lord Byron's *Marino Faliero*, written in 1820. Aside from the banal idea of transforming the wife of the old doge into an adulteress, whom Byron portrays as the imperturbable victim of a calumny, Delavigne feebly followed his model, claiming an originality that was not really there.[18] This was noted even by Stendhal, who, in an anonymous article in the *New Monthly Magazine*, spoke coldly of the play by Delavigne, a writer whom he did not esteem.[19] Stendhal, as he often does, misleads his readers: his own views differ from those of his protagonist, Julien Sorel, and the specific mention of Delavigne in the article conceals an implicit reference to Byron.

Stendhal had known Byron in Milan between 1816 and 1817. Many years later Stendhal recalled him perpetually "agitated . . . by some passion or other": he saw him beset, without cease, in turn, by the genius of the poet, the fatuity of the aristocrat, and a vanity pushed to the extremes of madness.[20] But when Stendhal surrendered to one of his infantile whims, he would list the three greatest men he had ever met: Napoleon; invariably accompanied by Lord Byron; followed by, depending on the circumstances, Antonio Canova or Gioacchino Rossini.[21] As long as Byron was alive, Stendhal awaited his writings impatiently. In December 1820 he wrote to a friend asking him to send a copy of the second edition of Byron's *Marino Faliero* (the first was already out of print), providing that the book did not cost too much.[22] Sooner or later Stendhal would have read it. I shall try to explain the identification of Julien Sorel with Israël Bertuccio in the light of this likely reading. But first something needs to be said about the plot of Byron's *Marino Faliero*.[23]

In the very title Byron announced that the play would have notes to substantiate the historical truth of various details. The notes were followed by an appendix reproducing passages from a number of chroniclers and historians concerning the story of Marin Falier. In the chronicles, at least in some of them, the antiaristocratic conspiracy of 1355 was described as the reaction to a twofold offense which had victimized, respectively, the old doge Marin Falier, derided as a cuckold in the placards concocted by some young noblemen, and Israël Bertuccio, head of the Arsenal, who had been struck a blow by one of them after a frivolous altercation. Byron takes up this parallelism: the destinies of the two men, seemingly so distant, merge in the course of the events of one night. The conspirators are ready. The next morning, 15 April, the doge will sound the great bell, the warning of impending danger (in fact, there is a war on with Genoa). The nobility will rush to the ducal palace, where they will be massacred, followed by the sacking of their residences. But one of the conspirators betrays the plan, the plot is uncovered, and its leaders—Israël Bertuccio and Filippo Calandra, who are not of aristocratic birth—are hanged; the old doge is beheaded.

For Byron, as well as for his readers, the contemporary echoes of this episode were obvious. This has been stated repeatedly.[24] Byron wrote *Marino Faliero* in 1820, in Ravenna, where he was living with Teresa Guiccioli (but the idea for it went back three years earlier). Through Guiccioli's family Byron had come into contact with the underground political movement of the Carbonari. To be sure, what was good for Italy was not necessarily good for Great Britain. In 1820, for example, Byron vigorously condemned the Cato Street conspiracy, which intended to assassinate a number of ministers. His reaction supports the traditional view that *Marino Faliero* should be read in an autobiographical key: in the uncertainty of the old doge, who hesitates before the prospect of the slaughter of the Venetian nobility, Lord Byron was projecting his ambivalence due to his own aristocratic birth.[25]

These hypotheses, all of them plausible, take us to the beginning of the work. Byron substantially followed the traditionally recognized history, but parted from it (as he indicated in the preface) where he presented the plot as already formed. In his tragedy the doge joins an existing conspiracy, whereas in reality it had been he, together with Israël Bertuccio, who had set it in motion. The desire to construct a tragedy modeled on Aristotelian unity, thereby avoiding the irregularity that constituted a weak point in the English theater, prompted Byron to situate Israël Bertuccio at the center of the action.[26] Critics have missed the importance of this structural choice, even those who have shown how Byron, at the same time that he was rejecting Shakespeare in the name of Aristotelian unity, was writing a tragedy rich in echoes from Shakespeare, especially *Macbeth*.[27] It has been noted that *Marino Faliero*'s dependence on this play is marked by a bloody trail. After Banquo's assassination, Macbeth, torn with guilt, exclaims: "Will all great Neptune's ocean wash this blood / Clean from my hand? No; this my hand will rather / The Multitudinous seas incarnadine, / Making the green one red."[28] Here *incarnadine* is used as a verb. In *Marino Faliero* the word returns to being an adjective: "When all is over," the doge says to Israël Bertuccio, "you'll be free and merry, / and calmly wash those hands incarnadine."[29] The analogy between the two passages brings out their difference. Macbeth is rent by remorse for what he has done; the doge, for that which he is about to do—the slaughter of the nobles who will be summoned to the palace. The contrast between the tormenting indecision of the doge and the implacable firmness of Israël Bertuccio repeats the contrast between the irresolute will of Macbeth and the ferocious determination of Lady Macbeth. But Byron rereads and rewrites Shakespeare while looking back at the French Revolution and, contemporaneously, forward to an approaching future. Israël Bertuccio incarnates a new reality: the pitiless innocence of the revolutionary. In a dialogue in which solidarity and class hate violently oppose each other, the doge, turning to Israël Bertuccio, blurts out: "You are a patriot, a plebeian Gracchus."[30] It is with this "plebeian Gracchus" that Julien Sorel, *plébéien révolté*, identifies himself: a Jacobin outside his time, whose desperate energy erupts tragically, wretchedly, in an act of personal violence.[31] And like Israël Bertuccio, Julien Sorel, who also rebuffs the priest sent to visit him before his execution, does not feel any pangs of guilt. This, too, may have been one of his "atrocious" traits which shocked even such an intelligent and somewhat cynical reader as Prosper Mérimée.[32]

Byron's writings appeared scandalous as well (not to mention the author himself). In 1822 a harsh critic of his *Cain*, who concealed himself under the pseudonym "Philo-Milton," suggested that invented works ("fiction") were much more dangerous than essays and books of history, because they were sold more cheaply and were accessible to a much larger public. In the case of works that on the whole were harmful, wrote "Philo-Milton," their circulation had to be impeded at all costs.[33] This had happened, just the year before, with *Marino Faliero*, performed on Drury Lane in London in a mutilated version. The copy of Byron's tragedy owned by the Huntington Library shows that the censor had suppressed half the text, focusing especially on the exchanges between the doge and Israël Bertuccio.[34] A play like *Marino Faliero* was doubly dangerous in the eyes of the censors, because it combined the dangers of history with the attractions of invention. For us, the personages created by Stendhal, Delavigne, and Byron belong to the world of literary fiction. For Byron it was a different matter: in the preface to *Marino Faliero* he observed that with the exception of Angiolina, the wife of the doge, all the personages were "strictly historical," and, as far as "real facts" were concerned, he invited readers to look closely at the texts published in the appendix.[35]

Let us do just that. Byron's principal source for the conspiracy was Marin Sanudo's multivolume *Vite dei dogi*, which he cited from the edition in Muratori's *Rerum Italicarum Scriptores*.[36] In the Sanudo text used by Byron we find Israël Bertucci: "They sent for Filippo Calendario, a seafaring man and one of great consequence, and for Bertucci Israello, engineer and a most astute man."[37] There are two problems with this. The first, apparently negligible, is the reversal of the name: Bertucci Israello instead of Israël Bertuccio (or Bertucci, as we might expect). The second has to do with the profession: engineer instead of admiral, as we read in Byron's play. The latter difficulty has an easy solution. The "ancient chronicle" copied by Sanudo recounts, in the paragraph preceding the just-quoted passage, that a nobleman of the Barbaro family had struck the admiral of the Arsenal, who then had gone to the doge to protest this affront. Byron combined the two passages, tacitly identifying the admiral with Israël Bertuccio. But the first difficulty is more serious. If we compare the passage in Sanudo quoted in the appendix of *Marino Faliero* with the corresponding passage in the *Rerum Italicarum Scriptores*, we discover that Byron's transcription (or that of whoever copied it for him) is incorrect. The text published by Muratori speaks of a "Bertucci Isarello, Engineer and most astute man."[38]

Israello or Isarello? This is not a trivial choice. If we opt for "Isarello," the possibility or probability that we might have been dealing with a Jew vanishes (and, for that matter, could a Jew in fourteenth-century Venice become, though certainly not an admiral, even an "engineer," or whatever the exact meaning of this term is?). We need to look at the texts more closely. Today the edition of the *Vite dei dogi* in the *Rerum Italicarum Scriptores* seems wholly unreliable, an Italianized version full of lacunae and errors.[39] Comparing the printed text with a manuscript copy of the corresponding passage of the *Vite dei dogi* (the second volume of Sanudo's original autograph has been lost), the name "Isarello" emerges once again.[40] But we need to press further. One of the oldest pieces of evidence concerning the conspiracy of Marin Falier is provided by the incomplete Latin chronicle of Lorenzo de' Monaci, chancellor of Crete, written shortly after 1420 but not printed until 1758. Among the events reported in this work we find the blow struck by a nobleman (here identified as Giovanni Dandolo) against a "Bertucium Israelo" of San Basilio, an affluent man among mariners ("notabilis conditionis inter marinarios"), perhaps a ship owner or shipbuilder. In the index of names to Lorenzo de' Monaci's chronicle we find a reference to "Bertuccius Israel rebellis,"[41] the very name recorded (perhaps independently) in the appendix to Byron's *Marino Faliero*. Is this the actual designation for the person whose tracks we are following? Or is this a humanistic disguise transforming "Isarello" into "Israelo"? And if this was an act of dissimulation, who was responsible? Lorenzo de' Monaci, or the eighteenth-century erudite who published his work? The manuscripts of de Monaci's *Chronicon de rebus Venetis* may provide an answer. Kristeller's *Iter Italicum* records a seventeenth-century copy housed in the British Library.[42] But the remaining questions would persist.

This long discussion takes us far from the notion (shared by Byron—not a historian) that chronicles contain "real facts," things as they really happened. To untangle the contradictions among these accounts we must try to read them critically, by inserting them into a broader documentary context. In effect, we have to go backward, retracing our steps along a path that, by following the name of Israël Bertuccio, brought us from a literary romance to a tragedy (two in fact), and from there to the chronicles. But before moving on to the next stage, it might be useful to clarify the overall significance of this journey.

We began from the literary echoes of Marin Falier's conspiracy; by dint of retrogressing we came to the conspiracy itself. Numerous studies deal with aspects of this subject, some of them excellent, but there is no satisfactory comprehensive and comparative overview; this is highly desirable in view of the extraordinary nature of the event and of Venetian history itself. For the moment, at any rate, we need to question an interpretation, put forward in the last few decades by reliable scholars, that the conspiracy of Marin Falier was a clash between aristocratic parties or factions.[43] This view seems to be definitely incompatible with the participation in the plot, along with the doge, of persons belonging to the well-to-do populace ("populares pinguis conditionis," as they were dubbed by Lorenzo de' Monaci).[44] The detailed descriptions (later developed by the literary tradition) of the insult inflicted contemporaneously on the doge and on a person of the popular classes obviously are an attempt to explain anecdotally the anomalous social alliance behind the conspiracy.

Can we suppose that in some cases these anecdotes reworked a real event, expanding it? Vittorio Lazzarini, who contributed the most to our knowledge of the Falier conspiracy, has not ruled this out. In one of his admirable, erudite pieces of research from the end of the nineteenth century and finally collected in a volume in 1963, Lazzarini analyzed that page from Lorenzo de' Monaci's chronicle which discussed the blow the nobleman Giovanni Dandolo was said to have inflicted on Bertucci Isarello.[45] (Actually, de' Monaci, as we saw, spoke of a Bertuccio *Israelo*—a variant form not recorded by Lazzarini.) In succeeding chronicles the episode was repeated and expanded. The names of the protagonists change: in the so-called Barbaro chronicle it is Marco Barbaro who administers the slap, and the person receiving it is Stefano Giazza nicknamed Gisello, admiral of the Arsenal, who says to Marin Falier: "Meser lo dose, le bestie maligne se liga, e se ne le se pol ligar le se ammazza" ("My Lord, doge, we tie up malignant beasts, and if we cannot tie them up, we butcher them"). Lazzarini comments: "We suspect that the two different accounts are the reports of a single fact, and, anyway, we accept the one that refers to Dandolo and to Bertuccio Isarello, because it is narrated by a chronicler who is almost contemporary, as is the case with de' Monaci, and because Giovanni Dandolo was at the time *sopracomito* and councillor of the *capitano da mar* and Bertuccio Isarello is a historical person, whereas Stefano Giazza never appears in contemporary documents and chronicles. . . ."[46]

"Bertuccio Isarello is a historical person": the statement is supported by careful research conducted on Venetian notarial documents. Of the five texts discovered by Lazzarini, it suffices to mention two, both conserved in the *fondo Grazie* in the Venetian State Archives. From the first, dated 13 July 1330, it emerges that Bertuccio Isarello was at the time a *nauclero*, the master of a vessel, together with Jacobello Lambardo.[47] The second, dated 22 February

1345, reveals that Bertuccio Isarello was sentenced to a fine equal to half the value of a cargo of pepper.[48]

This is the name of the man who is supposed to have participated, with his father-in-law Filippo Calendario, in Doge Marin Faliero's conspiracy. In a fine essay Lazzarini refuted the tradition which identified Filippo Calendario as the architect of the ducal palace.[49] In the documents Filippo is always referred to as "taiapiera" ("stone cutter"), except in the aforementioned "ancient chronicle" transcribed by Sanudo, which speaks of a "Filippo Calendaro seafarer and man of great consequence and . . . Bertuzzi Isarello engineer and a most astute man."[50] Lazzarini shrewdly supposes that in this passage the professions of the father-in-law and of the son-in-law were reversed: Bertuccio Isarello would have been the "seafarer and man of great consequence."[51] To grasp the significance of this last point it will suffice to recall how the conspiracy was supposed to have unfolded. Nicolò Trevisan, who at the time sat on the Council of Ten, wrote in his chronicle that "Philippo Calendario with all those of the castle, namely the seafaring men, that very night [of the conspiracy] were to rush to shore."[52] Of the ten men hanged by the neck as participants in the conspiracy, five were variously described as "seafaring men."[53] Four other "seafaring men, who were principal actors and traitors in said betrayal," managed to escape and were declared outlaws.[54] Only in-depth research may be able to tell us what drove "the seafaring men," after the Genoese victory at Porto Longo, to support Marin Falier's attempt to make himself "sovereign" of Venice. To be sure, the conspirators were not isolated figures. The four magistrates appointed by the Council of Ten to deal with the situation acted with extreme dispatch. They had to set an example, impede the contagion from spreading: "The earth was set in motion," a contemporary chronicle cryptically mentions.[55]

The sentences reveal a symbolic hierarchy. At the summit we find Bertuccio Isarello and Filippo Calendario. On 16 April, a day after the discovery of the conspiracy, they were hanged by the neck "with iron gags (*sparange*) over their mouths," presumably to prevent them from haranguing the crowd.[56] None of the other condemned men received this macabre treatment. On 17 April the doge's cap was cast to the ground and he was decapitated.

3. Our journey backward from libraries to archives, from Julien Sorel to the conspiracy of Marin Falier, has been highly discontinuous. Between Israël Bertuccio and Bertuccio Isarello there is more than the divide separating

fiction from historical reality. In the continuous variation of the contexts, everything—from names to social status—dissolves. An aphorism from the eighteenth-century satirist Georg Christoph Lichtenberg comes to mind: "If I first change the blade and then the handle of my knife, do I still have the same knife?"

One of Lichtenberg's devoted readers invites us to examine the question differently. I refer to Ludwig Wittgenstein and to his notion of "family resemblances." Wittgenstein began from the "composite portraits" of Francis Galton, images created by the superimposition of photographs of members of the same family, or of a determinate social group.[57] Earlier Wittgenstein had used Galton's "composite portraits" to illustrate the possibility of isolating a common element, running like a red thread (a metaphor borrowed from Goethe's novel *Elective Affinities*) within a determinate whole. Later, Wittgenstein, in writings published after his death with the title *Philosophische Untersuchungen*, returned to Galton's experiment, but now suggesting a totally different point of view. The shaded contours of the "composite portraits," the result of partial intertwining and superimpositions, suggested a different, nonessentialist notion of family resemblances. The metaphor of the red thread running the length of the fiber was replaced by a much more complex web. In a series of perceptive essays the British anthropologist Rodney Needham identified the historical precedents of Wittgenstein's idea, demonstrating that the eighteenth-century botanist Michel Adanson had already worked out a similar classification. The series which Needham called "polythetic" can include components characterized by distinctive traits of the type aba, bcb, dcd. . . . In a case of this sort, the first and last elements in the series do not have any trait in common.[58]

4. The long shadow thrown over the centuries by Bertuccio Isarello is a fictional shadow, the shadow of someone else. His voice, suffocated on the scaffold, has not come down to us. But precisely because it is important to distinguish between reality and fiction, we must learn to recognize when one becomes joined to the other, each transmitting something that we might call "energy"—that word so dear to Stendhal.[59]

CHAPTER 10

The Bitter Truth

Stendhal's Challenge to Historians

1. Balzac issued an explicit challenge to historians of his day; Stendhal, an implicit one to future historians. The first of these is known; the second is not. This is an attempt to examine an aspect of the latter.

Erich Auerbach devoted one of the central chapters in his *Mimesis* to the relationships of both Stendhal and Balzac with historians.[1] To evaluate this properly we need first to point out a fact strangely neglected by critics: in the long series of passages that have been studied in *Mimesis*, poets and novelists— Homer, Dante, Stendhal, Balzac, Proust, and many others—alternate with such historians as Tacitus, Ammianus Marcellinus, and Gregory of Tours, or with a memorialist such as Saint-Simon.

Today, a coexistence of this sort may seem unremarkable. Many readers assume without question that all the texts discussed by Auerbach are to a greater or lesser degree works of fiction. This interpretation of *Mimesis*, which undoubtedly has contributed to his continuing fame in American universities, would have horrified Auerbach himself.[2] After all, the subtitle of his book is *The Representation of Reality in Western Literature* (*Dargestellte Wirklichkeit in der abendländischen Literatur*).[3] Auerbach had a strong sense of reality and especially of social reality. His approach, inspired by Giambattista Vico (even if its nucleus was, in my opinion, a secularized version of an idea belonging to St. Augustine), was based on the notion that historical development tends to generate multiple approaches to reality.[4] But Auerbach was not a relativist. When he commented on the descriptions of the military revolts which we read in Tacitus and Ammianus, Auerbach stressed that these historians were not concerned with "objective problems" such as the "condition of the Roman populace," and he remarked that ". . . a modern historian would have taken up the question of how such a state of affairs had come about, he would have discussed the problem of the mob's corruption, or at the very least have touched upon it. But this does not interest Ammianus at all; and in this attitude he goes much further than Tacitus."[5]

Thus, Auerbach reaches the point of characterizing the specific nature of passages in Tacitus and Ammianus, opposing their points of view to some that are more modern and truthful. It is not a matter of just one isolated instance. Even when he is studying fictional works Auerbach always considers, explicitly or implicitly, historical reality as it has been perceived by the modern conscience. He writes, for example, in the chapter on Stendhal, ". . . the element of time perspective is evident everywhere. . . . Insofar as the serious realism of modern times cannot represent man otherwise than as embedded in a total reality, political, social, and economic which is concrete and constantly evolving—as is the case today in any novel or film—Stendhal is its founder."[6]

But, according to Auerbach, Stendhal's serious, "modern" realism was not, after all, fully modern: "However, the attitude from which Stendhal apprehends the world of events and attempts to reproduce it with all its interconnections is as yet hardly influenced by historicism [Historismus] . . . his representation of events is oriented, wholly in the spirit of classic ethical psychology, upon an *analyse du cœur humain*, not upon discovery or premonitions of historical forces; we find rationalistic, empirical, sensual motifs in him, but hardly those of romantic Historicism."[7]

To discover an authentic historicist point of view, Auerbach notes, we must turn to Balzac. In him novelist and historian converge, demonstrating the truth of the romantic notion that the many cultural forms of a period are joined by a hidden coherence: "Atmospheric Historism and atmospheric realism are closely connected; Michelet and Balzac are borne on the same stream. . . . It is needless to cite historical motifs, for the spirit of Historism with its emphasis upon ambient and individual atmospheres is the spirit of his [Balzac's] entire work."[8] At this point we might be tempted to equate Auerbach's position with German *Historismus*, a category which should not be confused either with Italian historicism or with the American New Historicism.[9] To be sure, many passages in *Mimesis* point in this direction. But just before it ends, the book takes another tack. Auerbach actually states what the reader had already come to suspect—namely, that the protagonists of the final chapter in *Mimesis*, Marcel Proust and Virginia Woolf, also inspired the formal principles on which the book was constructed. From *To the Lighthouse* and from the *Recherche* Auerbach took the idea, totally foreign to traditional literature, that through an accidental event, an ordinary life, a random passage, we can attain a deeper understanding of the whole.[10]

How can we reconcile this historical perspective with the qualities of the passages from history and fiction examined in *Mimesis*? Auerbach, who was suspicious of explicit theoretical formulations, did not ask himself the question.[11] We, instead, can try to answer it by putting Auerbach himself, a master of the art, into perspective. The starting point for this game of Chinese boxes or *mise en abîme* will be the passage in Stendhal's *The Red and the Black* which launched Auerbach into one of his more celebrated analyses.[12] But first it may be useful to establish the context.

2. On the flyleaf of the copy of *The Red and the Black* housed in the Bucci collection of the Sormani Municipal Library in Milan, Stendhal scribbled a few words: "Rome, 24 May 1834. When I was young I wrote a few biographies (Mozart, Michelangelo) which in some way were histories. I regret having written them. I believe that the *truth* in small as in large things, is almost unattainable—at least a truth that is *somewhat circumstantial*. Monsieur de Tracy used to say to me: truth can be found only in novels. With every passing day I can see more clearly that everywhere else we encounter only ostentation."[13]

The inscriptions at the opening of each of the two volumes of *The Red and the Black* shed some light on these words. The first is attributed to Danton: "Truth, the bitter truth." The second, to Sainte-Beuve: "She's not pretty, she's not wearing rouge." For Stendhal, "truth" meant, above all, rejection of every sort of ornamentation. My book, he proudly declared, is not pretty: it is immediate, direct, harsh. A harsh chronicle: the subtitle of the first edition of the novel (1831) reads "Chronicle of the 19th Century," altered a few pages later into "Chronicle of 1830." More recent editions occasionally eliminate one of the two subtitles.[14]

Naturally, no reader has ever taken the word *chronicle* seriously. *The Red and the Black* has always been read as a novel. But Stendhal's intentions are clear. Through a story based on fictional persons and events he hoped to reach a deeper historical truth. This was an aspiration shared by other early nineteenth-century novelists, and principally by Balzac—"that great historian," as Baudelaire called him.[15] But Stendhal had different objectives and went in another direction.

3. In that passage of *The Red and the Black* which Auerbach selected as the starting point for his examination, the protagonist of the novel, Julien Sorel, and his protector, the Jansenist abbé Pirard, are conversing in the chateau of the Marquis de la Mole. Julien is now working for the nobleman, who had invited him to join him in his meals. Julien asks the *abbé* to arrange for him to be excused from this obligation; he found the meals too boring. Pirard, "a true snob," is scandalized by the insolence of this son of peasants. "A slight noise" reveals that the daughter of the marquis, Mademoiselle de la Mole, has overheard the conversation: "She had come to fetch a book and had heard everything. She began to entertain some respect for Julien. He has not been born servile, she thought, like that old abbé. Heavens! how ugly he is."[16]

We shall return to this passage, but, meanwhile, here is Auerbach's comment:

> What interests us in the scene is this: it would be almost incomprehensible without a most accurate and detailed knowledge of the political situation, the social stratification, and the economic circumstances of a perfectly definite historical moment, namely, that in which France found itself just before the July Revolution; accordingly, the novel bears the subtitle, *Chronique de 1830*. Even the boredom which reigns in the dining room and salon of this noble house is no ordinary boredom. It does not arise from the fortuitous personal dullness of the people who are brought together there; among them there are highly educated, witty, and sometimes important people, and the master of the house is intelligent and amiable. Rather, we are confronted, in their boredom, by a phenomenon politically and ideologically characteristic of the Restoration period. In the seventeenth century and even more in the eighteenth, the corresponding salons were anything but boring.[17]

Auerbach's are astute observations, but his conclusions are debatable. It can be demonstrated that Stendhal considered boredom not only a phenomenon of the past, associated with French society during the Restoration, but a phenomenon that characterized both the present—in other words, the society that succeeded the July (1830) Revolution—and the foreseeable future. We can add to support this interpretation Stendhal's own review of his *The Red and the Black* prepared for the journal *L'Antologia* in 1832. The review, as well as Vincenzo Salvagnoli's article based on information gleaned from Stendhal, appeared posthumously.[18] Auerbach wrote *Mimesis* in exile, at Istanbul, where access to secondary sources was precluded and primary sources were limited. The selection of the passage in question from *The Red and the Black* and Auerbach's comment might have been influenced by a vague recollection of Stendhal's review of his own work.

It is an extraordinary document, an undoubted exercise in estrangement. In addressing a foreign audience under the veil of a pseudonym, Stendhal reflected, from the vantage points of geography and culture, on the novel he had published two years earlier. The customs and moral attitudes described in *The Red and the Black* had taken root in France, Stendhal observed, "between 1806 and 1832." Provincial life before the Revolution was lighthearted, as emerges from that "charming, little novel" by Pierre Victor Besenval entitled *Spleen*. Today, Stendhal continues, "in a city numbering between six- and eight-thousand inhabitants everything is sad and correct. The foreign visitor does not know how to get through an evening, just like in England."[19]

Stendhal's readers will find it worthwhile to peruse Besenval's *Spleen*. The novel takes place at Besançon, one of the places where the events of *The Red and the Black* unfold; the name of the protagonist, Madame de Rennon, recalls that of Madame de Rênal; the protagonist hates her father, just like Julien Sorel (and, for that matter, Stendhal himself).[20] But even more notable is the fact that Stendhal starts from Besenval's *Spleen* in making boredom the central theme of *The Red and the Black*. As Auerbach correctly notes, boredom for Stendhal is a historical phenomenon, tied to specific space and time. But the period indicated—between 1806, shortly after the inauguration of Napoleon's empire, and 1832, the year of Stendhal's review of his own work— and also the parallel with England cannot be reconciled with Auerbach's idea that the boredom described by Stendhal should be placed in "France just prior to the July Revolution."

What, then, is boredom? It is the product (explains Stendhal's self-review) of morality, of a "moral France" still unknown to foreigners, but which is getting ready to become the model for all of Europe:

> Moral France is unknown abroad. That is why before beginning to speak of the novel by M. de S[tendhal] it has been necessary that the gay, amusing, somewhat libertine France, which from 1715 to 1789 was the model for Europe, no longer exists: nothing resembles it less than the France, serious, moral, gloomy, which the Jesuits have bequeathed to us, the congregations and the government of the

Bourbons from 1814 to 1830. Since it is extremely difficult, where novels are concerned, to depict what is true and not *copy from books*, no one, before M. de S[tendahl] had dared to describe those so unattractive customs, which, nevertheless, since Europe is populated by sheep, will spread quickly from Naples to St. Petersburg.[21]

That is how Stendhal perceived himself in 1832. Could he possibly retrospectively have distorted the significance of his own work? This immediately raises a long-standing question: when was *The Red and the Black* written? In his self-review Stendhal wrote that because he focused on "the society of 1829 (the time when the novel was written)," the author had risked imprisonment.[22] In the "Editor's Note" which precedes the book it is suggested that Stendhal had indicated a different date: "We have reason to believe that the following pages were written in 1827."[23]

These two slightly divergent dates are both incorrect. We know from Stendhal himself that the idea for *The Red and the Black* had come to him in Marseilles, the night between 25 and 26 October 1829. He worked on the novel during the winter of 1829–1830 and signed a contract with the publisher Levavasseur on 8 April 1830. In May he corrected the first proofs, but on 1 June of that year he was still "dictating" the scene in the Besançon Cathedral which appears in chapter 28 of book 1. The importance of these final additions did not escape Victor Del Litto.[24] Clearly, Stendhal kept returning to the novel while he was correcting the proofs. An enigmatic footnote dated "11 August 1830" reveals that the correction of the proofs (perhaps accompanied by moments of writing or rewriting) was still in progress after the July Revolution. Michel Crouzet has suggested that *The Red and the Black* was "written entirely before July 1830, and thus is intrinsically connected to the agony of the Restoration." This is not convincing. Crouzet himself in a footnote mentions a fact which clashes with his own chronology: Louis Lablache, the singer portrayed by Stendhal under the name of Géronimo, Julien Sorel's friend, performed to great acclaim the role of Géronimo in Cimarosa's *Matrimonio segreto* in Paris on 4 November 1830.[25] This fact supposes, as Henri Martineau suggests, that Stendhal "continued to work editing and revising the novel until November." He could have dictated the passage mentioning Géronimo's triumph on 6 November, the eve of his own departure from Paris for Trieste, where he had been named consul. The publication of *The Red and the Black* was announced on 15 November.[26]

This minute chronological excursus may seem pedantic and even irrelevant. But the evidence which we have just reviewed explains why Stendhal dated the writing of the novel as 1827 in the editorial note and as 1829 in his own review of the work. The two dates, both incorrect, intended to suggest to readers—and even Auerbach was misled—that *The Red and the Black* accurately portrayed French society during the Restoration. Accurate it undoubtedly was; but the characteristics described were destined to endure much beyond their original setting, as Stendhal suggested indirectly in one of the two subtitles to the work: "Chronicle of the Nineteenth Century." In a footnote at the end of the novel, which seemingly intended to signal the purely arbitrary value of the places where the events unfold (Verrières, Besançon), Stendhal alluded to the more general historical implications of the story: "The inconvenience of the reign of public opinion is that though, of course, it secures liberty, it meddles with what it has nothing to do with—private life, for example. Hence the gloominess of America and England."[27]

By using such terms as *opinion* and *liberty*, which evoked the political atmosphere of the 1830 revolution, Stendhal was suggesting the importance of the novel for the France of the period following the Restoration. The mention of England and America was equally significant. For Stendhal, the two countries symbolized the future—a somber future in which all passions would disappear except one: the passion for wealth.[28] Boredom and melancholy, produced by the intrusion of morality into private life, were the characteristics of modern industrial societies, among which France was about to be numbered.[29]

4. Auerbach wrote that Balzac "far outdoes the former [Stendhal] in organically connecting man and history."[30] The remark does not do justice to Stendhal. Auerbach, misled by *Historismus*, had not noticed that in Stendhal's novels the absence of an organic connection between man and history results from a deliberate choice, expressed through a specific formal procedure. The isolation of Stendhal's heroes is underlined and strengthened by their internal reflections, which, alternating with the description of their actions, create a sort of counterpoint. This procedure, which has been called "free direct discourse," usually presents itself in this way: a narration in the third person is interrupted brusquely by a series of brief sentences attributed to one of the protagonists of the narration.[31] Free direct discourse, while more highly structured than the

formless flow of the internal monologue, places the reader in a close, almost intimate, relationship with the principal characters in the novel: Julien Sorel, Madame de Rênal, Mademoiselle de la Mole. Let us return to the passage which describes the reaction of Mademoiselle de la Mole to the conversation between Julien and the abbé Pirard: "She had come to fetch a book and had heard everything; she began to entertain some respect for Julien. He has not been born servile, she thought, like that old abbé. Heavens! how ugly he is."[32]

We can see that Stendhal does not overpunctuate.[33] No quotation marks introduce the last two sentences, even if both are characterized by direct sentences or by interjections: "thought" in the first, the cry "Heavens!" followed by an exclamation mark in the next. When there are no quotation marks, the shift from the third to the first person—whether this occurs in a single sentence or in two contiguous sentences—is more abrupt and startling. Here are two more examples, referring respectively to Julien Sorel and to Mathilde de la Mole, quoted first in the original French, and then in an English translation: "A force d'examiner le comte Norbert, Julien remarqua qu'il était en bottes et en éperons; [semicolon] et moi je dois être en souliers, apparemment comme inférieur." And: "Ce Sorel a quelque chose de l'air que mon père prend quand il fait si bien Napoléon au bal. [period] Elle avait tout à fait oublié Danton. [period] Décidément, ce soir, je m'ennuie. [period] Elle saisit le bras de son frère...."[34]

In the M. R. B. Shaw English translation the two passages become more conventional: "After taking a good look at Count Norbert, Julien noticed that he was booted and spurred; and I, *he thought* [my italics], am obliged to wear shoes, apparently as an inferior." "This man Sorel has something of the air my father adopts when he gives such a good imitation of Napoleon, at a ball. She had completely forgotten Danton. I'm certainly feeling bored tonight, *she thought* [my italics]. She caught hold of her brother's arms."[35]

The translator must have feared that the reader could feel lost, if only for a fraction of a second: hence the addition of "he thought," "she thought." But this was precisely Stendhal's aim: to give his narrative a feverish, dizzy pace by using broken punctuation, which introduces a sudden change of viewpoints.[36]

5. In the passage analyzed by Auerbach, Julien uses Mathilde to justify the boredom he feels at the dinners of the marquis: "Sometimes I see even Mademoiselle de la Mole yawn." A few chapters later Mathilde reappears, yawning and fixing on Julien "these fine eyes, which were the home of the deepest

ennui."[37] Mathilde asks Julien to accompany her to a ball. Julien realizes that he must accept; but as soon as the dancing begins, his interest in her ceases. At this point the scene, one of the most extraordinary in the entire novel, is seen through the eyes of Mathilde. The only thoughts to which we have access are hers: "Yes, I am decidedly bored tonight" and so forth. Julien enters into an impassioned discussion with Count Altamira, an exile from Naples who had fled (as Domenico Fiore, a friend of Stendhal's, had done) to escape from a death sentence imposed for political motives. The two men draw near. Mathilde "did not lose a syllable of their conversation. Her ennui had vanished."[38]

Both Mathilde and Julien are fascinated by Altamira. His impassioned political commitment is the true antithesis to boredom. Altamira tells Julien: "There are no longer any real passions in the nineteenth century; that's why one is so bored in France."[39]

Altamira talks of the nineteenth century as if Restoration France was a particular case confirming a more general law. In this sense he is only echoing the two different subtitles of the novel: "A Chronicle of 1830," "Chronicle of the Nineteenth Century." Altamira is speaking for Stendhal. Someone could object that the first readers of *The Red and the Black* might have read these pages—in fact, the entire novel—in the context of the July Revolution. The passage in which Altamira expresses the wish that the experiences of the South American countries might transmit to Europe their ideals of liberty is accompanied by a footnote from the publisher (undoubtedly written by Stendhal himself) in which it is laconically stated that this section of the novel, "sent to press 25 July 1830," "was printed 4 August." This has made Michel Crouzet argue that the scene at the ball and Altamira's remarks "agree in every detail with the [July] Revolution, of which they are both the augury and the announcement. Stendhal is telling the reader that his novel leads to the barricades, although without mentioning them."[40] But the footnote and the novel have completely different meanings. Julien Sorel is not a liberal, he is a Jacobin, a throwback to another age; *The Red and the Black* relates the story of a tragic individual defeat, not of a victorious revolution. Stendhal thought that politics, as he had lived it under Napoleon during the Russian campaign, was a thing of the past, which the tiresome age of industry and commerce had rendered obsolete. And historiography, traditionally identified with the history of public life, was by this point surpassed by novels, as Destutt de Tracy had explained to Stendhal. Historical events were destined to repeat themselves, but in diminished and distorted form. Mathilde distractedly is aware of this as she gazes pensively at Altamira: "I think being condemned to death is the only real distinction," said Mathilde. "It is the only thing which cannot be bought."[41]

Here—a frequent recurrence in Stendhal's novels—future events are anticipated, obscurely and symbolically. Mathilde will bury Julien's decapitated head, just as Queen Marguerite of Navarre had buried the head of her lover, Boniface de la Motte, at the time of the Wars of Religion. Julien will die not for a political cause but for attempting to murder his lover, Madame de Rênal. He will die not as a hero but as a criminal. In "a degenerate and tedious age," in the words of Mathilde, everything can be bought and heroism is impossible.[42]

6. Let us return to the scene at the ball. Mathilde is listening to the conversation between Julien and Altamira: "Mademoiselle de la Mole, who was leaning her head forward with keenest interest, was so near him that her beautiful hair almost touched his shoulder."[43]

Once again, Mathilde is portrayed in the act of listening, of eavesdropping— just as Stendhal was all ears to the conversations of his characters, compelling his readers to do the same. For Stendhal, the "I" is synonymous with multiplicity. On some occasions he scrutinized with an amused, perplexed, or annoyed air, as when he wrote in a copy of *Armance*: "Tedious Sunday, I walked along the *Corso* with Mister Sten[dhal] and so shall it be for my entire life, *till the death*."[44]

Over half a century ago in a brilliant essay Jean Starobinski investigated Stendhal's passion for pseudonyms, of which we know almost two hundred, used on both public and private occasions. Starobinski, a critic and psychoanalyst, stresses the voyeuristic side of Stendhal, supporting his interpretation with a passage from the diaries in which Stendhal speaks of his romantic longings. In that essay Starobinski does not discuss Stendhal's writings. The connection between the literary work and the psychology of the author is obscure; the critic, observed Starobinski, should investigate the space that separates them.[45] Stendhal's novels are imbued with eroticism, but the amorous encounters between his personages are always left to the reader's imagination.[46] As a writer, Stendhal always abstained from voyeurism in a strict sense: but acoustic voyeurism, instead, as we have seen, was crucial to his narrative.[47] Free, direct discourse had been used, occasionally, by Goethe in his

Elective Affinities, a novel which Stendhal read and loved, and to which he paid homage by making it the title of a chapter in *The Red and the Black* (book 1, chapter 7). But an element of psychology may have contributed to Stendhal's systematic use of the process.

7. Stendhal reread *The Red and the Black* in 1834–1835 with mixed feelings. He scrawled some comments on the manuscript of *Lucien Leuwen*. Among other things, he criticized "certain broken sentences, and the lack of those small words which assist the imagination of the benevolent reader to imagine what is happening."[48] The novel appeared to him "truthful, but dry"; the style, "too brusque, too disconnected"; "when I was writing it," he remarked, "I was only concerned with the substance of things."[49]

Stendhal, who usually wrote in a state of excitement, was incapable of revising his text.[50] His dissatisfaction with the dryness of *The Red and the Black* seems to anticipate the more lavish style of *The Charterhouse of Parma*. But that "dryness" was the very point of an intellectual project which went back to Stendhal's youth. On 29 March 1805, when he was in his twenties, he wrote in his diary:

> I feel the urge to show everyone a decorticated figure. Like a painter who wants to attempt the style of Albani, and properly begins by studying anatomy, but then this, from useful instrument[,] becomes so satisfying that, instead of painting a beautiful bosom for men's pleasure, [he] depicts the exposed and bloody muscles in the breasts of a lovely woman; and so much more horrible is the result when one, instead, expected an agreeable object. A new disgust results from the veracity of the subjects presented. If they were not real it would be possible to ignore them, but they are real and they haunt the imagination.[51]

Twenty-five years later Prosper Mérimée wrote to Stendhal, who was one of his closest friends, to tell him what he thought of the recently published *The Red and the Black*. Mérimée repeated the metaphor used by the youthful Stendhal, which he may have heard during one of their conversations; but instead of identifying himself with the painter, he put himself in the place of the horrified public. In the first part of the letter, now lost, Mérimée stated that someone had accused Stendhal of the most serious crimes: "that of having bared and exposed to the light of day certain sores of the human heart which are too disgusting to behold."

"This observation seemed fair to me," Mérimée wrote. "Julien's character possesses some atrocious traits; they are undoubtedly real, but they are horrible just the same. It is not the purpose of art to shed light on these aspects of human nature." And Mérimée compared *The Red and the Black* to Swift's *The Lady's Dressing Room*, remarking: "You are full of these intolerable truths."[52]

8. Mérimée's comparison of Stendhal to Swift should not be taken literally. There is nothing eschatological about *The Red and the Black*. What irritated Mérimée was Stendhal's independent views about social conventions, and the impulse to lay them bare. But the juxtaposition with Swift needs to be examined further. In a marginal note on the manuscript of *Mina de Vanghel*, left unfinished, Stendhal remarked that "in a novel, the description of uses and customs leaves us cold. We get the impression of an attempt to moralize. Description has to provoke astonishment, introduce a foreign woman who feels amazement, and transform the description into a sentiment."[53] Stendhal had already made use of this device. Julien Sorel, the son of a peasant, moves bewilderingly between the home of Madame de Rênal, the seminary, and the palace of the Marquis de la Mole. Stendhal was looking at contemporary French society from afar, through the eyes of a young man lacking experience and socially out of his depth. Mérimée shared Stendhal's attraction for concrete, ethnographic details: but the "bitter truth" of *The Red and the Black* was too much for him.

The two friends differed greatly, as writers and as people. In an ironically affectionate sketch which appeared a few years after Stendhal's death, Mérimée wrote: "For his entire life he was enslaved by his imagination; he did everything without premeditation, with enthusiasm. He claimed he did everything without reason. 'In every thing one should let himself be guided by LO-GIC' he used to say pausing between the first syllable and the rest of the word. But he suffered impatiently when the logic of others was not the same as his."[54]

In this psychological trait, picked up intuitively by Mérimée, we see Stendhal's twofold, contradictory connection with the Enlightenment and Romanticism, with rationality and with the emotions, with logic and with beliefs. This interlacing, as we perceive in the *Vie d'Henry Brulard*, was already present in the fourteen-year-old Stendhal. He had begun to study mathematics, and he was unable to understand how, multiplying negative numbers, one obtained a positive number. But the worst was yet to come:

At the beginning of geometry it is said: "We give the name parallel to two lines which extended to infinity, would never meet." And from the very beginning of *Statics*, that beast of a Louis Monge more or less tells us this: "Two parallel lines can be considered as meeting, if we extend them to infinity." I thought I was reading a catechism, and, in fact, one of the most pointless. I asked M. Chabert [another mathematics instructor] for an explanation: Son, he said, assuming that paternal tone which does not well suit that foxy heir apparent, the air of Edouard Mounier [peer of France in 1836]—son, you shall know later. And the monster, drawing near the blackboard of waxed cloth, drew two parallel contiguous lines. See, he told me, that at the point of infinity we can say that they meet. I was on the point of dropping everything. A confessor, a good and able Jesuit that moment could have converted me by commenting this maxim: See everything is in error, or, better, there is nothing which is false, nothing that is true, everything is convention. Adopt the convention which will make you more acceptable in this world. The populace is patriotic and will always soil this aspect of the question; turn yourself into an aristocrat like the members of your family and we shall find the way to send you to Paris and recommend you to influential ladies. To say this with élan, I would have become a rogue and today, in 1836, I would be very rich.[55]

Looking back at this episode, Stendhal connected his own precocious passion for logic to his hate for the conventional. But what kept that scene alive for almost forty years in Stendhal's memory must have been the discovery of a flaw in Euclid's geometry which had seemed to him as solid as a rock. This finding may have contributed to his enduring fascination with irrational phenomena—the passions, for instance—which reason must learn to analyze. The young Stendhal nurtured a great admiration for Pascal, whom he compared not only to Shakespeare but to himself: "When I read Pascal," he wrote, "I have the impression I am reading myself.... I believe that among all the writers he is the one closest to my soul."[56] This claim (which seems to have passed unobserved) is less startling than it may appear at first glance. To the simple provincials who inquired what his profession might be, Stendhal usually replied, "Observer of the human heart."[57] He may have had in mind Pascal's famous dictum "The heart has its reasons which reason does not know." In a letter to his sister Pauline, to whom he was very close, Stendhal translated Pascal's words in Montaigne's *Que sais-je:* "I reread the *Logique* by de Tracy with great pleasure; I try to reason correctly to find the right answer to this question: 'What do I desire?'"[58]

In his *Souvenirs d'égotisme* Stendhal wrote: "We can know everything except ourselves."[59]

9. Free direct discourse gives a voice to the isolation of Stendhal's characters, to their ingenuous vitality defeated by a historical process which overturns and humiliates their illusions.[60] It is a process which seems to be unavailable to historians because free direct discourse by definition leaves no documentary traces. We are in territory that lies beyond historical knowledge, and is inaccessible to it. But narrative processes act like magnetic fields: they provoke questions and potentially attract documents.[61] In this sense, a procedure such as free direct discourse, which came into being to respond, on the terrain of fiction, to a number of historical questions, may be considered as an indirect challenge to historians. One day they may be able to confront it in ways which at this moment we cannot even imagine.

CHAPTER 11

Representing the Enemy

On the French Prehistory of the Protocols

1. The present chapter concerns two texts and the relationship between them: the first is known almost exclusively to scholars; the second has circulated throughout the world. The first, *Dialogue aux Enfers entre Machiavel et Montesquieu,* appeared anonymously in Brussels in 1864.[1] On the title page the unnamed author, Maurice Joly, called himself "contemporary." The following year he was identified by the French police, tried, and sentenced to fifteen months in prison for having written seditiously and offensively against Napoleon III. The *Dialogue* was promptly translated into German; in 1868 it was twice reprinted in Brussels, with the author's name appearing.[2] Following the collapse of the Second Empire, Joly, who was practicing law without great success, attempted a political career. After a violent conflict with Jules Grévy, who for a time had been his patron, Joly found himself totally isolated. In 1878, not quite yet fifty years of age, he committed suicide.

A Spanish translation of the *Dialogue aux Enfers* appeared in Buenos Aires in 1898. Then the book fell into oblivion, only to be rediscovered in 1921, when (as we shall see) it was identified as the source for the *Protocols of the Elders of Zion,* the anti-Semitic pamphlet first published in Russia in 1903.

For a long time the miserable success of the *Protocols,* today more virulent than ever, has obscured the originality of the *Dialogue aux Enfers.* Recently, however, Joly's book has been recognized, especially in France, as an important example of nineteenth-century political thought. It has even been called "a classic." It seems appropriate to analyze the reasons for and implications of its late success.

2. In an autobiographical piece written in 1870 Joly described the genesis of his *Dialogue*:

> One evening, while walking on the terrace along the river near Pont Royal in bad weather suddenly the name of Montesquieu came to mind, as someone who would have been able to incarnate fully some of the ideas I wanted to express. But who could have been his interlocutor? I was struck by an idea: Machiavelli, of course! Machiavelli would have personified the politics of force against Montesquieu, who would have represented the policy of justice; and Machiavelli would have been Napoleon III describing his own abominable policies.[3]

The police and the judges who condemned Joly read the *Dialogue aux Enfers* in line with the author's intentions. Thus, we could conclude that the meaning of the work is clear, free of any ambiguity. But a closer inspection brings out a different and more complex story.

Literary critics have long tried to teach us to look at writers' intentions with skepticism. Obviously, to ignore them would be absurd, but, on the other hand, an author is not necessarily the best judge of his own work. The case of Maurice Joly is a perfect example of this.

The first thing to ask ourselves is to which literary or subliterary genre the *Dialogue* belongs. The passage we have just examined shows that Joly had intended to write a dialogue even before the names of Machiavelli and Montesquieu crossed his mind. The idea had come to him while thinking of the *Dialogue sur le commerce des bleds*, by Ferdinando Galiani, which had first appeared anonymously in 1770 and was then reprinted many times. But the presumed connection between the two texts, recalled by everyone who commented on the *Dialogue aux Enfers*, is not convincing. In Galiani's pamphlet, the knight Zanobi, who speaks for the author, carries on a discussion with two unidentified persons, one of whom is known only by his initials.[4] Joly's allusion elsewhere to the *Satyre Ménippée*, the anti-Catholic pamphlet inspired by Lucian of Samosata that had appeared during the Wars of Religion, seems much more pertinent.[5] The imaginary dialogue between two famous personages, Machiavelli and Montesquieu, immediately calls to mind the dialogues of the dead, made famous (if not actually invented) by Lucian of Samosata in the second century after Christ.[6] As we shall see, this early attempt at contextualization highlights, rather than diminishes, the originality of Joly's *Dialogue*.

3. A genre is defined by a series of characteristics which imply at the same time restrictions and possibilities. In the past the characteristics were called

"laws"—which, as happens to actual laws, can be broken or amended. In Lucian's *Dialogues of the Dead* one encounters real persons next to mythical figures, such as in the comparison, inspired directly by Plutarch, between Hannibal and Alexander the Great (with Minos sitting in judgment and Scipio, who turns up at the end of the dialogue).[7] But at the end of the seventeenth century, Bernard Bovier de Fontenelle, in his *Nouveaux dialogues des morts*, eliminated the mythological figures and treated the real persons exclusively. By doing so he reinvented and modified a genre which offered him the possibility of emphasizing with ironic levity the superiority of the moderns over the ancients.[8] This literary formula spread rapidly throughout Europe, from France to England, from Germany to Russia.[9]

Joly, who would have been well acquainted with Fontenelle's *Nouveaux dialogues des morts*, adopted the genre but treated it differently. The discussion in the underworld between Machiavelli and Montesquieu unfolds throughout twenty-five dialogues, with the addition of an epilogue, written some years later and only recently reprinted as an appendix to the main text.[10] Montesquieu begins by recalling the ideas which he had formulated in the *Esprit des lois*, first among which was the reciprocal autonomy of the three powers— legislative, executive, and judicial. Montesquieu is of the opinion that the triumph of this principle, which characterizes the modern European states, is by now an accepted fact; but his information on recent history stops at 1847. With malignant pleasure Machiavelli brings Montesquieu up to date on what has transpired since then, delineating in a veiled manner more recent French happenings: the revolution of 1848 and its bloody aftermath; the coup d'état of 2 December 1851; the plebiscite and the proclamation of the Second Empire a year later. So, Machiavelli concludes, in one of the most progressive countries in Europe, torn by political and social tensions, one person (Louis Napoleon) has seized power by force, installing a new government which efficiently combines social peace and prosperity. It is the best solution to the fragile situation that threatens all modern societies, as Machiavelli explains in an eloquent apology for the regime of Napoleon III:

> I don't see any salvation for such societies, veritable colossuses with feet of clay, except by instituting extreme centralization, placing all public power at the disposal of those who govern. What is needed is a hierarchical administration similar to that of the Roman Empire, which regulated with machine-like precision all the movements of the individual. It calls for a vast system of legislation that takes back bit by bit all the liberties that had been imprudently bestowed—in sum a

gigantic despotism that could strike immediately and at any time all who resist and complain. I think the Caesarism of the late Empire answers fairly well to what I would want for the well-being of modern societies. I have been told that such vast apparatuses already exist in more than one country in Europe, and thanks to them, these countries can live in peace, like China, Japan, and India. It's only vulgar prejudice that makes us look down on these oriental civilizations whose institutions one learns to appreciate more every day. The Chinese, for example, are very good businessmen, and their lives are very well regulated.[11]

For the earliest readers of the *Dialogue aux Enfers*, Machiavelli's words had an obvious meaning. In 1850 Auguste Romieu had coined the term *Caesarism* to define a regime which was "the necessary result of a phase of extreme civilization . . . neither monarchy nor empire, neither despotism nor tyranny, but something peculiar that still is not well understood."[12] A year later Romieu wrote a pamphlet entitled *Le spectre rouge de 1852* which presented the imminent coup d'état by Louis Napoleon as the only solution that might be able to avert a lower-class revolt. Romieu exalted force and eliminated disparagingly the concept of natural law: "I believe in social needs, not in natural laws. In my opinion the word LAW has no meaning at all, since there is nothing of the sort in nature. It is a mere human invention. . . ."[13]

On this point Joly's Machiavelli mirrored Romieu: "All sovereign powers find their origin in force, or, what is the same thing, in the negation of justice. . . . Don't you see that this word—'justice'—is infinitely vague?"[14] But Joly's Machiavelli brutally associated "Caesarism" with a gigantic despotism. In effect this was a challenge directed at Montesquieu—the real one—who had seen in Oriental despotism the very antithesis of the progress incarnated in European civilization.[15] Joly must certainly have thought of Tocqueville's bitter reflections on the future of democratic societies, in which a new form of servitude, "regulated, mild, calm," might have been able to be joined with "some of the external forms of liberty . . . in the shadows of popular sovereignty."[16] But Tocqueville still saw in the freedom of the press the strongest antidote against the ills of equality.[17] Joly, instead, who had lived through the experience of the Second Empire, had no illusions on this point. According to his Machiavelli, the best future for modern society would be a form of despotism (we could call it Western despotism) which would leave intact the parliamentary system and freedom of the press: "One of my great principles," says Joly's Machiavelli, "is to set things against themselves. Just as I use the press against the press, I would use oratory to counter oratory. . . . In my Assembly, I will control nineteen

out of twenty men, all of whom will follow my instructions. In the meantime, I would pull the strings of a sham opposition, clandestinely enlisted to
my cause."[18]

This strategy, observed his interlocutor, Montesquieu, will lead "to the
annihilation of parties and the destruction of other collective forces," even if
political liberty will remain formally intact.[19] Machiavelli declares himself
in agreement. He proposes to use a similar strategy with the press:

> My scheme envisions neutralizing the press by the press itself. Because journalism
> wields such great power, do you know what my government will do? It will be-
> come like them. It will be journalism incarnate. . . . Like the god Vishnu, my press
> will have a hundred arms, and these arms will stretch out their hands throughout
> the country delicately giving form to all manner of opinion. Everyone will belong
> to my party without knowing it. Those who think they are speaking the language
> of their party will be acting for mine. Those who think they are marching under
> their own banner will be marching under mine. "Are these ideas possible or only
> wild fantasies? They make the head swim," murmured Montesquieu.[20]

4. Montesquieu, hammered by Machiavelli's implacable logic, wavers bewildered between stupor and horror. Montesquieu is a man of the past; Machiavelli is of the present and perhaps of the future. The paradoxical reversal
of the placement in history of the two personages overturns the significance
that, from the time of Fontenelle, had often been attributed to the genre "dialogues of the dead." More generally it seems to liquidate the idea of progress.
But Joly employs the dialogical form so subtly that it conceals his own attitude,
to the point of rendering it almost indecipherable. When Joly states that he
has cancelled himself out as author, perhaps he was affirming more than the
obvious literal meaning of the prudent decision not to exhibit his name on
the title page of his *Dialogue aux Enfers*.[21]

As we recall, Joly declared retrospectively that the idea of bringing Montesquieu onstage had made him think that Machiavelli "would be Napoleon
III, describing his own abominable politics."[22] In quoting these words we
have forgotten to mention what Joly had written a few lines earlier— namely,
that he had thought of Montesquieu "as of someone who could have *fully incarnated an aspect* of the ideas I wanted to express." Just as Montesquieu did
not incarnate all of Joly's ideas, so Machiavelli did not incarnate all the ideas
and policies of Napoleon III.

A passage will demonstrate the truth of this statement. Machiavelli explains to Montesquieu that the new constitution emerging from the coup

d'état will be submitted to a popular vote, which will accept or reject it in its entirety. Obviously, this is an allusion to the plebiscite of 2 December 1852 which made of Louis Napoleon an emperor legitimized by the electorate: a hybrid without precedent in history.[23] Machiavelli immediately rejects the example of America: we are in Europe, and the idea of discussing the constitution before voting on it would be absurd. "A constitution can only be the work of a single man. Things have never happened otherwise, as the histories of all the founders of empire testify—Sesostris, Solon, Lycurgus, Charlemagne, Frederick II, Peter the First, for example."

"You are about to expound upon a chapter from one of your disciples," Montesquieu observes.

"Who?" Machiavelli asks.

"Joseph de Maistre," Montesquieu replies. "Some general points you make are not without merit but I find them inapplicable here."[24]

Montesquieu is implicitly alluding to a passage from de Maistre's *Considérations sur la France*. In chapter 6, entitled "On divine influence in constitutions," we read: "No mere assembly of men can form a nation, and the very attempt exceeds in folly the most absurd and extravagant things that all the *Bedlams* of the world might put forth."[25]

In support of this scornful statement de Maistre cited in a note a passage taken from Machiavelli's *Discorsi sulla prima deca di Tito Livio* (1:9): "... it is even necessary that he whose mind has conceived such a constitution should be alone in carrying it into effect."[26] A bit later, in the same chapter of the *Considérations*, de Maistre ironically compared Montesquieu to a pedantic poet, and Lycurgus, he who had given Sparta its laws, to Homer. Thus, in regard to constitutions de Maistre actually appealed to the authority of Machiavelli rather than Montesquieu, whom he considered an abstract theoretician, lacking a grip on reality.

Joly shared this opinion, since on the matter of constitutions he cited the authority of the ultrareactionary de Maistre, not Montesquieu. A year before the *Dialogue aux Enfers*, Joly published a book entitled *Le barreau de Paris: Études politiques et littéraires*, a series of general reflections, mixed in with profiles, often written in a satirical tone, of lawyers, sometimes designated by pseudonyms. In a note to *Le barreau de Paris* Joly alluded disdainfully to the "folly of constitutions and to their incapacity to construct anything." Immediately afterward he praised de Maistre, calling him an "author whose prophetic voice, at the beginning of the century, enjoyed undisputed authority." He cited approvingly several passages taken from de Maistre's *Essai sur le principe générateur des constitutions politiques et des autres institutions humaines* which recalled the just-cited passage from the *Considérations sur la France,* including the reference to Machiavelli's *Discourses.*[27]

Allow me to recapitulate this rather complicated discussion. I have contrasted four books, two by de Maistre (*Considérations sur la France* and *Essai sur le principe générateur des constitutions*) and two by Joly (*Le Barreau de Paris* and *Dialogue aux Enfers entre Machiavel et Montesquieu*). De Maistre's first book is cited in his second; both make an appearance, implicitly or explicitly, in Joly's two books, written almost contemporaneously (readers of the *Dialogue aux Enfers* will not have missed an allusion to that "machiavélisme infernal" in the *Barreau de Paris*).[28] We can look at the four works as fragments of a whole. But if we place them side by side we notice an ambiguous figure emerging. The boundaries between invention and reality become less rigid: the imaginary Machiavelli develops ideas already proposed by the real de Maistre, who in turn advances arguments suggested by the real Machiavelli. The praise of de Maistre as one of the most "illustrious partisans" of the true Machiavelli, which Joly in his *Dialogue aux Enfers* puts in the mouth of Montesquieu, should be extended, in the final analysis, even to the imaginary Machiavelli.[29] Consequently, one might say that Joly has projected something of himself into both speakers of the dialogue. On the one hand, Joly shared Montesquieu's liberal ideas; on the other, he presented Machiavelli's arguments as the stronger ones, if not actually irrefutable. This painful disjuncture places the reader before a dialogue based on an unbridgeable chasm between ideals and reality, between desires and ideas: a tension that is just the opposite of self-consolatory thought.[30]

5. Joly felt undoubted hostility toward the regime of Napoleon III. But the *Dialogue aux Enfers* is much more than a polemical work. Joly attacked Louis Napoleon and his cynical use of power, but at the same time he tried to understand a form of government that he viewed as unprecedented. Joly paid much more attention to the plebiscite of 2 December 1852 than to the coup d'état of 2 December 1851. The violence used by Louis Napoleon to crush his opposition was much less original than what followed: a hybrid jumble of police control and freedom of the press, of despotism and popular legitimacy. To understand this novel situation (Joly implicitly says) requires the detached, unsentimental attitude of a modernized Machiavelli, not the illusions of a

Montesquieu. But in Machiavelli's bitter foretelling of the more recent past there is no trace of that sense of triumph that one might expect from a spokesman for Napoleon III. Joly's Machiavelli is a much more complex figure, on which the true Machiavelli (especially as author of the *Prince*), Napoleon III, and Joly himself are superimposed, creating a composite portrait which recalls the photographic experiments carried out just a few years later by Francis Galton.[31]

The unfocused image created by Galton can suggest a visual equivalent to the ambiguity which permeates the *Dialogue aux Enfers*. In attempting to understand the Second Empire, Joly entered into a complex and ambivalent relationship with the personage who, under the name of Machiavelli, was intended to assume the role of Napoleon III. At the same time, however, the dialogical form permitted the author to keep a certain distance from the characters he had created. It is as if Joly were listening to himself, in the guise of Montesquieu, in the act of being aggressively criticized by himself in the guise of Machiavelli.

The voice of this imaginary Machiavelli is the voice of the enemy. I shall not repeat here the celebrated words of Carl Schmitt about the enemy (*hostis*) who incarnates our questions. I prefer to recall a verse from Ovid (*Metamorphoses* 4:428), perhaps familiar even to Joly: *Nam et fas est ab hoste doceri*— one must learn even from one's enemy.[32] Joly could have said: *especially* from the enemy, from whom we must learn the reasons for our defeat.

6. The modern form of despotism, Joly wrote, includes free elections and freedom of the press. About either he certainly did not share the illusions of the liberals; in his eyes, true power resided elsewhere. In 1864, when the *Dialogue aux Enfers* first appeared, a statement of this sort would have seemed paradoxical to most readers. It seems much less so today. I agree with Winston Churchill, who said democracy is the worst form of government, with the exception of all the others. But when in the United States, the greatest democracy in the world, only a small minority of its citizens exercise their right to vote in elections (a right which often is the extent of their participation in politics), the self-legitimization of democracy is badly shaken. More doubtful yet is the capacity of voters to have an impact on the actual centers of power and on their decisions. At the dawn of the twenty-first century the democracies appear to be much more powerful than they were a hundred and fifty years earlier, when Joly published his analysis of modern despotism: their control

over society is much more sophisticated and efficient; the power of the citizen, infinitely diminished.

All this sheds some light on the twentieth-century reception of the *Dialogue aux Enfers*. During the 1920s and '30s, as we shall see, it was discussed exclusively in terms of its connection with the *Protocols*. After World War II the *Dialogue* was published three times in France, four in Germany, twice in Spain, once each in Italy and in the United States.[33] Some readers have seen in the *Dialogue* a clear foretelling of the totalitarian regimes of the twentieth century.[34] But the most recent French edition, reprinted in 1987, 1992, and 1999, presents the *Dialogue* in a different light. For the author of the preface, Michel Bounan, it is "a political classic which exposed, a hundred years before its time, the true face of the modern despotism" which emerged from the ruins of the totalitarian regimes.[35] This conclusion, further developed by Bounan in a series of later essays, interprets Joly's *Dialogue aux Enfers* through the prism of its unforeseeable, distorted posthumous fate: the *Protocols of the Elders of Zion*. To express an opinion on Bounan's views, we must first examine the relationship between the two works.

7. It has been said that in the world ranking of best sellers, the *Protocols* stand second, right after the Bible. This may be an exaggeration, but new editions of the *Protocols* appear yearly, in the Middle East, in Latin America, in Japan, in Europe; I recall seeing copies in the window of a bookstore in Budapest. The *Protocols*, we know, claim to be the proceedings of a secret meeting of a group of Jewish conspirators planning to infiltrate society at every level: finance, publishing, the military, politics, and so forth. The conspiracy, if successful, would lead to a Jewish monarchy and world domination. The *Protocols* contain a translator's *postscriptum* which explains that the text is an updated version of a plot that went back to Solomon and to the Wise Men of Zion in 929 B.C.

The composition and extraordinary publishing history of the *Protocols* have been studied often and in depth. Here are the essential data.[36] The basic facts are that the *Protocols* were published for the first time in Russia in 1903; other Russian versions, with variants, appeared in the following years. But their worldwide circulation began only after the October revolution, an event that some of the reactionary press interpreted as a consequence of a Jewish conspiracy. The German translation of 1919 was greeted by the *Times* of London a year later as an important document and, thus, implicitly, believable. In 1921 Philip Graves, correspondent for this paper in Istanbul, wrote three articles demonstrating that the *Protocols* were a forgery. He showed that many passages borrowed closely from a book, then forgotten, that had appeared a century and a half earlier: Maurice Joly's *Dialogue aux Enfers entre Machiavel et Montesquieu*. Graves had learned of the connection between the two texts from someone he chose not to name, a Russian émigré later identified as Mikhail Raslovlev. Although some of the "sources" of the *Protocols* had been ascertained earlier, Graves's articles caused a sensation.[37] Nevertheless, the booklet's circulation continued without pause. The protonotary apostolic Monsignor Ernest Jouin, who had translated it into French, commented: "It does not matter whether the *Protocols* are authentic; it is enough that they be true" ("Peu importe que les *Protocoles* soient authentiques; il suffit qu'ils soient vrais").[38] Medieval clerics had fabricated their *piae fraudes* in the same spirit: forgeries inspired by true religion. When, in 1934, Jewish organizations in Switzerland brought legal action for libel against two local National Socialist officials who were circulating the *Protocols* as the confessed truth of the existence of a Jewish world conspiracy, the discussion once again focused on the passages from Joly's *Dialogue* plagiarized in the *Protocols*.[39]

"Like the god Vishnu, my press will have a hundred arms," says Joly's Machiavelli; "like the Indian idol Vishnu, we will have a hundred hands," say the Elders of Zion, in a chapter of the *Protocols* urging the infiltration of the publishing organs of every political stripe.[40] The list of plagiarized material is endless.[41] Whoever concocted the *Protocols* used the *Dialogue aux Enfers* as a model, frequently succumbing to some clumsiness or other, as we note in another chapter of the *Protocols* where the metaphor evoking Vishnu is repeated.[42] There is a strong structural similarity between the strategies to control society that are proposed, respectively, by the Elders of Zion and by Joly's Machiavelli: for example, the former say that anti-Semitism will end up strengthening the occult power of Jews, while the latter holds that the political opposition will end up serving as an instrument of the regime of Napoleon III. How can these similarities be explained?

Until not so long ago it was thought that the *Protocols* had been assembled in France between 1894 and 1899.[43] De Michelis's aforementioned recent book *Il manoscritto inesistente*, on the basis of other internal elements, has suggested a different thesis: the *Protocols* originated in Russia in 1902–1903.[44] But the work's hypothetical Russian ancestry cannot easily be reconciled with the close dependence of the *Protocols* on Joly's *Dialogue aux Enfers*—a forgotten text, difficult to come upon.[45] De Michelis objects that the *Dialogue* was not at all "a practically forgotten text." But to support this claim he can only point to the Spanish translation that had appeared, after thirty years of silence, in Buenos Aires in 1898.[46] However, De Michelis, who considers Joly's book a subtext of the *Protocols*, even going so far as to use the former to reconstruct the textual transmission of the latter, is then forced to suppose, if only in vague terms, that the authors of the forgery, presumably Russian, must have enjoyed a number of links with France, from which they would have obtained either Joly's book or, at least, a host of excerpts taken from it.[47] This potpourri would presumably have included passages from French authors such as Tarde or Chabry echoed in the *Protocols*.[48]

So now we are back in France. But can we really discover a French link tying Joly's *Dialogue* to the *Protocols*? Curiously, De Michelis does not mention an attempt to reply to this question, admittedly conjectural but interesting, in a book which he correctly defined as the bedrock of the literature on the *Protocols*, *L'Apocalypse de notre temps: Les dessous de la propagande allemande d'après des documents inédits*, by Henri Rollin.[49] This truly notable work, written by a nonacademic historian who worked for the French Secret Services, appeared in 1939, immediately after the onset of World War II, and was reprinted in 1991. With remarkable intelligence and erudition Rollin reconstructed the context from which the *Protocols* had emerged, including the fact that in 1872 Joly, not surprisingly, had begun to collaborate with an ultrarightist newspaper, *La liberté*. Among the journalists working there, one, Edouard Drumont, later became the spokesman of a particularly virulent anti-Semitism through books such as *La France juive* (1886) and the daily *La libre parole*, which he directed.[50] Drumont mentioned Joly ("ce bon Jolly"), slightly distorting his name, in *La France juive*, as well as in his autobiography, entitled *Le testament d'un antisémite* (1891).[51] In 1894, when the president of the French Republic, Sadi Carnot, was assassinated by an Italian anarchist, Drumont fled to Brussels, to avoid the consequences from some of his articles which contained vaguely pro-anarchist thoughts. In fact, Drumont successfully combined themes of both Catholic and socialist anti-Semitism.[52] In an interview appearing in *Figaro* on 18 July 1894 Drumont threatened to revive the anti-Napoleonic pamphlets which had circulated during the Second Empire: "We must prepare some new *Propos de Labiénus*," he exclaimed. Then, mentioning a large box: "Documents—authentic documents! Until now I have kept silent inspired by compassion or Christian charity. I have fought a war by the rules. But if an unjust law will turn us into outlaws, I shall declare a war without mercy." Rollin supposes that Drumont had discovered the *Dialogue aux Enfers*, written by his former colleague, Joly. To be sure, the book would have been easier to stumble upon in Brussels, where it had been published, than in Paris.[53] Especially telling is Drumont's allusion to "some new *Propos de Labiénus*," a satire against Napoleon III which had appeared the year before. It was presented in the form of an imaginary dialogue between two ancient Romans and was obviously inspired by Joly's *Dialogue*.[54] On 10 January 1896 Drumont once again raised in the pages of *La libre parole* the possibility of writing a "gracious pamphlet" which would have been a continuation of the *Propos de Labiénus*. Ten days later he mentioned this again: "If the *Dialogues of the Dead* were still fashionable. . . ."[55] These things do not prove that Drumont had adopted the *Dialogue aux Enfers* as a potentially anti-Semitic work, presenting an invented text as if it were a real document; nor does it prove that Drumont had passed Joly's text to someone in Russia, who came up with the *Protocols*. But the Drumont trail, suggested by Rollin, deserves to be examined further. In 1898, the "Jewish year," as Drumont bitterly wrote as the year drew to an end, a series of dramatic events suddenly reopened the Dreyfus *affaire*. The document used to prove the guilt of Dreyfus turned out to be a forgery; Colonel Henry, imprisoned as the author of the falsification, killed himself. At this point Drumont went on the attack. *La libre parole* announced a great subscription to raise funds for a monument to Colonel Henry, a man who naively, Drumont wrote, had committed a stupidity which was infinitely less serious than the "infamous means employed by Jews to enrich themselves and become our masters."[56] Shortly after, on 26 February 1899, *La libre parole* published on its front page an article signed "Gyp." The pseudonym concealed the identity of Sibylle Gabrielle Marie Antoinette, countess of Mirabeau-Martel, celebrated author of dazzling ultranationalist and anti-Semitic writings. The article, entitled "L'affaire chez les morts," grotesquely evoked the genre of "dialogues of the dead" which had inspired Joly's *Dialogue aux Enfers*. Gyp portrayed Calvin, Joan of Arc, Catherine de' Medici, Voltaire, Napoleon, Gavroche in the act of insulting and assaulting Moses, Jeremiah, Mayer Rothschild, Jacques de Reinach—all of whom spoke French with a German accent. It was a vulgar joke which, when read today, has a sinister, prophetic ring. "I have been so criticized over the course of history," says Catherine de' Medici, "and yet if there had been a Jewish St. Bartholomew's I would not be at all surprised."[57] The *Protocols*, based on Joly's *Dialogue aux Enfers*, a book which was no longer read, must have originated in this climate, and perhaps during these very months.[58]

8. But the similarity between Joly's *Dialogue* and the *Protocols* also needs to be discussed from a perspective that touches the present directly. The *Dialogue* contains a single hostile allusion to Jews, in a passage borrowed by the *Protocols* (but where the mention of Jews has been dropped).[59] But this single point of convergence has little importance. Much more relevant, and disturbing, is the general conformity between the two texts for anyone who accepts the notion that Joly, through his analysis of the Second Empire, conceived as an example of "modern despotism," succeeded in revealing a long-standing phenomenon which in diverse forms has come down to our own day.[60] If this is how things are, how should we interpret the *Protocols*? As a caricature? Michel Bounan has come up with a different notion: the *Protocols* were "a police forgery of a revolutionary tumult."[61] Such a view seems to presuppose the famous definition by August Bebel—"antisemitism is the socialism of imbeciles"—but it goes well beyond it. According to Bounan, the real conspiracy which inspired the false one—the *Protocols*—is a classic example of a characteristic which earmarks the system described by Joly: "*An occult and permanent plot* of the modern state intended to maintain subjection indefinitely" (but Bounan uses, perhaps deliberately, de Tocqueville's harsher term: *servitude*).[62]

Little is known of Michel Bounan's life. From a few hints in his writings, and from a bit of information on the Internet, we are informed that he had been close to Guy Debord and to the Situationists, that small band which played a leading role in the Parisian rebellion of May '68. Today, Bounan seems to be the key figure in a small publishing house which has reprinted two books important to the present research, Joly's *Dialogue aux Enfers* and Rollin's *L'Apocalypse de notre temps*. In a number of elegant articles explicitly inspired by these works, Bounan has developed a coherent vision of history as conspiracy. In modern societies power pervades everything; everyone's energies (with the exception of those of a small privileged elite) are derailed by false conspiracies and false designs; even the feeling of being the victims of injustice has been cancelled out by the awareness of the victims—in other words, of everyone. Bounan's most recent pamphlet, *Logique du terrorisme*, published in 2003, examines the events of the last few years from this perspective.

I have never subscribed to that rather widespread notion which automatically disqualifies as absurd all explanatory theories based on conspiracy. To be sure, the majority of these theories are effectively nonsense, and in a few cases they are something worse. But as I tried to bring out some time ago in a book on the stereotype of the witches' Sabbath, conspiracies exist, and false conspiracies often conceal true ones[63] (an observation that Bounan also makes). After the events of 11 September 2001 in America, to which we could add others, including 11 March 2004 in Madrid, the idea that conspiracies actually exist encounters less resistance. But I am well aware that the attempts to identify false plots that may conceal real ones may lead, at the very least, to wild conclusions. Is it possible to trace a dividing line between a healthy skepticism toward certain official versions and a conspiratorial obsession? In my opinion, Bounan transgressed that boundary, letting himself be guided by that destructive principle *is fecit cui prodest*, which retroactively transforms, illogically, an achieved end into a causal relationship. The fact that a government used the political prospects created by a terrorist attack to make war on another country does not prove that the attack had been concocted by that government. One might say that Bounan has been hypnotized by the subject of his research, the *Protocols*, and by their source, Joly's *Dialogue aux Enfers*. Still, it is not sufficient to reject a conspiratorial view of history because it is an inverse version of the *Protocols*. To clarify this point, we must return once more to what connects the two books.

Joly finished by paying a price for using the literary form on which his ideas were constructed. The Machiavelli of the *Dialogue aux Enfers* describes in detail, in the first person, the political strategies he will adopt, thereby giving the impression that reality (which has already occurred) will only be able to conform to his wishes. Fleeting allusions to vast anonymous phenomena, such as the fragility of modern societies, are immediately dropped. Imagining an omnipotent individual who models society in accordance with his own wishes, Joly involuntarily made possible the deplorable, posthumous fortune of the *Dialogue aux Enfers*. The compilers of the *Protocols* poured the materials from Joly's work into a preexistent mold, the delusional Jewish conspiracy. But elements which were part of the formal model used by Joly also contributed to this transformation. Any trace of ambiguity vanished, and a polished political parable was turned into a crude falsification.

CHAPTER 12

Just One Witness

The Extermination of the Jews and the Principle of Reality

FOR PRIMO LEVI

1. On 16 May 1348, the Jewish community of La Baume, a small Provençal village, was exterminated. This event was just one link in a long chain of violence which had started in southern France with the first eruption of the Black Death just one month before. The hostilities against the Jews, who were widely believed to have spread the plague by poisoning wells, fountains, and rivers, had first crystallized in Toulon during Holy Week. The ghetto had been assaulted; men, women, and children had been killed. In the following weeks similar violence took place in other towns in Provence—Riez, Digne, Manosque, and Forcalquier. In La Baume there was a single survivor, a man who ten days before had departed for Avignon, summoned by Queen Jeanne. He left an emotional recollection of the episode in a few lines written in a copy of a Torah now preserved in the Austrian National Library in Vienna. In an excellent essay Joseph Schatzmiller, by combining a new reading of the passage inscribed in the Torah with a document extracted from a fiscal register, has succeeded in identifying the survivor: Dayas Quinoni. In 1349 Quinoni had settled in Aix, where he had received his Torah. We do not know if he ever went back to La Baume after the massacre.[1]

Let us turn briefly to a different, though not unrelated, case. The accusations against Jews in 1348 that they had spread the plague closely imitated a pattern which had been established a generation before. In 1321, during Holy Week, a rumor suddenly spread throughout France and some neighboring regions (western Switzerland, northern Spain). According to the different versions, lepers, or lepers influenced by Jews, or lepers urged on by Jews inspired by the Muslim kings of Tunis and Granada, had concocted a plot to poison Christians. The Muslim kings were obviously out of reach, but for two years lepers and Jews became the targets of violent acts by mobs but also by religious and political authorities. I have tried elsewhere to disentangle this complex muddle of events.[2] Here I would just like to analyze a passage from a Latin chronicle written in the early fourteenth century by the so-called continuator of William of Nangis, an anonymous monk who, like his predecessor, lived in the convent of Saint-Denis.

Many Jews were killed, most of them in northern France, after the discovery of the alleged conspiracy. Near Vitry-le-François, according to the chronicler, approximately forty Jews were confined in a tower. To avoid perishing at the hands of the Christians they decided, after long deliberations, to take their own lives. The execution of the deed was to be carried out by an elder who enjoyed great authority among them, and a youth. The older man then asked the younger man to kill him. The latter reluctantly did so but then, instead of committing suicide himself, took the gold and silver from the pockets of the bodies on the ground. He then tried to escape from the tower by knotting sheets together as a rope, but it was not long enough and the young man fell to the ground, broke a leg, and was subsequently put to death.[3]

The episode is not implausible. However, it resembles closely two passages from Flavius Josephus's *The Jewish War*. The first passage (3:8) speaks of forty persons who, after hiding in a cave near Jotapata in Galilee, all commit suicide, with two exceptions: Josephus himself and a fellow soldier who agrees not to kill him. The second passage describes the celebrated siege of Masada, the desperate resistance of the Jews who had taken refuge inside the fortress, followed by a collective suicide, here also with two exceptions, both women (7:8–9).[4] How should we explain the analogies between Josephus's texts and the aforementioned passage in the chronicle by William of Nangis? Should we assume a factual convergence or, on the contrary, the presence of a historiographical topos (which in the more recent version also included an allusion to another topos, Jewish greed)?

The hypothesis of a historiographical topos has already been cautiously formulated in regard to Josephus's reconstruction of the events at Masada.[5] Flavius Josephus's work, either in Greek or in the famous Latin version prepared under the direction of Cassiodorus, circulated widely in the Middle Ages, especially in northern France and Flanders (if we can judge from the many extant manuscripts).[6] Although we know that Flavius Josephus was mandatory reading during Lent at the monastery of Corbie c. 1050, his works are not included in a fourteenth-century list of required books for the monks of Saint-Denis, among whom was, as we have seen, the continuator of William of Nangis.[7] Moreover, we have no direct proof that manuscripts of Josephus's *Jewish War* existed in the library of Saint-Denis at all.[8] But the anonymous chronicler could have consulted them without difficulty: among the many manuscripts housed in the Bibliothèque Nationale in Paris there is one (a twelfth-century copy) from the library of Saint-Germain-des-Prés.[9] We can conclude that the continuator of William of Nangis could have been familiar with Flavius Josephus's *Jewish War* (or its fourth-century adaptation known as "Hegesippus").[10] But it does not necessarily follow from this that the collective suicide near Vitry-le-François never took place. More work is needed on this question, although it may be impossible to reach a definitive conclusion.

2. These events dating back to a distant and largely forgotten past are connected by myriad threads to the theme expressed in the subtitle of this chapter. Pierre Vidal-Naquet was acutely aware of this when he decided to republish, in two essays in the same volume (*Les juifs, la mémoire, le présent*, Paris, 1981), "Flavius Josephus and Masada" and "A Paper Eichmann," a detailed discussion of the so-called revisionist school which claims that the Nazi extermination camps never existed.[11] The similarity of content—the persecution of Jews in the Middle Ages, the extermination of Jews in the twentieth century—is less important, in my opinion, than the similarity in the theoretical issues posed in both cases. Let me try to explain why.

The analogies between the two passages from Josephus, describing the Jotapata and Masada episodes, concern, in addition to the collective suicide, the survival of two people: Josephus and his fellow soldier in the first case, the two women in the second.[12] The survival of at least one person was logically required by the necessity to provide a witness, but why two? I think that the well-known rejection of a single witness in court, shared by the Jewish and Latin legal traditions, explains the choice of two witnesses.[13] Both traditions were familiar, of course, to Flavius Josephus, a Jew who became a Roman citizen. Later, the emperor Constantine transformed the rejection of the single witness into a formal law, later included in the Justinian Code.[14] In the Middle Ages the implicit reference to Deuteronomy 19:15, *Non stabit testis unus contra aliquem* ("A single witness shall not prevail against a man"), became *testis unus, testis nullus* ("one witness, no witness"), a recurring maxim, implicitly or explicitly, in trial records and the legal literature.[15]

Let us try to imagine for a moment what would happen if such a criterion were applied to the field of historical research. Our knowledge of the events which took place at La Baume in May 1348, near Vitry-le-François sometime during the summer of 1321, and in the cave near Jotapata in July A.D. 67 is based, in each case, on a single, more or less direct witness. That is, respectively, the person (identified as Dayas Quinoni) who wrote the lines in the Torah now in the National Library in Vienna, the continuator of William of Nangis, and Flavius Josephus. No sensible historian would dismiss this evidence as intrinsically unacceptable. According to normal historiographical practice, the value of each document will have to be tested by way of comparison—that is, by constructing a series including at least two documents. But let us assume for a moment that the continuator of William of Nangis, in his account of the collective suicide near Vitry-le-François, was merely echoing Josephus's *Jewish War.* Even if the supposed collective suicide should evaporate as a fact, the account itself would still give us a valuable piece of evidence about the reception of Josephus's work (which is also, except to an inveterate positivist, a "fact") in early fourteenth-century Île-de-France.

Law and history, it seems, have different rules and different epistemological foundations which do not always coincide. Consequently, legal principles cannot be transposed in their entirety into historical research.[16] Such a conclusion would seem to contradict the close contiguity stressed by such sixteenth-century scholars as François Baudouin, the legal historian who solemnly declared that "historical studies must rest on a solid legal foundation, and jurisprudence must be joined to history."[17] From a different perspective, related to antiquarian research, the Jesuit Henri Griffet, in his *Traité des differentes sortes de preuves qui servent à établir la verité de l'histoire* (1769), compared the historian to a judge testing the reliability of different witnesses.[18]

Such an analogy today has a definitely unfashionable ring. Many historians would probably react with a certain embarrassment to the crucial word *preuves*, "proofs," in Griffet's title. But some recent discussions show that the connection among proofs, truth, and history cannot be easily dismissed.

3. I have mentioned "A Paper Eichmann," the essay that Pierre Vidal-Naquet wrote to refute the notorious thesis, advanced by Robert Faurisson and others, that Nazi extermination camps never existed.[19] This essay has been republished in a small volume, *Les assassins de la mémoire*, which Vidal-Naquet dedicated to his mother, who died at Auschwitz in 1944. It is not difficult to imagine the moral and political motives which drove him to engage in a detailed discussion, involving, among other things, a punctilious analysis of the evidence (witnesses, technological possibilities, and so on) concerning the gas chambers. Other, more theoretical implications have been spelled out by Vidal-Naquet in a letter to Luce Giard which was included in a volume in memory of Michel de Certeau which appeared a few years ago. Vidal-Naquet writes that the collection of essays, *L'écriture de l'histoire*, published by de Certeau in 1975, was an important book which contributed to the dismantling of historians' proud innocence: "Since then, we have become aware that the historian *writes*; that he produces space and time, being himself intrinsically embedded in a specific space and time." But we should not dismiss, Vidal-Naquet goes on, that old notion of "reality," meaning "precisely what happened," as evoked by Ranke a century ago.

> I became very conscious of all this when the *affaire Faurisson*, which unfortunately continues, began. Naturally, Faurisson is the antithesis of de Certeau. The former is a crude materialist, who, in the name of the most tangible reality, transforms everything he deals with—pain, death, the instruments of death—into something unreal. De Certeau was deeply affected by this perverse folly, and wrote me a letter about it . . . I was convinced that there was an ongoing discussion on gas chambers, that everything should necessarily pass through discourse [*mon sentiment était qu'il y avait un discours sur les chambres à gaz, que tout devait passer par le dire*]; but beyond this, or rather, before this, there was something irreducible which, for better or worse, I shall continue to call reality. Without this reality, how can we tell the difference between fiction and history?[20]

In the United States the question regarding the difference between fiction and history usually seems to spring from the work of Hayden White, or, at least, is associated with it. That there are differences in the historiographical practices of the two writers is obvious: but it cannot be denied that there is a certain convergence between White's *Metahistory* (1973) and de Certeau's *L'écriture de l'histoire* (1975, but which includes essays published earlier). To fully comprehend Hayden White's contribution, it seems essential to sketch out first his intellectual biography.[21]

4. In 1959, introducing to an American audience the translation of *Dallo storicismo alla sociologia*, by Carlo Antoni, one of Benedetto Croce's closest followers, White spoke of Croce's youthful essay "La storia ridotta sotto il concetto generale dell'arte," ("History subsumed under a general concept of the arts") as a "revolutionary" contribution.[22] The significance of this essay, published in 1893 when the author was twenty-seven years old, had already been emphasized by Croce himself in his intellectual autobiography (*Contributo alla critica di me stesso*) ("Contribution to a critique of myself"), as well as later by R. G. Collingwood (*The Idea of History*).[23] Not surprisingly, the chapter on Croce in *Metahistory* includes a detailed discussion of "La storia ridotta."[24] But at a distance of sixteen years White's appreciation of this essay had cooled considerably. He declared that he still agreed with certain crucial statements in Croce's essay, such as the sharp distinction between historical research, deemed a purely propaedeutic activity, and history proper, equated with narrative history. But then he concluded in this vein:

> It is difficult not to think of Croce's "revolution" in historical sensibility as a retrogression, since its effect was to sever historiography from any participation in the effort—just beginning to make some headway in sociology at the time—to construct a general science of society. But it had even more deleterious implications for historians' thinking about the artistic side of their work. For, while Croce was correct in his perception that art is a way of knowing the world, and not merely a physical response to it or an immediate experience of it, his conception of art as literal *representation* of the real effectively isolated the historian as artist from the most recent—and increasingly dominant—advances made in representing the different levels of consciousness by the Symbolists and Post-Impressionists all over Europe.[25]

This passage already points to some elements of Hayden White's later work. Since writing *Metahistory* he has become interested less and less in the construction of a "general science of society," and more and more "in the artistic side of the historian's work"—a shift not far removed from Croce's long battle against positivism, which inspired, among other things, his scorn toward the social sciences. But in *Metahistory* Croce had already ceased to be the crucial influence he had been in the early stages of White's intellectual development. Undoubtedly his esteem of Croce remained high, and he continued to define him as "the most talented *historian* of all the philosophers of history of the century"; even on the last page of the book he is warmly praised for his allegedly "ironical" attitude.[26] But the global evaluation cited above testifies to the existence of significant disagreement with Croce's theoretical perspective.

The principal motive for White's dissatisfaction with Croce's thought hinged, as we have seen, on his "conception of art as a literal *representation* of the real"—in other words, on his "realistic" attitude.[27] The term, which in this context has a cognitive and not merely aesthetic meaning, may sound a bit paradoxical when applied to a neo-idealist philosopher like Croce. But the latter's idealism was of a rather special sort: the term "critical positivism," as applied to him by a highly discerning critic of his work, seems more appropriate.[28] The most distinctly idealistic phase of Croce's thought has to be traced back to the strong influence exerted over him by Giovanni Gentile, to whom he was linked for two decades by a close intellectual bond.[29] In a note added to his *Logica come scienza del concetto puro* ("Logic as the science of pure concept") (1909) Croce traced a retrospective reconstruction of his own intellectual development, moving from his "La storia ridotta" to the recent recognition of the identity between history and philosophy achieved under the influence of Gentile ("my very dear friend . . . to whose help and stimulation my intellectual life owes much").[30] Some years later, however, the intrinsic ambiguities of this identity (as well as, on a general level, of the alleged theoretical convergence between Croce and Gentile) emerged fully.[31] Croce, by interpreting philosophy as "the methodology of history," seemed to be dissolving the former in the latter. Gentile moved in the opposite direction. "Ideas without facts are empty," he wrote in 1936 in his *Il superamento del tempo nella storia* ("The overcoming of time in history"); "philosophy which is not history is the vainest abstraction. But facts are simply the life of the objective moment of self-consciousness, outside of which there is no real constructive thought." He emphasized that history (*res gestae*) "must not be a presupposition of historiography (*historia rerum gestarum*)." Gentile vigorously rejected "the metaphysical theory of history (or historicism) based directly on the idea that historical writing presupposes historical fact, an idea as absurd as those of other metaphysics, and pregnant with worse consequences; for no enemy is so dangerous as one who has managed to creep into your house and hide there."[32]

By identifying that unnamed "metaphysical theory of history" with "historicism," Gentile was reacting to a polemical anti-Fascist essay by Croce, "Antistoricismo," which had just appeared.[33] The theoretical core of Gentile's essay went back to his *Teoria generale dello spirito come atto puro* (1918), a response to Croce's *Teoria e storia della storiografia* (1915).[34] But by 1924 the philosophical dispute between the two old friends had transformed itself into a bitter political and personal feud.

This apparent digression was required to clarify the following points:

a. Hayden White's intellectual development can be understood only by considering his exposure, at an early stage of his career, to Italian philosophical neo-idealism.[35]

b. White's "tropological" approach, suggested in *Tropics of Discourse*, his 1978 collection of essays, still showed the impact of Croce's thought. In 1972 White had written that Croce

> moved from his study of the epistemological bases of historical knowledge to a position in which he sought to subsume history under a general concept of art. His theory of art, in turn, was constructed as a "science of expression and general linguistics" (the subtitle of his *Aesthetics*). In his analysis of the linguistic bases of all possible modes of comprehending reality, he came closest to grasping the essentially tropological nature of interpretation in general. He was kept from formulating this near perception, most probably, by his own "ironic" suspicion of system in any human science.[36]

Such an approach started from Croce but then proceeded in a totally different direction. When we read that "tropics is the process by which all discourse *constitutes* [the emphasis is in the text] the objects which it pretends to describe realistically and to analyze objectively" (a passage from the introduction to *Tropics of Discourse* [1978]),[37] we recognize the aforementioned criticism of Croce's "realism."

c. This subjectivist stand was certainly reinforced by White's encounter with the work of Michel Foucault. But it is significant that White tried to "decode" Foucault through Giovanbattista Vico, the alleged founding father of Italian philosophical neo-idealism.[38] In fact, White's statement about discourse creating its own objects seems to be echoing—with a major difference discussed immediately below—Croce's emphasis on expression and general linguistics combined with Gentile's extreme subjectivism, according to which historiography (*historia rerum gestarum*) creates its own object: history (*res gestae*). "Le fait n'a jamais qu'une existence linguistique" ("A fact never has anything but a linguistic existence"): these words by Roland Barthes, used by White as an epigraph for *The Content of the Form* (1987), could be ascribed to this imaginary combination of Croce and Gentile to which I have just alluded. Even White's reading of Barthes in the early eighties (he was still barely mentioned in *Tropics of Discourse*)[39] reinforced a preexisting pattern.

5. There is a questionable element in this reconstruction—namely, the role attributed to Gentile. As far as I know, White never studied his writings or even mentioned him (with one relevant exception, as we shall see). But familiarity with Gentile's work can be safely assumed in a scholar such as White, who, through Carlo Antoni, had been introduced to the philosophical tradition of Italian neo-idealism. (On the other hand, a direct knowledge of Gentile's work must be ruled out in the case of Barthes. The crucial role played by Barthes in de Certeau's intellectual development can explain, but only to a certain extent, the partial convergence between the latter and Hayden White.)

Gentile's close association with Fascism, right up to his violent death, has somewhat darkened, at least outside Italy, the first phase of his philosophical career. His adherence to Hegelian idealism resulted from a firsthand reading of Marx's early philosophical writings (*La filosofia di Marx*, 1899).[40] In his analysis of Marx's *Theses on Feuerbach*, Gentile interpreted Marxist praxis through Vico's famous dictum *verum ipsum factum*, or rather through the neo-idealistic interpretation of it. Praxis, therefore, was regarded as a concept implying the correspondence between subject and object, insofar as the Spirit (the transcendental subject) creates reality.[41] Even Gentile's much later statement on historiography creating history was just a corollary to this principle. The presentation of Marx as a fundamentally idealistic philosopher had a lasting impact on Italian intellectual and political life. To be sure, Antonio Gramsci, by using an expression such as "philosophy of praxis," instead of "historical materialism," in his *Prison Notebooks*, was obviously trying to circumvent Fascist censorship. But he was also echoing the title of Gentile's second essay on Marx ("La filosofia della praxis") as well as, more significantly, Gentile's emphasis on "praxis" as a concept which diminished materialism, almost to the point of eliminating it, as a crucial element in Marxist thought. Other echoes of Gentile's interpretation of Marx have been detected in Gramsci's early idealistic Marxism.[42] It has been proposed that even the well-known passage in the *Prison Notebooks* suggesting that Gentile's philosophy is closer to Futurism than Croce's implied a favorable opinion of Gentile: had not Futurism been regarded by Gramsci in 1921 as a revolutionary movement which had been able to respond to a need for "new forms of

art, of philosophy, of behavior, of language"?[43] A similar closeness between
Gentile's philosophy and Futurism, both seen as negative examples of "antihis-
toricism," had instead been implicitly suggested by Croce in a liberal-conservative
anti-Fascist perspective.[44]

In light of a left-wing reading of Gentile's work (or at least of part of it),
the quasi-Gentilian flavor detectable in Hayden White's writings beginning
with *The Burden of History*—his 1966 plea for a new historiography written
in a modernist key—sounds less paradoxical.[45] One can easily understand
the impact (as well as the intrinsic weakness) of this attack launched against
liberal and Marxist orthodoxies. In the late 1960s and early '70s subjectivism,
even in an extreme form, had a definitely radical flavor. But if one regarded
desire as a left-wing slogan, then *reality* (including the emphasis on "real facts")
would have looked definitely right-wing. Such a simplistic, not to mention
self-defeating, view has largely been superseded—in the sense that attitudes
implying a basic flight from reality are certainly not restricted today to a few
factions of the left. This should be taken into account in any attempt to explain the rather extraordinary appeal of contemporary skeptical ideologies,
even outside the academic world. In the meantime Hayden White has declared that he is "against revolutions, whether launched from 'above' or 'below'
in the social hierarchy."[46] This statement was elicited, he explains in a footnote, by the fact that "the relativism with which I am usually charged is conceived by many theorists to imply the kind of nihilism which invites revolutionary activism of a particularly irresponsible sort. In my view, relativism is
the moral equivalent of epistemological skepticism; moreover, I conceive relativism to be the basis of social tolerance, not a license to 'do as you please.'"[47]

Skepticism, relativism, tolerance: at first the distance between this self-
presentation of White's thought and Gentile's theoretical perspective seems
as though it could not be greater. Gentile's attacks against positivist historians did not have skeptical implications, since his philosophical position implied a transcendental Spirit, not a multiplicity of empirical subjects.[48] He
was never a relativist; on the contrary, he strongly advocated a religious commitment, intransigent in both philosophical and political matters.[49] And, of
course, he never theorized tolerance, as his support of Fascism—including
squadrismo, its most violent aspect—shows.[50] The notorious statement describing the truncheons of the punitive squads as a "moral force" comparable
to preaching—a remark Gentile made during a speech in the 1924 electoral
campaign[51]—was consistent with his strictly monistic theory: in a reality

created by the Spirit there is no place for a real distinction between facts and values.

These are not minor theoretical divergences. Any argument suggesting intellectual contiguity between Gentile's and White's approaches must account for these major differences. So we may wonder on what ground White stresses, in his article "The Politics of Historical Interpretation," that his own historical perspective shares something with "the kind of perspective on history . . . conventionally associated with the ideologies of Fascist regimes," whose "social and political policies" he simultaneously rejects as "undeniably horrible."

6. This contradiction, so clearly perceived, leads us to the moral dilemma implicit in White's approach. "We must guard," he says, "against a sentimentalism that would lead us to write off such a conception of history simply because it has been associated with Fascist ideologies. One must face the fact that when it comes to apprehending the historical record, there are no grounds to be found in the historical record itself for preferring one way of constructing its meaning over another."[52] No grounds? In fact, in discussing Faurisson's views on the extermination of Jews, White does not hesitate to suggest a criterion according to which we must judge the validity of conflicting historical interpretations. Let us look at his argument.

White's above-mentioned statement is based (1) on the distinction (even better, disjunction) between "'positive' historical inquiry" and "proper history"— that is, narrative—advocated by Croce in La storia ridotta; and (2) on a skeptical interpretation of this distinction, converging in many ways with Gentile's transcendental subjectivism. Both elements can be detected in White's reaction to the refutation, provided by Vidal-Naquet "on the terrain of positive history," of Faurisson's "lies" about the extermination of Jews. Faurisson's claim is as "morally offensive as intellectually bewildering"; but the notion of a "lie," insofar as it implies concepts such as "reality" and "proof," is clearly a source of embarrassment for White, as this remarkably twisted sentence shows: "The distinction between a lie and an error or a mistake in interpretation may be more difficult to draw with historical events less amply documented than the Holocaust." In fact, even in this latter case White is unable to accept Vidal-Naquet's conclusion, suggesting that there is a big difference "between an interpretation that would 'have profoundly transformed the reality of the massacre' and one that would not. The Israeli interpretation leaves the 'reality' of the events intact, whereas the revisionist interpretation dereal-izes it by redescribing it in such a way as to make it something other than what the victims know the Holocaust to have been."[53] The Zionist historical interpretation of the Holocaust, White says, is not a *contre-verité* (as has been suggested by Vidal-Naquet) but a truth: "its truth, as a historical interpreta-tion, consists precisely in its *effectiveness* in justifying a wide range of current Israeli political policies that, from the standpoint of those who articulate them, are crucial to the security and indeed the very existence of the Jewish people." In the same way, "the effort of the Palestinian people to mount a po-litically *effective* response to Israeli policies entails the production of a simi-larly *effective* ideology, complete with an interpretation of their history capa-ble of endowing it with a meaning that it has hitherto lacked."[54] We can conclude that if Faurisson's narrative were ever to prove *effective*, it would be regarded by White as true as well.

Is this conclusion the result of a tolerant attitude? As we have seen, White argues that skepticism and relativism can provide the epistemological and moral foundations for tolerance.[55] But this claim is historically and logically untenable. Historically, because tolerance has been theorized by people who had strong intellectual and moral convictions (Voltaire's assertion "I will fight in order to defend my opponent's freedom to speak" is typical). Logically, be-cause absolute skepticism would contradict itself if it were not extended also to tolerance as a regulating principle. Moreover, when moral and intellectual differences are not ultimately related to truth, there is nothing to *tolerate*.[56] In fact, White's argument connecting truth and effectiveness inevitably reminds us not of tolerance but of its opposite—Gentile's evaluation of a truncheon as a moral force. In the same essay, as we have seen, White invites us to consider without "sentimentalism" the association between a conception of history which he has implicitly praised and the "ideologies of Fascist regimes." He calls this association "conventional." But the mention of Gentile's name (along with Heidegger's) in this context does not seem at all conventional.[57]

7. Since the late 1960s the skeptical attitudes of which we are speaking have become more and more influential in the humanities and social sciences. This broad diffusion is only partially related to their presumed novelty. Only an encomiastic impulse could have suggested to Pierre Vidal-Naquet that "[s]ince then [i.e., the publication of Michel de Certeau's *L'écriture de l'histoire*

in 1975] we have become aware that the historian *writes;* that he produces space and time, being himself intrinsically embedded in a specific space and time." As Vidal-Naquet knows perfectly well, the same point (leading sometimes to skeptical conclusions) was strongly emphasized, for instance, in a not particularly bold methodological essay of 1961 by E. H. Carr, *What Is History?*, as well as at a much earlier date by Benedetto Croce.

By looking at these issues in historical perspective, we obtain a better grasp of their theoretical implications. As a starting point I would suggest a brief essay written by Renato Serra in 1912 but not published until 1927, after his untimely death in 1915. Its title, "Partenza di un gruppo di soldati per la Libia" ("The departure of a group of soldiers for Libya"),[58] gives only a vague idea of its content. It begins with a description, written in a daringly experimental style reminiscent of Umberto Boccioni's Futuristic paintings from the same era, of a railway station full of departing soldiers surrounded by a large crowd.[59] At this point a series of anti-Socialist observations intrude, followed by a reflection on history and historical writing, which abruptly leads to a passage couched in a metaphysical tone, full of Nietzschean echoes. This unfinished essay, which certainly deserves a longer and deeper analysis, reflects the complex personality of a man who, besides being the best Italian critic of his generation, was an erudite person with pronounced philosophical interests. In his correspondence with Croce (to whom he was personally very close, without being a follower) he explained the genesis of the pages we are discussing here.[60] They had been elicited by "Storia, cronaca e false storie" (1912), an essay by Croce which later was included, in revised form, in the latter's *Teoria e storia della storiografia.* Croce had mentioned the gap, emphasized by Tolstoy in *War and Peace*, between an actual event, such as a battle, and the fragmentary and distorted recollections of it on which historical accounts are based. Tolstoy's view is well known: the divide could be overcome only by collecting the memories of every individual (even the humblest soldier) who had directly or indirectly participated in the battle. Croce dismissed this suggestion and the skepticism which it seemed to involve as absurd. "At every moment we know all the history that we need to know"; therefore, the history we do not know is identical to "the eternal ghost of the thing itself."[61] Serra, ironically defining himself as "a slave of the thing itself," wrote to Croce that he felt much closer to Tolstoy; however, he added, "my difficulties are—or at least seem to be—much more complicated."[62] It is impossible not to agree with him. "There are people who imagine in good faith that a document can be an expression of reality. . . . As if a document could express something different from *itself*. . . . A document is a fact. The battle is another fact (an infinity of other facts). The two cannot become *one*. . . . The person who acts is *a fact*. The person who tells a story is *another fact*. . . . Every piece of testimony is only a testimony of itself; of its immediate moment, of its own origin, of its own purpose, and of nothing more."[63]

These were not the reflections of a pure theoretician. Serra knew what erudition was. In his incisive critiques he did not artificially oppose historical narratives to the materials on which they are constructed. He was well aware that any document, regardless of how direct it is, always has a highly problematic relationship with reality. But reality ("the thing in itself") exists.[64]

Serra explicitly rejected simple, positivist attitudes. But his thoughts also help us to reject a point of view which brings together positivism (in other words, "positivist historical inquiry" based on a literal reading of documents) and relativism (namely, "historical narratives" based on figurative, incomparable, and irrefutable interpretations).[65] In fact, the narratives based on one witness discussed earlier in this chapter can be regarded as experimental cases which deny such a clear-cut distinction: a different reading of the available evidence immediately affects the resulting narrative. A similar although usually less visible relationship can be assumed also on a general level. An unlimited skeptical attitude toward historical narratives is therefore groundless.

8. On Auschwitz, Jean-François Lyotard wrote:

> Suppose that an earthquake destroys not only lives, buildings, and objects but also the instruments used to measure earthquakes, directly and indirectly. The impossibility of quantitatively measuring it does not prohibit, but rather inspires in the minds of the survivors the idea of a great seismic force. . . . With Auschwitz, something new has happened in history (which can only be a sign and not a fact), which is that the facts, the testimonies which bore the traces of *here's* and *now's*, the documents which indicated the sense or senses of the facts, and the names, finally the possibility of various kinds of phrases whose conjunction makes reality, all this has been destroyed as much as possible. Is it up to the historian to take into account not only the damages, but also the wrong? Not only the reality, but also the meta-reality, that is the destruction of reality? . . . Its name [Auschwitz] marks the confines wherein historical knowledge sees its competence impugned.[66]

I am not at all certain that this final observation is true. Memory and the destruction of memory are recurring elements in history. "The need to tell our story to 'the rest,' to make 'the rest' participate in it," Primo Levi wrote, "had taken on for us, before our liberation and after, the character of an immediate and violent impulse, to the point of competing with our other elementary needs."[67] As Emile Benveniste has shown, one of the Latin words for "witness" is *superstes*—survivor.[68]

CHAPTER 13

Details, Early Plans, Microanalysis

Thoughts on a Book by Siegfried Kracauer

History: The Last Things before the Last, the posthumous, unfinished book by Siegfried Kracauer, appeared in paperback for the first time in 1995. For the occasion, Paul Oskar Kristeller, who had presented the first edition in 1969, wrote a new preface. In the twenty-six years that transpired between Kristeller's two texts, an actual Kracauer renaissance had occurred, with reprintings, translations, and essays of various types in several languages. But for Kristeller in 1995 this late recognition was debased by the attempt to eliminate from Kracauer's work everything that could not be traced back to the Frankfurt School. As examples of this distorted interpretation, Kristeller cited essays by Gertrud Koch and Inka Mülder-Bach on *History: The Last Things before the Last*, appearing in the issue which the journal *New German Critique* had devoted to Kracauer in 1991. Kristeller wrote that the "... two papers neither summarize the book nor indicate that its content fundamentally differs from his earlier writings. Their footnotes cite only books and articles unknown to Kracauer and refer to Kracauer's earlier books as if the books on history were in complete agreement with them. They also fail to indicate that Kracauer, in the footnotes and bibliography of this book, cites for the most part historical, philological, and philosophical sources, never mentions his earlier writings, and very seldom refers to the sociologists that predominate in his earlier works. And worst of all, they imply and even state that history was not his major concern. An adequate scholarly interpretation of Kracauer's last work is yet to be written."[1]

This harsh critique from the great scholar who left us that monument of precision and academic probity, the *Iter Italicum*, contains a few factual errors. Even a cursory inspection reveals that the notes to the essays by Koch and Mülder-Bach cite virtually exclusively writings by Kracauer or those known to him—with the exception of two or three obvious references to recent articles on his work. Moreover, contrary to what Kristeller says, the piece by Mülder-Bach emphasizes the elements of *divergence* between the posthumous book on history and some of Kracauer's previous writings. To what should we attribute this uncharacteristic inaccuracy on Kristeller's part? Perhaps to indignation. The allusion by Mülder-Bach to the "extreme cultural and scholarly isolation" in which Kracauer allegedly wrote his book on history tacitly ignores Kristeller's claim (which we have no reason to question) that the book had come into being thanks to intense discussions between the two friends over many years.[2] But the point I should like to underline is yet another: the idea of a clear-cut break which, Kristeller argued, separated *History: The Last Things before the Last* from Kracauer's earlier writings is totally indefensible.

Kracauer's posthumous book opens with an autobiographical statement: ". . . recently I suddenly discovered that my interest in history—which began to assert itself about a year ago and which I had hitherto believed to be kindled by the impact of our contemporary situation on my mind—actually grew out of the ideas I tried to implement in my *Theory of Film*. In turning to history, I just continued to think along the lines manifest in that book." Kracauer then continued, ". . . I realized in a flash the many existing parallels between history and the photographic media, historical reality and camerareality. Lately I came across my piece on photography and was completely amazed at noticing that I had compared historism with photography already in this article of the 'twenties."[3]

The identification of the parallelism between history (in the twofold sense of process and narration, of *res gestae* and of *historia rerum gestarum*) and the photograph (in a broad sense, including the cinema) as an element of continuity between the earlier and later Kracauer, the caesura marked by the exile experience notwithstanding, comes from Kracauer himself. We should not ignore such an assertion, as Kristeller implicitly seems to do when he contrasts the posthumous book to the earlier writings. However, this needs to be confirmed, since the passage I have just quoted assimilates, without undue hairsplitting, history and historicism: a contiguity difficult to reconcile with the critique of historicism repeatedly offered by Kracauer. The continuity as well as the contiguity concentrated in the adverb *already* are thus debatable. Is this a minute discrepancy perhaps caused by the unfinished state of the manuscript? Or is it a clue suggesting the presence of an unresolved problem in Kracauer's thought?

2. To settle this our search must begin with some texts, cited by Kracauer himself, around which discussions have shed a little light but also produced many doubts in the last few years. We can begin with the article on photography appearing in 1927 in the *Frankfurter Allgemeine Zeitung*, which Kracauer later included in his collection *Die Ornament der Masse* (1963).[4] Here Kracauer observes that "historicist thinking . . . emerged at about the same time as modern photographic technology," insinuating that both were the products of a capitalist society. But this coincidence, according to the author, concealed an even more profound parallelism. Representatives of historicism such as Wilhelm Dilthey (a reference which Kracauer omitted when he reprinted the essay in a volume) believe "they can explain any phenomenon purely in terms of its genesis. They believe that they can grasp historical reality by reconstructing the course of events in their temporal succession without leaving anything out. Photography, instead, offers a spatial continuum; historicism seeks to provide the temporal continuum." To historicism and to photography Kracauer contrasted memory and its images. The latter, by definition, are fragmentary: "*Memory* encompasses neither the entire spatial appearance of a state of affairs nor its entire temporal course."[5] And here is where the profound significance of the juxtaposition between historicism and photography on the one hand, and memory and its images on the other, made its appearance: "That the world devours them is a sign of the *fear of death*. What the photographs by their sheer accumulation attempt to banish is the recollection of death, which is part and parcel of every memory image."[6]

Admittedly, in the conclusion of his essay, with a sudden dialectical reversal, Kracauer projected an emancipation of the photograph from the one-dimensional recording of events, from the accumulation of the detritus of nature: a possibility attributed to film, which (alongside the dream and Kafka's work) would be in a position to reunite in an unforeseeable manner the fragments of reality, bringing to light a superior order. But basically the Kracauer of 1927 condemned photography and historicism equally. He opposed them to "history" in quotation marks: a history to be written, a history that in fact did not yet exist.

3. Is it correct to see these reflections, as Kracauer retrospectively suggested, as the seed of his posthumous book on history? Yes and no: in between there is a discontinuity, which can be summed up, as has been noted, in reference to Proust—or, better yet, to a specific passage in his work. The 1927 photography article does not mention Proust at all, although it discusses memory and the images of memory.[7] Instead, in *Theory of Film* (1960) and in *History: The Last Things before the Last*, Kracauer analyzed, respectively, the characteristics of film and of historiography, recalling again and again that page in *The Guermantes Way (Le côté de Guermantes)* in which the narrator, returning home from a trip unexpectedly, sees his grandmother without being seen himself and for an instant does not recognize her.[8] Here is a passage from that unforgettable page:

> Of myself—thanks to that privilege which does not last but which one enjoys during the brief moment of return, the faculty of being a spectator, so to speak, of one's own absence,—there was present only the witness, the observer, with a hat and traveling coat, the stranger who does not belong to the house, the photographer who has called to take a photograph of places which one will never see again. The process that mechanically occurred in my eyes when I caught sight of my grandmother was indeed a photograph. . . . For the first time and for a moment only, since she vanished at once, I saw sitting on the sofa, beneath the lamp, red-faced, heavy and common, sick, lost in thought, following the lines of a book with eyes that seemed hardly sane, a dejected old woman whom I did not know.[9]

Through the estranged, mechanical gaze which Proust compares to the impassive lens of the camera, the narrator grasps instantly, in spite of himself, what love had hitherto prevented him from seeing: his grandmother was dying. The photograph which for Kracauer in 1927 was the token of the fear of death became, through Proust, the instrument which permitted the overcoming of that fear, of looking death in the face. Furthermore, the premonition of death was already at the heart of that passage of Saint-Simon's *Mémoires* which, if I am not mistaken, had inspired Proust. The Duke of Saint-Simon enters to visit the dauphin and finds him "seated on a chair among his gentlemen-in-waiting and two or three of his high officials. I was horrified. I saw a man with a lowered head, his face of a purple, reddish complexion, with an inane air, who did not even notice my approach."[10] Apart from the perception of physical decadence attributed to skin coloring by both writers (*rouge pourpre, rouge*) the process used in the two passages to convey the lack of recognition is similar: "Je vis un homme" (Saint-Simon), "j'aperçus . . . une vieille femme" (Proust). Behind the altered physiognomy of the individual stands the anonymous destiny of the species, its moral condition.

"The face in the film has no value if it does not bring out the skull beneath it. '*Danse macabre.*' To what end? This remains to be seen." In these enigmatic words attempts have been made to see an early reaction on Kracauer's part to the Proustian text. They are taken from a notebook containing a preliminary version of an introduction to a book on the cinema. It was the project on which Kracauer had begun to work in Marseilles in November 1940 during the agonizing wait for the permit that would allow him to emigrate with his wife to the United States.[11] A new version of the project begun at Marseilles, which Kracauer wrote in English in 1949, opens with a direct reference, later developed in the final version of the book, to Proust's text.[12] In the French city Kracauer had met Walter Benjamin, who a few months later fled to Spain and ultimately suicide. We know that during their stay in Marseilles the two friends spoke of Kracauer's film project.[13] There is no risk in supposing that in the course of these conversations Benjamin mentioned the passage in Proust, which some years before he had translated, in collaboration with Franz Hessel.[14] The comparison between the look with which the narrator mechanically registers the physical decay of the grandmother without recognizing her, and the indifference of the camera, clarifies the implications of the notion of optical unconsciousness which Benjamin had proposed in his historical essay on photography (1931).[15]

4. Through Proust, perhaps mediated by Benjamin, Kracauer substituted for the analogy which he had proposed in 1927 between photography and historicism one that was completely different and in some ways the opposite, between photography and history (in the sense of *historia rerum gestarum*, or historiography), which he fully discussed in *History: The Last Things before the Last*. But to understand the full significance of the juxtaposition, Kracauer was suggesting, we need to recall that in the page from Proust, the photographer is the final element in a series composed of more or less similar figures: "the witness, the observer, with a hat and traveling coat, the stranger who does not belong to the house, the photographer who has called to take a pho-

tograph of places which one will never see again." For Kracauer the exile, it was natural to identify with the stranger, or actually even with the wandering Jew Ahasuerus, who appears in the title of one of the chapters in his posthumous book on history.[16] But the identification, at least on the surface, was not intended to convey pathos. Kracauer emphasized that the stranger, he who is marginalized, he who "does not belong to the house," is in a position to understand more, and more deeply. The instant in which recognition fails opens to the estranged gaze of the spectator the way to cognitive awareness.[17] It is not pure coincidence, Kracauer remarks, that great historians, from Thucydides to Napier, were exiles: "It is only in this state of self-effacement, or homelessness, that the historian can commune with the material of his concern. . . . A stranger to the world evoked by the sources, he is faced with the task—the exile's task—of penetrating its outward appearances, so that he may learn to comprehend that world from within."[18]

All this helps us to understand why Kracauer presented his unfinished book on history as a development of the theses he had formulated in *Theory of Film*. The identification of the historian with the exile is the destination of his extended reflections on photography. The attitude of active passivity which Kracauer recommends to historians builds on (as Volker Breidecker has pointed out) a page from *Theory of Film* on the desolate urban photographs of Charles Marville or of Eugène Atget. The "melancholy" which has been recognized in those Parisian scenes, Kracauer notes, "favors self-estrangement, which, on its part entails identification with all kinds of objects. The dejected individual is likely to lose himself in the incidental configurations of his environment, absorbing them with a disinterested intensity no longer determined by his previous preferences. His is a kind of receptivity which resembles that of Proust's photographer cast in the role of a stranger." But this is a receptivity which is interwoven with the choice, the construction: the photograph is not a simple mirror image of reality. The photographer could be compared, Kracauer observes, to "the imaginative reader intent on studying and deciphering an elusive text."[19] These words, contained in the first part (by far the most important) of *Theory of Film*, explain why Kracauer would write to Adorno that the cinema, in that book, was only a pretext.[20] Kracauer, who for years had read, along with the young Adorno, *The Critique of Pure Reason*, wanted to explore a cognitive model using the cinema.[21] This research continued in the posthumous book on history—the final phase, destined to remain unfinished, of an intellectual journey that was remarkably single-minded, in spite of the many different research areas it touched.

5. The influence of Kant is identifiable even in Panofsky's famous essay on film, especially where he mentions ". . . the fascinating spectacle of a new artistic medium gradually becoming conscious of its legitimate, that is, exclusive possibilities and limitations. . . ."[22] And yet, as has been convincingly demonstrated by Tom Levin, that essay promptly took a different and less ambitious turn.[23] Much more fruitful, according to Levin, are the reflections on the cinema in Panofsky's essay on perspective as symbolic form published in 1927 in the *Warburg Vorträge*.[24] An oblique allusion to this essay can be found, as noted above, in a 1928 letter from Walter Benjamin to Kracauer.[25] But even if Kracauer did not read the essay on perspective, he could have grasped its gist from Panofsky's other writings. The preparatory material for Kracauer's *History: The Last Things before the Last* includes a page of notes to which Volker Breidecker has justly called attention. It is entitled "Emphasis on minutiae—Close-up—micro-analysis." As an example of "close-up" Kracauer mentioned the "principle of disjunction" illustrated by Panofsky—in other words, the divarication, typical of medieval art, between classical themes represented anachronistically and ancient images Christianized.[26] In his *History: The Last Things before the Last*, Kracauer offers a twofold clarification. Panofsky's "principle of disjunction" is offered first as an example of a perfect equilibrium between "realistic tendency" and "formative tendency," together with a photo by Alfred Stieglitz; and second as a paradigmatic example of "microhistory," or "small-scale histories," compared to a close-up.[27] In both cases the photograph (or the photographic frame) emerges as the object on which to base comparisons; but here it is the latter model that is of interest.[28]

Without the cinema, without the "close-up," could Kracauer have spoken about microhistory? Obviously, this is a rhetorical question. It is no accident that Kracauer, to underline the connection between macrohistoric investigation and close-ups based on microresearch, should quote a passage from Vsevolod Pudovkin on the plurality of points of view imposed by film narration.[29] The photograph and its extensions (the cinema, television) have opened up, just as linear perspective did in the past, a series of cognitive possibilities: a new way to see, to narrate, to think.[30] Kracauer's reflections collected in his posthumous book on history spring from an awareness of the emergence of a world which, more than ever, is still ours today.

A new world to behold: but to what degree is it really new? As T. S. Eliot wrote, every innovation in expression constructs its own genealogy backwards. The cinema is no exception to this rule. Sergei Eisenstein argued that the early inventions of the film pioneer D. W. Griffith had literary antecedents: the isolated representation of details in the novels of Dickens.[31] In another essay Eisenstein used the encounter between Emma and Rodolphe in *Madame Bovary* as an exceptional example of the alternating editing of dialogues.[32] I had failed to notice this when, some years ago, I analyzed a series of devices used by Flaubert in *L'éducation sentimentale*, especially the famous *blanc* so admired by Proust, inserting it in a context molded by the photograph, by the panorama, by the train.[33] I had also forgotten an early reaction to *L'éducation sentimentale*, which I should like to address now—a digression which may better help us to understand Kracauer's way of thinking.

6. In December 1869 a long essay entitled "Le roman mysanthropique" appeared in the *Revue des Deux Mondes*. It dealt with *L'éducation sentimentale*, which had just appeared.[34] In his youth, the author of the piece, Saint-René Taillandier, had written a monograph, *Scot Erigène et la philosophie scholastique* (1843), with an eye to Hegel and Schilling; later he taught literature at the Universities of Strasbourg and Montpellier, closing out his career in the Académie Française.[35] In 1863 he had published, always in the *Revue des Deux Mondes*, a paper on *Salammbô* entitled "Le réalisme épique dans le roman."[36] From an academic critic of Catholic background and conservative tastes such as Taillandier one might expect a condemnation of Flaubert's "immorality" and stylistic audacity. And the expected condemnation did come, but at the center of a critical discussion that holds some surprises, especially for those of us accustomed to reading *L'éducation sentimentale* as a classic. Taillandier, who read it as a freshly minted novel by an established and scandalous author, conveys to us, unexpectedly, astonishment over what is new: "Imagine an artist who pretends to reproduce reality most faithfully, and who begins by casting over this reality the bizarre veil of his system. Uselessly he proposes to show everything, similar to the ray of sun which traverses the darkroom of the photographer. . . ." (p. 988).

The comparison between Flaubert and a photographer, which may seem banal, actually is not, as we see from what follows immediately:

> In vain he tries to be pointed, biting, like a blade that slices through rock, like nitric acid which cuts into copper: wholly concerned with the effect he thinks

only of the process, of the equipment, of the instruments, of the acids. Nature's rich variety is forgotten: here he is secluded in an unsanitary laboratory. The unrefined artisan of realism will rapidly lose the sense of the real world. He has a small number of examples before his eyes, and these examples, fatigued, disfigured, bored and boring, will become for him an image of human destiny. (p. 988)

Taillandier recognizes that Flaubert "certainly is not a mediocre writer . . . he produces little, but each one of his works testifies to intense thought and demanding execution." But a book such as *Madame Bovary* "is a knowledgeable dissection executed with glacial aplomb" which has scandalized not because of its subject matter but for "the indifference of the thought" which inspired it (pp. 988–989). "The epic realism of *Salammbô* had the same characteristic of *inhuman* fantasy" (in the previous article Taillandier had spoken without mincing his words of "*a sadistic element of the imagination*").[37] This raised the question: "What was this writer then, who, while devoting such care to his work, nevertheless remained so totally estranged from it? What was the significance of this impassible portrait?" (p. 989).

Impassibilité, impassible: these recurring terms in the article emanate from the initial juxtaposition between writer and photographer. Taillandier sees this impassibility as "the result of a system, the expression of a concealed philosophy," misanthropy in the broadest sense of the term. "To inflict on man outrages of this sort means offending the world and him who created it, if we admit that the world is someone's work. . . . A sort of atheism: that is the book's philosophy" (p. 990). But this philosophical intention is joined by "the desire to write a page of history." Flaubert seems to have wanted to suggest "the idea of a work in which the public events [of the last twenty-five years] are explained by individual behavior. The education of the protagonist would thus correspond to the education of Parisian society during a period of our history."

> It is difficult not to accept this hypothesis, extravagant as it may be, the moment we realize unquestionably that the author is imitating the style of Michelet in the final volumes of his *History of France*. We find the same broken, convulsed way of splitting the narration, of passing brusquely from one scene to another accumulating details and suppressing the transitions. A novel has never spoken a similar language; one has the impression of confronting a chronicle, a dry and hurried diary, a collection of notes, of signs, of words. But the difference is this: that in the case of the historian the signs are incisive, the words express, the notes summarize sometimes well, sometimes badly, relevant events, while in the case of the

novelist these forms, wisely, laboriously expressed, are applied to totally tasteless adventures. (pp. 993–994)

I shall return presently to the pairing of Michelet and Flaubert. But Taillandier realizes that the antithesis which came to him spontaneously between the "relevant events" described by the former and the "totally tasteless adventures" recounted by the latter is inexact. The reader of *L'éducation sentimentale* is struck by something quite different from the mingling of private lives and public events: Taillandier perceives in this "the intention of confusing great things with the small, the serious with the ridiculous, so as to establish on this promiscuity the doctrine of universal scorn" (p. 999). Everything is placed on the same plane: "It is no longer the case of a banal indifference, but of a deliberate will to disenchant the world and degrade human nature" (p. 1002). The term *désenchanter* recurs toward the conclusion: with the book completed, "we tell ourselves that all this is false, that the author has not represented either love or action, that he has slandered humanity, that life is something of value, and that art betrays itself when it persists in disenchanting God's work" (p. 1003).

7. Dissociation of the author from his work; narrative processes which are their own end; impassibility; indifference; history in which public events and private happenings lacking in importance are interwoven; general irrelevance; disillusionment with the world. It would not be difficult to find in Kracauer's *History: The Last Things before the Last* themes similar to those Taillandier identified in *L'éducation sentimentale*: estrangement, detachment, the interweaving of micro- and macrohistory, a rejection of the philosophy of history—in other words, of the search for a comprehensive sense in human history. Kracauer may not have read Taillandier's article; however, he had read Flaubert and, during the Weimar period, regarded Flaubert's impassibility as an ideal. Toward the end of World War II he contemplated an essay (which he never wrote) on the pessimism of Flaubert and the intellectuals of the Third Republic.[38] But these similarities suggest something more complex than the reading of an author by two very different persons, a century apart. Here we are dealing not simply with reception, but with reception and production together. In an extraordinary book which has not received the attention it deserves, Michael Baxandall has shown that Italian Quattrocento

painters applied themselves to a public which knew how to understand their work thanks to a series of shared social experiences: the abacus, sermons, the dance.[39] The experiment could be repeated with photography, choosing a specific sector: France toward the mid–nineteenth century, Germany in the first decades of the twentieth, Europe in the early years of the twenty-first. Let there be no doubt, however: this research perspective has nothing to do with determinism. If man is (among the many possible definitions) a metaphorical animal, then we could say that the abacus, photography, and such suggest to the artist and to his public experiences that can be treated as metaphors, as worlds *als ob* (as if), with respect to the fictional world of which the work is composed. In the present case, the photograph offered Flaubert the possibility of developing a series of cognitive and narrative experiments, and to his readers the possibility of deciphering them. When Taillandier hypothesizes, without providing concrete citations, that Flaubert tried to emulate Michelet's later style—". . . it is the same broken, convulsed way of splitting the narration, of passing brusquely from one scene to another accumulating details and suppressing the transitions . . ."—it is impossible not to think of photography and (anachronistically) of cinematic cutting and splicing.

Let us try to test Taillandier's hypothesis on a passage taken, almost haphazardly, from the final volume of Michelet's *Histoire de France*. It is the description of an episode from the revolt of the nobles which preceded the great revolution itself: the so-called *journée des tuiles*, an uprising at Grenoble on 7 June 1788. Michelet had direct access to numerous accounts of that event: "The best, provided by a monk, is of an enchanting simplicity." It would be worthwhile to see how he reorganized this material (beginning with the punctuation). But let us listen to Michelet:

> It was noon. At that sinister rumble, which resounded throughout every nook and cranny of that high valley, the rough peasants of Tronche and surrounding villages, with a terrible surge, grabbed their firearms and began to run. But the gates were nailed shut. They search for ladders. Unfortunately, they were too short. They end up opening a breach in a wall which blocked a fake door. It took a long while: but their presence sufficed to convey the idea that the countryside was as one with the city.[40]

To this succession of visual and auditory sensations, articulated with brief phrases, interrupted by photographic frames, which go on page after page, we could compare the splendid scene of the killing of Dussardier in *L'éducation sentimentale*.[41] Instead, I shall quote a passage written in the plain prose of a manual for film directors: "In order to receive a clear and definite impression of a demonstration, the observer must perform certain actions. First he must climb upon the roof of a house to get a view from above of the procession as a whole and measure its dimensions; next he must come down and look out through the first-floor window at the inscriptions carried by the demonstrators; finally, he must mingle with the crowd to gain an idea of the outward appearance of the participants."

This is the passage in Pudovkin quoted by Kracauer to support his thesis about the reciprocal implication between macro- and microhistory, between long shots and close-ups.[42] I, in turn, would quote certain pages in Kracauer in support of the thesis of the cognitive implications (and not just rhetorical or ornamental) in any narrative.[43] On this point Kracauer stands out, more than ever, as an essential protagonist in the discussion.

8. "There is no cosmos on the screen" wrote Roger Caillois. Kracauer, who quoted these words with emphatic approval, went so far as to say that "art in film is reactionary because it symbolizes wholeness."[44] This obstinate refusal of totality, which fed Kracauer's diffidence toward the philosophy of history, sheds an ironic light to words which he penned in Marseilles in November 1940: "The face in film has no value if it does not allow the skull beneath it to surface. 'Danse macabre.' To what end? This remains to be seen." "Zu welchem Ende?" The question mark leaves open the possibility that, along with the end, which is a given, there also exists a *telos*, a purpose. But the title—it, too, ironical—of the unfinished book, *History: The Last Things before the Last*, evokes the world of contingency, the disenchanted world for which Flaubert (as Taillandier wrote) and Max Weber had contended.[45] All this, it seems to me, counsels against enrolling Kracauer, as has been done on occasion, among the devotees of messianicism, even in a paler version.[46] The emphatic "NO" which Kracauer applied to his copy of Benjamin's writings published in 1955, next to the last sentence of the seventh thesis on the philosophy of history, attests to a dissent which his friend's tragic death had not extinguished.[47] It may be worthwhile to reread what Benjamin had written:

> Addressing himself to the historian who wishes to relive an era, Fustel de Cou-langes recommends that he blot out everything he knows about the later course of history. There is no better way of characterizing the method with which his-torical materialism has broken. It is a process of empathy. Its origin is indolence of the heart, that *acedia* which despairs of appropriating the genuine historical

image as it briefly flashes up. Among medieval theologians, *acedia* was regarded as the root cause of melancholy. Flaubert, who was familiar with it, wrote: "Few will guess how much sadness it took to resuscitate Carthage" *(Peu de gens devineront combien il a fallu être triste pour resusciter Carthage)*. The nature of this melancholy becomes clearer if we ask: With whom does historicism actually sympathize? The answer is inevitable: with the victor.[48]

Kracauer, who thought of himself as a champion of lost causes and associated the theme of David and Goliath with the close-up—namely, the conviction that the most significant forces reveal themselves in what is small and insignificant—could not accept Benjamin's conclusion.[49] Nor could he accept what preceded it: the condemnation of melancholy, of empathy, of Flaubert assimilated into historicism. As for historicism, Kracauer was of two minds. But faith in the notion of progress, as expressed by Dilthey with reservations, seemed unacceptable.[50] Flaubert's pessimism was much more congenial to him. And yet in the antimessianical idea of the redemption of physical reality one discerns, in spite of everything, a subdued utopian accent.[51]

CHAPTER 14

Microhistory

Two or Three Things That I Know about It

1. It must have been 1977 or 1978 when I heard of "microhistory" for the first time from Giovanni Levi, and I adopted this previously unheard-of word without asking what it meant literally; I suppose I contented myself with the reference to a reduced scale suggested by the prefix *micro-*. I well remember, too, that in those early conversations we spoke of "microhistory" as if it were a label attached to an empty vessel waiting to be filled.[1]

Sometime later Levi, Simona Cerutti, and I began working on a series entitled precisely *Microstorie* for the Einaudi publishing house in Turin. Twenty-odd volumes by both Italian and foreign authors have appeared; a few of the Italian works have been translated into other languages. In some quarters there has been talk of an Italian school of microhistory. Recently, thanks to a small retrospective investigation into terminology,[2] I discovered that this word, which we thought was free of connotation, had already been used by others.

2. To the best of my knowledge, the first person to dredge up the word *microhistory* as a self-defined term was an American scholar, George R. Stewart, in 1959. Stewart, who lived from 1895 to 1980, and who for many years was a professor at the University of California, Berkeley, must have been an exceptional person. The vast bibliography of this liberal polymath includes, in addition to various novels (which I have not read), a precocious ecological manifesto (*Not So Rich as You Think*, 1968); a recapitulation of universal history in the form of an autobiography of the human species (*Man, an Autobiography,*

1946); a chronicle, written in collaboration with others, of the resistance by Stewart and colleagues, including Ernst Kantorowicz, to the loyalty oath imposed by the University of California during the McCarthy era (*The Year of the Oath*, 1950).[3] Stewart's best-known books (*Names on the Land*, 1945, 1967; *American Place-Names*, 1970) are dedicated to the toponymy of the United States.[4] In a lecture, taking as his point of departure the place-names mentioned in a Horatian ode, he asserted that to interpret a literary text it is necessary first of all to decipher the background references—places, vegetation, meteorological conditions—that it contains.[5] Stewart's passion for microscopic detail also inspired the book that interests me here: *Pickett's Charge: A Microhistory of the Final Charge at Gettysburg, July 3, 1863* (1959). In it Stewart analyzed minutely for over three hundred pages the decisive battle of the American Civil War. The title refers to an event lasting only about twenty minutes: the desperate, unsuccessful assault led by a Confederate battalion under Major General Edward Pickett. The account unfolds within a narrow time frame, a period of fifteen hours. The maps and diagrams that accompany the text have captions such as "The Cannonade (1:10–2:55 P.M.)." The outcome of the battle of Gettysburg is played out in a matter of seconds, between a clump of trees and a stone wall.[6] Within this compressed compass in time and space, Stewart analyzes in almost obsessive detail what he defines as "the climax of the climax, the central moment of our history"—and, as such, part of universal history. If George Edward Pickett's failed charge had instead succeeded, Stewart suggests, the battle of Gettysburg might have ended differently, and "the existence of two rival republics would probably have prevented the United States from turning the balance of two World Wars and becoming a global power."[7] Stewart's dogged kind of microhistory might induce a contemplation of Cleopatra's nose.

3. A few years later, wholly independently of Stewart, a Mexican scholar, Luis González y González, inserted the word *microhistory* into the subtitle of a monograph published in Mexico City in 1968 (*Pueblo en vilo: Microhistoria de San José de Gracia* [A village in tumult]). The book investigates, within the span of four centuries, the transformation experienced by a tiny "forgotten" village. But the minute dimensions are redeemed by its representative characteristics. Besides the fact that González y González was born and lived there, this is the element that justifies the choice of San José de Gracia over a thousand other villages just like it. Here microhistory is synonymous with local

history, written, as González y González stressed, citing Paul Leuilliot, from a qualitative rather than a quantitative perspective.[8] The success enjoyed by *Pueblo en vilo* (reprinted and translated into English and French) persuaded its author to theorize about its methodology in two essays, "El arte de la microhistoria" and "Teoria de la microhistoria," which were included in two collections entitled, respectively, *Invitación a la microhistoria* (1973) and *Nueva invitación a la microhistoria* (1982). In these pages, echoes of which are discernible in other Mexican publications from these years,[9] González y González distinguished microhistory from the anecdotal and discredited *petite histoire*; and he reiterated its identity with what in England, France, and the United States was called "local history," and which Nietzsche had defined as "antiquarian or archeological history." Finally, to counteract the objections provoked by the word *microhistory*, González y González suggested two alternatives: *matria* history, suitable for evoking that "small, weak, feminine, sentimental world of the mother" which revolves around the family and the village; and *yin* history, the Taoist term that recalls all that is "feminine, conservative, terrestrial, sweet, obscure and painful."[10]

4. Even while claiming for himself the basic paternity of the word *microhistory*, González y González recalled that it had already appeared in Fernand Braudel's introduction to the *Traité de sociologie* edited by Georges Gurvitch (1958), but "sin significación concreta reconocida."[11] Actually, for Braudel *microhistoire* had a precise but negative connotation. It was synonymous with that "history of events" [*histoire événementielle*], with that "traditional history," that saw the "so-called history of the world" dominated by protagonists who resembled orchestra directors. Braudel held that, within the limits of brief and convulsive time, this traditional history was less interesting than microsociology on the one hand, and econometrics on the other.

As we know, Braudel had declared his hostility with regard to *histoire événementielle*, identified with political history, even from the time of his *Méditerranée* (1949). Ten years later he once again demonstrated his displeasure. But he was too intelligent, too impatient to content himself with repeating what had now become for many, because of his own authority, an accepted truth. Suddenly putting aside what at this point seemed to him "old misunderstandings," Braudel wrote: "The incident (if not the event, the sociodrama) exists in repetition, regularity, multitude, and there is no way of saying absolutely whether its level is quite without value or scholarly promise. It must be given closer examination."[12] Twenty-five years had to pass before this suggestion would be acted upon.[13] Braudel excluded the possibility of scholarly recognition of singularity: the incident, the *fait divers*, could, perhaps, find acceptance simply because it was considered repetitive—an adjective that in González y González became "typical." But microhistory remained condemned.[14] The word, obviously modeled on *microeconomics* and *microsociology*, remained clothed in a technicist aura, as emerges from this passage of *Les fleurs bleues*, arguably Raymond Queneau's finest novel. The two speakers are the duke of Auge and his chaplain:

> "What is it exactly that you want to know?"
>
> "What you think about universal history in general and of general history in particular. I'm listening."
>
> "I'm really tired," said the chaplain.
>
> "You can rest later. Tell me, for example, is this Council of Basel universal history?"
>
> "But of course: it is universal history in general."
>
> "And what about my small cannon?"
>
> "General history in particular."
>
> "And the marriage of my daughters?"
>
> "Scarcely 'the history of events.' At the most, microhistory."
>
> "What kind of history?" the duke of Auge stormed. "What the devil kind of language is this? What is today anyway? Pentecost?"
>
> "Please excuse me, sire. The effects of exhaustion, as you can see."[15]

The duke of Auge, probably just like many readers of Queneau in 1965, had never heard of microhistory. For this reason, perhaps, ignoring the chaplain's precise classification, the publisher of the 1977 French translation of González y González's *Pueblo en vilo* did not hesitate to substitute in the subtitle and in the text the words *histoire universelle* for *microhistoire*, with unintended comic effects.[16]

5. *Microhistory, microhistoria, microhistoire*: from which of these independent traditions did the Italian *microstoria* derive? On the level of strict terminol-

ogy that has occupied us thus far, the answer would seem to be clear: from the French *microhistoire*. I am thinking first of all of the splendid translation by Italo Calvino published by Einaudi in 1967 of *Les fleurs bleues* (*I fiori blu*); second, of a passage in Primo Levi in which, to the best of my knowledge, the word *microstoria* appears in Italian for the first time in an autonomous manner.[17] It occurs at the beginning of the chapter titled "Carbon," with which *The Periodic Table* concludes:

> The reader, at this point, will have realized for some time now that this is not a chemical treatise: my presumption does not reach so far—"ma voix est faible, et même un peu profane." Nor is it an autobiography, save in the partial and symbolic limits in which every piece of writing is autobiographical, indeed every human work; but it is in some fashion a history. It is—or would have liked to be—a micro-history, the history of a trade and its defeats, victories, and miseries, such as everyone wants to tell when he feels close to concluding the arc of his career, and art ceases to be long.[18]

There is nothing in these calm and melancholy words to suggest that twelve years later their author would take his life. The reduction of scale suggested by the word *microhistory* fits in with the acknowledgment of the limits of existence, with the sense of one's own capacities that dominates this passage. Primo Levi probably encountered it in Calvino's Italian translation, which he may have checked against Queneau's original text. That Levi knew of Calvino's version of *Les fleurs bleues* seems certain given the closeness between the two men; moreover, the last page of "Carbon" in *The Periodic Table* echoes closely the last page of Calvino's *Il barone rampante*.[19] A fresh encounter between Calvino and Primo Levi, by way of Queneau, occurred a few years later due to the Italian translation of the latter's *Petite cosmogonie portative*.[20]

Shortly after its appearance in *The Periodic Table*, the word *microhistory* entered Italian historical usage, losing, as often happens, its original negative connotation. Giovanni Levi (a distant cousin of Primo Levi) was undoubtedly behind this transposition.[21] *Microhistory* rapidly replaced *microanalysis*, which had been used in these years by Edoardo Grendi, more or less with the same meaning.[22]

6. There is a point that still needs defining: the history of a word, obviously, determines its possible application only in part. This is proved indirectly by the "Zaharoff lecture" that Richard Cobb dedicated to Raymond Queneau in 1976—a species of historiographical manifesto that fits none of the usages

discussed thus far. Cobb began with the ironic sympathy felt by Queneau for the timid, modest, provincial personages in his novels. He appropriated their words in order to counterbalance news of local happenings—the only ones that were of interest—with political events; and he concluded by assuming as his own slogan the colorful curse hurled by Zasie at Napoleon.[23] Basically, this is an exaltation of minor historiography (Cobb does not use the term *microhistory*) against that of the great and the powerful. The naïveté of this interpretation is obvious. Queneau does not identify in any way with his characters. The fondness he felt for the provincial life of Le Havre coexisted in him with an omnivorous, encyclopedic passion for the most random knowledge. His mocking curiosity for the *faits divers* did not stop him from proposing a drastic remedy for the prescientific nature of historiography, and he elaborated a rigorous mathematical model in which to trap the disordered course of human acts.[24] But neither the author of *Une histoire modèle* nor the auditor and later editor of Alexandre Kojève's courses on Hegel's *Phenomenology* appears in the portrait simplified by Cobb to the point of distortion. Totally missing is the tension that runs through all of Queneau's work between the warmth of the narrator's intimate glance and the coldness of the scientist's detached observation.[25]

There is nothing strange about this. Cobb is an empiricist who claims to be superior to theoretical questions; and, after all, for him the use of Queneau is a mere pretext.[26] But the proposal of a minor historiography made in the name of Queneau has a symptomatic importance that Cobb, confirmed cultivator of his own eccentricity, would be the first to reject. The contrast between Historiography with a capital H and Zasie's "Napoléon mon cul" might suggest, apart from the obvious difference in tone, the contrast between *storia patria* and *storia matria* as outlined by Luis González y González. To be sure, the latter's *microhistoria* focuses on typical phenomena, whereas Cobb's *petite histoire* focuses on the unpredictable and the unrepeatable *fait divers*. But in both cases the choice of a circumscribed and close-up perspective reveals a dissatisfaction (explicit and aggressive in Cobb's case, tactful and almost imperceptible in the case of González y González)[27] with the macroscopic and quantitative model that dominated the international historiographical scene between the mid-1950s and mid-1970s, primarily through the activities of Braudel and the historians of the *Annales* school.

7. None among that relatively heterogeneous group of Italian scholars of microhistory would recognize himself in George Stewart's close-up "history

of events," in the local history of González y González, or in the *petite histoire* of Richard Cobb. However, it cannot be denied that even Italian microhistory, though very different (beginning with its theoretical goals), originated in opposition to the historiographical model just mentioned. The latter was presented in the mid-1970s, with Braudel's backing, as the culmination of the functional-structural approach, the supreme historiographical paradigm, the third to have occurred in the course of the more than two millennia that began with Herodotus.[28] But a few years earlier, the ceremony marking the publication of the *Mélanges* honoring Braudel (1973) revealed the existence of hidden tensions and anxieties at the very moment of the celebration. A parallel reading of two essays published on that occasion—"Un nouveau champ pour l'histoire sérielle: Le quantitatif au troisième niveau," by Pierre Chaunu; and "Histoire et ethnologie," by François Furet and Jacques Le Goff—seems instructive twenty years later. In both cases a historiographical program was being introduced and justified by some general historical reflection.[29] Chaunu spoke of the end of the anticolonial wars (referring only to France) and to student revolts (in America and in Europe); of a disoriented Roman Church following Vatican II; of an economic crisis in the most advanced countries that brought into question the very idea of progress; of a challenge to the ideals of the Enlightenment that he interpreted consistently as a secularized transposition of an eschatological ideal. Furet, with words that we can suppose were shared by Le Goff, observed that the worldwide phenomenon of decolonization had placed the great nineteenth-century historiography, in its Manchesterian and Marxist versions, face-to-face with nonhistory: progress and change had run into inertia, stagnation. Common to both essays was a clear-cut rejection of theories of modernization (such as W. W. Rostow's, then in vogue, mentioned by Furet and Le Goff) that in Chaunu was coupled with a repudiation of modernity *tout court*. The research projects resulting from these essays varied greatly. Chaunu proposed analyzing the traditional societies of the Ancien Régime, observing that the "great continuity of Latin Christendom which has unconsciously . . . been transformed into a Europe of the West" was "infinitely more attractive than the Nambikwaras or the Dogons"—a statement that lumped together disdainfully peoples from various continents being studied by ethnologists (Claude Lévi-Strauss and Marcel Griaule, respectively) from very different intellectual worlds.[30] Instead, Furet and Le Goff suggested reconnecting the long-sundered bonds between history and ethnology by adopting a generally comparative perspective based on the explicit rejection, especially by Le Goff, of a Eurocentric approach. But at this point the two positions began to converge: both Chaunu and Furet were aiming at a "serial history" based on the analysis of phenomena, according to Furet, "selected and constructed as a function of *their* repetitive character."[31] Le Goff subscribed to the rejection of the single event on the part of the ethnologists and their concentration on "events repeated or awaited": Le Roy Ladurie's analysis of the carnival in Romans, though praised, was evidently considered an exception. Chaunu insisted that after studying economies and societies, the time had come, using similar methods, to deal with the third level, that of civilizations; and he spoke with strong approval of Michel Vovelle's examination of Provençal testaments. Le Goff stressed that the attention to everyday man suggested by ethnology "naturally leads to the study of mentalities, considered as 'that which changes least' in historical evolution."[32] Both essays ended up supporting the validity of the Braudelian paradigm, at the same time extending the range of its applicability.

8. It is not a simple matter to evaluate the import of this "at the same time." In all institutions, innovations, while rupturing with the past, make headway by means of the reaffirmation of a certain continuity with what has gone before. In the years that followed, precisely while Braudel's work was being translated into many languages (beginning with English) and was reaching a public far beyond the world of specialists, the paradigm that for the sake of convenience I have called Braudelian was rapidly declining. After Le Roy Ladurie had proclaimed that the French historical school founded by Bloch and Febvre must accept the American challenge and convert to the computer, he published the enormously successful *Montaillou*: a piece of research conducted in craftsmanlike fashion on a medieval village, population two hundred.[33] Even Furet was dedicating himself to these themes of political history and the history of ideas that he had previously judged intrinsically resistant to serial history.[34] Questions that had been considered peripheral were cropping up at the center of the discipline, and vice versa. The pages of the *Annales* (and the journals of half the world) were beset by themes proposed by Le Goff in 1973: the family, the human body, relations between the sexes, age groups, factions, charismatics. Studies on the history of price fluctuations went into a brusque decline.[35]

In France one has spoken of *nouvelle histoire* to describe this change in the intellectual climate that coincides significantly with the end of the long period of economic development that had begun in 1945.[36] The term is debatable, but the basic characteristics of the phenomenon are clear. In the course of the 1970s and 1980s the history of mentalities to which Braudel attributed a marginal significance grew in importance, often under the name "historical anthropology."[37] The ideological "ambiguity" emphasized by Le Goff in 1974 undoubtedly contributed to this success.[38] Philippe Ariès has devoted some telling words to the subject: "The criticism of progress has passed from a reactionary right that had, moreover, abandoned it, to a left, or, rather, a leftism with poorly drawn borders, rough, but vigorous. I do indeed believe (it's a hypothesis) that there is a connection between the new reticence of the 1960s in regard to development, progress, modernity, and the passion brought by young historians to the study of preindustrial societies and their mentalities."[39]

These words were implicitly autobiographical; as a young man Ariès had been a follower of Charles Maurras and active in the ranks of Action Française. Beginning in the 1970s this "Sunday painter" (*historien du dimanche*), as Ariès ironically described himself, gradually became integrated into the group of *Annales* historians; he even was elected to the École Pratique des Hautes Études.[40] This academic event can be viewed as one of the many symptoms of a much greater transformation that was neither solely French nor academic. The frequently unconscious resumption of the themes of romantic opposition to capitalism on the part of leftist ecological currents is a component of it.[41]

The "new reticence" to which Ariès alluded could become transformed into divergent positions. It may be remembered that Furet had proposed fighting the ethnocentric abstraction of theories of modernization with a dose of ethnology.[42] Chaunu had suggested throwing overboard the ideals of modernity tied to the Enlightenment together with theories of modernization. The latter alternative—more radical than the ideological point of view—refused to bring the historian's research tools into the discussion. The former alternative was moving in this direction but stopped halfway. Retrospectively, speaking primarily from my personal experience, I think that Italian research into microhistory began from a diagnosis that agreed in part with Furet's but that arrived at a totally different prognosis.

9. The element of agreement lies in the rejection of ethnocentrism and of the teleology that for Furet characterized the historiography transmitted by the nineteenth century. The affirmation of a national entity, the advent of the

bourgeoisie, the civilizing mission of the white race, and economic development furnished to historians a unifying principle of both a conceptual and a narrative order, depending on the point of view and the scale of observation adopted. Ethnographic history conceived along serial lines proposed breaking with this tradition. Here the paths traveled by serial history and microhistory diverge—a divergence that is at once intellectual and political.

To select as a cognitive object only what is repetitive, and therefore capable of being serialized, means paying a very high price in cognitive terms. First of all, on the chronological plane, ancient history, as Furet himself observed, precludes such treatment;[43] and medieval history renders it very difficult (for many of the themes suggested by Le Goff the documentation is fragmentary). Second, on the thematic level, areas such as the history of ideas and political history (again as Furet would have it) by definition elude this type of investigation. But the most serious limitation of serial history emerges precisely through what should be its basic objective: "the equalization of individuals in their roles of economic or sociocultural agents." This idea of equalization is doubly deceiving. On the one hand, it distorts an obvious element: in any society the conditions of access to the production of documentation are tied to a situation of power and thus create an inherent imbalance. On the other hand, it cancels out many particulars in the existing documentation for the benefit of what is homogeneous and comparable. With a trace of scholarly pride, Furet affirmed: "the document, 'facts,' no longer exist for themselves, but in relationship to the series that precedes them and follows them; it is their relative value that becomes objective, and not their relationship to an ungraspable 'real' substance."[44] It is therefore not surprising if the twice-filtered data in the series become "incomprehensible" in their relation to reality.

Historical knowledge, obviously, involves the construction of documentary series. Less obvious is the attitude that the historian must assume with regard to the anomalies that crop up in the documentation.[45] Furet proposed ignoring them, observing that the *hapax* (that which is unique documentation) is not usable in the perspective of serial history. But the *hapax*, strictly speaking, does not exist. Any document, even the most anomalous, can be inserted into a series; but not only that: it can, if properly analyzed, shed light on a still-broader documentary series.

10. In the early 1960s I began to study inquisitorial trials, hoping to reconstruct, in addition to the attitudes of the judges, those of the men and women ac-

cused of witchcraft. I quickly realized that this nonethnocentric approach would require comparison with the work of anthropologists, first among whom was Claude Lévi-Strauss. But the historiographical, conceptual, and narrative implications of such a choice became clarified for me only gradually, in the course of the years that separated *I benandanti* (1966) from *Storia notturna* (1989).[46] Along the way I wrote a book in which I attempted to reconstruct the ideas and attitudes of a sixteenth-century Friulian miller who was tried and condemned to death by the Inquisition, *Il formaggio e i vermi* (1976). The rejection of ethnocentrism had brought me not to serial history but to its opposite: the minute analysis of a circumscribed documentation, tied to a person who was otherwise unknown. In the introduction I took issue with an essay by Furet in the *Annales* in which he asserted that the history of the subaltern classes in preindustrial societies can be studied only from a statistical point of view.[47]

Recently, Michel Vovelle rejected as fictitious the alternative between individual biography and serial research.[48] In principle, I agree. But in practice the choice does assert itself: it is a question of evaluating risks and advantages on a practical and, even more, on an intellectual plane. Roger Chartier wrote about *The Cheese and the Worms* that "it is on this reduced scale, *and certainly only on this scale*, that we can understand, without deterministic reduction, the relationship between systems of belief, of values and representations on one side, and social affiliations on another."[49] Even someone not disposed to accept such an uncompromising conclusion has to admit that the experiment was not only legitimate but useful, if only for analyzing the results.

By reducing the scale of observation, that for which another scholar could have been a simple footnote in a hypothetical monograph on the Protestant Reformation in the Friuli was transformed into a book. The motives that impelled me at that time to make this choice are not totally clear to me. I am suspicious of those that come to mind today (and naturally there are many) because I would not like to project into the past intentions that have been maturing over the years. Gradually I came to realize that many events and connections of which I was totally unaware influenced the decisions that I thought I had made independently—a banal fact in itself, but always surprising, because it contradicts our narcissistic fantasies. How much does my book owe (to take an obvious example) to the political climate in Italy during the early 1970s? Something, perhaps a lot; but I suspect that the motives for my choices should be searched for elsewhere.

To discover them, at least in part, I shall begin by stating what may not be totally obvious. *The Cheese and the Worms* does not restrict itself to the reconstruction of an individual event; it narrates it. Furet had rejected narrative—and, more specifically, literary narrative—as an expression, typically teleological, of the "history of events," whose time "is made up of a series of discontinuities described in the mode of the continuous: the classic subject matter of the narrative [*récit*]."[50] Against this type of "literary" narration Furet contrasted the examination of serial ethnographic history, problem by problem. He thus appropriated that widely accepted commonplace that still today tacitly identifies a specific form of narration, based on late-nineteenth-century realist novels, with historical narrative *tout court*.[51] Granted, the figure of the omniscient historian-narrator, who unravels the slightest details of an event or the hidden motivations that inspire the behavior of individuals, social groups, or states, has gradually established itself. But it is only one of the many possibilities, as the readers of Marcel Proust, Virginia Woolf, and Robert Musil should well know.[52]

Before beginning *The Cheese and the Worms* I had at length mulled over the relationship between research hypotheses and narrative strategies. Reading Queneau's *Exercices de style* had powerfully whetted my desire to experiment.[53] I had set out to reconstruct the intellectual, moral, and fantastic world of the miller Menocchio on the basis of sources produced by persons who had sent him to the stake. This in some way paradoxical project *could* evolve into an account that transforms the gaps in the documentation into a smooth surface.[54] It could, but it seemed to me it should not, for reasons that were of a cognitive, ethical, and aesthetic order. The obstacles interfering with the research were integral elements in the documentation and thus had to become part of the account; the same for the hesitations and silences of the protagonist in the face of his persecutors' questions—or mine.[55] Thus the hypotheses, the doubts, the uncertainties became part of the narration; the search for truth became part of the exposition of the necessarily incomplete truth attained. Could the result still be defined as "narrative history"? For a reader with the slightest familiarity with twentieth-century fiction, the reply is obviously yes.

11. But the impetus toward this type of narration (and more generally toward occupying myself with history) came to me from further off: from *War and Peace*, from Tolstoy's conviction that a historical phenomenon can become

comprehensible only by reconstructing the activities of *all* the persons who participated in it.[56] This notion, and the sentiments that had spawned it (populism, fierce disdain for the vacuous and conventional history of historians), left an indelible impression on me from the moment I first read it. The *Cheese and the Worms*, the story of a miller whose death is decreed from afar, by a man (a pope) who one minute earlier had never heard his name, can be considered a small, distorted product of Tolstoy's grand and intrinsically unrealizable project: the reconstruction of the numerous associations linking Napoleon's head cold before the battle of Borodino, the disposition of the troops, and the lives of all the participants in the battle, down to the most humble soldier.

In Tolstoy's novel the private world (peace) and the public world (war) now run along parallel lines, now intersect; Prince André participates in the battle of Austerlitz, Pierre at Borodino. Thus Tolstoy proceeds along a path that had been opened up to him splendidly by Stendhal in his description of the battle of Waterloo seen through the eyes of Fabrizio del Dongo.[57] The romanticized personages were bringing to light the painful inadequacy with which historians had dealt with a historical event *par excellence* (or presumed such). It was a formidable intellectual challenge that seemed to pertain to a past now vanished, just as are *l'histoire-bataille* and the polemic against it.[58] But reflecting on the battle as a historiographical theme can still be useful. From it emerges indirectly a fundamental problem in the historian's trade.

12. In *The Battle between Alexander and Darius at the River Issus*, the artist Albrecht Altdorfer, to represent the battle, selected a towering and distant vantage point, like that of an eagle in flight. As if with the bird's keen sight he painted the light resplendent on armor, trappings, and harnesses, the banners' brilliant colors and white plumes swaying on warriors' helmets, the hordes of knights with their lances raised, resembling an immense porcupine, and then, gradually receding toward the background, the mountains behind the battlefield, the encampments, the waters and mists, the horizon arching to suggest the shape of the terrestrial sphere, the immense sky in which burn the setting sun and waxing moon. No human eye will ever succeed in catching at once, as did Altdorfer, the historical specificity (real or presumed) of a battle and its cosmic irrelevance (figure 10).[59]

A battle, strictly speaking, is invisible, as we have been reminded (and not only thanks to military censorship) by the images televised during the first Gulf War. Only an abstract diagram or a visionary imagination such as

FIGURE 10. Albrecht Altdorfer, *The Battle between Alexander and Darius at the River Issus* (Munich, Alte Pinakothek, 1929).

Altdorfer's can convey a global image of it. It seems proper to extend this conclusion to any event and with greater reason to whatever historical process. A close-up look permits us to grasp what eludes a comprehensive viewing, and vice versa.

This contradiction is at the heart of a chapter ("The Structure of the Historical Universe") in Siegfried Kracauer's final book, published posthumously with a foreword by Paul Oskar Kristeller: *History: The Last Things before the Last.* Although avowing himself to be more optimistic on this point than his friend Kracauer, Kristeller had to admit that "the discrepancy between general and special history, *or as he calls it,* macro and micro history, represents a serious dilemma."[60] Queneau's *Les fleurs bleues* dates from 1967; Kracauer's death, from a year before. We probably find ourselves in this instance facing an independent invention. But what is important is not the term *microhistory;* it is the significance that it gradually comes to assume in Kracauer's mind.

At first for Kracauer, *"microhistory"* seems to be synonymous with *monographic research.* But the comparison between "microhistory" and cinematographic close-up (an obvious thing for the author of *From Caligari to Hitler* and *Theory of Film*) introduces new elements. Kracauer observes that some research of a specific character, such as Hubert Jedin's on the Councils of Constance and Basel, is capable of modifying the comprehensive visions delineated by macrohistory. Are we compelled to conclude, then, with Aby Warburg, that "God is in the detail"? It is the thesis sustained by "two great historians," the Tolstoy of *War and Peace* and Sir Lewis Namier (the pairing suggested by Kracauer is significant). But despite Kracauer's sympathy for these positions, he recognizes that certain phenomena can be grasped only by means of a macroscopic perspective. This suggests that the reconciliation between macro- and microhistory is not at all taken for granted (as Toynbee wrongly believed). And yet it needs to be pursued. According to Kracauer, Marc Bloch offered the best solution in his *Feudal Society:* a constant back-and-forth between micro- and macrohistory, between close-ups and extreme long shots, so as to continually thrust back into discussion the comprehensive vision of the historical process through apparent exceptions and cases of brief duration. This methodological prescription led to an affirmation of a decisively ontological nature: reality is fundamentally discontinuous and heterogeneous. Consequently, no conclusion attained apropos a determinate sphere can be transferred automatically to a more general sphere (what Kracauer calls the "law of levels").[61]

These posthumous pages of Kracauer's, who was not a professional historian, still constitute today, in my opinion, the best introduction to microhistory. As far as I know, they have had no influence on the emergence of this
historiographical current.[62] Certainly not on me, since I learned about them
with deplorable delay only a few years ago. But when I read them they seemed
strangely familiar for two reasons. First, an indirect echo of them had reached
me long before by way of my decisive encounter with *Minima moralia*, the
masterpiece in which Theodor Adorno, despite his belief in the idea of totality, and one he never renounced, implicitly demonstrated his own indebtedness to the micrological tradition inaugurated by Georg Simmel, a tradition
carried on by Adorno's friend (and, in a sense, master) Siegfried Kracauer.[63]
Second, the latter's ideas on history, beginning with the crucial one of the
discontinuity of reality, are an explicit and conscious development of key
phenomena in the culture of this century, from Proust to the cinema. The
fact that certain ideas are in the air signifies, after all, that even when starting from the same premises, it is possible to arrive at similar conclusions
independently.

13. It is often difficult to demonstrate the existence of intellectual convergence and, at the same time, the lack of direct contact. So, if I am not mistaken,
the interest (going well beyond the relevance of the object) in the intellectual
genealogy that I have attempted to reconstruct thus far is in part true, in
part fictional; in part conscious, and in part unconscious. Looking at things
from a distance, I realize that the researches of our original Einaudi *"microstorie* group" were a fragment of a more general tendency, the parameters of
which almost totally escaped me at the time. It may not be pure chance that
the word *microhistory* was used first in the title of a work that, in almost ma-
niacal detail, describes a battle (although the conclusion of Stewart's book on
Gettysburg seems to evoke Conrad rather than Tolstoy). Even less casual is the
fact that some years later, undoubtedly independently, Kracauer identified
microhistory with Tolstoy; I read this, I must confess, with pleasure mingled
with some disappointment (my approach had not been so unusual after all).

I am aware of a difficulty. Tolstoy's extraordinary capacity to communicate to the reader the physical, palpable certainty of reality seems incompatible with the wholly twentieth-century idea that I have placed at the core of
microhistory—namely, that the obstacles interfering with research in the
form of lacunae or misrepresentations in the sources must become part of

the account. In *War and Peace* just the opposite happens. Everything that precedes the act of narration (from personal reminiscences to the memorials of the Napoleonic age) is assimilated and fused to permit the reader to enter into a relationship of special intimacy with the characters and participate directly in their lives.[64] Tolstoy leaps over the inevitable gap between the fragmentary and distorted traces of an event (a battle, for instance) and the event itself. But this leap, this direct contact with reality, can take place only on the terrain of invention. It is precluded by definition from the historian, who has at his disposal only fragments of things and documents. The historiographical frescoes that seek to communicate to the reader, through frequently mediocre expedients, the illusion of a vanished reality tacitly remove this constituent limitation of the historical vocation. Microhistory chooses the opposite approach. It accepts the limitations while exploring their gnoseological implications and transforming them into a narrative element.

This approach had been anticipated in some respects by the Italian critic Renato Serra, in a brief but important essay written in 1912 and published posthumously: "Partenza di un gruppo di soldati per la Libia."[65] In a letter to Benedetto Croce, Serra explained that he had started from Tolstoy's ideas on history as expressed in *War and Peace*.[66] In an article later included in the volume *History: Its Theory and Practice*, Croce had repudiated Tolstoy's position, calling it absurd and skeptical: "we know at every moment all the history that we need to know"; consequently, the history that we do not know is identical to "the eternal phantom of the 'thing itself.'"[67] Serra, in calling himself "a slave to the thing itself," confessed to Croce that he felt much closer to Tolstoy, "only that," he added, "my difficulties are, or seem to be, more complex."[68]

In effect, "Partenza" harks back to ideas of Tolstoy (without naming him) but takes them in a completely different direction. Gruff letters from soldiers to their families, newspaper articles written for the pleasure of a distant public, accounts of military actions hurriedly scribbled by a harried captain, the reworking by historians full of superstitious veneration for each of these documents—all these narratives, independently of their more or less direct character, have (Serra explains) a highly problematic relationship with reality. In phrases that become little by little more hurried and almost feverish, Serra registers the rhythm of a thought that revolves around the unresolved contradiction between the certainty of the existence of the "thing itself" and distrust in the possibility of encompassing it by means of the evidence:

There are people who imagine in good faith that a document can be the expression of reality.... As if a document could express something different *from itself*.... A document is a fact. The battle is another fact (an infinity of other facts). The two cannot make *one*.... The man who acts is *a fact*. And the man who narrates is *another fact*.... Every piece of evidence provides testimony only of itself; of its proper moment, of its proper origin, of its proper end, and of nothing else.... All the critical judgments to which we subject history involve the concept of true history, of absolute reality. It is necessary to face up to the question of memory; not insofar as it is forgetfulness, but insofar as it is *memory*. Existence of things in themselves.[69]

14. I read Serra's work only at the beginning of the 1980s. But the gist of it had reached me more than two decades earlier through Arsenio Frugoni's teaching in Pisa. In his book *Arnaldo da Brescia nelle fonti del secolo XII* (1954) he had shown how the specific perspective of each narrative source contributes to present the same personage in an alternating, different light.[70] Today I feel that Frugoni's sarcasm over the naive efforts by positivist erudites to make the pieces fit together had as its point of departure Serra's antipositivist polemic ("Every piece of evidence provides testimony only of itself; of its proper moment, of its proper origin, of its proper end, and of nothing else"), which it sought to surpass in its skeptical implications.

I am not certain that Frugoni knew Serra's "Partenza di un gruppo di soldati per la Libia." But that it had been read or reread recently by Italo Calvino seems obvious from his "Memories of a Battle" ("Ricordo di una battaglia") (1974), a writing of a completely different kind.[71] "It is necessary to face up to the question of memory," Serra had written. Calvino takes up the question, even if his battle is an episode of partisan warfare that he is recalling at a distance of almost thirty years. At first everything seems clear to him, easily within reach: "It is not true that I no longer remember anything, my memories are still there, hidden in the gray matter of the brain." But the negative statement "It is not true" shows that he is already assailed by doubt, that recollections crumble as memory brings them to light: "And my fear now is that as soon as some remembrance forms, it will immediately appear in a faulty light, contrived, sentimental, as war and youth always are, and become a segment in the story with the style of that time, which cannot tell us how things really were but only how we thought we saw them and said them." Can memory abolish the mediation of the illusions and distortions of the self of a bygone time in order to attain "things" ("the things themselves")? The conclusion echoes, with a bitter ironic twist, the false confidence of the beginning: "Everything that I have written thus far serves to make me understand that I remember almost nothing of that morning."

The closing words of "Memories of a Battle" ("The sense of everything that appears and disappears") insist on the precariousness of our relationship with the past. And yet that "almost nothing" suggests that the past, in spite of everything, is not unattainable. This conclusion is important subjectively for me, having learned much from Calvino, but also objectively, since it explodes the current image of him (of the later Calvino) as a postmodernist writer. The laborious and painful autobiographical reflection that emerges from "Memories of a Battle" provides a different image than the one now in fashion of the euphoric skeptic.

15. In a recent essay, F. R. Ankersmit, a Dutch student of historiographical theory, argued that the tendency to focus attention on scraps rather than on larger entities is the most typical expression of "postmodernist historiography."[72] To elucidate this point Ankersmit used a vegetal metaphor (one that actually goes back to Lewis Namier, and perhaps to Tolstoy).[73] In the past historians were preoccupied with the trunk of a tree or its branches; their postmodernist successors busy themselves only with the leaves—namely, with minute fragments of the past that they investigate in an isolated manner, independently of the more or less larger context (branches, trunk) of which they were a part. Ankersmit, who accepts the skeptical notions formulated by Hayden White in the early 1970s, looks with great favor on this shift toward the fragmentary. In his opinion it expresses an antiessentialist or antifoundationalist attitude that brings to light (Ankersmit is not frightened by formal contradictions) the "fundamentally postmodernist nature" of historiography: activity of an artistic type that produces narratives incommensurable among themselves. The ambition to know the past has waned: the significance of the fragments is sought in the present, the way "in which their pattern can be adapted to other forms of civilization existing today." As examples of this historiographical tendency Ankersmit cites two French books (Emmanuel Le Roy Ladurie's *Montaillou* and Georges Duby's *Sunday of Bouvines*), an American work (Natalie Zemon Davis's *The Return of Martin Guerre*), and a nonexistent book (*Microhistories*, by the undersigned).

In the past decade Giovanni Levi and I have unceasingly argued against the relativist positions, including the one warmly espoused by Ankersmit, that reduce historiography to a textual dimension, depriving it of any cognitive value.[74] There is no contradiction between this polemic and the debt I have acknowledged in these pages toward Calvino and more generally toward the nineteenth- and twentieth-century novel. The experimental attitude that brought together, at the end of the 1970s, the group of Italian students of microhistory ("a history with additives," as Franco Venturi ironically dubbed it) was based on a definite awareness that all the phases through which research unfolds are *constructed* and not *given*: the identification of the object and its importance; the elaboration of the categories through which it is analyzed; the criteria of proof; the stylistic and narrative forms by which the results are transmitted to the reader. But this accentuation of the constructive moment inherent in the research was combined with an explicit rejection of the skeptical implications (postmodernist, if you will) so largely present in European and American historiography of the 1980s and 1990s. In my opinion the distinctive quality of Italian microhistory must be looked for in this cognitive wager.[75] I should like to add that my own work during these years, even if in large part absorbed by a book decisively macrohistoric in approach (*Ecstasies*), proceeded, at least in my intentions, along this twofold track.

16. Piero della Francesca, Galileo, a community of nineteenth-century Piedmontese weavers, a Ligurian valley in the sixteenth century: these examples selected at random show that Italian research in microhistory has looked at subjects of acknowledged importance as well as themes that had been previously ignored or relegated to spheres considered inferior, such as local history.[76] What all these investigations have in common programmatically is the insistence on context—exactly the opposite of the isolated contemplation of the fragmentary advocated by Ankersmit. But although the choice of Galileo does not require any prior justification, we have to ask ourselves: why precisely that community, why precisely that valley? In these cases, the reference, explicit or implicit, to a comparative dimension is inevitable. Franco Ramella (*Terra e telai*, 1984) and Osvaldo Raggio (*Faide e parentele*, 1990) have shown us that the in-depth study of the Val di Mosso and of the Fontanabuona compel us to look differently at such problems as protoindustry and the birth of the modern state. But to recognize the richness of the results is still not enough. An object, as we saw, may be chosen because it is typical (González y González) or because it is repetitive and therefore capable of being serialized (Braudel, apropos the *fait divers*). Italian microhistory has confronted the question of comparison with a different and, in a certain sense, opposite approach:

through the anomalous, not the analogous. First of all, it hypothesizes the more improbable sort of documentation as being potentially richer: the "exceptional normal" of Edoardo Grendi's justly famous quip.[77] Second, it demonstrates, as was done, for example, by Giovanni Levi (*L'eredità immateriale*) and by Simona Cerutti (*La Ville et les métiers*), that any social structure is the result of interaction and of numerous individual strategies, a fabric that can be reconstituted only from close observation.[78] Significantly, the relationship between this microscopic dimension and the larger contextual dimension became in both cases, though so diverse, the organizing principle in the narration.[79] As Kracauer had already foreseen, results obtained in a microscopic sphere cannot be automatically transferred to a macroscopic sphere (and vice versa). This heterogeneity—we are just beginning to perceive the implications—constitutes both the greatest difficulty and the greatest potential benefit of microhistory.[80]

17. Giovanni Levi, speaking recently of microhistory, concluded: "this is a self-portrait, not a group portrait."[81] I had proposed doing the same, but did not succeed. Both the boundaries of the group to which I belonged and my own boundaries of self seemed retrospectively shifting and uncertain. To my surprise I discovered how important to me, unknowingly, were books I had never read, events and persons I did not know existed. If this is a self-portrait, then its model are the paintings of Umberto Boccioni in which the street enters into the house, the landscape into the face, the exterior invades the interior, the I is porous.

POSTSCRIPTUM

Domenico Scarpa, whom I thank with pleasure, brought to my attention that the word *microhistory* appears in writings by Andrea Zanzotto that date back to the 1960s, specifically:

1. In a passage of *Retorica su: lo sbandamento, il principio "resistenza"* (VI), published in the collection *La beltà* (1968), containing poems written between 1961 and 1967 ("most from the last four years": see *Le poesie e prose scelte*, ed. Stefano Dal Bianco and Gian Mario Villalta [Milan: Mondadori, 1999], p. 309).

2. In the "Author's notes" (p. 352) Zanzotto writes: "And this is a way of entering in the *templum-tempus* of a history that finally is 'true,'

which nevertheless, from a certain perspective, can appear outside maximum time, in the shadow of the possible evanescence of the idea of history itself, current today. In this shadowy realm everything tends to flatten out into microhistory (a tale). The *templum-tempus* is a term from Heidegger, here used freely."

3. "Microhistory" makes an appearance with a similar meaning in Zanzotto's, "Alcune prospettive sulla poesia oggi," *L'approdo Letterario* 35 (1966): 1137: "Science and technology have created an obstruction, a congestion of 'revelations' (invention and discovery), enough to justify in large part the appellation of apocalyptic given to our age. The final unmasking, the demystifying-demythologizing have finally turned themselves particularly against that which just yesterday understood as 'macrohistory' (oriented by transcendence or by dialectic), has transfigured itself into 'microhistory' fading into ahistoricity."

In these passages, as we see, Zanzotto used the word *microhistory* in a very different sense from that which Italian historians would give to it subsequently. But Scarpa notes that as far back as 1962, in his critical review of the anthology *I novissimi*, Zanzotto contraposed to Sanguinetti's "archhistory" a history that "actually tended to take the form of tales, *nugae*, dynamics (*moto*) of depressed areas" (*Le poesie e prose scelte*, p. 1110). I wonder if Zanzotto, who obviously for quite some time had been contemplating the idea of the transformation of greater history into fables, might not have obtained the word *microhistory* from Queneau (*Les fleurs bleues*, 1965), a hypothesis that cannot be verified at the moment, as Gian Mario Villalta kindly informs me.

CHAPTER 15

Witches and Shamans

The path which brought me metaphorically from northeastern Italy, where my research on witchcraft began, to the Central Asian steppes is a tortuous one. I shall try to trace the journey.

The great French sinologist Marcel Granet once said that "la méthode, c'est le chemin après qu'on l'a parcouru": method is the path after one has already taken it.[1] The word *method* actually comes from the Greek, even if the etymology proposed by Granet—*meta-hodos*, "after the path"—may be imaginary. But Granet's quip had a serious—in fact, polemical—side to it: in any scholarly situation a discussion on method has some value only when it is an a posteriori reflection on concrete research, not when it shows up (by far the most frequent case) as a series of a priori prescriptions. Perhaps the following account of the way in which my research began and subsequently developed may offer some confirmation, however slight and negligible, of Granet's ironic remark.

To recount the itinerary of a piece of research when it has already reached a conclusion (even if, by definition, a provisional conclusion) always brings a risk with it: a teleological one. Retrospectively, the uncertainties and errors vanish, or, rather, they become transformed into the steps which lead directly to the goal: the historian knows from the start what he wants, he searches for it, and finally finds it. But things do not happen like this in actual research. Life in any laboratory as described by Bruno Latour, a historian of science with an anthropological background, is much more confusing and untidy.[2]

1. The experience that I am about to describe is itself fairly confused and untidy, though it pertains not to a group but to an individual—myself. It begins with an illumination, a research topic (witchcraft) which suddenly suggests itself to a student in his twenties at the University of Pisa toward the end of the 1950s. Until that very moment I was not at all certain that I wanted to become a historian, but as soon as the subject presented itself I no longer had any doubts. This was *my* topic, the topic I would be willing to work on for years (little did I imagine how many).

I have asked myself often about the reasons for this unexpected enthusiasm, which, to me, retrospectively, seems to have all the characteristics of falling in love: the suddenness, the enthusiasm, the lack of awareness (at least initially). I knew nothing about the history of witchcraft: my first move, later repeated many times for other research projects, was to look up the entry on *witchcraft* in the *Enciclopedia italiana* to obtain a bit of basic information. It may have been the first time I really experienced what I would call "the euphoria of ignorance": the sensation of not knowing anything but being on the verge of beginning to learn something. I think that the intense pleasure associated with that moment helped to keep me from becoming a specialist, of delving into a well-defined or limited field of study. Not only have I preserved the urge to confront periodically themes and areas of research of which I am totally ignorant, but it has grown more marked with the passing of time.

It happens often enough that a second-year university student chooses a research topic of which he is totally ignorant. But it is perhaps less common to note that a similar disparity between little or no preliminary knowledge and the importance of the objective probably characterizes all or almost all the truly important choices that a person makes in the course of a lifetime. (Retrospectively we call this disparity destiny). But what is it then that drives us to choose? At the time, behind my enthusiasm for the research theme that had suddenly loomed before my eyes, I think I can guess now that there lurked a congeries of childhood memories and experiences confusedly muddled with much more recent anxieties and prejudices.

How greatly was my choice influenced by the fairy tales that were recounted to me as a child? My mother used to read to me fables that had been collected at the end of the nineteenth century by the Sicilian writer Luigi Capuana. They were filled with every imaginable sort of magic and horror: she-dragons whose mouths were bloodied from the flesh of "lambs and kids who looked like children"; tiny beings innocent in appearance, bedecked in plumed turbans, who, after the page was turned, became transformed into monstrous werewolves with cavernous jaws. Crocetta, a young girl of the village in the Abruzzi where my parents lived for three years, used to tell my brother and me (as I discovered in something my mother, Natalia Ginzburg, had written in her *Inverno in Abruzzo*) stories not very different from those collected by Capuana. In one of them a boy is killed by his stepmother and given to his father to eat: at which point his bones, stripped of flesh, begin to sing: "And my dismal stepmother / Has cooked me in a kettle / While my gluttonous father / Has made a nice mouthful out of me."[3] Through the sinister ambiguities of such tales I, like all children, must have begun to decipher reality, beginning with the mysterious world of adults.

Cannibalism and animal metamorphoses are at the heart of *Storia notturna*.[4] The decision to study witchcraft immediately signified for me concentrating on the revelations of witches, in many respects so similar to the fables I heard in my early childhood. But the underlying motives for that choice, barely discerned at the time, were joined by others of an emotional and ideological order. I was born into a family that politically leaned to the left. My father, Leone Ginzburg, born in Odessa, who emigrated to Italy with his family, lost his position in the Department of Russian Literature at the University of Turin in 1934 because of his refusal to swear an oath of loyalty to the Fascist regime imposed on all academics. He was twenty-five at the time. Not long after that he was arrested for anti-Fascist activities and passed two years in prison. When Italy entered the war in 1940 as Germany's ally, as a Jew and as an anti-Fascist he was interned at Pizzoli, a village in the Abruzzi near L'Aquila, where he was joined by his family. At the fall of the Fascist regime he went to Rome, where he resumed his political activities. Arrested and recognized by the Nazis, he died in 1944 in the wing of the prison Regina Coeli which was under German control. In his book *Il populismo russo* Franco Venturi, the Turin historian, spoke of the writings and person of my father, whom he had known and been close to in the circles of anti-Fascist émigrés in Paris, as "a new and original incarnation" of the spirit of the *narodniki*.[5] At the heart of the Russian populist experience one finds a strong moral and intellectual affinity for the values expressed by peasant society. I discovered a similar perspective in a book which was published after the war and then promptly translated into several languages, *Cristo si è fermato a Eboli (Christ Stopped at Eboli)*. The author—the writer, physician, and painter Carlo Levi, had been a friend of my father's, and had participated with him

in the anti-Fascist activities of the group Giustizia e Libertà. He, too, was
condemned by the regime to internal exile in a small village in Lucania.[6]
Undoubtedly, these affinities contributed to the profound impact that *Christ
Stopped at Eboli* had on me when I read it as an adolescent. A feeling of identification was inevitable, even if the village described by Levi was much more
isolated and primitive than the one where I had passed a part of my early
childhood. But I was struck by more than the circumstances of the writing of
the book. Levi never conceals the differences between himself and the peasants of southern Italy, from their ideas and beliefs; but he never assumes a tone
of superiority toward them. He takes everything seriously, including their
charms and magic rituals. From *Christ Stopped at Eboli* I think I learned that
intellectual detachment and emotional participation, passion for rationality
and respect for cultural diversity, are not only compatible attitudes but also
capable of sustaining one another. From my mother I learned something
even more important (not limited to my research)—namely, that there is no
relation between intelligence and social and cultural position.

Looking back, I think that both the lasting impression made by the fables
I listened to in my childhood and the populism I imbibed from my family
milieu contributed to my research becoming oriented from the outset toward the study of the victims of persecution rather than to the persecution
itself. Historiographically it was an anomalous choice in two ways. At the
end of the 1950s, witchcraft, which had long before entered the canon of anthropological study, was still considered by the majority of historians (as the
Englishman Keith Thomas observed with some irony) a marginal and bizarre area of research.[7] At most, one admitted the legitimacy of studying the
persecution of witchcraft as an aberrant episode in the intellectual history of
late medieval and early modern Europe. During the 1970s and '80s this actually became a fashionable historiographical current: but the interest of historians, even though much more complex than in the past, has continued to
focus almost exclusively on the persecution and its cultural and social mech-
anisms. The victims almost always have remained in the shadows.[8]

These are some of the motives that impelled me in this direction. At this
point, I should add another: the difficulty of research of this type. Some of
the most serious obstacles emerged along the way: at the time I noticed one
especially—the apparently similar forms assumed by the practice of witchcraft
(not by its persecution) in ages and places far removed from one another. I
thought that it would be necessary, in order to reintroduce witchcraft into

history, to historicize its apparently atemporal features. Obviously there was an inevitable trace of youthful arrogance in this willingness to confront a cognitive challenge: the desire to prove to others, and especially to oneself, what we are capable of, on the threshold of the shadowy edge discussed by Conrad.

I have left for last an element which struck me many years later, when a friend brought to my attention that the choice to study witchcraft, and especially the victims of the persecution of witchcraft, was not so strange after all for a Jew who had experienced persecution himself.[9] I was dumbfounded by this simple remark. How could such an obvious fact have eluded me? And yet for years the analogy between Jew and witch, and the resulting possibility that I could have identified myself with the subject of my research, had never dawned on me. Today I am inclined to view in this the effect of repression. What is at once both evident and hidden, Freud taught us, is that which we do not want to behold.

2. Although I have gone on at some length in discussing these personal circumstances, I should like to resist the narcissistic temptation which is in all of us and look at them as the data of an experiment in vitro. It is or should be obvious that the biography of a historian—from family circumstances to education and, of course, friendships—is not irrelevant to an understanding of his or her work. But usually one does not go beyond the mere stating of this fact. I should like to take advantage of what, conventionally, we call *identity*, in a sense that is both biological and personal (even if a term like *contiguity* would be preferable), between the person I am now and the person I was then to examine retrospectively the role these elements played in my actual research. Those I have mentioned thus far contributed to the selection of a theme (witchcraft) from a particular vantage point (the victims of persecution). But none of these factors, from the most subconscious (my being a Jew) to the most conscious (the desire to cross over disciplines), implied a specific research hypothesis. The idea with which I began—namely, that witchcraft in some cases could have been a rough and elementary form of class struggle—today simply seems like an attempt to justify, to myself and to others, research lacking true historiographical legitimacy. My willingness to transgress disciplines, in other words, was not boundless.

Behind my hypothesis was an encounter with essays by Eric Hobsbawm, those collected in his *Primitive Rebels* (1959), but especially a survey of studies entitled "Per la storia delle classi subalterne" ("For the History of the Subaltern Classes"), which he published in 1960 in *Società*, the ideological journal of the Italian Communist Party. The title of the survey echoed a term used by Antonio Gramsci in his *Prison Notebooks*. For me, as for so many other Italian students of my generation, reading Gramsci had been a decisive event. But the Gramsci that Hobsbawm proposed was a Gramsci read and interpreted through the prism of British social anthropology.[10] The works of anthropology into which I delved in those years were actually others: first of all there was Lévi-Strauss, who thirty years later was to serve as the principal interlocutor of my *Storia notturna*.

I began by reading the inquisitorial trials housed in the Archivio di Stato in Modena. Among those documents I came upon a 1519 trial against a peasant woman, Chiara Signorini, accused of having tried to murder, through magic, her mistress, a woman who had chased her and her husband away from the piece of land which they worked.[11] "Historians usually find what they are looking for, a fact that makes me uneasy," wrote Morton Smith, the American student of Judaism and Christian origins.[12] I am not certain whether I, too, may have experienced some embarrassment in the face of the unexpected confirmation of my hypothesis that witchcraft was a basic instrument of class warfare, but, in any case, my research promptly took another direction.

Early on, by the time of the conclusion to the essay I wrote on that trial, I emphasized that it might be possible to discern in inquisitorial documents not only the overlay in the text that could be attributed to the judges, but also (and this was much more unexpected) the voices of the accused, expressions of a starkly different culture.[13] The struggle and conflict remained central, but they were transferred to a cultural plane, capable of being deciphered by a close reading of the texts. The writings of some of the Romance philologists—Erich Auerbach, Leo Spitzer, Gianfranco Contini—encouraged me to proceed in this direction. I tried to learn from them the art of "slow reading" (this, as Roman Jakobson has reminded us, is philology),[14] applying it to nonliterary texts.

I say all this with the wisdom of hindsight: I do not want to project into the past a clarity that I certainly lacked then. In 1961–1962 I went about Italy on the trail of inquisitorial archives. There were moments of doubt and disappointment when I thought I was wasting time. My initial hypothesis of perceiving witchcraft as an elementary form of class struggle no longer pleased me, but I could not seem to replace it with a more satisfactory one. I came to

Venice, to the State Archives which house one of Italy's richest inquisitorial collections: more than one hundred and fifty large bundles *(buste)* of more than three thousand trials, which span over two and a half centuries from the mid-sixteenth to the end of the eighteenth, at which time the Inquisition was suppressed in Venice. Each day scholars request a limited number of bundles: at the time I believe the limit was three. Since I did not know, literally, what I was searching for, I put in my request at random—for example, bundles no. 8, 15, and 37—and then I began to leaf through the trial records. I had the feeling I was playing a sort of Venetian roulette. These trivial details underline the total unpredictability of my discovery: the proceedings in 1591 against a young drover of Latisana, a small village not too far from Venice. The herdsman, named Menichino della Nota, recounted to the inquisitor that four times yearly he went out at night in spirit, together with some others who, like him, had been born with the caul and were called *benandanti* (at the time a completely new and incomprehensible word to me), to fight against warlocks in a vast field of roses, the field of Josaphat. If the *benandanti* prevailed, the harvest would be abundant; if the warlocks conquered, there would be famine.

I remember vividly that after reading the document, of not more than three or four pages, I became so agitated that I had to interrupt my work. While I strolled up and down outside the archive smoking one cigarette after another it struck me that I had had a wonderful stroke of luck. I still think so, but today this observation seems insufficient. A totally unexpected document had been laid before me by pure chance: why, I ask myself, did I react with such excitement? It is as though I had *recognized* instantly a text that had been totally unknown to me until a moment before—not only that, but one that was completely unlike any other trial of the Inquisition that I had ever seen. And this is precisely the point.

As a student I had the good fortune of taking a seminar with Gianfranco Contini. At one point, he began telling us an anecdote. There were two Romance philologists, both French, but otherwise very dissimilar. The first had a long beard and a passion for morphological, grammatical, and syntactical irregularities; when he encountered one he would stroke his beard and murmur with pleasure: "*C'est bizarre*." The second philologist, a true representative of the Cartesian tradition, with a highly lucid mind and totally bald, tried in every way possible to lead every linguistic phenomenon back to a rule: and when he succeeded he rubbed his hands, saying "*C'est satisfaisant pour l'esprit.*" I am willing to admit that the conflict between anomaly and analogy embodied in Contini's two philologists (a contest that began more than two thousand years ago with the grammarians of the Alexandrine age) is a conflict in name only. In truth, they are complementary positions. And yet I have to confess that my impulse is to identify with the bearded philologist, the one who loved anomalies: this is due to a psychological inclination which, however, I would consider justifying even on rational terms. The violation of the norm contains even the norm itself, inasmuch as it is presupposed; the opposite is not true. Anyone who studies the functioning of a society beginning from the entirety of its norms, or from statistical fictions such as the average man or the average woman, inevitably remains on the surface of things. I think that the in-depth analysis of an anomalous case is much more fruitful, though the contemplation of an isolated oddity does not usually interest me.

This is the course that I ended up pursuing with witchcraft. I started from an anomalous document (the questioning of the *benandante* Menichino della Nota) and ended up reconstructing an anomalous and geographically peripheral phenomenon (the beliefs of the Friulian *benandanti*). This, in turn, provided the key to decipher the origins of the witches' Sabbath on a huge scale—the whole of Eurasia.[15] *Storia notturna,* just like *I benandanti* twenty years earlier, literally originated from these three pages found by chance so many years ago in the Archivio di Stato in Venice. What was it that induced me, I asked myself, to react so strongly to a totally unexpected document? I think I can answer: the same sort of reasoning that might have persuaded someone else to consider the same document as largely irrelevant, if not actually to push it aside altogether. Today, and even more so thirty years ago, the account of an ecstatic experience offered by a sixteenth-century herdsman in fairy-tale and absolutely exceptional terms most likely would be treated by a serious historian as colorful evidence of the ignorance of people who obstinately ignored the instruction imparted by ecclesiastical authorities.[16]

The chance which brought me to the inquisitorial dossier of the *benandante* Menichino della Nota might never have occurred. And yet at times it crossed my mind that the document was there waiting for me, and that my entire past life had predisposed me to find it. I believe there is a nucleus of truth in all this absurd fantasizing. Knowing, as Plato wrote, is always an act of *recognizing.* It is only that which we already know, that which is already part of our myriad experiences, that permits us to apprehend what is new, isolating it from the mass of miscellaneous and casual pieces of information that continually plummet down on us.

3. In the witchcraft trials celebrated in Europe over two and a half centuries, from the beginning of the fifteenth to the middle of the seventeenth century and beyond, we behold in almost every instance communication—coerced, propped up by psychological influences and the menace of torture—which moves unilaterally. The judges, whether lay or ecclesiastical, knew what they could expect from the accused, and they pressed for it by suggestive questioning or by force. They did not always obtain what they wanted: occasionally, the defendants persisted in proclaiming their innocence, or succumbed to the torture. To be sure, not everything that was confessed resulted from the pressure exerted by the judges: the descriptions of charms and magic intended to achieve some illicit end clearly emanated from the different culture of the defendants. But in the case of the Sabbath—that nocturnal gathering filled with orgies, banquets, and the paying of homage to the devil—the men and women accused of witchcraft seem to be only reproducing, with just a few variations, a scheme developed by demonologists and then imposed during the persecution of witchcraft in most of Europe and eventually the Americas.

The picture that emerges from the *benandanti* trials is entirely different. These proceedings are dominated (especially the earlier ones) by a total failure to communicate between judges and defendants. The *benandanti* spoke, often without even being asked, of the battles for fertility which they fought at night, in spirit, armed with stalks of fennel, against witches and warlocks armed with canes of sorghum. For the inquisitors this was all incomprehensible; the very term *benandante* was new to them, and for over fifty years they kept asking what it meant. It is this inability to communicate that brought to the surface a deep and hidden stratum of beliefs: an ecstatic cult hinging on fertility, which was still very much alive in the sixteenth and seventeenth centuries among the peasants in a northeasterly region like the Friuli, then under Venetian domination.

After an initial bafflement, the inquisitors tried to orient themselves. Since the tales of the nocturnal fertility battles made them think of the Sabbath, they tried to coax the *benandanti*, without recourse to torture, to admit they were warlocks. The *benandanti* at first protested vigorously in the face of this pressure: but gradually they gave in. In their revelations, given over a fifty-year span, we see bit by bit the image of the witches' Sabbath insinuate itself. This mutation, which we can trace step-by-step, as if in slow motion, made me wonder if a similar phenomenon—namely, the imposition of the image of the sabbat on a stratum of beliefs extraneous to it—could be verified elsewhere.

But this hypothesis, which I attempted to verify in *Storia notturna*, still does not tell us anything about the ecstatic experiences recounted by the *benandanti* with such an abundance of colorful details. Unlike the inquisitors, I was not in a position to influence their accounts. But I, too, just like the inquisitors, tried to turn into an analogy the anomaly I had stumbled upon, inserting it into an appropriate category. The similarity between *benandanti* and shamans struck me with what seemed irresistible evidence. In both instances we are dealing with individuals whose physical or psychological characteristics, frequently tied to the circumstances of their birth, designate them as highly skilled in achieving states of ecstasy. In both cases the ecstasy is accompanied by the going forth of the spirit, often in the shape of an animal. In both cases the spirit, whether of the shaman or the *benandante*, becomes involved in hazardous activities on which the health or material wellbeing of the community depends.

In the preface to *I Benandanti: The Night Battles*, I tried to explain that I had not dealt with the relationship between *benandanti* and shamans, which I pronounced unquestioned, so as not to sink to the level of a purely typological comparison. I stated that by doing so I was following the example of Marc Bloch, who, in his *Rois thaumaturges*, had juxtaposed strictly historical comparisons between phenomena belonging to societies that were historically contiguous and to anthropological studies of societies without documented historical ties. Bloch, writing in 1924, cited J. G. Frazer as an example of this second type of correlation. But almost a half century later, I was not able to deal with the question in the same terms. The ahistorical comparison to be reckoned with was that of Lévi-Strauss, or at least so I thought. For a time, while writing *The Night Battles*, I played around with the idea of presenting my documentation in two different ways: the first, historical; the second, formal-structural. I was under the impression that by choosing the first of the alternatives (as I ended up doing), I could not succeed in dealing satisfactorily with the elements which seemed to be historically intractable, the first of which were the analogies between *benandanti* and shamans.

The dilemma "history or structure" cropped up anew in the mid-1970s when I decided to confront the problems I had left unresolved in the book on the *benandanti*, but on a much larger scale than just the area of the Friuli. Meanwhile, my position had changed, now taking two apparently opposing directions. On the one hand, I was no longer willing to exclude from my research possible ahistorical connections. On the other, I was no longer so convinced that the relationship between *benandanti* and shamans was purely typological. The first path took me away from historiography; the second led me back in, but through a problem that any historian would have judged simply inappropriate.

The book which I ended up writing, *Storia notturna (Ecstasies: Deciphering the Witches' Sabbath)*, is the result of these contrasting pressures. It opens with a first, definitely historical part founded on the emergence of the idea of the conspiracy, the mainstay of the inquisitorial stereotype of the Sabbath. This is followed by a second part, organized about purely morphological criteria. It analyzes a number of ecstatic cults of a shamanic type, which can be documented over much of Europe. The Friulian *benandanti* reappear in this context, in a maze of cults which includes the *kresniki* of the Balkan Peninsula, the *burkudzäutä* of the Caucasus, the Hungarian *táltos*, the *noajdi* of Lapland, and so forth. The inclusion of Hungary and Lapland are especially significant because these areas belong to the linguistic Finno-Ugric sphere, inhabited by peoples whose distant ancestors came or could have come from central Asia. In the cases of the Hungarian *táltos* and of the Lapp *noajdi* the resemblance to shamans is especially close. We can consider them a bridge between central Asia and such regions as the Friuli, the Balkan Peninsula, or Caucasian Ossetia, inhabited by peoples speaking Indo-European languages. How can we explain this geographical distribution? Chapter 1 in the third part of *Storia notturna* proposes a historical solution consisting of a possible diffusion of shamanistic beliefs and practices from Asia to Europe, by way of the Scythians, who spoke an Iranian language, thus belonging to Indo-European stock, perhaps originating in central Asia. A few centuries before the Christian era they settled in an area north of the Black Sea, whence they entered into contact with Greeks and Celts. But this chapter, entitled "Eurasian Conjectures," ends by stressing the limitations in diffusion theories. As Claude Lévi-Strauss wrote, cultural transmission can be explained by external connections, but only internal connections can explain their permanence.

This objection thrusts to the foreground once again the dilemma "history or structure." I have thought for quite some time that the impossibility of choosing between them was connected to a lessening within me (and around me) of the ideological motivations which in the past had urged me on toward an explanation in historical terms. In my mind I have often compared myself to Buridan's donkey (forced to die from hunger), renouncing the completion of my book, stuck between two interpretations that from the documentary aspect were equally valid.

Not long ago this dilemma appeared to me in a new light. It took the form of a possibility suggested to me by Adriano Sofri when he connected a sentence in my book on the Sabbath that dealt with the possibility of demonstrating experimentally the existence of human nature with what has been called my mother's "personal doctrine of natural law."[17] I asked myself if the opposite thesis, the one from which I had set out twenty-five years earlier, could instead be traced back to the historicism of my father. I do not think I can rule this out even if the historicism that initially guided my research was not Croce's (whose books I read in copies belonging to my father, who had been very attached to him), but its radical version, disowned by Croce, as proposed by Ernesto De Martino in his *Il mondo magico*.[18] The existence of this psychological dimension, of which I was at first totally unaware, could have influenced my work in two ways. First, the dilemma which confronted me for so long could have become simply paralyzing in the same way that the child feels unable to choose when he is asked whom he loves more, his mother or his father; second, I might have felt impelled to find some solution which might be compatible not only with the required documentation, but with my psychological demands as well.

4. One thing should be clear: I certainly do not think that the specific answers with which I ended up in my research were psychologically determined. I ask myself, however, if, to become acceptable to me, they perhaps had to be reconciled with a subconscious psychological veto that might have rejected them as absurd or unfounded. If this veto indeed exists, as I believe it does, and not just in my case, I can understand in hindsight why my decision to evade the whole dilemma seemed acceptable. The second chapter in part 3 of *Storia notturna*, the longest in the book, attempts to combine the two perspectives—the historical and the structural or morphological—by analyzing a single element in that complex of beliefs that became absorbed in

the stereotype of the sabbat: the devil's lameness. I cannot recapitulate here the exceedingly complex argument which led me to find a common thread binding apparently very different personages like Oedipus and Cinderella. But even this hasty recounting of *Storia notturna* must have demonstrated that history and morphology are not juxtaposed in it (as in the project, later abandoned, of a twofold version of *I benandanti*), but rather interwoven: two alternating voices in debate, finally finding agreement. It was a choice that reflects that incessant inner discussion during the fifteen years that it took me to write *Storia notturna*.

NOTES

INTRODUCTION

I am happy to thank all the librarians who aided me in my research, in particular the staffs of the Archiginnasio in Bologna and the Charles E. Young Research Library, University of California, Los Angeles.

1. François de la Mothe Le Vayer, *Discours sur l'histoire*, in his *Œuvres*, 15 vols. (Paris: L. Billaine, 1669), 2:152: "C'est le temps qui compose ce qu'on nomme proprement le fil de l'Histoire. Car la Chronologie est un filet plus necessaire à se démeller d'une narration historique, que ne fut iamais à Thesée celuy qui le tira de tous les détours du Labyrinthe."

2. A. Frugoni, *Arnaldo da Brescia nelle fonti del secolo XII* (Rome: Istituto Storico Italiano per il Medio Evo, 1954); new ed., with an introduction by Giuseppe Sergi (Turin: Einaudi, 1989).

3. Marc Bloch, *Apologie pour l'histoire; ou, Métier d'historien* (Paris: Armand Colin, 1949); trans. Peter Putnam as *The Historian's Craft* (New York: Knopf, 1953), pp. 63–64.

4. Carlo Ginzburg, *I benandanti: Stregoneria e culti agrari tra Cinquecento e Seicento* (Turin: Einaudi, 1966); trans. John Tedeschi and Anne C. Tedeschi as *The Night Battles: Witchcraft and Agrarian Cults in the Sixteenth and Seventeenth Centuries* (Baltimore: Johns Hopkins University Press, 1983).

5. Carlo Ginzburg, "Spie: Radici di un paradigma indiziario" (1979), later included in *Miti, emblemi, spie* (Turin: Einaudi, 1986), pp. 158–209: 166–167; trans. John Tedeschi and Anne C. Tedeschi as "Clues: Roots of an Evidential Paradigm," in *Clues, Myths, and the Historical Method* (Baltimore: Johns Hopkins University Press, 1989), pp. 96–125: 102–104. Cf. also idem, *Nessuna isola è un'isola: Quattro sguardi sulla letteratura inglese* (Milan: Feltrinelli, 2002), pp. 13–14; trans. as *No Island Is an Island;*

Four Glances at English Literature in a World Perspective (New York: Columbia University Press, 2000).

6. The same thing is true of the three books that are intertwined with the present one: *Occhiacci di legno; Nove riflessioni sulla distanza* (Milan: Feltrinelli 1998) (trans. Martin Ryle and Kate Soper as *Wooden Eyes: Nine Reflections on Distance* [New York: Columbia University Press, 2001]); *Rapporti di forza: Storia, retorica, prova* (Milan: Feltrinelli, 2000); and *Nessuna isola è un'isola*. I should also like to mention the thought-provoking 1993 conference organized by Anthony Grafton and Sue Marchand, "Proof and Persuasion in History" (Davis Center for Historical Studies, Princeton University, Princeton, NJ).

7. The most obvious example is that of Paul Feyerabend. Cf. Ginzburg, *Occhiacci di legno*, pp. 155–159; *Wooden Eyes*, pp. 131–135.

8. Bloch, *Historian's Craft*, pp. 63–64.

9. Ibid., p. 104. On this passage, see Ginzburg, "A proposito della raccolta dei saggi storici di Marc Bloch," *Studi medievali*, ser. 3, vol. 6 (1965): 335–353: 338–340.

10. Ginzburg, *Rapporti di forza*, pp. 47, 87–108.

11. A. Jolles, "Forme semplici," chap. "Il caso," in his *I travestimenti della letteratura: Scritti critici e teorici (1897–1932)*, ed. Silvia Contarini (Milan: Mondadori, 2003), pp. 379–399: 393.

12. See the fine essay by Yan Thomas, "L'extrême et l'ordinaire: Remarques sur le cas médiéval de la communauté disparue," in Jean-Claude Passeron and Jacques Revel, eds., *Penser par cas* (Paris: École des Hautes Études en Sciences Sociales, 2005), pp. 45–73. The mental experiment which Hobbes proposes in his *De corpore*, describing the *annihilatio* of the world with the exception of one individual, may have been rooted in an actual case: see G. Paganini, "Hobbes, Gassendi und die Hypothese von Weltvernichtung," in Martin Mulsow and Marcelo Stamm, eds., *Konstellationsforschung* (Frankfurt a. M.: Suhrkamp, 2005), pp. 258–339.

13. "Of history," as the grammarian Asclepiades of Myrlea wrote, "one division is true, one false, one as if true: the factual is true, that of fictions and legends is false, and as if true are such forms as comedy and mimes": Sextus Empiricus, *Adversus Mathematicos* (1:252). See Sextus Empiricus, trans. R.G. Bury, vol. 4, *Against the Professors* (London: Heinemann; Cambridge, MA: Harvard University Press, 1961), 141–143. See also below, chap. 3.

CHAPTER 1. DESCRIPTION AND CITATION

1. On this point, cf. chap. 12 below, "Just One Witness," esp. what is said apropos Renato Serra's "Partenza di un gruppo di soldati per la Libia."

2. Walter Benjamin, *Understanding Brecht*, trans. Anna Bostock (London and New York: Verso, 1988), p. 121; originally published as *Versuche über Brecht* (Frankfurt a. M.: Suhrkamp, 1966).

3. See chap. 12 below, "Just One Witness."

4. E. Benveniste, "Les relations de temps dans le verbe française," in idem, *Problèmes de linguistique générale*, 2 vols. (Paris: Gallimard, 1966), 1:237–250; trans. Mary Elizabeth Meek as *Problems in General Linguistics* (Coral Gables, FL: University of Miami Press, 1971).

5. R. Caillois, *Ponce Pilate: Récit* (Paris: Gallimard, 1961); trans. Charles Lam Markmann as *Pontius Pilate* (Charlottesville: University of Virginia Press, 2006).

6. This expression goes back to Roland Barthes's "effect of the real," but from an opposite perspective. For Barthes, who identifies reality and language, "a fact has nothing but a linguistic existence," and the "truth," between quotation marks, is assimilated to polemic against "realism." See Roland Barthes, "Il discorso della storia," in his *Il brusio della lingua: Saggi critici* (Turin: Einaudi, 1988), 4:138–149: 147, 149; see also pp. 151–159; trans. Richard Howard as *Critical Essays* (Evanston: Northwestern University Press, 1972). I think that facts have an extralinguistic existence and that the notion of truth is part of a very long story, which may coincide with the history of the species. But the procedures used to control and communicate the truth have changed over the course of time.

7. *The Histories of Polybius*, trans. from the text of F. Hultsch by Evelyn S. Shuckburgh, introd. by F. W. Walbank, 2 vols. (Bloomington: Indiana University Press, 1962), 2:482. Cf. Attilio Roveri, *Studi su Polibio* (Bologna: Zanichelli, 1964), at the entry "*enargeia*" in the index; and, esp., G. Schepens, "Emphasis und *enargeia* in Polybios' Geschichtstheorie," *Rivista Storica dell'Antichità* 5 (1975): 185–200. For a different reading of Polybius 24:3 (*energeia* rather than *enargeia*), see Kenneth Sacks, *Polybius on the Writing of History* (Berkeley: University of California Press, 1981), p. 154n8.

8. Terence Cave, *The Cornucopian Text* (Oxford: Clarendon Press, 1979), p. 28n39; André Wartelle, *Lexique de la "Rhetorique" d'Aristote* (Paris: Les Belles Lettres, 1982), pp. 142–144; P. Pirani, *Dodici capi pertinenti all'arte historica del Mascardi* (Venice, 1646), pp. 56, 84; S. L. Alpers, "Ekphrasis and Aesthetic Attitudes in Vasari's Lives," *Journal of the Warburg and Courtauld Institutes* 23 (1960): 194n18, led into error by Franciscus Junius, *The Painting of the Ancients* (London, 1638), p. 300 (*Energia*): but see the original text, *De pictura veterum* (Amsterdam, 1637), p. 185 (*enargeia*). I have not been able to consult Colette Nativel, "La théorie de l'enargeia dans le 'De pictura veterum' de Franciscus Junius: Sources antiques et développements modernes," in René Demoris, ed., *Hommage à Elizabeth Sophie Chéron: Texte et peinture à l'age classique* (Paris: Presses de la Sorbonne Nouvelle, 1992), pp. 73–85.

9. The confusion had already been noted by Agostino Mascardi (1636); see n. 70 below.

10. The following pages, corresponding to sections 3 through 6, are basically unchanged in respect to the original 1988 version of this essay. In the notes I have added citations to studies that have since appeared on the subject of *enargeia* (many cited in Bernard Vouilloux, "La description des œuvres d'art dans le roman français au XIXe siècle," in *La description de l'œuvre d'art: Du modèle classique aux variations contemporaines*, Acts of a colloquium organized by Olivier Bonfait, Rome, 2004

[Paris: Somogy, 2004], pp. 153–184: 179n13; but the entire volume is important). I have found especially useful Claude Calam, "Quand dire c'est faire voir: L'évidence dans la rhétorique antique," *Études de Lettres* 4 (1991): 3–20; A. D. Walker, "*Enargeia* and the Spectator in Greek Historiography," *Transactions of the American Philological Association* 123 (1993): 353–377; and Perrine Galand-Hallyn, *Les yeux de l'éloquence: Poétiques humanistes de l'évidence* (Orléans: Paradigme, 1995).

11. Gioia M. Rispoli, "*Phantasia ed enargeia* negli scoli all'*Illiade*," *Vichiana* 13 (1984): 311–339; Graham Zanker, "*Enargeia* in the Ancient Criticism of Poetry," *Rheinisches Museum*, n.s., vol. 124 (1981): 296–311, esp. p. 304n29 and p. 310n57.

12. P. Chantraine, *Dictionnaire étymologique de la langue grecque*, 4 vols. (Paris: Klincksieck, 1968), 1:104. See also D. Mülder, "Götteranrufungen in Ilias und Odyssee," *Rheinisches Museum* 79 (1930): 7–34: 29. *Enargés* is not mentioned in Charles Mugler, *Dictionnaire historique de la terminologie optique des grecs* (Paris: Klincksieck, 1964).

13. *Histories of Polybius*, 2:261.

14. *The Institutio Oratoria of Quintilian*, trans. H. E. Butler, Loeb Classical Library (Cambridge, MA: Harvard University Press; London: Heinemann, 1977), 2:84–85: "Evidentia in narratione, quantum ego intelligo, est quidem magna virtus, cum quid veri non dicendum, sed quodammodo etiam ostendendum est."

15. Ibid., 2:434–437: "... quae non tam dicere videtur quam ostendere; et adfectus non aliter, quam si rebus ipsis intersimus sequentur." See also the notes to Quintilian, *Institution oratoire*, ed. Jean Cousin, 7 vols. (Paris: Belles Lettres, 1977), vol. 4, bks. 6 and 7, pp. 194–195, on the importance of *enargeia* in Greek and Roman historical thought.

16. Cicero, *Partitiones Oratoriae* 20: "Haec pars orationis, quae rem constituat paene ante oculos."

17. [Cicero], *Ad C. Herennium De ratione dicendi (Rhetorica ad Herennium)*, trans. Harry Caplan, Loeb Classical Library (London: Heinemann; Cambridge, MA: Harvard University Press, 1964), pp. 404–408: "Demonstratio est cum ita verbis res exprimitur ut geri negotium et res ante oculos esse videatur.... Statuit enim rem totam et prope ponit ante oculos."

18. Jacqueline de Romilly, *Magic and Rhetoric in Ancient Greece* (Cambridge, MA: Harvard University Press, 1975).

19. On this notion, see G. Schepens, *L'"autopsie" dans la méthode des historiens grecs du Ve siècle avant J.-C.* (Brussels: AWLSK, 1980).

20. [Demetrius], *On Style*, Loeb Classical Library (Cambridge, MA: Harvard University Press; London: Heinemann, 1982), p. 429. Cf. W. Rhys Roberts, *Demetrius on Style: The Greek Text of Demetrius "De elocutione"* (Cambridge: The University Press, 1902; reprint Hildesheim, 1969), pp. 209ff.; Bernard Weinberg, "Translations and Commentaries of Demetrius 'On Style' to 1600: A Bibliography," *Philological Quarterly* 30 (1951): 353–380; Dirk M. Schenkeveld, *Studies in Demetrius on Style* (Amsterdam: Hakkert, 1964), p. 61; Paul Oskar Kristeller and F. Edward Cranz, *Catalogus translationum et commentariorum* (Washington, DC: Catholic University of Amer-

ica Press, 1971), 2:27–41 (B. Weinberg); Guido Morpurgo Tagliabue, *Demetrio dello stile* (Rome: Ateneo, 1980).

21. Luciano Canfora, *Totalità e selezione nella storiografia classica* (Bari: Laterza, 1972).

22. E. H. Gombrich, *Art and Illusion: A Study in the Psychology of Pictorial Representation*, 3rd ed. (London: Phaidon, 1968), pp. 99ff. (1st ed., 1960); Hermann Strasburger, *Die Wesenbestimmung der Geschichte durch die antike Geschichtsschreibung*, Sitzungsberichte der wissenschaftlichen Gesellschaft an der Johann Wolfgang Goethe Universität Frankfurt a. M., vol. 5, no. 3, 1966 (Wiesbaden: Steiner, 1978), p. 78n1, p. 79n3.

23. Strasburger, *Die Wesensbestimmung*. In a more limited perspective, see Erich Burck, *Die Erzählungskunst des T. Livius* (Berlin: Weidmann, 1934); and Gert Avenarius, *Lukians Schrift zur Geschichtsschreibung* (Meisenheim/Glan: Hain, 1956), pp. 130ff. *Enargeia* is mentioned in Josef Martin, *Antike Rhetorik: Technik und Methode* (Munich: Beck, 1974), pp. 252–253, 288–289. For a broader perspective, see Heinrich Lausberg, *Handbuch der literarischen Rhetorik* (Munich: Hueber, 1960), paragraphs 810–819; trans. as *Handbook of Literary Rhetoric: A Foundation for Literary Study*, ed. David E. Horton and R. Dean Anderson (Leiden and Boston: Brill, 1998); and in Perrine Galand, "L'enargia' chez Politien," *Bibliothèque d'Humanisme et Renaissance* 49 (1987): 25–53. (Both are very useful even if they do not treat the relationship with historiography.) On the philosophical implications of *enargeia*, see A. A. Long, "Aisthesis, Prolepsis and Linguistic Theory in Epicurus," *Bulletin of the Institute of Classical Studies* 18 (1971): 114–133. On Duride, in addition to Strasburger, *Die Wesensbestimmung*, see the discussion between Schepens, "Emphasis," and Sachs, *Polybius*, pp. 149ff. For additional bibliography, see J. R. Morgan, "Make-Believe and Make Believe: The Fictionality of the Greek Novels," in Christopher Gill and T. P. Wiseman, eds., *Lies and Fictions in the Ancient World* (Austin: University of Texas Press, 1993), pp. 175–229: 184n15.

24. Plato, *The Statesman*, in *The Dialogues of Plato*, trans. B. Jowett (Oxford: Clarendon Press, [1953]), 3:489.

25. Philostratus the Elder, *Imagines*; Philostratus the Younger, *Imagines*; Callistratus, *Descriptions*; trans. Arthur Fairbanks, Loeb Classical Library (Cambridge, MA: Harvard University Press; London: Heinemann, 1969), p. 339.

26. Plutarch, *On the Fame of the Athenians*, in *Plutarch's Moralia*, trans. Frank Cole Babbitt, Loeb Classical Library (London: Heinemann; Cambridge, MA: Harvard University Press, 1972), p. 501.

27. Strasburger, *Die Wesensbestimmung*, p. 80, p. 87n3. Calame ("Quand dire," pp. 5, 13–14) suggests that the relationship between the *ekphrasis* and the description was marginal: but the *ekphrasis* in a broad sense included the detailed descriptions.

28. The presence of these notions in the aesthetic discussions of the time is attested to in Murray Krieger, *Ekphrasis: The Illusion of the Natural Sign* (Baltimore: Johns Hopkins University Press, 1992), pp. 67–112 (on *enargeia*).

29. The same juxtaposition has been suggested, independently, in T. P. Wiseman, "Lying Historians: Seven Types of Mendacity," in Gill and Wiseman, *Lies and Fiction*, pp. 122–146: 145–146.

30. The *Institutio oratoria of* Quintilian 2:84–85: ". . . quia in quibusdam causis obscuranda veritas esset; quod est ridiculum. Nam qui obscurare vult, narrat falsa pro veris, et in iis quae narrat debet laborare ut videantur quam evidentissima."

31. Arnaldo Momigliano, "Ancient History and the Antiquarian," *Journal of the Warburg and Courtauld Institutes* 13 (1950): 285–315; idem, "The Rise of Antiquarian Research," in his *The Classical Foundations of Modern Historiography*, foreword by Riccardo Di Donato (Berkeley and Los Angeles: University of California Press, 1990), pp. 54–79. The Italian translation, *Le radici classiche della storiografia moderna*, ed. R. Di Donato (Florence: Sansoni, 1992), contains a new introd. by the volume's editor (pp. 59–83).

32. Francesco Robortello, *De convenientia supputationis Livianae Ann. cum marmoribus Rom. quae in Capitolio sunt. Eiusdem de arte, sive ratione corrigendi veteres authores, disputatio. Eiusdem Emendationum libri duo*, Patavii [Padua], 1557. Cf. Antonio Carlini, "L'attività filologica di Francesco Robortello," *Atti dell'Accademia di Scienze, Lettere ed Arti di Udine*, ser. 7, vol. 7 (1966–1969): 53–84; E. J. Kenney, *The Classical Text: Aspects of Editing in the Age of the Printed Book* (Berkeley: University of California Press, 1974), pp. 29–36 (to whom Sebastiano Timpanaro was perhaps alluding when he observed that Robortello's writing "deserves to be remembered without anachronistic severity": *La genesi del metodo del Lachmann* (1963) (Turin: UTET, 2003), p. 13n1; trans. Glenn W. Most as *The Genesis of Lachmann's Method* (Chicago: University of Chicago Press, 2005). For Robortello's life, see Gian Giuseppe Liruti, *Notizie delle vite ed opere scritte da' letterati del Friuli* (Venice, 1762), 3:413–483 (reprinted Bologna: Forni, 1971). But Robortello's denunciation of Celio Secondo Curione as a heretic will bear further scrutiny, especially in light of what is said in the next note.

33. F. Robortello, *De historica facultate disputatio. Eiusdem Laconici, seu sudationis explicatio. Eiusdem de nominibus Romanorum. Eiusdem de rhetorica facultate. Eiusdem explicatio in Catulli Epithalamium*, Florentiae, Apud L. Tolentinum, 1548. The *Disputatio* was edited and reprinted by the Pole Stanislaus Ilovius, a student of Curione, in two volumes: see Dionysius of Halicarnassus, *Nonnulla opuscula*, ex officina Roberti Stephani, Lutetiae [Paris] 1556, pp. 42–62, followed by a letter to Curione; Demetrius of Phalerum, *De elocutione liber*, Basileae, per Ioannem Oporinum, 1557 (pp. 226–246). This collection contains a piece by Ilovius which recalls, even by its very title, Robortello's (*De historica facultate libellus*, pp. 215–226). The continuation of Robortello's ideas on the part of Francesco Patrizi, who called him "master" (*Della historia, diece dialoghi*, Venetia, A. Arrivabene, 1560, fol. 6r), is a subject I hope to return to elsewhere. Robortello and Patrizi are both present in the *Artis historicae penus*, ed. Johann Wolff, Basileae, officina Petri Pernae, 1579. The importance of Robortello's *Disputatio* (and what Speroni and Patrizi owed to it) was missed in Giorgio Spini, "I trattatisti dell'arte storica nella Controriforma italiana," in *Con-*

tributi alla storia del Concilio di Trento, "Quaderni di Belfagor" 1 (1948): 109–136; see also below at n. 47). More useful, even if partly influenced by the preceding essay, is Girolamo Cotroneo, *I trattatisti dell' "ars historica"* (Naples: Giannini, 1971), pp. 121–168 (on Robortello).

34. *Sexti philosophi Pyrrhoniarum hypotiposeon libri III . . . latine nunc primum editi, interprete Henrico Stephano,* Parisiis, 1562. On all this, see Richard Popkin, *The History of Scepticism from Savonarola to Bayle,* rev. and expanded ed. (Oxford and New York: Oxford University Press, 2003), esp. pp. 17ff. Cf. also Arno Seifert, *Cognitio historica* (Berlin: Duncker & Humblot, 1976), pp. 17–18; and Luciano Floridi, *Sextus Empiricus: The Transmission and Recovery of Pyrrhonism* (Oxford and New York: Oxford University Press, 2002), p. 31.

35. Gian Francesco Pico, *Examen vanitatis doctrinae gentium, et veritatis Christiane disciplinae, distinctum in libros sex,* impressit Mirandulae Joannes Maciochius, 1520, fol. lxxxii r (bk. 3, chap. 3): "Quid sceptici contra grammaticam soleant disputare: ubi et quaepiam ex aliis auctoribus"). Cf. Charles B. Schmitt, *Gian Francesco Pico della Mirandola (1450–1533) and His Critique of Aristotle* (The Hague: Nijhoff, 1967), p. 49.

36. H. Mutschmann, "Die Überlieferung der Schriften des Sextus Empiricus," *Rheinisches Museum,* n.s., vol. 64 (1909): 244–283.

37. On this point, see chap. 5 below.

38. The first edition of Sextus Empiricus, *Adversus mathematicos,* dates to 1569; the *Artis historicae penus* followed ten years later.

39. See, for example, Eckhard Kessler, *Theoretiker humanistischer Geschichtsschreibung* (Munich: Fink, 1971) (superficial). Jean Jehasse, *La Renaissance de la critique: L'essor de l'humanisme érudit de 1560 à 1614* (Paris: Champion, 2002), p. 101, is totally off the mark, attributing to Robortello a "radical subjectivism" which excludes the possibility of even ascertaining factual truths.

40. "Thucydides nobis exemplo sit, qui libro sexto omnem antiquitatem urbium, ac populorum Siciliae diligentissime ac verissime explicit. Et quoniam ad hanc antiquitatem cognoscendum multum nos iuvant vetustorum aedificiorum reliquiae, atque aut marmoribus, aut auro, aere, et argento incisae literae haec quoque teneat oportet. Idem Thucydides (quid enim opus est ab huius tanti praeclari historici authoritate discedere?) ex inscriptione marmoris, quod in arce fuerat positum, ut posteris esset monimentum, probat, quod multi aliter recensebant: Hippiam Atheniensium fuisse tyrannum, et liberos quinque suscepisse."

41. Luciano [Lucian of Samosata], *Come si deve scrivere la storia,* ed. Franco Montanari and A. Barabino (Milan, 2002), paragraphs 19, 34.

42. F. Robortello, *Emendationum libri duo,* in the collective volume *De convenientia,* fols. 34v–37r; see also fol. 22v etc. For a minute reconstruction of the controversy, see William McCuaig, *Carlo Sigonio: The Changing World of the Late Renaissance* (Princeton, NJ: Princeton University Press, 1989), pp. 28ff., 43ff.

43. I have discussed this in my *Rapporti di forza: Storia, retorica, prova* (Milan: Feltrinelli, 2000). Cotroneo (*I trattatisti dell' "ars historica"*) emphasizes the Aristotelian

and rhetorical dimension of Robortello's *Disputatio*, without, however, grasping the connection between rhetoric and proof.

44. I have not been able to see G. Lloyd, "Annalen, Geschichten, Mythen," in M. Teich and A. Müller, eds., *Historia Magistra Vitae?* in *Österreichische Zeitschrift für Geschichtswissenschaften* 16, n. 2 (2005): 27–47.

45. "Historiam ab annalibus quidam differre eo putant, quod, cum utrumque sit rerum gestarum narratio, earum tamen proprie rerum sit historia quibus rebus gerendis interfuerit is qui narret"; Aulus Gellius, *Attic Nights*, trans. John C. Rolfe, Loeb Classical Library (Cambridge, MA: Harvard University Press, 1954), 1:433.

46. Isidore of Seville, *Etymologiae*, 1:44: "Historia est eorum temporum quae vidimus, annales vero sunt eorum annorum quos aetas nostra non vidit." I have used the Italian translation, *Etimologie o origini*, ed. A. Vilastro Canale (Turin: UTET, 2004), 1:183.

47. Sperone Speroni degli Alvarotti, *Dialogo della Istoria*, in *Opere . . .*, ed. Natale delle Laste and Marco Forcellini, 5 vols. (Venice, 1740), 2:210–328. The two editors called a previous edition "monstrous" (*Dialoghi* [Venice, Meietti, 1596], pp. 361–502). The passage is cited in Mario Pozzi, ed., *Trattatisti del Cinquecento* (Milan and Naples: Ricciardi, 1978), 1:503. Actually, as was observed by Jean-Louis Fournel ("Il *Dialogo della Istoria: Dall'oratore al religioso*," in *Sperone Speroni, Filologia Veneta*, no. 2 [1989]: 139–167: 150–151 [Padua: Editoriale Programma, 1989]), the first part of the dialogue printed by Meietti in 1596, which was based on a manuscript now lost, reproduces an earlier, quite different version. (Subsequently Fournel spoke, with unjustified caution in my opinion, of a probable, rather than a certain, priority: *Les dialogues de Sperone Speroni: Libertés de parole et règles de l'écriture* (Marburg: Hitzeroth, 1990), p. 235. This chronology is verified by the series of notes at the end of part 1 (*Dialoghi*, pp. 411–412) and developed in the subsequent edition—namely, the last (*Opere*, 2:250ff.). The letters which Alvise Mocenigo wrote to Speroni between 27 August 1585 and 11 October 1587 (*Opere*, 5:378–381) to bring him up-to-date on the copying of the *Dialogo della Istoria* concern the penultimate edition, as emerges from the passage (later suppressed) in which Pomponazzi's old student, Speroni himself, born in 1500, is described as an "old man more than eighty-six years of age" (p. 373). Between October 1587 and 2 June 1588 (the date of his death) Speroni was strong enough to work on a new edition of part 1 of the *Dialogo*. This work, erroneously dated 1542, has been portrayed as the inspiration of the *Disputatio* on history written by "another of the big guns of sixteenth-century pedantry, Francesco Robortello" (G. Spini, "I trattatisti dell'arte storica," pp. 113–114). A little pedantry would have permitted the reconstruction of the chronology of the two works, and their relationship.

48. On these personages, see the prefatory remarks by Mario Pozzi to the second part of Speroni's *Dialogo della Istoria*, in *Trattatisti del Cinquecento*, pp. 725–727.

49. Speroni, *Opere*, 2:222. This piece of evidence did not attract the attention of the scholars (from Bruno Nardi to Paul Oskar Kristeller) who have studied the work of Pomponazzi. That the "booklet" appears to be irreparably lost is confirmed

in A. Daniele, "Sperone Speroni, Bernardino Tomitano e l'Accademia degli Infiammati di Padova," in *Sperone Speroni,* p. 16.

50. Speroni, *Dialoghi* (1596 ed.), p. 373. The passage does not appear in the edition of the *Opere,* a fact which did not prevent J. L. Fournel ("Il *Dialogo della Istoria,*" p. 163) from recognizing the identity of the former student.

51. Speroni, *Dialoghi* (1596 ed.), pp. 386, 392.

52. Speroni, *Opere,* 2:201. The dialogue was printed for the first time in the posthumous *Dialoghi* in 1596. The statement attributed to Trapolino resurrected, even more aggressively, a passage in which Julius Caesar Scaliger defined Livy as a poet for having, like Thucydides, inserted speeches which were total fabrications. (See J. C. Scaliger, *Poetices libri septem* [Genevae], Apud Antonium Vincentium, 1561, p. 5.)

53. On Trapolino, see Bruno Nardi, *Studi su Pietro Pomponazzi* (Florence: Le Monnier, 1965), pp. 104–121; and Eugenio Garin, *Storia della filosofia italiana,* 2 vols. (Turin: Einaudi, 1966), 2:564–565 (1st ed. Turin: Vallecchi, 1949); trans. Giorgio A. Pinton as *History of Italian Philosophy* (Amsterdam and New York: Rodopi, 2008).

54. Mario Pozzi, "Sperone Speroni e il genere epidittico," in *Sperone Speroni,* pp. 55–88.

55. Speroni, *Opere,* 2:319.

56. Ibid., pp. 319–320.

57. Reprinted in Mario Pozzi, ed., *Discussioni linguistiche del Cinquecento* (Turin: UTET, 1988).

58. Speroni, *Dialoghi* (1596 ed.), p. 387.

59. Ibid., p. 389.

60. Speroni, *Opere,* 5:380. For reasons explained above (n. 47), the letter should be referenced to the penultimate version of the *Dialogo.*

61. Beginning in 1578, Baronius resided at Santa Maria della Vallicella, where Antoniano preached weekly (a document from 1581 called him "one of our men, but who does not reside with us"): see Louis Ponnelle and Louis Bardet, *Saint Philippe Néri et la société romaine de son temps, 1515–1595* (1929) (Paris: La Colombe, 1958). I have used the Italian version: *San Filippo Neri e la società romana del suo tempo (1515–1595)* (Florence: Ferrari, 1931), p. 352n10. Trans. Ralph Francis Kerr as *St. Philip Neri and the Roman Society of His Times (1515–1595)* (London: Sheed & Ward, 1932). See also the entries in the *Dizionario Biografico degli Italiani* by Alberto Pincherle ("Baronio, Cesare" [6:470–478]) and by Paolo Prodi ("Antoniano, Silvio" [3:511–515]). The "myth" of the influence of the *Filippini* on Baronius's *Annales* transfigured a real situation (see Stefano Zen, *Baronio storico: Controriforma e crisi del metodo umanistico* [Naples: Vivarium, 1994], pp. 117ff.).

62. Pincherle limits himself to recording the title change ("Baronio, Cesare," p. 472). In 1581, in the draft of a letter to Charles Borromeo, Filippo Neri mentioned "the *Historia ecclesiastica*" among the obligations of the Oratory (Ponnelle and Bardet, *San Filippo Neri,* p. 277).

63. C. Baronius, *Annales Ecclesiastici* (Romae: Ex typografia Vaticana, 1593), vol. 1, introd.: "Relinquemus historicis Ethnicis locutiones illas per longiorem ambitum

periphrastice circumductas, orationesque summa arte concinnatas, fictas, ex senten-
tia cuiusque compositas, ad libitum dispositas; et Annales potius quam Historiam
scribemus." Cf. also Cyriac K. Pullapilly, *Caesar Baronius, Counter-Reformation Historian* (Notre Dame, IN: University of Notre Dame Press, 1975), p. 171. On the simplicity of preaching desired by the Oratory, see Ponnelle and Bardet, *San Filippo
Neri*, pp. 328–329.

64. St. Jerome to Eustochius, *Patrologia Latina* 22:7, 30.

65. This echoes a letter from Cicero to Atticus: "Horridula mihi atque incompta
visa sunt" (2:1).

66. Baronius, *Annales Ecclesiastici*, 1:4–5. Both A. Pincherle ("Baronio, Cesare,"
p. 476) and Anthony Grafton (*The Footnote. A Curious History* [Cambridge, MA:
Harvard University Press, 1999], p. 164) refer to this passage.

67. Anna Laura Lepschy and Giulio Lepschy, "Punto e virgola: Considerazioni
sulla punteggiatura italiana e europea," in Ilona Fried and Arianna Carta, eds., *Le
esperienze e le correnti culturali europee del Novecento in Italia e in Ungheria* (Budapest: Eötvös Lorand University, 2003), pp. 9–22: 20–21. A. Castellani ("Le virgolette
di Aldo Manuzio," *Studi Linguistici Italiani* 22 [1996]: 106–109) notes that the introduction of quotation marks is an example of the dependence of the printed book on
the manuscript: the marginal marks (") are taken, in fact, from the *diple* used in
Greek and Roman manuscripts: see P. McGurk, "Citation Marks in Early Latin
Manuscripts," *Scriptorium* 15 (1961): 3–13. For a precocious discussion on the *diple*,
see Pietro Vettori, *Explicationes suarum in Ciceronem castigationum*, Parisiis 1538, p. 48
(apropos Cicero, *Ad Atticum*, 8: 2). C.J. Mitchell ("Quotation Marks, National
Compositional Habits and False Imprints," *The Library*, ser. 6, vol. 5 [1983]: 360–384:
362–363) will have to be corrected on the basis of Castellani's findings.

68. An example of both (1597) is reproduced in Malcolm B. Parkes, *Pause and Effect: Punctuation in the West* (Berkeley and Los Angeles: University of California Press,
1993), p. 261. Much research remains to be done on the history of the note (perhaps
located in the margin rather than at the foot of the page: but the difference does not
affect the essential point). In Grafton's brilliant "flashback" (*The Footnote*), what
preceded "the Cartesian origins of the footnote"—namely, Pierre Bayle (chap.
7)—receives inadequate attention.

69. Agostino Mascardi, *Dell'arte historica* (Rome: Facciotti, 1636), pp. 25, 313–314.

70. Ibid., pp. 419ff, esp. pp. 426–427. Julius Caesar Scaliger, inadequately distinguishing between the two terms, had translated *energeia* as "efficacy" (*efficacia*) (*Poetices*, pp. 116ff.).

71. Mascardi, *Dell'arte historica*, pp. 122–123.

72. Ibid., pp. 125ff. Also by Mascardi, see *La congiura del Conte Gio: Luigi de'
Fieschi* (Venice: G. Scaglia, 1629); *Oppositioni e difesa alla "Congiura del Conte Gio:
Luigi de' Fieschi" descritta da Agostino Mascardi* (Venice, 1630).

73. The passage is quoted from Francis Haskell, *History and Its Images: Art and
the Interpretation of the Past* (New Haven, CT: Yale University Press, 1993), pp. 93–
94. Curiously, Haskell does not mention the allusion to a figure whom he studied

admirably in his *Patrons and Painters: A Study in the Relations between Italian Art and Society in the Age of the Baroque* (London: Chatto & Windus, 1963; many times reprinted with additions and corrections). There is much new material on Cassiano dal Pozzo and his activities in David Freedberg, *The Eye of the Lynx: Galileo, His Friends, and the Beginnings of Natural History* (Chicago: University of Chicago Press, 2002). Several volumes of the *Museo cartaceo* have appeared in a beautifully illustrated series edited by Francis Haskell and Jennifer Montagu.

74. See Manuel Chrysoloras, *Roma, parte del cielo: Confronto tra l'Antica e la Nuova Roma*, ed. Enrico V. Maltese, trans. Guido Cortassa (Turin: UTET, 2000), p. 59n2 (for the identification of the addressee of the letter). The volume has a rich bibliography. See also Michael Baxandall, "Guarino, Pisanello and Manuel Chrysoloras," *Journal of the Warburg and Courtauld Institutes* 28 (1985): 183–204: 197–199; idem, *Giotto and the Orators: Humanist Observers of Painting in Italy and the Discovery of Pictorial Composition* (Oxford: Clarendon Press, 1971), pp. 80–81.

75. Chrysoloras, *Roma*, pp. 59–98: 65–66. In view of the mention of "Herodotus and other historians," I do not follow Peter N. Miller, who proposes to translate *historian* with "description." See his "Description Terminable and Interminable," in Gianna Pomata and Nancy G. Siraisi, eds., *Historia: Empiricism and Erudition in Early Modern Europe* (Cambridge, MA: MIT Press, 2005), pp. 357–358.

76. According to Maltese this statement "has no precedent in classical literature" (introd. to Chrysoloras, *Roma*, p. 20).

77. Ibid., p. 96.

CHAPTER 2. THE CONVERSION OF THE JEWS OF MINORCA

I am grateful to Peter Brown, Sofia Boesch Gajano, Pier Cesare Bori, Augusto Campana, and Richard Landes for their valuable suggestions.

1. See Peter Brown, *The Cult of the Saints: Its Rise and Function in Latin Christianity* (Chicago: University of Chicago Press, 1981), pp. 103–105.

2. Ibid., p. 104.

3. On "emic" and "etic," see Kenneth L. Pike, *Language in Relation to a Unified Theory of Structure of Human Behaviour*, 2nd rev. ed. (The Hague and Paris: Mouton, 1967), pp. 37ff.; and Ernest Gellner, *Relativism and the Social Sciences* (Cambridge and New York: Cambridge University Press, 1985), pp. 144–145. For Brown's praise of another work by Mary Douglas (*Natural Symbols*), see *Cult of the Saints*, p. 177n102. Douglas's seminal *Purity and Danger* is mentioned in Brown's "The Saint as Exemplar in Classical Antiquity," *Representations* 2 (1983): 1–25: 11, in a context suggesting the author's growing distance from "a strand of post-Durkheimian and of British functionalist anthropology."

4. See, for example, Maurice Kriegel, "Un trait de psychologie sociale," *Annales, E.S.C.* 31 (1976): 26–30.

5. Arnaldo Momigliano, in *La contraddizione felice? Ernesto De Martino e gli altri*, ed. Riccardo Di Donato (Pisa: ETS, 1990), p. 198. (This final sentence was

Momigliano's last-minute addition: see editor's note, p. 11.) For a similar rejection of "history of historiography as history of political thought (*pensiero storico*)," see Delio Cantimori, "Storia e storiografia in Benedetto Croce" (1966), reprinted in Cantimori's *Storici e storia* (Turin: Einaudi, 1971), pp. 397–409: 407–409. Momigliano was alluding implicitly to Hayden White and his followers, whereas Cantimori was directing himself to some unnamed followers of Croce, as well as, to a certain extent, to Croce himself. I have tried to explore the reasons behind this convergence in "Just One Witness" (see chap. 12).

6. See B. Croce, *La storia ridotta sotto il concetto generale dell' arte* (1895), now in Croce's *Primi saggi*, 2nd ed. (Bari: Laterza, 1927), pp. 38ff. The importance of this early essay has been underlined in Hayden White, *Metahistory: The Historical Imagination in Nineteenth-Century Europe* (Baltimore: Johns Hopkins University Press, 1975), pp. 381ff.

7. See, in this connection, my "Just One Witness" (chap. 12).

8. See G. Seguí Vidal, *La carta-encíclica del obispo Severo . . .* (Palma de Majorca: Seminario de los Misioneros de los Sagrados Corazones de Jesús y María, 1937), pp. 1ff. Translations in Castillian: Juan Bautista Dameto, *La historia general del reyno balearico* (Majorca: en casa de Gabriel Guasp, 1632), pp. 150ff.; J. de la Puerta Vizcaino, *La sinagoga Balear, ó Historia de los Judíos de Mallorca* (Palma de Majorca: Editorial Clumba, 1951 [reprint of 1857 ed.]). For the Latin text, followed by Castilian and Catalan translations, see *Epistola Severi episcopi—Carta del Obispo Severo—Carta del Bisbe Sever*, ed. E. Lafuente Hernandez (Minorca, 1981). But see now Severus of Minorca, *Letter on the Conversion of the Jews*, ed. and trans. Scott Bradbury (Oxford: Clarendon, 1996), with an excellent introduction.

9. Bernhard Blumenkranz, "Altercatio Ecclesiae contra Synagogam. Texte inédit du Xe siècle," *Revue du Moyen Age Latin* 10 (1954): 5–159: 46; idem, *Juifs et Chrétiens dans le monde occidental (430–1096)* (Paris and The Hague: Mouton, 1960), pp. 282–284; idem, *Les auteurs chrétiens latins du Moyen Age* (Paris and The Hague: Mouton, 1963), pp. 106–110; idem, "Juden und Jüdische in christliche Wundererzählung," in idem, *Juifs et Chrétiens: Patristique et Moyen Age* (London: Variorum, 1977), pp. 419–420.

10. To the best of my knowledge, the question of the letter's authenticity was not raised by any of the numerous reviewers of *The Cult of the Saints*.

11. See Seguí Vidal, *La carta-encíclica*, pp. 130ff.

12. See G. Seguí-Vidal and J. N. Hillgarth, *La "Altercatio" y la basilica paleocristiana de Son Bou de Menorca* (Palma de Majorca: Sociedad Arqueológica Lulliana, 1955).

13. José Vives, review of Seguí Vidal and Hillgarth, *La "Altercatio,"* in *Hispania Sacra* 9 (1956): 227–229.

14. See Blumenkranz, "Altercatio."

15. Idem, *Les auteurs*, p. 108n14. On the letter of Severus studied from a linguistic point of view, see C. Paucker, "De latinitate scriptorum quorundam saeculi quarti et ineuntis quinti p. C. minorum observationes," *Zeitschrift für die Oesterreichischen*

Gymnasien 32 (1881): 481–499 (not cited by Blumenkranz). Strangely, no scholar has discussed the word *argistinum*, which, according to Severus, in the dialect of Minorca meant "small hail" (Severus, *Letter on the Conversion*, ed. Bradbury, p. 112: "grando minutissima, quam incolae insulae huius gentili sermone 'argistinum vocant'"). To the best of my knowledge, *argistinum* is a hapax legomenon.

16. See L. Cracco Ruggini, "Note sugli ebrei in Italia dal IV al XVI secolo (a proposito di un libro e di altri contributi recenti)," *Rivista Storica Italiana* 76 (1964): 926–956: 936–938.

17. See M. C. Díaz y Díaz, "De patristica española," *Revista española de teologia* 17 (1956): 3–12.

18. *Patrologia Latina* 41:833–854.

19. See Díaz y Díaz, "De patristica," p. 12n30.

20. Some unconvincing doubts about this identification have been raised in Raymond Van Dam, "'Sheep in Wolves' Clothing': The Letters of Consentius to Augustine," *Journal of Ecclesiastical History* 37 (1986): 515–535.

21. St. Augustine, *Œuvres*, Bibliothèque Augustinienne (Paris: Desclée, De Brouwer, 1936-), vol. 46B, *Lettres* 1*–29* (ed. J. Divjak, 1987), pp. 184ff. For the relevant passage, see pp. 248–250: "Eodem tempore accidit, ut quaedam apud nos ex praecepto domini mirabilia gererentur. Quae cum mihi beatus antistes, frater paternitatis tuae Severus episcopus cum ceteris qui affuerant rettulisset, irrupit propositum meum summis viribus caritatis et, ut epistolam quae rei gestae ordinem contineret ipse conscriberet, sola a me verba mutuatus est." Consentius mentions also that he wrote an anti-Jewish treatise (one that apparently has not survived), which he asks his correspondent not to reveal. Peter Brown has kindly brought to my attention the importance of Consentius's letter, as well as articles about him.

22. J. Wankenne, in St. Augustine, *Œuvres*, 46B:492.

23. Madeleine Moreau, "Lecture de la lettre 11* de Consentius à Augustin," in *Les lettres de Saint Augustin decouvertes par Johannes Divjak, communications présentées au colloque des 20 et 21 septembre 1981* (Paris: Études Augustiniennes, 1983), pp. 215–223.

24. E. D. Hunt, "St. Stephen in Minorca: An Episode in Jewish-Christian Relations in the Early 5th Century A.D.," *Journal of Theological Studies*, n.s., vol. 33, pt. 1 (1982): 106–123; L.-J. Wankenne and B. Hambenne, "La lettre-encyclique de Severus évêque de Minorque au début du Ve siècle," *Revue Bénédictine* 103 (1987): 13–27. Both articles take for granted the early date as well as the authenticity of Severus's letter; only the second of the two, more limited in scope, takes into account the letter by Consentius (12*). For an early discussion of it, see J. Amengual i Batle, "Noves Fonts par a la història de les Balears dins el Baix Imperi," *Bolletí de la Societat Arqueològica Lulliana*, ser. 2, vol. 37 (1980): 99–111.

25. Not in order to "acquire relics of St. Stephen" (they had not been discovered yet), as stated in W. H. G. Frend, "The North-African Cult of Martyrs," in idem, *Archeology and History in the Study of Christianity* (London: Variorum, 1988), chap. 11, p. 164.

26. *Patrologia Latina* 41:805–816.

27. On this date, corresponding to 2 February 418, see Victor Saxer, *Mort, martyrs, reliques en Afrique chrétienne aux premiers siècles* (Paris: Beauchesne, 1980), p. 246.

28. I am very grateful to Richard Landes for having pointed this out to me. See, in general, his essay "Let the Millennium Be Fulfilled: Apocalyptic Expectations and the Pattern of Western Chronography, 100–800 CE," in W. Verbek, D. Verhelst, and A. Welkenhuysen, eds., *The Use and Abuse of Eschatology in the Middle Ages* (Louvain: Louvain University Press, 1988), pp. 137–211, esp. pp. 156–160, on the epistolary discussion, which took place in either 418 or 419 (i.e., at approximately the time of Severus's letter), between Augustine and Hesychius, a Dalmatian bishop, concerning the end of the world. On the date of Orosius's work, see Adolf Lippold's introduction to Orosius, *Le storie contro i pagani*, trans. A. Bartalucci, 2 vols. (Milan: Fondazione L. Valla, 1976), 1:xxii.

29. P. Brown, *Augustine of Hippo, a Biography* (Berkeley and Los Angeles: University of California Press, 1967), passim; Paul Monceaux, *Histoire littéraire de l'Afrique chrétienne depuis les origines jusqu'à l'invasion arabe* (Paris: E. Leroux, 1923), 7:42–45.

30. L. Cracco Ruggini, "Ambrogio e le opposizioni anticattoliche fra il 383 e il 390," *Augustinianum* 14 (1974): 409–449; Manlio Simonetti, "La politica antiariana di Ambrogio," in Giuseppe Lazzati, ed., *Ambrosius episcopus . . . Atti* (Milan: Vita e Pensiero, 1976), 1:266–285; A. Lenox-Conyngham, "The Topography of the Basilica Conflict of A.D. 385/6 in Milan," *Historia* 31 (1982): 353–363; Gérard Nauroy, "Le fouet et le miel: Le combat d'Ambroise en 386 contre l'Arianisme milanais," *Recherches Augustiniennes* 23 (1986): 3–86.

31. *De vera religione* 25:47: "Cum enim Ecclesia catholica per totum orbem diffusa atque fundata sit, nec miracula illa in nostra tempora durare permissa sunt, ne animus semper visibilia quaereret, ut eorum consuetudine frigesceret genus humanum" (quoted by G. Bardy in a note on miracles included in his edition of *The City of God* [Augustine, *Œuvres*, Bibliothèque Augustinienne 37, pp. 825–831]); Pierre Courcelle, *Recherches sur les "Confessions" de Saint Augustin*, enlarged ed. (Paris: E. de Boccard, 1968), pp. 139ff.

32. Carlo Cecchelli, "Note sopra il culto delle reliquie nell'Africa romana," *Rendiconti della Pontificia Accademia Romana di Archeologia* 15 (1939): 125–134: 131–132.

33. Saxer, *Mort, martyrs, reliques*, pp. 245ff. See also Cyrille Lambot, "Collection antique de sermons de S. Augustin," *Revue Bénédictine* 57 (1947): 89–108: 105–106; idem, "Le sermons de saint Augustin pour les fêtes des martyrs," ibid. 79 (1969): 82–97: 94; Pierre Patrick Verbraken, *Études critiques sur les sermons authentiques de Saint Augustin* (The Hague and Steenbergen: In Abbatia S. Petri, 1976), sermons 314–320.

34. Saxer, *Mort, martyrs, reliques*, pp. 293–294.

35. Michel van Esbroeck, "Jean II de Jérusalem et les cultes de S. Etienne, de la Sainte-Sion et de la Croix," *Analecta Bollandiana* 102 (1984): 99–134.

36. *Patrologia Latina* 41:813, 815–816.

37. On the two versions, see P. Peeters, "Le sanctuaire de la lapidation de S. Etienne," *Analecta Bollandiana* 27 (1908): 359–368: 364–367; J. Martin, "Die revelatio S. Stephani und Verwandtes," *Historisches Jahrbuch* 77 (1958): 419–433. On the entire event, see E. D. Hunt, *Holy Land Pilgrimage in the Later Roman Empire*, A.D. 312–460 (Oxford: Clarendon; New York: Oxford University Press, 1982), pp. 212–220.

38. Marcel Simon, *Verus Israel: Étude sur les relations entre Chrétiens et Juifs dans l'empire romain (135–425)*, 2nd ed. (Paris: E. de Boccard, 1964).

39. Theodor Mommsen and Paul M. Meyer, eds., *Codex Theodosianus*, 2 vols. in 3, 3rd ed. (Berlin: Weidmann, 1962), pp. 892–893.

40. Jean Juster, *Les Juifs dans l'Empire romain: Leur condition juridique, économique et sociale* (Paris: P. Geuthner, 1914), 1:391ff.; Alfredo M. Rabello, "The Legal Condition of the Jews in the Roman Empire," in H. Temporini, ed., *Aufstieg und Niedergang der römischen Welt* (Berlin and New York: De Gruyter, 1980), pp. 713–716 (but in A.D. 415 patriarch Gamaliel was not "deposed," as we read at p. 714n212); Bernard S. Bachrach, "The Jewish Community of the Later Roman Empire," in Jacob Neusner and Ernest S. Frerichs, eds., *"To See Ourselves as Others See Us": Christians, Jews, "Others" in Late Antiquity* (Chico, CA: Scholars Press, 1985), pp. 399–421: 412–415; Günther Stemberger, *Juden und Christen im Heiligen Land* (Munich: C.H. Beck, 1987), pp. 208–213.

41. St. John Chrysostom, *Discourses against Judaizing Christians*, trans. P. W. Harkins (Washington, DC: Catholic University of America Press, 1979). See also Robert L. Wilken, *John Chrysostom and the Jews: Rhetoric and Reality in the Late 4th Century* (Berkeley: University of California Press, 1983); and Wayne A. Meeks and Robert L. Wilken, *Jews and Christians in Antioch in the First Four Centuries of the Common Era* (Missoula, MT: Scholars Press, 1979).

42. Marcel Simon, "La polémique antijuive de Saint Jean Chrysostome et le mouvement judaïsant d'Antioche," in idem, *Recherches d'histoire Judéo-Chrétienne* (Paris and The Hague: Mouton, 1962), pp. 140–153.

43. Cardinal M. Rampolla [del Tindaro], "Martyre et sépulture des Macchabées," *Revue de l'Art Chrétien*, ser. 4, vol. 10 (1899): 290–305; 377–392; 457–465: 388ff.

44. Elias J. Bikerman ("Les Macchabées de Malalas," *Byzantion* 21 [1951]: 63–83: 74–75) remarks that synagogues were regarded as holy places in Roman law, not in Jewish ritual; but the attitude of the Christians (including those who seized the Antioch synagogue) was presumably closer to the Roman model.

45. St. Ambrose, Ep. 40, 16, quoted in Lellia Cracco Ruggini, "Ebrei e Orientali nell'Italia settentrionale fra il IV e il VI sec. d.C.," *Studia et Monumenta Historiae et Iuris* 25 (1959): 198–199.

46. William H.C. Frend, "Blandina et Perpetua: Two Early Christian Heroines," in Jean Rouge and Robert Turran, eds., *Les martyrs de Lyon (177)* (Paris: Editions du CNRS, 1978), pp. 167–177: 173.

47. W. H.C. Frend, *Martyrdom and Persecution in the Early Church* (Garden City, NY: Anchor, 1967). I cite from the Oxford (1965) ed., pp, 21, 87.

48. Marcel Simon, "Les Saints d'Israël dans la dévotion de l'Église ancienne," in *Recherches d'histoire*, pp. 154–180:157 (Gregory of Nazianzus, *Hom. 3 in Mach.*, in *Patrologia Graeca* 35:627).

49. "Judaei igitur exemplis se Machabaei temporis cohortantes, mortem quoque pro defendendis legitimis suis desiderabant" (Severus, *Letter on the Conversion*, ed. Bradbury, p. 86).

50. Marcel Simon made a stimulating attempt in this direction: *St. Stephen and the Hellenists in the Primitive Church* (London and New York: Longmans, Green, 1958).

51. The importance of this theme had been underlined by Bernhard Blumen-kranz (*Les auteurs*, p. 108n14).

52. Brown, "The Saint as Exemplar," p. 12.

53. On the subject of the foregoing pages, see now the comprehensive critical survey in I. Amengual i Batle, "Consentius/Severus de Minorca: Vint-i-cinc anys d'estudis, 1975–2000," *Arxiu de Textos Catalans Antics* 20 (2001): 599–700.

CHAPTER 3. MONTAIGNE, CANNIBALS, AND GROTTOES

1. M. de Montaigne, *Essais*, ed. Albert Thibaudet (Paris: Gallimard, 1950), p. 24; *The Essays*, trans. E. J. Trechmann (Oxford: Oxford University Press, n.d.), p. 1. [Translators' note: In some instances below, the Penguin edition of the *Essays*, in the translation by J. M. Cohen, is followed.] In the first volume of his *Recherches de la France* (Orléans, 1567), Étienne Pasquier emphasized that he was addressing himself neither to patrons nor to friends, but simply to "his reader." Montaigne's address "au lecteur," coming from a nobleman, is understandable, but this takes nothing away from the provocative character of his subject.

2. Montaigne, *Essais*, pp. 262–263; *The Essays*, p. 224. See also *Essais*, "Apologie de Raimond Sebond," pp. 502–503.

3. For another allusion to the parallel between the Golden Age and the American natives, see "De l'experience" (*Essais*, p. 1196).

4. Gerard Genette, *Seuils* (Paris: Éditions du Seuil, 1987).

5. Montaigne, *Essais*, p. 545; *The Essays*, "Apology for Raimond Sebond," p. 487.

6. Torquato Tasso, *Aminta*, vv. 656ff. The parallel between Montaigne and Tasso has been noted in Richard Cody, *The Landscape of the Mind* (Oxford: Clarendon Press, 1969), p. 57. See also Ronsard, *Discours contre fortune*, in which he addresses the explorer Nicolas Durand de Villegaignon in the following terms: "Comme ton Amérique, où le peuple incognu / Erre innocentement tout farouche et tout nu, / D'habit tout aussi nu qu'il est nu de malice, / Qui ne cognoist les noms de vertu ny de vice, / De Senat ny de Roy, qui vit à son plaisir / Porté de l'appetit de son premier desir, / Et qui n'a dedans l'ame ainsi que nous emprainte / La frayeur de la loy qui nous fait vivre en crainte: / Mais suivant sa nature est seul maistre de soy / Soy-mesme est sa loy, son Senat et son Roy: / Qui de coutres trenchans la terre n'importune, / Laquelle comme l'air à chascun est commune, / Et comme l'eau d'un fleuve, est commun tout leur

bien, / Sans procez engendrer de ce mot *Tien et Mien*" ("Le second livre des poèmes," in *Œuvres complètes*, ed. Gustave Cohen [Paris: Gallimard, 1994], p. 778). Cf. Elizabeth Armstrong, *Ronsard and the Age of Gold* (Cambridge: Cambridge University Press, 1968), and, more generally, Nicole Pellegrin, "Vêtements de peau(x) et de plumes: La nudité des Indiens et la diversité du monde au XVIe siècle," in *Voyager à la Renaissance*, Actes du Colloque de Tours 1983, sous la direction de Jean Céard et Jean-Claude Margolin (Paris: Éditions Maisonneuve & Larose, 1987), pp. 509–530.

7. L. F. Benedetto, "Il Montaigne a Sant'Anna," *Giornale Storico della Letteratura Italiana* 73 (1919): 213–234: 218–219n2; Isida Cremona, *L'influence de l'Aminta sur la pastorale dramatique française* (Paris: Vrin, 1977), pp. 33ff. (who ignores the previously cited article).

8. Richard A. Sayce and David Maskell, *A Descriptive Bibliography of Montaigne's "essais," 1580–1700* (London: Bibliographical Society, 1983). Tasso received the first copies of the first edition of the *Aminta*, published in Cremona, on 3 December 1580 (cf. *La raccolta tassiana della Biblioteca Civica "A. Mai" di Bergamo* [n.p., n.d.], p. 261).

9. Montaigne, *Essais*, p. 546; *The Essays*, "Apology for Raimond Sebond," p. 487; Benedetto, "Il Montaigne a Sant'Anna."

10. *La métamorphose d'Ovide figurée* (Lyon: Jean de Tournes, 1557; facsimile reprint 1933, Collection d'unica et de livres rares, no. 3, with R. Brun's descriptive leaflet on the illustrations). Cf. Harry Levin, *The Myth of the Golden Age in the Renaissance* (Bloomington: Indiana University Press, 1969), first page, and the appendix, pp. 197–198. On the author of the etchings, see Natalis Rondot, *Bernard Salomon, peintre et tailleur d'histoire à Lyon, au XVIe siècle* (Lyon: Imprimerie de Mougin-Rusand, 1897), who remarks (p. 53) that the grotesques accompanying the French translation of Ovid are similar to the illustrations of *La plaisante et joyeuse histoire de Gargantua et Pantagruel* (see *Les songes drolatiques de Pantagruel* [La Chaux-de-Fonds, 1989], with a brilliant introduction by M. Jeanneret, "Rire à la face du monstre"). Salomon, who frequently used a five-pointed star as a signature (ibid., p. 27), might have been a converted Jew. See also M. D. Henkel, "Illustrierte Ausgaben von Ovids Metamorphosen im XV., XVI., und XVII. Jahrhundert," *Bibliothek Warburg Vorträge 1926–1927* (Leipzig: Teubner, 1930), pp. 58–144: 77ff. Some of Salomon's grotesques, despite their occasional obscenity, were also used in Clement Marot and Théodore de Bèze, *Les Pseaumes mis en rime françoise*, à Lyon, par Jean de Tournes, 1563, ff. Q i v (ps. LICX), R 5v (ps. LXVIII), etc.

11. Levin (*Myth of the Golden Age*, pp. 197–198) notices that "the second of the two summarizing quatrains, departing from Ovid and foreshadowing Tasso, sounds the praise of free love."

12. Nicole Dacos, *La découverte de la Domus Aurea et la formation des grotesques à la Renaissance*, Studies of the Warburg Institute 31 (London and Leiden, 1969); idem, in N. Dacos-Caterina Furlan, *Giovanni da Udine*, vol. 1 (Udine: Casamassima, 1987). See also H. de Geymüller, *Les du Cerceau, leur vie et leur œuvre* (Paris and London: J. Rouam & G. Wood, 1887). More evidence can be found in Carlo Ossola, *Autunno del Rinascimento* (Florence: Olschki, 1971), pp. 184–207.

13. Montaigne, *Essais*, "De l'amité," p. 218 (*The Essays*, pp. 182–183). André Chastel chose this passage as a starting point for his essay *La grottesque* (Paris: Le Promeneur, 1988).

14. François Enaud, "Peintures murales de la seconde moitié du XVIe siècle decouvertes au château de Villeneuve-Lembrun (Puy-de Dôme)," in André Chastel, ed., *Actes du colloque international sur l'art de Fontainebleau* (Paris: Éditions du Centre National de la Recherche Scientifique, 1975), pp. 185–197: 194. See also Jean Adhémar, "L'estampe et la transmission des formes maniéristes," in *Le triomphe du Maniérisme Européen* (Amsterdam: Rijks-Museum, 1955), pp. 34–36.

15. J. Céard, *La Nature et les prodiges: L'insolite, au XVIe siècle en France* (Geneva: Droz, 1977), pp. 387ff. (chap. 16: "L'idée de variété dans les *Essais*"); Imbrie Buffum, *L'influence du voyage de Montaigne sur les "Essais"* (Princeton, NJ: Princeton University Press, 1946), pp. 121–133 (chap. 5, "Unité et diversité"). For a remarkable parallel, see Cristina Del Lungo, "La *Zucca* del Doni e la struttura della 'grottesca,'" *Paradigma* 2 (1978): 71–91.

16. M. de Montaigne, *Journal de voyage . . . en Italie . . .* , ed. Alessandro D'Ancona (Città di Castello: Lapi, 1895), pp. 163–164, 177–178, 527–530 (still important even after the recent edition of François Rigolot [Paris: Presses Universitaires de France, 1992]). See also Lino Pertile, "Montaigne in Italia: Arte, tecnica e scienza dal *Journal* agli *Essais*," *Saggi e Ricerche di Letteratura Francese*, n.s., vol. 12 (1973): 49–82; Richard A. Sayce, "The Visual Arts in Montaigne's Journal de Voyage," in Raymond C. La Charité, ed., *O un amy! Essays on Montaigne in Honor of Donald M. Frame* (Lexington: University of Kentucky Press, 1977), pp. 219–241.

17. Montaigne, *Essais*, p. 344.

18. See André Chastel, *The Palace of Apollidon* (The Zaharoff Lecture for 1984–1985) (Oxford: Oxford University Press, 1986), p. 3.

19. Vitruvius, *De architectura*, ed. Carol Herselle Krinsky (photostatic reprint of the 1521 edition) (Munich: Fink Verlag 1969), introduction pp. 5–6; text, fol. 31v. See also *Architecture ou art de bien bastir, de Marc Vitruve Pollion, Autheur Romain Antique, mis de latin en François par Ian Martin . . .* à Paris 1547, fols. C ii v ff.

20. Montaigne, *Journal de voyage*, pp. 163–164 (*The Works of Michel de Montaigne*, ed. W. Hazlitt, 2nd ed. [London 1845], p. 565).

21. Detlef Heikamp, "La grotta grande del giardino di Boboli," *Antichità Viva* 4, no. 4 (1965): 27–43; Emil Maurer, "Zwischen Gestein und Gestalt: Zur grossen Grotte im Boboli-Garten in Florenz" (1977), in *Manierismus: Figura serpentinata und andere Figurenideale* (Zürich: Fink, 2001), pp. 131–137; Ida Maria Botto, "Buontalenti, Bernardo," *Dizionario Biografico degli Italiani* 15:280–284. See also W. Smyth, "Pratolino," *Journal of the Society of Architectural Historians* 20 (1961): 155–168; *Boboli '90: Atti del convegno internazionale di studi*, 2 vols. (Florence: Edifir, [1991]). On Castello, see also L. Châtelet-Lange, "The Grotto of the Unicorn and the Garden of the Villa of Castello," *Art Bulletin* 50 (1968): 51–58.

22. Quoted from Heikamp, "La grotta grande," p. 43.

23. One of Montaigne's recurrent appreciations of Plutarch reads: "Il me semble avoir veu en Plutarque (qui est de tous les autheurs que je cognoisse celuy qui a mieux meslé l'art à la nature et le jugement à la science) . . ." (*Essais*, p. 1006); *Essays* (Penguin ed.), p. 264: "I think that it was in Plutarch—who of all the authors I know is the best at combining art with nature, and judgement with knowledge—that I read. . . ."

24. E. Kris, "Der Stil 'rustique': Die Verwendung des Naturabgusses bei Wenzel Jamnitzer und Bernard Palissy," *Jahrbuch der Kunsthistorischen Sammlungen in Wien*, n.s. 1 (1926): 137–208.

25. Ibid., p. 196: ". . . der grosse Man zeigt sich hier im kleinen als echtes Kind seiner Zeit." See also the perceptive pages in Michel Butor, *Essai sur les Essais* (Paris: Gallimard, 1968), pp. 66–71, 114–119. Cf. Naomi Miller, "Domain of Illusion: The Grotto in France," in *Fons Sapientiae: Renaissance Garden Fountains* (Washington, DC: Dumbarton Oaks, 1978), pp. 175–205; J. Céard, "Relire Bernard Palissy," *Revue de l'Art* 78 (1987): 77–83.

26. S. Serlio, *Regole generali di architettura*, 3rd ed. (Venice, 1551), book 4, fols. xiv–xiir. See James S. Ackerman, "The Tuscan/Rustic Order: A Study in the Metaphoric Language of Architecture," in *Distance Points: Essays in Theory and Renaissance Art and Architecture* (Cambridge, MA: Harvard University Press, 1991), pp. 495–545. Cf. *Natura e artificio: L'ordine rustico, le fontane e gli automi nella cultura del Manierismo europeo*, ed. Marcello Fagiolo (Rome: Officina Edizioni, 1981).

27. This point was emphasized in E. H. Gombrich, "Zum Werke Giulio Romanos," *Jahrbuch der Kunsthistorischen Sammlungen in Wien*, n.s., vol. 8 (1934): 79–104; vol. 9 (1935): 121–150: 86–87 (an essay to which I am greatly indebted). See also idem, "Architecture and Rhetoric in Giulio Romano's Palazzo del Te," in *New Light on Old Masters* (Chicago: University of Chicago Press, 1986), pp. 161–170.

28. The importance of Serlio's *Libro estraordinario* has been underlined in John Onians, *Bearers of Meaning: The Classical Orders in Antiquity, the Middle Ages, the Renaissance* (Princeton, NJ: Princeton University Press, 1988), pp. 263–286. For a useful overview of the literature on Serlio (and a less useful attempt to present him as a postmodernist), see idem, "Serlio and the History of Architecture," in Giovanna Perini, ed., *Il luogo e il ruolo della città di Bologna tra Europa continentale e mediterraneo* (Bologna: Nuova Alfa, 1992), pp. 181–199. See also Christof Thoenens, ed., *Sebastiano Serlio: Sesto seminario internazionale di storia dell'architettura* (Milan: Electa, 1989).

29. I have used the Venice 1566 edition. Ackerman's quotation (*Distance Points*, p. 543, with a reference to the forest at Fontainebleau) seems to have been taken from the first edition, which I have not seen. On the presence at Fontainebleau of Rosso, Primaticcio, and other Italian painters, see Sylvie Béguin, *L'École de Fontainebleau: Le Maniérisme à la cour de France* (Paris: Éditions Gonthier-Seghers, 1960).

30. See Bernard Palissy, *Architecture et Ordonnance de la grotte rustique de Monseigneur le duc de Montmorency connestable de France, réimprimé d'après l'édition de La Rochelle 1563* (Paris, 1919).

31. Antoine Compagnon, *La seconde main, ou le travail de la citation* (Paris: Éditions du Seuil, 1979), pp. 299ff.

32. "Nos vero, ut captus noster est, incuriose et inmeditate ac prope etiam subrustice ex ipso loco ac tempore hibernarum vigiliarum Atticas noctes inscripsimus" (Aulus Gellius, *Noctes Atticae*, preface).

33. Here I am developing some of the implications in "Les après midi périgourdins," the title chosen by Compagnon for his chapter on Montaigne (*La seconde main*, pp. 299ff.).

34. S. Serlio, *Libro estraordinario, nel quale si dimostrano trenta porte di opera rustica mista con diversi ordini*, in Venetia 1566, fols. 29v–30r.

35. S. Serlio, *Libro primo (-quinto) d'architettura*, in Venetia 1566, bk. IV, chap. 11, fol. 192r.

36. S. Serlio, *Regole generali*, fol. XI v.

37. Montaigne, *Essais*, p. 242; *Essays* (Penguin ed.), p. 108.

38. M. Eyquem de Montaigne, *Essais, réproduction photographique de l'édition originale de 1580*, ed. D. Martin (Geneva and Paris: Droz, 1976), p. 303v.

39. Montaigne, *Essais*, p. 1078. See A. Chastel, "Le fragmentaire, l'hybride, l'inachévé," in *Fables, formes, figures* (Paris: Flammarion, 1978), 2:33–45; Jean Lafond, "Achèvement, inachèvement dans les *Essais*," *Bulletin de la Société des Amis de Montaigne*, ser. 7, nos. 13–16 (July–December 1988/January–June 1989): 175–188; Arnaud Tripet, "Projet, développement, achèvement dans les *Essais*," ibid., pp. 189–201.

40. Erwin Panofsky, *Galileo as a Critic of the Arts* (The Hague: Nijhoff, 1954), pp. 17–18. Galileo's *Considerazioni* have been dated between 1595 and 1609 (ibid., pp. 19–20n2). See also G. Galilei, *Scritti letterari*, ed. Alberto Chiari (Florence: Le Monnier, 1970), pp. 493–494. For other pertinent references, see Ossola, *Autunno del Rinascimento*, pp. 86–94.

41. Arnold Hauser, *Der Manierismus* (Munich: Beck, 1964), pp. 325–327; R. A. Sayce, "Renaissance et Maniérisme dans l'œuvre de Montaigne," in *Renaissance, Maniérisme, Baroque* (Paris: Vrin, 1972), pp. 137–151.

42. G. Galilei, *Scritti letterari*, pp. 502–503.

43. Panofsky, *Galileo*, pp. 60–61.

44. Montaigne, *Essais*, p. 46; *The Essays*, p. 208. Cf. also Kris, *Der Stil "rustique*," p. 143. See also Julius von Schlosser, *Die Kunst- und Wunderkammern der Spätrenaissance* (Leipzig, 1908) (I have consulted the Italian translation, accompanied by useful notes: *Raccolte d'arte e di meraviglie del tardo Rinascimento*, ed. Paola di Paolo [Florence: Sansoni, 1974]).

45. For the moral implications of the style, see E. H. Gombrich, "Visual Metaphors of Value in Art," in *Meditations on a Hobby Horse* (London: Phaidon, 1963), pp. 12–29, 163–165. Cf. also my "Stile," in *Occhiacci di legno: Nove riflessioni sulla distanza* (Milan: Feltrinelli, 1998), pp. 136–170.

46. On this point, see R. A. Sayce, "Renaissance Mannerism and Baroque," in *The Essays of Montaigne: A Critical Exploration* (London: Weidenfeld & Nicolson, 1972), pp. 319–320.

47. Montaigne, *Essais*, p. 242. See Frank Lestringant, *André Thevet, cosmographe des derniers Valois* (Geneva: Droz, 1991) (with abundant bibliography).

48. A. Thevet, *Les vrais pourtraits et vies des hommes illustres* (Paris, 1584), fol. b iv r. The editions and translations of the work are recorded in Lestringant, *André Thevet*, pp. 376–381. Cf. Francis Haskell, *History and Its Images: Art and the Interpretation of the Past* (New Haven, CT, and London: Yale University Press, 1993), pp. 51–52.

49. Thevet, *Les vrais pourtraits*, fol. 650r (reproduced in Frank Lestringant, ed., *Le Brésil de Montaigne: Le Nouveau Monde des "Essais" (1580–1592)* [Paris: Chandeigne, 2005], p. 204).

50. Cited in Jean Baudry, introduction to André Thevet, *Les singularitez de la France Antarctique, autrement nommée Amérique* (Paris: Le Temps, 1981), p. 40.

51. Lestringant, *André Thevet*, p. 380.

52. Eugene Müntz, "Le musée des portraits de Paul Jove: Contribution pour servir à l'iconographie du Moyen Age et de la Renaissance," *Mémoires de l'Académie des Inscriptions et Belles-Lettres* 36, pt. 2 (1900).

53. This was stressed in Federico Chabod, "Paolo Giovio," in idem, *Scritti sul Rinascimento* (Turin: Einaudi, 1967), pp. 243–267: 262ff.

54. Müntz, "Le musée," pp. 13–14. On a general level, see Christian F. Feest, "Mexico and South America in the European *Wunderkammer*," in Oliver Impey and Arthur MacGregor, eds., *The Origins of Museums* (Oxford: Oxford University Press, 1985), pp. 237–244.

55. Lestringant, *André Thevet*, pp. 38–39. See also Jean Adhémar, *Frère André Thevet. Profils Franciscains* 28 (Paris: Éditions Franciscaines, 1947), p. 28.

56. Lestringant, *André Thevet*, p. 378.

57. Montaigne, *Essais*, pp. 251–252.

58. This is the kind of terminology used, in general, in Tzvetan Todorov, *The Conquest of America: The Question of the Other* (New York: Harper & Row, 1984). But see the perceptive comments in Antoine Compagnon, *Chat-en-poche: Montaigne et l'allégorie* (Paris: Presses Universitaires de France, 1993), pp. 41ff. (on Todorov and R. Romano).

59. R. A. Sayce, "Imitation and Originality: Montaigne and Books," in Sayce, *The Essays of Montaigne*, pp. 31–32, where he has perceived an antiquarian element in the essay "Des coustumes anciennes."

60. Montaigne, *Journal de voyage*, pp. 274–275: "J'y vis aussi un Virgile ecrit à mein, d'une lettre infiniement grosse, & de ce caractere long & etroit que nous voïons ici aus inscriptions du tamps des ampereurs, come environ le siecle de Constantin, qui ont quelque façon//gothique, & ont perdu cete proportion carré, qui est aus vielles escritures latines."

61. Sebastiano Timpanaro considers it as an "enormity" that in the past these verses could have been considered authentic (*Per la storia della filologia virgiliana antica*, Quaderni di Filologia e Critica 6 [Rome: Salerno, 1986], pp. 16–17). In fact, this attitude is still shared, for example, by Jacques Perret (*Enéide* [Paris: Les Belles

Lettres, 1981], p. xlvi). See also the detailed discussion in Walter Schmid, *Vergil-Probleme*, Göppinger Akademische Beiträge 120 (Göppingen: Kümmerle, 1983), who attributes to Vergil the authorship of the four verses. Cf. also Remigio Sabbadini, *Le scoperte dei codici latini e greci nei secoli XIV e XV* (1905), edizione anastatica con nuove aggiunte e correzioni dell'autore a cura di Eugenio Garin, 2 vols. (Florence: Sansoni, 1967), 1:154.

62. Montaigne, *Journal de voyage*, p. 275n1.

63. Poliziano had dated the codex to approximately the sixth century: see Sabbadini, *Le scoperte dei codici*, 1:154, 169. A comparison between the illuminations of the Vat. lat. 3867 and sculptures of the age of Constantine was first proposed in C. Nordenfolk, *Der Kalender vom Jahre 354 und die lateinische Buchmalerei des IV. Jahrhunderts* (Göteborg, 1936), pp. 31–36. Cf. Earl Rosenthal, *The Illuminations of the Vergilius Romanus (Cod. Vat. Lat. 3867): A Stylistic and Iconographic Analysis* (Zürich: Urs Graf-Verlag, 1972), p. 9; and David H. Wright, *The Roman Vergil and the Origins of Medieval Book Design* (Toronto and Buffalo: University of Toronto Press, 2001). Wright leans toward a date about 480. Unless I am mistaken, none of the above mention Montaigne.

64. Claude de Bellièvre, *Souvenirs de voyage en Italie et en Orient: Notes historiques, pièces de vers*, ed. Charles Perrat (Geneva: Droz, 1956), pp. 4–5. (In his notebook Bellièvre reproduced the manuscript's peculiar lettering.) See also Anthony Grafton, "The Scholarship of Poliziano and Its Context," in idem, *Defenders of the Text* (Cambridge, MA: Harvard University Press, 1991), pp. 47–48.

65. Montaigne, *Essais*, p. 189; *Essays*, "On the Education of Children" (Penguin ed.), p. 61 (slightly modified).

66. On this point, see Arnaldo Momigliano, "Ancient History and the Antiquarian," *Journal of the Warburg and Courtauld Institutes* 13 (1950): 285–315.

67. I have dealt with this theme fleetingly in *Rapporti di forza: Storia, retorica, prova* (Milan: Feltrinelli, 2000), pp. 100–105.

68. Lucien Febvre, *Civilisation: Le mot et l'idée*, Publications du Centre International de Synthèse (Paris, 1930), pp. 1–55; E. Benveniste, "Civilisation: Contribution à l'histoire du mot," in *Éventail de l'histoire vivante: Hommage à Lucien Febvre* (Paris: A. Colin, 1953), 1: 47–54.

69. Montaigne, *Essais*, pp. 251–252. These observations had been prepared by the quotation from Plutarch that appears at the beginning of the essay: ". . . King Pyrrhus remarked 'I do not know what barbarians these are—for so the Greeks called all foreign nations—but the ordering of the army before me has nothing barbarous about it'" (Montaigne, *Essays* [Penguin ed.], p. 105). On this, see Edwin M. Duval, "Lessons of the New World: Design and Meaning in Montaigne's 'Des cannibales' (1:31) and 'Des coches' (3:6)," *Yale French Studies* 64 (1983): 95ff.

70. Montaigne, *Essais*, pp. 242–243; *Essays* (Penguin ed.), p. 108.

71. Montaigne, *Essais*, p. 248; *Essays* (Penguin ed.), pp. 113–114.

72. Montaigne, *Essais*, pp. 243–244; *Essays* (Penguin ed.), p. 109.

73. Montaigne, *Essais*, p. 251; *Essays* (Penguin ed.), p. 117.

74. Montaigne, *Essais*, p. 253; *Essays* (Penguin ed.), p. 119.

CHAPTER 4. PROOFS AND POSSIBILITIES

1. Michel de Montaigne, *Essais*, ed. Albert Thibaudet (Paris: Gallimard, 1950), p. 1156. See Natalie Zemon Davis, *The Return of Martin Guerre* (Cambridge, MA: Harvard University Press, 1983), p. 119, in which Davis uses the famous Renaissance translation of Montaigne by John Florio (1603): "I remember . . . that me thought he proved his imposture, whom he condemned as guiltie, so wondrous-strange and so-far exceeding both our knowledge and his owne, who was judge, that I found much boldness in the sentence, which had condemned him to be hanged" (facsimile reprint of the original edition [Menston: Scholar Press, 1969], p. 615).

2. Montaigne, *Essais*, p. 1159. "When all is done, it is an over-valuing of one's conjectures, by them to cause a man to be burned alive" (Florio translation, p. 1159). Leonardo Sciascia dwells on this passage in his *Sentenza memorabile* (Palermo: Sellerio, 1982), p. 11, where he reviews the various accounts produced by the case of Martin Guerre.

3. Montaigne, *Essais*, p. 1155. "I am drawne to hate likely things, when men goe about to set them downe as infallible. I love these words or phrases, which mollifie and moderate the temeritie of our propositions: 'It may be,' 'Peradventure,' 'In some sort,' 'Some,' 'It is saide,' 'I think,' and such like. . . ." (Florio translation, p. 614).

4. Davis, *The Return of Martin Guerre*, p. viii.

5. See now my preface to the Italian translation of Marc Bloch, *I re taumaturghi* (Turin: Einaudi, 1973).

6. See "Clues: Roots of an Evidential Paradigm," in Carlo Ginzburg, *Clues, Myths, and the Historical Method*, trans. John Tedeschi and Anne C. Tedeschi (Baltimore: Johns Hopkins University Press, 1989), pp. 96–125: 117.

7. Georges Duby, *Le dimanche de Bouvines* (Paris: Gallimard, 1973).

8. I have found stimulating the article by Luigi Ferrajoli on the so-called "Case of 7 April," *Il Manifesto*, 23 and 24 February 1983; see especially the first part. But the question of "judicial historiography" alluded to there will have to be studied further.

9. Davis, *The Return of Martin Guerre*, p. 5.

10. J. de Coras, *Arrest memorable, du Parlement de Tolose, Contenant une histoire prodigieuse, de nostre temps.* . . . (Lyon: Antoine Vincent, 1561), dedication.

11. In addition to the copy cited by Davis, another exemplar from this printing run with a misprint in the title (*Histoite* rather than *Histoire*) is housed in the Bibliothèque Nationale (call no. Rés. Z. Fontanieu 171, 12). The sonnet does not appear in a late printing, not mentioned by Davis (*Recit veritable d'un faux et supposé mary, arrivé à une Femme notable, au pays de Languedoc, en ce derniers troubles*, à Paris chez Jean Brunet, ruë neufve sainct Louys, à la Crosse d'Or, MDCXXXVI: BN 80. LN 27. 27815).

12. J. de Coras, *Arrest memorable* (Paris, 1572), Arrest CIIII. In the introduction to this expanded edition, the printer, Gaillot du Pré, in addition to defining the small work as a "tragicomédie," as Davis notes, also declares that he has not "changé un iota du langaige de l'autheur, à fin que plus facilement on puisse discerner cette presente coppie, avec plusieurs autres imprimées parcidevant: l'autheur desquelles s'estoit tellement pleu à Amadizer, qu'il avoit assez maigrement récité la verité du fait." It is not clear what is meant by this statement: the term "coppie" makes one think of previous defective editions of Coras's text. "Amadizer," instead, suggests actual fictional revisions of the Martin Guerre story on the model of the *Amadis of Gaul.* Favoring this second hypothesis is the fact that the first twelve books of the French translation of the *Amadis* had been reprinted between 1555 and 1560 by Vincent Sertenas and Estienne Groulleau, and that Sertenas himself had published Le Sueur's *Histoire admirable.* Thus, the person who had "maigrement récité la verité du fait" could be identified with Sertenas.

13. Coras, *Arrest memorable* (1572 ed.), pp. 146, 149.

14. [Guillaume Le Sueur], *Histoite* [sic] *admirable,* fol. Aiir.

15. Coras, *Arrest memorable* (1572 ed.), p. 39.

16. Tzvetan Todorov has embarked on this type of research with his excellent book *The Conquest of America: The Question of the Other* (New York: Harper & Row, 1984).

17. For two recent examples, see Jürgen Kocka and Thomas Nipperday, eds., *Theorie und Erzählung in der Geschichte.* Theorie und Geschichte 3 (Munich: Deutscher Taschenbuch Verlag, 1979); Hayden White, "La questione della narrazione nella teoria contemporanea della storiografia," in Paolo Rossi, ed., *La teoria della storiografia oggi* (Milan: Il Saggiatore, 1983), pp. 33–78. See also the ambitious work by Paul Ricœur, *Temps et récit* (Paris: Seuil, 1983), vol. 1; trans. Kathleen Blamey and David Pellauer as *Time and Narrative* (Chicago: University of Chicago Press, 1988).

18. Wolfgang J. Mommsen and Jorn Rüsen, in Rossi, *La teoria della storiografia oggi,* pp. 109, 200. However, they do not go as far as to reformulate the terms in which the question is generally posed.

19. Lawrence Stone, "The Revival of Narrative: Reflections on a New Old History," *Past and Present* 85 (1979): 3–24; E. J. Hobsbawm, "The Revival of Narrative: Some Comments," ibid. 86 (1980): 3–8.

20. Ed. J. Donald Crowley (London: Oxford University Press, 1972), p. [1].

21. Henry Fielding, *Tom Jones, an Authoritative Text, Contemporary Reactions, Criticism,* ed. Sheridan Baker (New York and London: Norton, 1973), p. 58.

22. See Fielding, *Tom Jones,* chap. 1 of bk. 8 (p. 304). On the antithesis between the age of the chronicle and of the epic and the age of the novel, see the enlightening essay by Walter Benjamin, "The Storyteller: Reflections on the Works of Nikolai Leskov," in *Illuminations* (extracts of *Angelus novus*), ed. Hannah Arendt, trans. Harry Zohn (New York: Harcourt, 1968), pp. 83–110. Karl-Heinz Stierle takes it as his point of departure in "Erfahrung und Narrative Form," in Kocka and Nipperday, *Theorie und Erzählung,* pp. 85ff.

23. Ian Watt, *The Rise of the Novel: Studies in Defoe, Richardson and Fielding* (1957) (Berkeley: University of California Press, 1967), p. 292.

24. Fielding, *Tom Jones*, 1:516.

25. Ibid., pp. 417–418.

26. The quotation is from Leo Braudy, *Narrative Form in History and Fiction* (Princeton, NJ: Princeton University Press, 1970), p. 13.

27. *Honoré de Balzac in Twenty-Five Volumes* (New York: Collier, 1900), 1:15. For the original text, cf. Honoré de Balzac, *La Comédie humaine* (Paris: Gallimard, 1951), p. 7: "La Société française allait être l'historien, je ne devais être que le secrétaire. . . . Peut-être pouvais-je arriver à écrire l'histoire oubliée par tant d'historiens, celle des mœurs. Avec beaucoup de patience et de courage, je réaliserais, sur la France au XIXe siècle, ce livre que nous regrettons tous, que Rome, Athènes, Tyr, Memphis, la Perse, l'Inde ne nous ont malheureusement pas laissé sur leurs civilisations. . . ."

28. *Balzac in Twenty-Five Volumes*, 21:12–13 (slightly modified); *La Comédie humaine*, pp. 12–13: "J'accorde aux faits constants, quotidiens, secrets ou patents, aux actes de la vie individuelle, à leurs causes et à leurs principes, autant d'importance que jusqu'alors les historiens ont attaché aux événements de la vie publique des nations."

29. Renato Bertacchini, ed., *Documenti e prefazioni del romanzo italiano dell'Ottocento* (Rome: Editrice Studium, 1969), pp. 32ff., which reprints the introduction to the 3rd ed. of the *Falco della rupe* (Milan, 1831).

30. Alessandro Manzoni, *Opere*, ed. Riccardo Bacchelli (Milan and Naples: Ricciardi, 1953), pp. 1056, 1068–1069. This passage is taken from Sandra Berman's translation of Manzoni's *On the Historical Novel* (Lincoln and London: University of Nebraska Press, 1984), pp. 63–64, 76–77.

31. *Balzac in Twenty-Five Volumes*, vol. 21. Cf. Balzac, *La Comédie humaine*, 1:13: "La bataille inconnue qui se livre dans une vallée de l'Indre entre *madame de Mortsauf* et la passion est peut-être aussi grande que la plus illustre des batailles connues."

32. Hayden White, *Metahistory: The Historical Imagination in Nineteenth-Century Europe* (Baltimore and London: Johns Hopkins University Press, 1973).

33. François Hartog, *The Mirror of Herodotus: The Representation of the Other in the Writing of History* (Berkeley: University of California Press, 1988). I have used the original text, *Le miroir d'Hérodote: Essai sur la représentation de l'autre* (Paris: Gallimard, 1980), pp. 23ff., 141–142.

34. White, *Metahistory*, p. 3n.

35. Ibid., pp. 432–433. The reference to Gombrich and to the notion of "realism" is repeated at the beginning of the essay "La questione della narrazione" (p. 33n1) but then diverges.

36. Arnaldo Momigliano, "L'histoire dans l'âge des idéologies," *Le Débat* 23 (1983): 129–146; idem, "Biblical Studies and Classical Studies: Simple Reflections upon Historical Method," *Annali della Scuola Normale Superiore di Pisa*, ser. 3, vol. 11 (1981): 25–32.

37. Idem, "Ancient History and the Antiquarian," *Journal of the Warburg and Courtauld Institutes* 13 (1950): 285–315.

38. Gibbon, *History of the Decline and Fall of the Roman Empire*, quoted by L. Braudy (*Narrative Form*, p. 216), who notes the importance of this passage, but in a different context.

39. Manzoni, *On the Historical Novel*, pp. 74–75; Manzoni, *Opere*, pp. 1066–1067.

40. Benedetto Croce, *La storia come pensiero e come azione* (Bari: Laterza, 1938), pp. 122–128 (there already is a hint of it in idem, "La storia ridotta sotto il concetto generale dell'arte," in *Primi saggi* [Bari: Laterza, 1927], pp. 39–40).

41. Piero Zerbi, "A proposito di tre libri recenti di storia: Riflessioni sopra alcuni problemi di metodo," *Aevum* 31 (1957): 524n17, where Frugoni's indebtedness to Croce is suggested cautiously as a question. I am indebted to Giovanni Kral, who brought this to my attention in a seminar at the University of Bologna.

42. Arsenio Frugoni, *Arnaldo da Brescia nelle fonti del secolo XII* (Rome: Istituto Storico Italiano per il Medioevo, 1954), p. ix.

43. Zerbi, "A proposito," p. 504.

44. On this problem as applied to the history of art, see the discussion between Antonio Pinelli and the present writer in *Quaderni Storici* 50 (1982): 682–727.

45. A. Manzoni, *La "Lettre à M. Chauvet,"* ed. Natalino Sapegno (Rome: Edizioni dell'Ateneo, 1947), pp. 59–60: "This invention is that which is most facile and coarse in the work of the spirit, that which calls for the least reflection, and even less imagination"; idem, *I promessi sposi*, chap. 13.

46. These words from Austen's *Northanger Abbey* (London: Richard Bentley; Edinburgh: Bell & Bradfute, 1848), p. 87, were adopted by Edward H. Carr as the half title of his *What Is History?* (New York: Knopf, 1963), p. [iii].

47. Henry James, "The Art of Fiction," in Hazard Adams, ed., *Critical Theory since Plato* (New York: Harcourt, 1971), p. 662.

48. Fielding, *Tom Jones*, 1:418.

CHAPTER 5. A DIALOGUE ON FICTION AND HISTORY

I should like to thank R. Howard Bloch, who read a preliminary version of this essay and who corrected a number of errors; and Peter Burke, who noticed the absence of La Mothe Le Vayer in a slightly later redaction of the paper which I presented at Cambridge and subsequently published.

1. Marcel Detienne, *The Creation of Mythology*, trans. Margaret Cook (Chicago: University of Chicago Press, 1986), pp. 23–26; p. 141n19; p. 142n32. According to Detienne, Vidal-Naquet's introduction to the *Iliad* "distances itself from [Moses] Finley's historical interpretation" (p. 56n29). Actually, Vidal Naquet's position is much more nuanced: see "L'Iliade sans travesti," in *La démocratie grecque vue d'ailleurs* (Paris: Flammarion, 1990), pp. 38–39; and, in the same volume, "Économie et société dans la Grèce ancienne: L'œuvre de Moses Finley," pp. 55–94: 59ff. Cf. also the review by

Arnaldo Momigliano of the original French edition of Detienne's work *Invention de la mythologie* (1981) in *Rivista Storica Italiana* 94 (1982): 784–787.

2. Detienne, *Creation of Mythology*, p. 150n75.

3. On its dating, I now follow Jean-Pierre Cavaillé, "Galanterie et histoire de l'antiquité moderne: Jean Chapelain, de la lecture des vieux romans, 1647," *XVIIe Siècle* 50 (1998): 387–415, reprinted as the introduction to Cavaillé's edition of *De la lecture des vieux romans* (Paris: Zanzibar, 1999).

4. Voltaire's parody *La Pucelle d'Orléans* delivered the coup de grâce to Chapelain's poem.

5. See *Lettres de Jean Chapelain*, ed. Philippe Tamizey de Larroque, 2 vols. (Paris: Imprimerie Nationale, 1880–1883); J. Chapelain, *Soixante-dix-sept lettres inédites à Nicolas Heinsius (1649–1658)*, ed. Bernard Bray (The Hague: Nijhoff, 1966). On his literary career, see Christian Jouhaud, *Les pouvoirs de la litterature: Histoire d'un paradoxe* (Paris: Gallimard, 2000), pp. 97–150.

6. Except for one small correction, I have used the following text: J. Chapelain, *Opuscules critiques*, ed. Alfred C. Hunter (Paris: Droz, 1936), pp. 205–241. Other editions: [Pierre Nicolas Desmolets], *Continuation des mémoires de littérature et d'histoire* (Paris: Simart, 1728); another, ed. A. Feillet, who reprinted the dialogue, assuming it to be unpublished (Paris, 1870; reprinted Geneva: Slatkine, 1968); Fabienne Gegou, *Lettre-traité de Pierre-Daniel Huet sur l'origine des romans . . . suivie de la Lecture des vieux romans par Jean Chapelain* (Paris: A.-G. Nizet, 1971) (with useful commentary); and especially the Paris 1999 edition by Jean-Pierre Cavaillé. See also J. de Beer, "Literary Circles in Paris, 1619–1660," *Publications of the Modern Language Association* 53 (1938): 730–780: 757–758; Jean Frappier, "Voltaire amateur de vieux romans," in *Amour courtois et Table Ronde* (Geneva: Droz, 1973), pp. 283ff.; C. Delhez-Sarlet, "Le Lancelot 'fabuleux et historique': Vraisemblance et crédibilité d'un récit au XVIIe siècle," in *Mélanges offerts à Rita Lejeune* (Gembloux, Belgium: Editions Duculot, 1969), 2:1535ff.

7. Toward the end of the seventeenth century, poets, critics, and antiquarians gathered around the cardinal de Retz: see J. de Beer, "Literary Circles." On the libertines, see René Pintard, *Le libertinage érudit dans la première moitié du dix-septième siècle* (Paris: Boivin, 1943; reprinted with a new introduction, Geneva and Paris: Droz, 1983). See also Tullio Gregory et al., eds., *Ricerche su letteratura libertina e letteratura clandestina nel Seicento* (Florence: La Nuova Italia, 1981).

8. Paul de Gondi was Ménage's patron at the time, but their relationship ended in 1652. Ménage rejected the invitation, offered immediately after by Sarasin, to enter the service of Monseigneur de Conti. See G. G., "Ménage et le Cardinal de Retz," *Revue d'Histoire Littéraire de la France* 38 (1931): 283–285; and B. Bray's introduction to Chapelain, *Soixante-dix-sept-lettres*, pp. 168–169n2. Ménage and Sarasin remained friends, but Chapelain broke with both (ibid., pp. 112, 285). Among Sarasin's works published by Ménage, we find a dialogue entitled *S'il faut qu'un jeune homme soit amoureux*, clearly modeled on the *De la lecture des vieux romans*, written a few months earlier

but never published (J.-F. Sarasin, *Œuvres* [Paris, 1694], pp. 139–235, esp. p. 208). Except for M. de Pille and Louis Aubry, sieur de Trilleport, the personages in the two dialogues are the same. In Sarasin's text the starting point of the discussion is the *Roman de Perceforest* instead of the *Lancelot*.

9. See *Catalogue de tous les livres de feu M. Chapelain*, ed. Colbert Searles (Stanford University, CA: The University, 1912), p. 70nn2328–2329. Chapelain possessed the *Histoire de Lancelot* (Paris, 1520, 1591) and *Le premier volume de Lancelot du Lac nouvellement imprimé* (Paris, 1633).

10. An echo of the conversations is caught in Ménage's letter dedicating to Jacques Dupuy the *Origines de la langue françoise* (Paris, 1650): "Et pour remonter jusques à la source . . . il faudroit avoir leu tous nos vieux Poëtes, tous nos vieux Romans, tous nos vieux Coustumiers, et tous nos autres vieux Escrivains, pour suivre comme à la piste et découvrir les altérations que nos mots ont souffertes de temps en temps. Et je n'ay qu'une légère connoissance de la moindre partie de toutes ces choses." We read this passage at the conclusion of an astounding list which includes "l'Hebreu et le Chaldée," "la langue qui se parle en Basse-Bretagne, et l'Alleman avec tous ses differens dialectes," "les diverses idiomes de nos provinces, et le langage des paysans, parmi lesquels les langues se conservent plus longuement."

11. "*Fable*," we read in the *Dictionnaire de l'Académie*, means "an invented narrative intended to teach or entertain. . . . *Fable* also means the subject of an epic or dramatic poem, or the subject of a romance . . ." (Charles Sorel, *De la connoissance des bons livres*, ed. Lucia Moretti [Rome: Bulzoni, 1974], p. 84n23).

12. Chapelain, *Opuscules*, p. 219. On this and similar expressions, see the still-fundamental treatment by Nathan Edelman, *Attitudes of Seventeenth-Century France toward the Middle Ages* (New York: King's Crown Press, 1946), pp. 1–23.

13. The dialogue is not mentioned in the collection *La querelle des Anciens et des Modernes*, ed. and with an introd. by Marc Fumaroli, and with a postscript by Jean-Robert Armogathe (Paris: Gallimard, 2001).

14. See Chapelain, *Opuscules*, p. 209. On the ambiguity of the word *histoire*, resembling the Italian *storia*, see Furetière's *Dictionnaire*: "*Histoire* can also refer to romances, and narratives based on invented events but not intrinsically impossible, as imagined by a writer or presented in a form not immediately recognizable" (Sorel, *De la connoissance des bons livres*, p. 84n23).

15. Chapelain, *Opuscules*, p. 217.

16. This point was misunderstood by Maurice Magendie in *Le roman française au XVIIe siècle* (1932) (Geneva: Slatkine Reprints, 1978), p. 131. Much more pertinent is Detienne's polemical reaction to Finley's statement that verisimilitude was one of the conditions imposed by the audiences of Homeric poems: "But what can it mean for an auditor to demand verisimilitude, probability? What does verisimilitude mean? Surely something other than what Aristotle meant" (*Creation of Mythology*, p. 142n33).

17. On this passage, see [Desmolets], *Continuation des mémoires de littérature et d'histoire*, pp. 6, 304, which permitted me to correct an error in the Hunter edition. For a reaction to the original publication of Chapelain's dialogue, cf. La Curne de

Sainte-Palaye, *Mémoires sur l'ancienne chevalerie* (1759), ed. Charles Nodier, 3rd ed. (Paris: Girard, 1826), 1:431–432. See, esp., "Mémoire concernant la lecture des anciens romans de chevalerie," ibid., pp. 436–437: "Je ne dissimulerai point qu'après avoir achevé ce mémoire, j'appris que j'avais été prévenu il y a long-temps par M. Chapelain. . . ." Cf. Lionel Gossman, *Medievalism and the Ideologies of the Enlightenment: The World and Work of La Curne de Sainte-Palaye* (Baltimore: Johns Hopkins University Press, 1968), p. 153.

18. Arnaldo Momigliano, "Storia antica e antiquaria," in idem, *Sui fondamenti della storia antica* (Turin: Einaudi, 1984), pp. 3–45.

19. Claude Fauchet, *Les œuvres . . . revues et corrigées* (Paris: Le Clerc & de Heuqueville, 1610), pp. 482ff. On this writer, see J. G. Espiner-Scott, *Claude Fauchet* (Paris: Droz, 1938) (where he notes at p. 372 that Fauchet's name does not appear in Chapelain's dialogue). See also Gossman, *Medievalism*, p. 153.

20. Fauchet, *Les œuvres*, p. 591.

21. L. Chantereau Le Fèvre, *Traité des fiefs et de leur origine avec les preuves tirées de divers autheurs anciens et modernes, de capitulaires de Charlemagne, de Louis le Débonnaire, de Charles le Chauve, et des ordonnances de S. Louis, et de quantité d'autres actes mss. extraicts de plusieurs cartulaires authentiques* (Paris: Billaine, 1662), pp. 87–89, apropos *meffaire* (although in the corresponding passage in *Lancelot* we find a synonym, *mesprendre*). The ample study by G. Baer Fundenburg, *Feudal France in French Epic: A Study of Feudal French Institutions in History and Poetry* (Princeton, NJ: Princeton University Press, 1918), omits the seventeenth-century antiquarian tradition. For a fuller perspective, one that takes into consideration the narrative dimension, see Donald Maddox, "Lancelot et le sens de la coutume," *Cahiers de Civilisation Médiévale* 29 (1986): 339–353, and idem, "Yvain et le sens de la coutume," *Romania* 109 (1988): 1–17.

22. Chapelain, *Opuscules*, p. 219. Almost a century later, moving in a similar direction, see Bernard de Montfaucon's observation "Ce différent goût de sculpture, et de peinture en divers siècles peut même être compté parmi les faits historiques" (*Les monuments de la monarchie françoise*, 5 vols. [Paris, 1729–1733], 1:11; quoted in Giovanni Previtali, *La fortuna dei primitivi dal Vasari ai neoclassici* [Turin: Einaudi, 1964], p. 70).

23. Chapelain, *Opuscules*, p. 221.

24. According to M. Magendie, they testify "un sens du relatif rare au XVIIe siècle" (*Le roman*, p. 121).

25. Chapelain, *Opuscules*, p. 217.

26. Richard Popkin, *The History of Scepticism: From Savonarola to Bayle*, rev. and expanded ed. (Oxford: Oxford University Press, 2003), pp. 36–37. For a description of the 1621 edition, see Luciano Floridi, *Sextus Empiricus: The Transmission and Recovery of Pyrrhonism* (New York: Oxford, 2002), pp. 53–54.

27. Even a valuable book, Carlo Borghero's *La certezza e la storia: Cartesianesimo, pirronismo e conoscenza storica* (Milan: Franco Angeli, 1983), begins by saying that the category "historical Pyrrhonism" has generated a "historiographical mirage" (p. 9). But then he does not discuss the writings of Sextus.

28. *Sexti Philosophi Opera quae extant* (Parisiis, in officina Abrahami Pacardi, 1621), in two separately paginated parts (see part 2: 49–53, and also chap. 1 in this book).

29. On Dionysius Thrax, see Peter Matthews, "La linguistica greco-latina," in Giulio C. Lepschy, ed., *Storia della linguistica* (Bologna: Il Mulino, 1990), 1:246–248. And on the presumed *techné* of Dionysius, see Rudolf Pfeiffer, *History of Classical Scholarship from 1300 to 1850* (Oxford: Clarendon Press, 1968), pp. 266–272; Pfeiffer has sustained the thesis of authenticity against the compelling arguments of Vincenzo Di Benedetto in "Dionisio Trace e la techné a lui attribuita," *Annali della Scuola Normale Superiore di Pisa*, Classe di Lettere, ser. 2, vol. 27 (1958): 169–210; vol. 28 (1959): 87–118.

30. Sextus Empiricus, *Against the Schoolmasters (Against the Mathematicians)*, 1:252. (I have consulted the Italian translation, *Contro i matematici*, by Antonio Russo [Bari: Laterza, 1972], p. 82). Gentian Hervet's Latin translation reads: "Ex historia enim aliam quidem dicit esse veram, aliam vero falsam, aliam autem tanquam veram. Et veram quidem, eam, quae versatur in rebus quae geruntur. Falsam autem, quae versatur in figmentis et fabulis. Tanquam veram autem, cuiusmodi est comedia et mimi."

31. Ibid., 1:265 (Russo ed., p. 86); Hervet translation: "Non est ars aliqua in iis quae sunt falsa et esse non possunt: falsa autem sunt et esse non possunt que sunt in fabulis et figmentis, in quibus maxime historicae partis versatur grammatica: non est ars aliqua in historica parte grammaticae."

32. F. La Mothe Le Vayer, "Du peu de certitude qu'il y a dans l'histoire," in *Œuvres*, 15 vols. (Paris: Billaine, 1669), 13:409–448. Cf. Momigliano, "Storia antica e antiquaria," pp. 17–18. On La Mothe Le Vayer, see A. Momigliano, *Le radici classiche della storiografia moderna*, trans. Riccardo Di Donato (Florence: Sansoni, 1992), pp. 60–61 (original ed., *The Classical Foundations of Modern Historiography*). There is an extended discussion in Borghero, *La certezza e la storia*, pp. 57ff., esp. p. 71, where the "Du peu de certitude" is called "fundamental."

33. Vittor Ivo Comparato, "La Mothe Le Vayer dalla critica storica al pirronismo," in T. Gregory et al., eds., *Ricerche su letteratura libertina*, pp. 259–279: 271–273.

34. Pierre Bayle, *Dictionnaire historique et critique*, 4:408ff.: 413nK: "[Le livre] des historiens est bon: mais comme Mr. Baillet le remarque finement, il ne lui a pas coûté beaucoup de peine" (referring to Adrien Baillet, *Jugemens des savans sur les principaux ouvrages des auteurs*, 7 vols. [Paris: Charles Moette et al., 1722], 2:121). Borghero (*La certezza e la storia*, p. 71n100) alludes to it implicitly: "A sort of critical catalogue."

35. F. La Mothe Le Vayer, *Jugement sur les anciens et principaux historiens grecs et latins, dont il nous reste quelques ouvrages* (Paris: Augustin Courbé, 1646), unpaginated.

36. There is a gap for the years 1641–1658 in the Chapelain correspondence published in Tamizey de Larroque, *Lettres inédites à Chapelain*, 1:xiv (cited in full below at n. 48). La Mothe Le Vayer is among the missing correspondents, although he is frequently mentioned in the letters to Guez de Balzac (1638–1640), often accompanied by critical judgments. We perceive a competitive relationship, especially at the

moment in which Chapelain is offered the post of tutor to the dauphin, later filled by La Mothe Le Vayer. A reconciliation must have occurred about 1660, brought about also by their common friendship with François Bernier, to whom La Mothe Le Vayer was very attached (see Tamizey de Larroque, *Lettres inédites à Chapelain*, 2:186–187 and passim).

37. A. Momigliano, "Il posto di Erodoto nella storia della storiografia," in idem, *La storiografia greca* (Turin: Einaudi, 1982), pp. 138–155.

38. La Mothe Le Vayer, *Jugement*, p. 11.

39. Herodotus, trans. A. D. Godley, Loeb Classical Library (Cambridge, MA: Harvard University Press, 1982), 2:463.

40. La Mothe Le Vayer attributes this opinion to Francesco Patrizi, perhaps confusing it with a passage in Jean Bodin which asserts that Polybius "donned the mask of both the philosopher and the historian." See "Methodus ad facilem histo-riarum cognitionem," in Bodin's *Artis historicae penus*, ed. Johannes Wolf (Basel: Perna, 1579), pp. 52–53. The volume contains both Patrizi's dialogues on history and Bodin's *Methodus*; the passage from this second work is indicated in the table with a cross-reference to Polybius as "nimis Philosophus."

41. La Mothe Le Vayer, *Jugement*, p. 50.

42. Ibid., pp. 48–49.

43. C. Ginzburg, "Mito," in idem, *Occhiacci di legno: Nove riflessioni sulla distanza* (Milan: Feltrinelli, 1998), pp. 40–81: 56.

44. See Casaubon's dedication to Henri IV of his Polybius edition (Frankfurt, 1609).

45. See also La Mothe Le Vayer's *Jugement*, p. 339, on the passages where Herodo-tus distances himself from the myths concerning the Abari and from the beliefs of the Scythians tied to werewolves (regarding a preface which the editor states he found among the author's papers).

46. Ibid., p. 58.

47. Ibid., pp. 64–65.

48. Guez de Balzac, in a letter to Chapelain, ironically described La Mothe Le Vayer as "the successor of Montaigne and Charron, and even, if it should please him, of Cardano and Vanini, whose memory is blessed in Toulouse" (Jean-Louis Guez de Balzac, *Lettres inédites à Chapelain*, ed. Tamizey de Larroque [Paris: Im-primerie Nationale, 1873], pp. 410, 418, cited in Pintard, *Le libertinage érudit*, pp. 145–146).

49. See the passage in G. C. Vanini, *De admirandis Naturae arcanis* (Lutetiae [Paris]: Apud A. Perier, 1616), cited in Marco Ferrari and Carlo Ginzburg, "La co-lombara ha aperto gli occhi," *Quaderni storici* 38 (1978): 631–639: 639n27.

50. La Mothe Le Vayer, *Jugement*, p. 68.

51. See Comparato, "La Mothe Le Vayer," p. 269: ". . . the 'fables' declined in standing from causes to ethnographic material. . . ."

52. C. Ginzburg, "Distanza e prospettiva: Due metafore," in idem, *Occhiacci di legno*, pp. 171–193.

53. Pintard, *Le libertinage érudit*, pp. 531–533; and see at pp. xxxv–xxxvi Pintard's critique of the concept of La Mothe Le Vayer as Christian skeptic, proposed by Richard Popkin. The latter's response (*History of Scepticism*, pp. 82–87) is unconvincing.

54. Anna Maria Battista, *Alle origini del pensiero politico libertino: Montaigne e Charron* (Milan: Giuffré, 1966); idem, "Come giudicano la 'politica' libertini e moralisti nella Francia del Seicento," in Sergio Bertelli, ed., *Il libertinismo in Europa* (Milan and Naples: Ricciardi, 1960), pp. 25–80 (new ed. 1980).

55. "De la diversité des religions," in *Cinq dialogues faits à l'imitation des anciens* (Mons: Paul de la Flèche, 1671): cf. Ginzburg, *Occhiacci di legno*, pp. 57–58.

56. The two positions are not mutually exclusive, as demonstrated by Marc Bloch in *Les rois thaumaturges* (1924). Cf. also C. Ginzburg, "A proposito della raccolta dei saggi storici di Marc Bloch," *Studi Medievali*, ser. 3, vol. 6 (1965): 335–353: 352–353.

57. See F. de Grenaille, Sieur de Chatounieres, *La Mode ou Charactère de la Religion. De la Vie. De la Conversation. De la Solitude. Des Compliments. Des Habits. Et du Style du temps* (Paris, 1642) (to which I hope to return in the near future).

58. J.-L. Guez de Balzac, *Œuvres*, publiées par Valentin Conrart (Paris: Billaine, 1665; Geneva: Slatkine Reprints, 1971), 1: fols. *iir (but the entire introduction is important).

59. Fauchet, *Les œuvres*, p. 591.

60. Chapelain, *Opuscules*, p. 221.

61. Samuel Coleridge, *Biographia Literaria* (London: Dent; New York: Dutton [1906]), chap. 14, II, p. 6. The passage pertains to the *Lyrical Ballads* of Coleridge and Wordsworth.

62. *Hamlet*, act 2, sc. 2. I am expanding, in a slightly different direction, an expression by Giacomo Magrini which Cesare Garboli used in *Pianura proibita* (Milan: Adelphi, 2002).

63. Markus Volkel, *"Pyrrhonismus historicus" und "fides Historica": Die Entwicklung der deutschen historischen Methodologie unter dem Gesichtspunkt der historischen Skepsis* (Frankfurt a. M.: Lang, 1987).

64. "Fede è sustanza di cose sperate / ed argomento delle non parventi" (Dante, *Paradiso*, 24:64–65, which translated Hebrews 11:1: "Est fides sperandarum substantia rerum, argumentum non apparentium" ["Now faith is the assurance of things hoped for, the conviction of things not seen"]).

CHAPTER 6. THE EUROPEANS DISCOVER THE SHAMANS

1. Venetia: P. & F. Tini, gli heredi di G. M. Bonelli, 1572 (1st ed., 1565), fols. 54v-55r (anastatic reprint, Graz: F. Anders, 1972; see at pp. xxv–xxxi for a listing of reprintings and translations). See also A. Martinengo in Paolo Collo and Pier Luigi Crovetto, eds., *Nuovo Mondo: Gli italiani (1492–1565)* (Turin: Einaudi, 1991), pp. 549–552; and the entry for "Benzoni, Girolamo" by Angela Codazzi, *Dizionario Biografico degli Italiani* 8:732–733, in which Codazzi quotes part of the passage reproduced here from the first edition of *La historia* (see also below at n. 16).

2. C. Ginzburg, "Straniamento: Preistoria di un procedimento letterario," in idem, *Occhiacci di legno: Nove riflessioni sulla distanza* (Milan: Feltrinelli, 1998), pp. 15–39.

3. Benzoni, *La historia del mondo nuovo*, fols. 55r–56r.

4. N. Monardes, *Primera y segunda y tercera partes de la historia medicinal, de las cosas que se traen de nuestras Indias occidentales, que sirven en Medicina* (Seville, 1580; 1st ed., 1571), fols. 32ff., especially fols. 36v–39r. See also Nardo Antonio Recco, *Rerum medicarum Novae Hispaniae Thesaurus* (Rome, 1648), pp. 173–177 (Bk. V, chap. L I, "De Pycielt, seu Tabaco").

5. Pietro Andrea Mattioli, *I discorsi . . . nelli sei libri di Pedacio Dioscoride Anazarbeo della materia medicinale* (Venice, 1568), p. 1476, on the "solatro maniaco over furioso," distinguished from the "doricnian" (p. 1132: Mattioli asserts that he did not succeed in identifying it), it, too, mentioned by Dioscorides.

6. Garcia da Orta, *Coloquio dos simples e drogas da India* (Lisbon: Imprensa Nacional, 1891), pp. 95–101 (annotated by Count de Ficalho). The first edition appeared in Goa in 1563 (not seen). The form used today is *bhang*.

7. Christovam da Costa, *Tractado de las drogas, y medicinas de las Indias Orientales, con sus plantas debuxadas al bivo* (Burgos: M. de Victoria, 1578), pp. 360–361. In the dedication to the reader Costa discreetly alludes to the imperfections in the work of his predecessor, Garcia de Orta.

8. Monardes, *Primera y segunda*, fol. 38r.

9. Benzoni, *La historia del mondo nuovo*, fol. 169r.

10. E. Le Roy Ladurie, "Un concept: l'unification microbienne du monde (XIVe–XVIIe siècles)," in idem, *Le territoire de l'historien*, 2 vols. (Paris: Gallimard, 1973–1978), 2:37–97.

11. *Relation de ce qui s'est passé en la Nouvelle France en l'année 1636, envoyée au R. Père Provincial de la Compagnie de Jésus en la province de France par le P. Paul Lejeune de la mesme Compagnie, supérieur de la Résidence de Kébec* (Paris, 1637), 1:199–200: ". . . monsieur Gand parlant aux Sauvages, comme i'ay dit cy-dessus, leur remonstroit, que s'ils mouroient si souvent, ils s'en falloit prendre à ces boissons, dont ils ne sçauroient user par mesure. Que n'écris tu a ton grand roy, firent-ils, qu'il defende d'apporter de ces boissons qui nous tuent. Et sur ce qu'on leur repartit, que nos François en avoient besoin sur la mer, et dans les grandes froidures de leur païs, Fais donc en sorte qu'ils les boivent tous seuls. On s'efforcera, comme j'espère, d'y tenir la main; mai ces Barbares sont importuns au dernier point. Un autre prenant la parole, prit la defense du vin et de l'eau de vie. Non, dit-il, ce ne sont pas ces boissons qui nous ostent la vie, mais vos écritures: car depuis que vous avez décry nostre païs, nos fleuves, nos terres, et nos bois nous mourons tous, ce qui n'arrivoit pas devant que vous vinssiez icy. Nous-nous mismes à rire entendans ces causes nouvelles de leur maladies. Ie leur dy que nous décrivions tout le monde, que nous décrivions nostre païs, celuy des Hurons, des Hiroquois, bref toute la terre, et cependant qu'on ne mouroit point ailleurs, comme on fait en leurs païs, qu'il falloit donc que leur mort provint d'ailleurs; ils s'y accordèrent." Father de Brebeuf was killed by the Iroquois (*Dictionnaire de biographie française*, s.v. "Brebeuf").

12. François de Dainville, *La Géographie des humanistes* (Paris: Beauchesne, 1940; Slatkine Reprints, 1969).

13. On the hostility of the Catholic hierarchy toward tobacco consumption, an attitude which lasted until the end of the seventeenth century, see John Tedeschi, "Literary Piracy in Seventeenth-Century Florence: Giovanni Battista Neri's *De iudice S. Inquisitionis Opusculum*," *Huntington Library Quarterly* 50 (1987): 107–118 (reprinted in idem, *The Prosecution of Heresy: Collected Studies on the Inquisition in Early Modern Italy* (Binghamton, NY: Medieval and Renaissance Texts and Studies, 1991), pp. 259–272.

14. Jerome E. Brooks, *Tobacco: Its History Illustrated by the Books, Manuscripts and Engravings in the Library of George Arents, Jr.* 5 vols. (New York: Rosenbach, 1937–1952).

15. G. Fernández de Oviedo, *Historia general y natural de las Indias*, ed. Juan Pérez de Tudela Bueso (Madrid: Ediciones Atlas, 1959), 1:116–118.

16. Benzoni's words, "smoke which in the Mexican language is called tobacco"—changed in the second edition to "this herb which" etc.—could have been suggested by something Oviedo had said: the *Indios* call tobacco the smoke or the tubes to inhale it, not (as some have believed) the herb or the sleep into which they fall after smoking it (*Historia*, p. 116). Successive authors—Monardes, for example—instead call the plant "tobacco," in line with a usage that was later in fashion. According to Adolfo Ernst, "On the Etymology of the Word Tobacco," *American Anthropologist* 2 (1889): 133–141, the instrument described and reproduced by Oviedo—in the *guaraní* language, *taboca*—was and still is used on the American continent to inhale not the smoke of tobacco but of plants of the leguminous family containing alkaloids. The hypothesis that Benzoni never took the voyages he described is discussed (and rejected) by A. Codazzi and A. Martinengo (in the works cited at note 3).

17. "Aquí me paresce que cuadra una costumbre viciosa e mala que la gente de Tracia usaba entre otros criminosos vicios suyos, segund el Abulensis escribe sobre Eusebio *De los tiempos* Bk. 3, chap. 168), donde dice que tienen por costumbre todos, varones e mujeres, de comer alrededor del fuego, y que huelgan mucho de ser embriagos, o lo parescer; e que como no tienen vino, toman simientes de algunas hierbas que entre ellos hay, las cuales, echadas en las brasas, dan de sí un tal olor, que embriagan a todos los presentes, sin algo beber. A mi parescer, esto es lo mismo que los tabacos que estos indios toman" (G. F. de Oviedo, *Historia*, 1:117).

18. *Tostado sobre el Eusebio* (Salamanca: Hans Gysser, 1506), vol. 3, fol. lix v (chap. 168); C. Julius Solinus, *Polyhistor rerum toto orbe memorabilium thesaurus locupletissimus* (Basel: M. Isingrinus & H. Petrus, 1538), p. 36: "Uterque sexus epulantes, focos ambiunt, herbarum quas habent semine ignibus superiecto, cuius nidore perculsi, pro laetitia habent, imitari ebrietatem sensibus sauciatis."

19. Pomponius Mela, *De orbis situ libri tres, accuratissime emendati, una cum commentariis Joachimi Vadiani . . .* (Paris: Claude Garamond, 1540), p. 90: "Vini usus

quibusdam ignotus est: epulantibus tamen ubi super ignes, quos circumsident, quaedam semina ingesta sunt, similis ebrietati hilaritas ex nidore contingit."

20. François du Creux, *Historiae Canadensis, seu Novae Franciae libri decem, ad annum usque Christi MDCLVI* (Paris: Cramoisy, 1664), p. 76: "... ebrietatemque enim inducunt, vini instar" (on a facing page an illustration shows a pipe-smoking native).

21. Ibid., p. 56.

22. P. Biard, Grenoblois, de la Compagnie de Jésus, *Relation de la nouvelle France, de ses terres, naturel du Païs, et de ses Habitans* . . . , à Lyon 1616, p. 78.

23. Ibid., pp. 78–79.

24. On the use of *bhang* in ritual contexts, see Robert G. Wasson, *Soma, Divine Mushroom of Immortality* (New York, n.d.), pp. 128ff., in which he discusses and rejects the suggestion of identifying *bhang* with the *soma* mentioned in Vedic poems (apropos B. L. Mukherjee, "The Soma Plant," *Journal of the Royal Asiatic Society* [1921]: 241–244). A pamphlet by this author, with identical title, appeared in Calcutta in 1922 (not seen).

25. Simon Schama, *The Embarrassment of Riches* (New York: Knopf, 1987), pp. 193ff. (2nd ed., New York: Vintage Books, 1997). But the counterattack against tobacco, its producers, and its consumers, is now in full force.

26. I. Vossius, *Observationes ad Pomponium Melam de situ orbis* (Hagae Comitis, apud Adrianum Ulacq, 1658), pp. 124–125.

27. The oldest representation of tobacco by a European botanist (the Dutchman Rembert Dodoens, 1554) identifies the plant with the *Hyosciamus luteus* described by Dioscorides: cf. Jerry Stannard, "Dioscorides and Renaissance Materia Medica," in Marcel Florkin, ed., *Materia Medica in the Sixteenth Century* (Oxford and New York: Pergamon Press, 1966), p. 113, and n. 93; F. Edelmann, "Nicotiniana," *Flammes et Fumées* 9 (1977): 75–128.

28. See Joseph-François Lafitau, *Mœurs des sauvages amériquains, comparées aux mœurs des premieres temps* (Paris, 1724), 2:126ff. Cf. Anthony Pagden, *The Fall of Natural Man: The American Indian and the Origins of Comparative Ethnology* (Cambridge and New York: Cambridge University Press, 1982), s.v. "Lafitau"; Alessandro Saggioro, "Lafitau e lo spettacolo dell' 'altro': Considerazioni iniziali in margine a un comparatista *ante literam*," *Studi e Materiali di Storia delle Religioni* 63 (1997): 191–208.

29. Maximus of Tyre, *Sermones sive disputationes XLI* (Paris, 1557), p. 90 (sermon 11).

30. J.-F. Lafitau, *Mémoire présenté à son Altesse Royale monseigneur le Duc d'Orléans concernant la précieuse plante de Gin Seng de Tartarie découverte au Canada* (Paris, 1718).

31. J.-F. Lafitau, *Mœurs*, 2:133: "Il est certain que le Tabac est en Amérique une herbe consacrée à plusieurs exercices, et à plusieurs usages de Religion, Outre ce que j'ai déjà dit de la vertu qu'ils lui attribuent pour amortir le feu de la concupiscence et les révoltes de la chair; pour éclairer l'âme, la purifier, et la rendre propre aux songes

et aux visions extatiques; pour évoquer les esprits, et les forcer de communiquer avec les hommes; pour rendre ces esprits favorables aux besoins des nations qui les servent, et pour guérir toutes les infirmités de l'âme et du corps. . . ."

32. G. Henning, "Die Reiseberichte über Sibirien von Heberstein bis Ides," *Mitteilungen des Vereins fur Erdkunde zu Leipzig* (1905): 241–394. Cf. Gloria Flaherty, *Shamanism and the Eighteenth Century* (Princeton, NJ: Princeton University Press, 1992).

33. Jan N. Bremmer, *The Rise and Fall of the Afterlife* (London and New York: Routledge, 2002), pp. 26–27; Bremmer has perfected my reconstruction on this point.

34. E. I. Ides, "Voyage de Moscou à la Chine," in *Recueil de voiages au Nord, contenant divers mémoires très utiles au commerce et à la navigation* (Amsterdam: Jean-Frédéric Bernard, 1727), 8:54 (in the catalogue of the Bibliothèque Nationale, Paris, the work is entered under the name of the publisher, Bernard): "'A' quelques journées de chemin d'*Ilinskoi* il y a une grande cascade, ou pente d'eau, qu'on appelle *Chute du Schaman*, ou *Chute du Magicien*, à cause que le fameux *Schaman*, ou magicien des *Tunguses*, a sa cabane auprès de cet endroit." The original Dutch version of Ides's report appeared in Amsterdam in 1704. On the term *shaman*, see S. M. Shirokogoroff, *Psychomental Complex of the Tungus* (London: Kegan, Paul, Trench, Trubner, 1935), pp. 268–269, which cites B. Laufer, "Origin of the Word Shaman," *American Anthropologist* 19 (1917): 361–371.

35. J. B. Müller, "Les mœurs et usages des Ostiackes et la manière dont ils furent convertis en 1712 à la religion chrétienne du rit grec," in *Recueil de voiages au Nord*, 10 vols. (Amsterdam: J. F. Bernard, 1715–1738), 8:382ff., 412 (the translation of a German version, which I have not seen).

36. J. G. Gmelin, *Reise durch Sibirien, vor dem Jahr 1733 bis 1743*, 3 vols. (Göttingen: Abram Bandenhoect, 1751–1752), esp. 1:283ff., 351, 397; 2:45–46, 82ff., 351; 3: preface, 69ff., 330ff., 347ff. For a very abridged French translation of this work, see *Voyage en Sibérie*, 2 vols. (Paris, 1767).

37. Idem, *Reise durch Sibirien*, 3:370ff., 522ff.

38. Idem, *Flora sibirica sive historia plantarum Sibiriae*, 4 vols. (Petropoli [St. Petersburg]: Typis Academiae Scientiarum, 1747), 1:184; 3:31. A biography of Gmelin by the rector of the University of Tübingen serves as preface to Gmelin's *Sermo academicus de novorum vegetabilium post creationem divinam exortu* (Tubingae: Litteris Erhardtianis, 1749).

39. Frank E. Manuel, *The Eighteenth Century Confronts the Gods* (Cambridge, MA: Harvard University Press, 1959).

40. Ibid., pp. 137–145.

41. Ibid., pp. 73–74. Cf. J. G. Georgi, *Bemerkungen einer Reise im russischen Reich im Jahre 1772*, 2 vols. (St. Petersburg: Kaiserliche Akademie der Wissenschaften, 1775).

42. C. Meiners, "Über die Mysterien der Alten, besonders über die Eleusinischen Geheimnisse," in *Vermischte Philosophische Schriften* (Leipzig: Weygand, 1776), 3:164–342. On Meiners (barely mentioned by Manuel), see Sergio Landucci, *I filosofi*

e i selvaggi, 1580–1780 (Bari: Laterza, 1972), pp. 463–465, passim. On the Eurocentric and racist tone of his writings, see Luigi Marino, *I maestri della Germania: Göttingen, 1770–1820* (Turin: Einaudi, 1975), pp. 103–112.

43. Meiners, "Über die Mysterien," pp. 169–171.

44. C. Peucer, *Commentarius de praecipuis generibus divinationum* (Francofurti: apud A. Wecheli haeredes, 1560); J. Scheffer, *Lapponia* (Frankfurt a. M. and Leipzig, 1674).

45. C. Ginzburg, *Ecstasies: Deciphering the Witches' Sabbath*, trans. Raymond Rosenthal (New York: Pantheon, 1991).

46. Vossius, *Observationes*, p. 124.

47. Herodotus, trans. A. D. Godley, Loeb Classical Library (Cambridge, MA: Harvard University Press, 1982), pp. 273–274.

48. Karl Meier-Lemgo, *Engelbert Kämpfer, der erste deutsche Forschungsreisende, 1651–1716* (Hamburg: Cram, De Gruyter, 1960). Cf. also idem, "Die Briefe Engelbert Kaempfers," *Akademie der Wissenschaften und der Literatur in Mainz. Abhandlungen der Mathematisch-Naturwissenschaftliche Klasse* 6 (1965): 267–314, and *Die Reisetagebücher Engelbert Kaempfers* (Wiesbaden: Steiner, 1968).

49. E. Kaempfer, *Amoenitatum Exoticarum politico-physico-medicarum fasciculi V* (Lemgoviae [Lemgo]: Typis et impensis Henrici Wilhelmi Meyeri, 1712), pp. 333–334, 528–529. See also Detlev Haberland, *Engelbert Kaempfer, 1651–1716: A Biography*, trans. Peter Hog (London: British Library, 1996), with abundant reference to the bibliography, which has grown exponentially in recent years.

50. Kaempfer, *Amoenitatum*, pp. 638ff., esp. p. 647. Kaempfer's source is Alessandro d'Alessandro, *Genialium dierum libri sex* (Paris: J. Petrus, 1561), fols. 137v–138r (l.iii.xi).

51. For a new, complete edition, see René Radrizzani, *Manuscript trouvé à Saragosse* (Paris: José Corti, 1989).

52. J. Potocki, *Histoire primitive des peuples de la Russie* (St. Petersburg: Imprimé à l'Académie Impériale des Sciences, 1802), p. 128. We read "chaman" in the new edition, containing an introduction and highly useful critical notes by the Orientalist Julius Klaproth, a student of Potocki: see J. Potocki, *Voyage dans les steps [!] d'Astrakhan et du Caucase: Histoire primitive des peuples qui ont habité anciennement ces contrées. Nouveau périple du Pont-Euxin*, 2 vols. (Paris: Merlin, 1829), 2:171.

53. J. Potocki, *Histoire primitive*, p. 134; idem, *Voyages en Turquie et en Egypte, en Hollande, au Maroc*, ed. Daniel Beauvois (Paris: Fayard, 1980) (with a useful introduction). I wonder whether the secret relationship, especially of a structural order, that I have always thought existed between the *Manuscrit trouvé à Saragosse* and *La civetta cieca* of Sadègh Hedayàt should not be looked for in the reworking, on a very different plane, of a similar hallucinatory experience. (On Hedayàt, see now Youssef Ishaghpour, *Le tombeau de Sadègh Hedayàt* [Paris: Diffusion Distique, 1991]).

54. Barthold Georg Niebuhr, "Untersuchungen über die Geschichte der Skythen, Geten, und Sarmaten (Nach einem 1811 vorgelesenen Aufsatz neu gearbeitet

1828)," in *Kleine historische und philologische Schriften* (Bonn: Eduard Weber, 1828), 1:352–398: 361–362.

55. A. Mickiewicz, *L'Église officielle et le messianisme. I. Cours de littérature slave au Collège de France (1842–1843)*, 2 vols. (Paris: Au Comptoir des imprimeurs-unis, 1845), pp. 123–125: ". . . le premier de tous les historiens de l'Europe moderne, il reconnut l'importance de la tradition orale. Niebuhr demandait aux paysans et aux vieilles femmes, sur les marchés de Rome, des explications sur l'histoire de Romulus et de Rémus. Longtemps avant lui, Potocki, dans les huttes des Tartares, méditait sur l'histoire des Scythes . . . Potocki le premier a tiré la science du cabinet. Il a voyagé, observé le pays, parlé avec les peuples, ce qu'aucun antiquaire n'avait fait avant lui. . . ." The passage is noted in E. Krakowski, *Le Comte Jean Potocki, un témoin de l'Europe des Lumières* (Paris: Gallimard, 1963), p. 149. On the importance ascribed to oral tradition by Niebuhr, see Arnaldo Momigliano, "Perizonio, Niebuhr e il carattere della tradizione romana primitiva," in idem, *Sui fondamenti della storia antica* (Turin: Einaudi, 1984), pp. 271–293.

56. Thanks to Bremmer (*Rise and Fall of the Afterlife*, p. 146n16), I am able to correct an error which had crept into an earlier version of this chapter.

57. K. Meuli, "Scythica," in *Gesammelte Schriften*, ed. Thomas Gelzer (Basel and Stuttgart: Schwabe Press, 1975), pp. 817–879 (with additions with respect to the first 1935 edition). See also my *Ecstasies*, p. 218n4. For a critique of Meuli's thesis, see now Bremmer, *Rise and Fall of the Afterlife*, pp. 27–40.

58. Ginzburg, *Ecstasies*, p. 208.

CHAPTER 7. TOLERANCE AND COMMERCE

I discussed earlier drafts of this paper in 1999 at UCLA with my students and with participants at a colloquium on European history and culture, with Pier Cesare Bori, Alberto Gajano, Francesco Orlando, and Adriano Sofri. The current version has profited from their observations and from the criticism of David Feldman. I am grateful to all.

1. Erich Auerbach, *Mimesis: The Representation of Reality in Western Literature*, trans. Willard R. Trask (Princeton, NJ: Princeton University Press, 1974), p. 402 (slightly modified); Voltaire, *Lettres philosophiques*, in *Mélanges*, ed. J. Van den Heuvel (Paris: Gallimard, 1961), pp. 17–18: "Entrez dans la bourse de Londres, cette place plus respectable que bien des cours; vous y voyez rassemblés les députés de toutes les nations pour l'utilité des hommes. Là le juif, le mahométan et le chrétien traitent l'un avec l'autre comme s'ils étaient de la même religion, et ne donnent le nom d'infidèles qu'à ceux qui font banqueroute; là le presbytérien se fie à l'anabaptiste, et l'anglican reçoit la promesse du quaker. Au sortir de ces pacifiques et libres assemblées, les uns vont à la synagogue, les autres vont boire; celui-ci va se faire baptiser dans une grande cuve au nom du Père par le Fils au saint-Esprit; celui-là fait couper le prépuce de son fils et fait marmotter sur l'enfant des paroles hébraïques qu'il n'entend point; ces autres vont dans leur église attendre l'inspiration de Dieu, leur chapeau sur la tête, et tous sont contents."

NOTES TO PAGES 96–98 ◆ 267

2. Auerbach, *Mimesis*, p. 402; Antoine Compagnon (*Le démon de la théorie* [Paris: Seuil, 1998], p. 103) states that in *Mimesis* "la notion de réalisme allait encore de soi." But in the epilogue of the book Auerbach wrote: "Not even the term 'realistic' is unambiguous" (p. 556). On a strictly factual plane Voltaire's description may have been fairly accurate. A ground plan of the London Stock Exchange dated "Août et septembre 1784" (École des Ponts et Chaussée, Ms. 8, *Le Sage*, 1784) indicates that specific sections were assigned to the various religious minorities ("Place des Quakers," "Place des Juifs"). This classification apparently intersected with another based on the professions or commercial activity ("Place des Drapiers," "Place de la Jamaïque," etc.). I am grateful to Margaret Jacob for a reproduction of the plan.

3. Auerbach, *Mimesis*, chap. 18, "In the Hôtel de la Mole" (on Stendhal, Balzac, Flaubert). Auerbach never explicitly clarified the connections between the various types of realism. This reticence has been interpreted incorrectly from an antitheoretical perspective: see René Wellek, "Auerbach's Special Realism," *Kenyon Review* 16 (1954): 299–307.

4. Auerbach, *Mimesis*, p. 404.

5. Ibid., p. 404; "Epilegomena zu Mimesis," quoted by Aurelio Roncaglia in his introduction to the Italian edition of *Mimesis* (Turin: Einaudi, 1964), 1:xx; I have corrected a small inaccuracy in the translation. (Translators' note: The English edition reads simply: "I may also mention that the book was written during the war and at Istanbul" [p. 557].) On the copyright page of the book one reads "written in Istanbul between May 1942 and April 1945." See the introduction by J. M. Ziolkowski to Auerbach's *Literary Language and Its Public in Late Latin Antiquity and in the Middle Ages* (Princeton, NJ: Princeton University Press, 1993), p. xxii.

6. See my *Occhiacci di legno: Nove riflessioni sulla distanza* (Milan: Feltrinelli, 1998), pp. 171–193.

7. B. de Spinoza, *Tractatus theologico-politicus*, chap. 20: "Urbs Amstelodamum exemplo sit, quae tanto cum suo incremento, et omnium nationum admiratione hujus libertatis fructus experitur; in hac enim florentissima Republica, et urbe praestantissima omnes cujuscunque nationis et sectae homines summa cum concordia vivunt, et ut alicui bona sua credant, id tantum scire curant, num dives, an pauper sit, et num bona fide, an dolo solitus sit agere" (*Opera*, ed. Carl Gebhardt [Heidelberg: Winter, 1925], 3:245–246).

8. [B. de Spinoza], *Traitté des ceremonies superstitieuses des Juifs tant Anciens que Modernes*, à Amsterdam 1678, p. 527. I have also used a copy with a different title page: *La clef du sanctuaire par un sçavant homme de notre siècle* (Leiden, 1678).

9. B. de Spinoza, *Tractatus theologico-politicus*, preface: "Fides jam nihil aliud sit quam credulitas et praejudicia"; chap. 14: "Superest jam, ut tandem ostendam, inter fidem, sive theologiam, et philosophiam, nullum esse commercium"; chap. 20: "Fides ejusque fundamentalia determinanda sunt; quod quidem in hoc capite facere constitui, simulque fidem philosophia separare, quod totius operis praecipuum intentum fuit" (*Opera*, 3:8, 179, 275–276). On all this, see Emilia Giancotti Boscherini, *Lexicon Spinozanum* (The Hague: Nijhoff, 1970), pp. 423–427.

10. Spinoza, *Opera*, 3:243.

11. Giuliano Procacci, *Machiavelli nella cultura europea dell'età moderna* (Bari: Laterza, 1995), pp. 275–276.

12. Luigi Lombardi, *Dalla "fides" alla "bona fides"* (Milan: Giuffré, 1961); Gérard Freyburger, *Fides: Étude sémantique et religieuse depuis les origines jusqu'à l'époque augustéenne* (Paris: Les Belles Lettres, 1986). In 1584 Johannes Molanus, on the faculty at the University of Louvain, published a work entitled *Libri quinque de fide haereticis servanda, tres de fide rebellibus servanda*: see Adriano Prosperi, "Fede, giuramento, inquisizione," in Paolo Prodi and Elisabeth Müller-Luckner, eds., *Glaube und Eid* (Munich: Oldenbourg, 1993), pp. 157–171.

13. I am grateful to Pier Cesare Bori, who brought this to my attention. The thesis convincingly proposed by Albert O. Hirschman in *The Passion and the Interests* (Princeton, NJ: Princeton University Press, 1977) can be extended to religion. About 1833 Stendhal made a scornful allusion to "the young America in which all passions, or almost all, can be reduced to the cult of the dollar" (draft of the introduction to "Chroniques italiennes" in *Romans et nouvelles*, ed. Henri Martineau (Paris: Champion & Slatkine, 1947), p. 544.

14. Paul Vernière, *Spinoza et la pensée française avant la Révolution* (Paris: Presses Universitaires de France, 1954), 2:498–499. René Pomeau, *La religion de Voltaire*, new ed. (Paris: Nizet, 1969), p. 54n82, claims instead that at the time Voltaire knew Spinoza's work only indirectly. See also Charles Porset, "Notes sur Voltaire et Spinoza," in Olivier Bloch, ed., *Spinoza au XVIIIe siècle* (Paris: Presses Universitaires de France, 1990), pp. 225–240.

15. "'Osent penser,' expression remarquable," observed R. Pomeau apropos the passage in Voltaire ("Les 'Lettres philosophiques': Le projet de Voltaire," *Studies on Voltaire and the Eighteenth Century* 179 [1979]: 11–24: 12). The importance of Horace for Voltaire has been underlined in Ira O. Wade, *The Intellectual Development of Voltaire* (Princeton, NJ: Princeton University Press, 1969), pp. 15–18. On "sapere aude," see the excellent account in Franco Venturi, "Contributi a un dizionario storico, I: Was ist Aufklärung? Sapere aude!" *Rivista Storica Italiana* 71 (1959): 119–128; idem, *Utopia e riforma nell'Illuminismo* (Turin: Einaudi, 1970), pp. 12–18. See also by the present writer, "The High and the Low: The Theme of Forbidden Knowledge in the Sixteenth and Seventeenth Centuries," in idem, *Clues, Myths and the Historical Method*, trans. John Tedeschi and Anne C. Tedeschi (Baltimore: Johns Hopkins University Press, 1989), pp. 60–76. Voltaire owned a copy of the Horace edition translated by André Dacier (Amsterdam, 1727), in which the passage is correctly interpreted in a moral rather than intellectual sense: "Ayez le courage d'être vertueux"; cf. Venturi, "Contributi a un dizionario storico," p. 120. The discovery that the distortion of Horace's words was traceable to Voltaire certainly would have pleased Venturi.

16. "Il y avait plus de politesse dans l'air ouvert et humain de son visage qu'il n'y en a dans l'usage de tirer une jambe derrière l'autre et de porter à la main ce qui est fait pour couvrir la tête" (Voltaire, "Lettres philosophiques," in *Mélanges*, p. 1).

17. "Nous sommes chrétiennes, et tachons d'être bons chrétiens; mais nous ne pensons pas que le christianisme consiste à jeter de l'eau froide sur la tête, avec un peu de sel" (ibid., p. 2).

18. "Notre Dieu, qui nous a ordonné d'aimer nos ennemis et de souffrir sans murmure, ne veut pas sans doute que nous passions la mer pour aller égorger nos frères, parce que des meurtriers vêtus de rouge, avec un bonnet haut de deux pieds, enrôlent des citoyens en faisant du bruit avec deux petits bâtons sur une peau d'âne bien tendue" (ibid., p. 4).

19. Ginzburg, *Occhiacci di legno*, pp. 18–20.

20. *Voltaire's Notebooks*, ed. Theodore Besterman (Geneva: Droz, 1968), 1:51, 65 (*Les œuvres complètes de Voltaire*, vol. 81).

21. Ibid., p. 43n2.

22. Jonathan Swift, *A Tale of a Tub*, ed. A.C. Guthkelch and D.N. Smith (Oxford: Clarendon, 1920), p. 139.

23. Ibid., pp. 345–346. See also J. Swift, *Journal to Stella. I. April 14, 1711*, ed. H. Williams (Oxford: Clarendon, 1948), pp. 254–255. R. Pomeau, *La religion de Voltaire*, new ed. (Paris: Nizet, 1969), pp. 131–132, affirms erroneously that until 1756 Voltaire knew Swift only as the author of *Gulliver's Travels*. Pomeau cites Wolff, *Elementa matheseos universae*, as the possible source for *Micromégas*, without mentioning *Gulliver's Travels* (Voltaire, *Romans et contes* [Paris: Imprimerie Nationale, 1966], p. 125). But see Ira O. Wade, *Voltaire's "Micromégas": A Study in the Fusion of Science, Myth, and Art* (Princeton, NJ: Princeton University Press, 1950), p. 28.

24. J. Swift, *Gulliver's Travels*, ed. Peter Dixon and John Chalker (Harmondsworth: Penguin, 1967), p. 70. See also Gianni Celati, "Introduzione" to J. Swift, *I viaggi di Gulliver* (Milan: Feltrinelli, 1997), p. xix.

25. The italics are mine.

26. "Ainsi presque tout est imitation. L'idée des *Lettres persanes* est prise de celle de l'*Espion turc*. Le Boiardo a imité le Pulci, l'Arioste a imité le Boiardo. Les esprits les plus originaux empruntent les uns des autres. . . . Il en est des livres comme du feu dans nos foyers; on va prendre ce feu chez son voisin, on l'allume chez soi, on le communique à d'autres, et il appartient à tous" (Voltaire, *Mélanges*, p. 1394).

27. R. Lachmann, "Die 'Verfremdung' und das 'Neue Sehen' bei Viktor Sklovskij," *Poetica* 3 (1969): 226–249.

28. Francesco Orlando, *Illuminismo e retorica freudiana* (Turin: Einaudi, 1982), p. 163.

29. Voltaire, *Mélanges*, pp. 157ff. For the date of the *Traité*, see Ira O. Wade, *Studies on Voltaire* (Princeton, NJ: Princeton University Press, 1947), pp. 87–129. See also W.H. Barber's edition in Voltaire, *Les œuvres complètes* (Oxford: Voltaire Foundation, 1989), vol. 14.

30. "Peu de gens s'avisent d'avoir une notion bien étendue de ce que c'est que l'homme. Les paysans d'une partie de l'Europe n'ont guère d'autre idée de notre espèce que celle d'un animal à deux pieds, ayant une peau bise, articulant quelques paroles, cultivant la terre, payant, sans savoir pourquoi, certains tributs à un' autre

animal qu'ils appellent *roi*, vendant leur denrées le plus cher qu'ils peuvent, et s'assemblant certains jours de l'année pour chanter des prières dans une langue qu'ils n'entendent point" (Voltaire, *Mélanges*, p. 157).

31. Voltaire, *La philosophie de l'histoire* (*Les œuvres complètes de Voltaire* 59), ed. J. H. Brumfitt, 2nd enlarged ed. (Geneva: Institut et Musée Voltaire, 1969), p. 109. For later versions of this passage, see Ginzburg, *Occhiacci di legno*, p. 28.

32. Wade, *Voltaire's "Micromégas,"* p. 28, proposes that the published text preserves traces of an older, lost version entitled *Voyage du baron de Gangan* (1739). W. H. Barber, "The Genesis of Voltaire's 'Micromégas,'" *French Studies* 11 (1957): 1–15, rejects most of Wade's arguments but agrees that the original idea for *Micromégas* stemmed from Voltaire's scientific interests in the decade 1730–1740.

33. "Des singes, des éléphants, des nègres, qui semblent tous avoir quelque lueur d'une raison imparfaite. . . . L'homme est un animal noir qui a de la laine sur la tête, marchant sur deux pattes, presque aussi adroit qu'un singe, moins fort que les autres animaux de sa taille, ayant un peu plus d'idées qu'eux, et plus de facilité pour les exprimer; sujet d'ailleurs à toutes les mêmes nécessités, naissant, vivant et mourant tout comme eux" (Voltaire, *Mélanges*, pp. 159–160).

34. Ibid., p. 180. Cf. Sergio Landucci, *I filosofi e i selvaggi, 1580–1780* (Bari: Laterza, 1972), pp. 80ff.

35. "La membrane muqueuse des nègres, reconnue noire, et qui est la cause de leur couleur, est une preuve manifeste qu'il y a dans chaque espèce d'hommes, comme dans les plantes, un principe qui les différencie. La nature a subordonné à ce principe ces différents degrés de génie et ces caractères des nations qu'on voit si rarement changer. C'est par là que les nègres sont les esclaves des autres hommes. On les achète sur les côtes d'Afrique comme des bêtes, et les multitudes de ces noirs, transplantés dans nos colonies d'Amérique, servent un très petit nombre d'Européens" (Voltaire, *Essai sur les mœurs*, ed. René Pomeau [Paris: Classiques Garnier, 1963], 2:335).

36. Michele Duchet, *Anthropologie et Histoire au siècle des lumières* (Paris: A. Michel, 1995); Claudine Hunting, "The Philosophes and Black Slavery: 1748–1765," *Journal of the History of Ideas* 39 (1978): 405–418. See also Giuliano Gliozzi, "Poligenismo e razzismo agli albori del secolo dei Lumi," *Rivista di Filosofia* 70 (1979): 1–31.

37. "La plupart des nègres, tous les Cafres sont plongés dans la même stupidité" (*La philosophie de l'histoire*, p. 96); "Et y croupiront longtemps" (ibid.). See also the racist quip in *Les lettres d'Amabed* (Voltaire, *Romans et contes*, ed., Fréderic Deloffre and Jacques Van den Heuvel [Paris: Gallimard, 1979], pp. 507–508). Hunting, "The Philosophes," p. 417n16, argues, not too convincingly, that the passage was attempting to ridicule current attitudes toward blacks. Deloffre disagrees (*Les lettres d'Amabed*, p. 1136n).

38. Hunting, "The Philosophes," denies this. But see Alberto Burgio, "Razzismo e lumi: Su un 'paradosso' storico," *Studi Settecenteschi* 13 (1992–1993): 293–329.

39. See the somewhat apologetic article by Emeka Abanime, "Voltaire antiesclavagiste," *Studies on Voltaire and the Eighteenth Century* 182 (1979): 237–252.

40. Voltaire, *Mélanges*, p. 203: "The superfluous, which is a very necessary thing, has reunited one hemisphere with the other. Do you not see perhaps those slender ships that from the Texel, from London, from Bordeaux, go forth to seek, by a happy exchange, new products from the banks of the Ganges, while far from us, conquerors of the Muslims, our wines of France inebriate the sultans?"

41. André Morize, *L'apologie du luxe au XVIIIème siècle et "Le mondain" de Voltaire* (1909) (Geneva: Slatkine Reprints, 1970); Wade, *Studies on Voltaire*, pp. 22–49; A. Owen Aldridge, "Mandeville and Voltaire," in Irwin Primer, ed., *Mandeville Studies* (The Hague: Nijhoff, 1975), pp. 142–156. Wade argues that Voltaire came to know *The Fable of the Bees* only in 1735 at the time he wrote *La défense du mondain*. It should be noted, however, that Wade himself showed that *Le mondain* had been influenced by Jean François Melon, *Essai politique sur le commerce* (1736), which, in turn, was indebted to Mandeville.

42. Although we still lack a biography of Auerbach, much useful information can be gleaned from Hans Ulrich Gumbrecht, "Pathos of the Earthly Progress," in Seth Lerer, ed., *Literary History and the Challenge of Philology* (Stanford, CA: Stanford University Press, 1996), pp. 13–35.

43. The verses are contained in Yosef Hayim Yerushalmi, "Assimilation and Racial Anti-Semitism: The Iberian and the German Models," *The Leo Baeck Memorial Lecture* 26 (1992): 21–22.

44. K. Barck, "5 Briefe Erich Auerbachs an Walter Benjamin in Paris," *Zeitschrift für Germanistik* 9 (1988): 688–694: 692. I am grateful to Stephen Greenblatt, who brought these letters to my attention.

45. Benedetto Croce, *La filosofia di Giambattista Vico*, 2nd rev. ed. (Bari: Laterza, 1922), p. 254. Auerbach translated into German the *Scienza Nuova* (1925), as well as Croce's monograph on Vico (1927), both in collaboration with Theodor Lücke.

46. E. Auerbach, "Philology and Weltliteratur," *Centennial Review* 13 (1969): 1–17 (which appeared originally as "Philologie der Weltliteratur" in Walter Henzen, Walter Muschg, and Emil Staiger, eds., *Weltliteratur: Festgabe für Fritz Strich* [Bern: Francke, 1952], pp. 39–50). See also J. M. Ziolkowski's remark in the introduction (p. xxv).

47. M. Horkheimer and T. W. Adorno, *Dialectic of Enlightenment: Philosophical Fragments*, ed. Gunzelin Schmid Noerr, trans. Edmund Jephcott (Stanford, CA: Stanford University Press, 2002), p. xviii.

48. Ibid., pp. 180–181.

49. H. Mason, "Voltaire's Sermon Against Optimism: The *Poème sur le désastre de Lisbonne*," in Giles Barber and C. P. Courtney, eds., *Enlightenment Essays in Memory of Robert Shackleton* (Oxford: Voltaire Foundation, 1988), pp. 189–203.

50. "Il est toujours malheureusement nécessaire d'avertir qu'il faut distinguer les objections que se fait un auteur de ses réponses aux objections" (Voltaire, *Œuvres*, ed. Louis Moland [Paris: Garnier, 1877], 9:469, henceforth cited as "Moland").

51. "A l'égard des reproches d'injustice et de cruauté qu'on fait à Dieu, je réponds d'abord que supposé qu'il y ait un mal moral (ce qui me paraît une chimère), ce mal moral est tout aussi impossible à expliquer dans le système de la matière que dans

celui d'un Dieu . . . nous n'avons d'autres idées de la justice que celles que nous nous sommes formées de toute action utile à la société, et conformes aux lois établies par nous, pour le bien commun; or, cette idée n'étant qu'une idée de relation d'homme à homme, elle ne peut avoir aucune analogie avec Dieu. Il est tout aussi absurde de dire de Dieu, en ce sens, que Dieu est juste ou injuste, que de dire que Dieu est bleu ou carré.

"Il est donc insensé de reprocher à Dieu que les mouches soient mangées par les araignées" (Voltaire, *Mélanges*, pp. 169–170).

52. Moland, 9:478n12.

53. Voltaire, *Mélanges*, p. 208.

54. "Des nègres qu'on achetait en Afrique, et qu'on transportait au Perou comme des animaux destinés au service des hommes" (Voltaire, *Essai sur les mœurs*, p. 360).

55. See, for example, Voltaire, *Correspondance*, ed. Theodore Besterman (Geneva: Droz, 1971), vol. 17: D 6709, 6738, 6758, 6776.

56. A similar argument appears to have been proposed by R. Arruda in his unpublished dissertation, "La réaction littéraire de Voltaire et ses contemporains au tremblement de terre de Lisbonne de 1755" (Middlebury College, 1977). See Frederick A. Spear, in collaboration with Elizabeth Kreager, *Bibliographie analytique des écrits relatifs à Voltaire 1966–1990* (Oxford: Voltaire Foundation, 1992), p. 294. I have used the Pomeau edition for the additions to the *Essai sur les mœurs*. In general, see Henri Duranton, "Les manuscrits et les éditions corrigées de l'*Essai sur les mœurs*," in Louis Hay and Winfried Woesler, eds., *Die Nachlassedition—La publication des manuscrits inédits* (Bern: Lang, 1979), pp. 54–62.

57. "On comptait, en 1757, dans la Saint-Domingue française, environ trente mille personnes, et cent mille esclaves nègres ou mulâtres, qui travaillaient aux sucreries, aux plantations d'indigo, de cacao, et qui abrègent leur vie pour flatter nos appétits nouveaux, en remplissant nos nouveaux besoins, que nos pères ne connaissaient pas. Nous allons acheter ces nègres à la côte de Guinée, à la côte d'Or, à celle d'Ivoire. Il y a trente ans qu'on avait un beau nègre pour cinquante livres; c'est à peu près cinq fois moins qu'un bœuf gras. . . . Nous leurs disons qu'ils sont hommes comme nous, qu'ils sont rachetés du sang d'un Dieu mort pour eux, et ensuite on les fait travailler comme des bêtes de somme: on les nourrit plus mal; s'ils veulent s'enfuir, on leur coupe une jambe, et on leur fait tourner à bras l'arbre des moulins à sucre, lorsqu'on leur a donné une jambe de bois. Après cela nous osons parler du droit des gens! . . . Ce commerce n'enrichit point un pays; bien au contraire, il fait périr des hommes, il cause des naufrages; il n'est pas sans doute un vrai bien; mai les hommes s'étant fait des nécessités nouvelles, il empêche que la France n'achète chèrement de l'étranger un superflu devenu nécessaire" (Voltaire, *Essai sur les mœurs*, 2:379–380).

58. François de La Rochefoucauld, *Maximes*, ed. Jacques Truchet (Paris: Garnier, 1967), p. 11.

59. Arthur O. Lovejoy, *The Great Chain of Being* (Cambridge, MA: Harvard University Press, 1961), pp. 252–253, 365n15. See also *Dictionnaire philosophique* (1764),

ed. Christiane Mervaud (Oxford: Voltaire Foundation, 1994), 1:513–521, article "Chaine des êtres crées."

60. "Il ya probablement une distance immense entre l'homme et la brute, entre l'homme et les substances supérieures" (Moland 9:47).

61. D 9289, D 9329 (Voltaire, *Correspondance*, ed. T. Besterman, vol. 22). D'Alembert's reply contains a sarcastic allusion to Rousseau, suggested by a print entitled *Repas de nos philosophes*, and by the comedy *Les philosophes*, by Charles Palissot, both dated 1760.

62. At any rate the dialogue appears in the frequently cited Pléiade anthology (Voltaire, *Mélanges*). See also Christiane Mervaud, *Voltaire à table: Plaisir du corps, plaisir de l'esprit* (Paris: Editions Desjonquères, 1998), pp. 154–156. Hester Hastings, *Man and Beast in French Thought of the Eighteenth Century* (Baltimore: Johns Hopkins University Press, 1936), pp. 257–258, rather offhandedly defines it as "humorous."

63. Voltaire, *Mélanges*, pp. 323–335.

64. E. Auerbach, "Remarques sur le mot 'passion,'" *Neuphilologische Mitteilungen* 38 (1937): 218–224; idem, "Passio als Leidenschaft," in *Gesammelte Aufsätze zur romanischen Philologie* (Bern and Munich: Francke, 1967), pp. 161–175.

65. "Une maudite servante m'a prise sur ses genoux, m'a plongé une longue aiguille dans le cul, a saisi ma matrice, l'a roulée autour de l'aiguille, l'a arrachée et l'a donnée à manger à son chat" (Voltaire, *Mélanges*, p. 679).

66. Renato Galliani, "Voltaire, Porphyre, et les animaux," *Studies on Voltaire and the Eighteenth Century* 199 (1981): 125–138.

67. Moland 10:140–148.

68. B. Mandeville, *The Fable of the Bees: or, Private Vices, Publick Benefits*, ed. F. B. Kaye (Oxford: Clarendon, 1924), 1:180–181. This passage should be added to the detailed examination by Wade (*Studies on Voltaire*, pp. 12–56) of traces of Mandeville in the work of Voltaire. On Descartes and the animals, see Hastings, *Man and Beast*; and Leonora Cohen Rosenfield, *From Beast-Machine to Man-Machine* (New York: Oxford University Press, 1940). I do not have a direct acquaintance with Mandeville's *De brutorum operationibus*.

69. Voltaire, *Mélanges*, p. 682.

70. Mervaud, *Voltaire à table*, pp. 153–168.

71. "Il est juste qu'une espèce si perverse se dévore elle-même, et que la terre soit purgée de cette race" (Voltaire, *Mélanges*, p. 681).

72. Nicholas Hudson, "From Nation to Race: The Origin of Racial Classification in Eighteenth-Century Thought," *Eighteenth-Century Studies* 29 (1996): 247–264 (kindly brought to my attention by Daniel Stolzenberg). On the alleged cannibalism of the Jews, see Voltaire, *Dictionnaire philosophique*, vol. 1, *Anthropophages*, pp. 347–349; vol. 2: *Jephté*, pp. 240–242; as well as B. E. Schwarzbach, "Voltaire et les Juifs: Bilan et plaidoyer," *Studies on Voltaire and the Eighteenth Century* 358 (1998): 27–91: 82–83.

73. "Aïe! On me prend par le cou. Pardonnons à nos ennemis" (Voltaire, *Mélanges*, p. 684).

74. Ginzburg, *Occhiacci di legno*, pp. 100–117.

75. "Tous les animaux s'égorgent les uns les autres; ils y sont portés par un attrait invincible . . . il n'est point d'animal qui n'ait sa proie, et qui, pour la saisir, n'emploie l'équivalent de la ruse et de la rage avec laquelle l'exécrable araignée attire et dévore la mouche innocente. Un troupeau de moutons dévore en une heure plus d'insectes, en broutant l'herbe, qu'il n'ya d'hommes sur la terre. . . . Ces victimes n'expirent qu'après que la nature a soigneusement pourvu à en fournir de nouvelles. Tout renaît pour le meurtre" (Moland 28:534).

76. Sade, *La philosophie dans le boudoir*, in *Œuvres*, ed. Michel Delon (Paris: Gallimard, 1998), 3:145–153. I will return to this elsewhere.

77. Moland 28:549.

78. "Les Cafres, les Hottentots, les nègres de Guinée, sont des êtres beaucoup plus raisonnables et plus honnêtes que les Juifs. . . . Vous [Juifs] l'avez emporté sur toutes les nations en fables impertinentes, en mauvaise conduite, et en barbarie; vous en portez la peine, tel est votre destin. . . . Continuez surtout à être tolérants: c'est le vrai moyen de plaire à l'Etre des êtres, qui est également le père des Turcs et des Russes, des Chinois et des Japonais, des nègres, des tannés et des jaunes, et de la nature entière" (ibid., p. 551).

79. Ibid.

80. *Disturbing the Universe* (New York: Harper & Row, 1979), p. 223. But see also the observations by Claude Lévi-Strauss (*Le regard éloigné* [Paris: Plon, 1983], pp. 11–17, 21–48) on the relationships among cultures.

CHAPTER 8. ANACHARSIS INTERROGATES THE NATIVES

I would like to thank François Hartog, to whom I owe my first encounter with the *Voyage du jeune Anacharsis en Grèce*, and Cheryl Goldman, who called my attention to the passage in Flaubert.

1. Gustave Flaubert, *Madame Bovary*, trans. Mildred Marmur, with a foreword by Mary McCarthy (New York: New American Library, 1964), p. 32; *Madame Bovary: Mœurs de province*, ed. Edouard Maynial (Paris: Garnier, 1947), p. 9: "Le soir de chaque jeudi, il écrivait une longue lettre à sa mère, avec de l'encre rouge et trois pains à cacheter; puis il repassait ses cahiers d'histoire ou bien lisait un vieux volume d'*Anacharsis* qui traînait dans l'étude."

2. On the connection between these elements, see Francesco Orlando, *Gli oggetti desueti nelle immagini della letteratura* (Turin: Einaudi, 1993).

3. This is how the entry "J. J. Barthélemy" ends in the *Dictionnaire de la biographie française*.

4. See the biographical sketch by C. A. Sainte-Beuve, *Causeries du lundi*, 3rd ed. (Paris, n.d.), 7:186–223. For other data, see Maurice Badolle, *L'abbé Jean-Jacques Barthélemy (1716–1795) et l'hellénisme en France dans la seconde moitié du XVIIIe siècle* (Paris: Thèse, 1927).

5. "Explication de la mosaïque de Palestrine," *Mémoires de littérature tirés des registres de l'Académie Royale des Inscriptions et Belles-Lettres* 30 (1764): 503–538.

6. A listing without any pretense to completeness gives an idea of the variety of themes treated by Barthélemy in this period: "Remarques sur une inscription grecque, trouvée par M. l'Abbé Fourmont dans le temple d'Apollon Amycléen, et contenant une liste des prêtresses de ce Dieu," *Histoire de l'Académie des Inscriptions avec les Mémoires de Littérature* (Paris: L'Imprimerie Royale, 1756), 23:394–421; "Essai d'une paléographie numismatique," *Mémoires de littérature tirés des registres de l'Académie Royale des Inscriptions et des Belles-Lettres* 24:30–48; "Dissertations sur deux médailles samaritaines d'Antigonus roi de Judée," ibid., pp. 49–66; "Mémoires sur les anciens monumens de Rome," ibid., 26: 532–556; "Dissertations sur les médailles arabes," ibid., pp. 557–576; "Réflexions sur l'alphabet et sur la langue dont on se servoit autrefois à Palmyre," ibid., pp. 577–597; "Réflexions sur quelques monuments phéniciens et sur les alphabets qui en résultent," ibid., 30:405–427; "Remarques sur quelques médailles publiées par differens autheurs," ibid. 22:671–684; "Explication d'un bas-relief égyptien et de l'inscription phénicienne qui l'accompagne," ibid., pp. 725–738.

7. J.-J. Barthélemy, *Voyage en Italie*, à Paris l'an X (1802); reprint (Geneva: Minkoff Reprints, 1972), pp 397ff.

8. Voltaire, *Essai sur les mœurs*, ed. René Pomeau (Paris: Garnier 1963), vol. 2, chap. 21, p. 168.

9. Barthélemy, *Voyage en Italie*, p. 402. See also Werner Kaegi, *Jacob Burckhardt, eine Biographie* (Basel and Stuttgart: Helbing & Lichtenhahn, 1956), 3:678–679.

10. Barthélemy, *Voyage en Italie*, p. 408. For similar use of the term *revolution* applied to the period 1453–1648, see Johann Koch, *Tableau des revolutions de l'Europe* (Lausanne and Strasbourg, 1771), quoted in Delio Cantimori, *Studi di storia* (Turin: Einaudi, 1959), pp. 355–356.

11. On 23 October 1771, Barthélemy's friend Madame du Deffand wrote to the duchess de Choiseul that she had read *Télémaque* and that she had found it "deathly boring. . . . The style is wordy, lacking in vigor; it seeks to attain a certain unction without ardor. . . ." Barthélemy, replying in the name of the duchess, acknowledged: "Granted, it is digressive, somewhat monotonous, too full of descriptions, but richly endowed with high morality . . ." (*Correspondance complète de Mme du Deffand avec la duchesse de Choiseul, l'abbé Barthélemy et M. Craufurt*, with an introd. by M. le M[arqu]is de Sainte-Aulaire [Paris, 1877], 2:75, 77).

12. Barthélemy, *Voyage en Italie*, pp. 403–404.

13. Idem, *Voyage du jeune Anacharsis en Grèce*, 3rd ed. (Paris, 1791), 1:i–iii. (I have also used the Italian translation, *Viaggio d'Anacarsi il giovine nella Grecia verso la metà del quarto secolo avanti l'era volgare* [Venice, 1791], 1:vii).

14. Keith Stewart, "History, Poetry and the Terms of Fiction in the Eighteenth Century," *Modern Philology* 66 (1968): 110–120.

15. J.-J. Barthélemy, *Œuvres diverses*, 2 vols., à Paris l'an VI, 1:lxxii.

16. J. Spon, *Voyage d'Italie, de Dalmatie, de Grèce et du Levant, fait és années 1675 et 1676* (Lyons, 1678–1680).

17. Sainte-Beuve, *Causeries du lundi*, 7:208: "Il est le Tillemont de la Grèce."

18. A. Momigliano, "Storia antica e antiquaria" (1950), in *Sui fondamenti della storia antica* (Turin: Einaudi, 1984), pp. 3–45.

19. J. Gronovius, *Thesaurus Antiquitatum Graecarum*, 13 vols. (Lugduni Batavorum [Leyden]: Pieter van der Aa et al., 1697–1702).

20. Barthélemy to Madame du Deffand, Chanteloup, 18 February 1771 (*Correspondance complète de Mme du Deffand*, 1:345–347 [letter CCX]). On the liaison between Barthélemy and the duchess de Choiseul, see the introduction, p. xlvii. When Barthélemy was arrested during the Terror, the duchess managed to have him freed (p. cxxix).

21. *Correspondance complète de Mme du Deffand*, 1:cxv–xxvi; *Horace Walpole's Correspondence*, ed. W. S. Lewis, *Madame du Deffand and Mlle Sanadon* (New Haven, CT: Yale University Press, 1939), vol. 5, tome 3, p. 155 (12 December 1771).

22. Barthélemy, *Œuvres diverses*, 1:163–195.

23. Idem, *Voyage*, 2:368.

24. For a careful biography based on a wide assortment of letters, see Benedetta Craveri, *Madame du Deffand e il suo mondo* (Milan: Adelphi, 1982).

25. Madame du Deffand to Walpole, 4 April 1767 (*Correspondance complète de Mme du Deffand*, 1:95).

26. Madame du Deffand to the duchess de Choiseul, 20 April 1775 (ibid., 3:167).

27. Madame du Deffand to the duchess de Choiseul, 2 September 1778 (ibid., 3:338).

28. Madame du Deffand to the duchess de Choiseul, 9 December 1773 (ibid., 3:48–49).

29. Ibid.

30. "On nous parle de Catherine, et le marquis Ginori nous est inconnu!" (ibid., 1:119).

31. "Les entreprises de ces peuples [Romans and Carthaginians] sont paisibles, mais présentent de grands mouvements, et c'est le mouvement qui fixe 'attention et qui intéresse. Il est vrai que cet intéret est tranquille, et tant mieux, car M. De Bucq prétend que le bonheur n'est autre chose que l'intérêt dans la calme. J'aime mieux voir les romains et les carthaginois, les espagnols et les portugais traverser les mers pour découvrir de nouveaux pays, que de voir les factions des Guelfes et Ghibellines et celles des Roses rouge et blanche mettre tout à feu et à sang pour gouverner des peuples qui se seraient bien passés d'elles" (ibid., 3:336).

32. This is the thesis of a splendid book by Albert O. Hirschman, *The Passions and the Interests* (Princeton, NJ: Princeton University Press, 1977).

33. Madame du Deffand to the duchess de Choiseul (*Correspondance complète de Mme du Deffand*, 1:422).

34. G. H. Gaillard, *Histoire de la rivalité de la France et de l'Angleterre* (Paris: J. J. Blaise [impr. de P. Didot ainé], 1771), 1:2 (preface): "L'Europe est polie, l'Europe se

NOTES TO PAGES 121–123 ◆ 277

croit éclairée, et l'Europe fait la guerre! Nous nous sommes trop pressés d'applaudir à nos lumières, l'Europe est encore barbare!"

35. Among the exceptions, see Pierre-Daniel Huet, *Histoire du commerce et de la navigation des anciens*, à Lyon, chez Benoit Duplain, 1763 (reprinting of the 1715 edition; the book had been written at the request of Colbert).

36. *Monthly Review* 81 (1789): 577–593 (app.), quoted also in J.-J. Barthélemy, *Travels of Anacharsis the Younger in Greece, during the Middle of the Fourth Century before the Christian Aera*, 4th ed., 4 vols. (London, 1806), 1:iii (translator's preface).

37. See the entry "Yorke, Philip," in *Dictionary of National Biography*. Cf. *Monthly Review* 81 (1789): 592 (app.).

38. I have consulted one of the twelve copies of the first edition housed in the Special Collections department of the Young Research Library, UCLA: *Athenian letters, or the Epistolary Correspondence of an Agent of the King of Persia, residing at Athens during the Peloponnesian War, Containing the History of the Times, in Dispatches to the Ministers of State at the Persian Court. Besides Letters on Various Subjects between Him and His Friends*, 4 vols. (London, 1741–1743). A manuscript note on the title pages of the third and fourth volumes cautions: "Supposed to be wrote [!] by Ld Ch [arles] N [Yorke] 12 copies printed not more." The copy contains manuscript notes and additions, presumably written by one of the authors, and then in part inserted in the subsequent editions. This emerges from a comparison between the first and third editions, in two volumes, published in Dublin in 1792. I have not been able to see the second edition, 1781, apparently identical to the third. See, for example, the 1741 edition (1:148); the 1792 edition (1:133); the 1741 edition (1:166); and the 1792 edition (1:149).

39. *Athenian Letters*, 3:91–92, where there is a reference to a dissertation on *Marmor Sandvicense*, which had but recently been published by John Taylor (Cantabrigiae, 1743).

40. *Athenian Letters*, 4:227ff.

41. I have seen neither the successive editions (1800, 1810) nor the French translation (*Lettres Athéniennes*, 1803).

42. *Athenian Letters* (Dublin, 1792), vol. 1, "Introduction," which mentions a work by Crebillon *fils* (*Lettres Athèniennes, extraites du porte-feuille d'Alcybiade*: see *Collection complète des œuvres*, vols. 12–14 [London (actually Paris), 1777]), a work of imagination. Another book, which I have not seen, seems to have a similar character (which in its title recalls Marana's mentioned earlier): *The Athenian Spy, Discovering the Secret Letters which were sent to the Athenian Society by the Most Ingenious Ladies of the Three Kingdoms, relating to Management of their Affections. Being a Curious System of Love Cases, Platonic and Natural* (London: R. Halsey, 1704; expanded ed., 1709).

43. See the following entries in the *Dictionary of National Biography*: Birch, Thomas; Coventry, Henry; Green, John; Heberden, William; Salter, Samuel; Talbot, Catherine; Wray, Daniel; Yorke, Charles; Yorke, Philip (which names among those who participated in the initiative Dr. Rooke, later Master of Christ's College;

278 NOTES TO PAGES 123-125

John Heaton [*recte* Eaton] of Christ's College; John Lawry). See also E. Heberden, *William Heberden, Physician of the Age of Reason* (London: Royal Society of Medicine, 1989).

44. On this subject, see Natalie Z. Davis, "History's Two Bodies," *American Historical Review* 93 (1988): 1–30.

45. *Monthly Review*, n.s., vol. 1 (1790): 477–478 (app.).

46. Walpole expressed a scornful opinion about one of them, Thomas Birch: see the apposite entry in *Dictionary of National Biography*.

47. J.-J. Barthélemy, *Voyage du jeune Anacharsis en Grèce*, 5 vols. (Paris: Firmin Didot, 1824), 4:117ff.

48. *Athenian Letters*, 1:viii.

49. *Athenian Letters* (1792 edition), p. xviii: "The general character of Cleander is taken from Mahmut, the Turkish Spy. . . ." See Gian Carlo Roscioni, *Sulle tracce dell' "Esploratore turco"* (Milan: Roth, 1933; new ed., 1992). We know of only one copy of the first Italian edition.

50. [G. P. Marana], *L'espion dans les cours des princes chrétiens, ou lettres et mémoires d'un envoyé secret de la Porte dans les cours d'Europe; ou l'on voit les découvertes qu'il a faites dans toutes les Cours où il s'est trouvé, avec une dissertation curieuse de leurs Forces, Politique, et Religion*, à Cologne, Erasmus Kinkius, 1739, 1:41: "C'est alors [during Lent] qu'ils s'appliquent d'avantage aux exercices de piété; et qu'après avoir purgé leur conscience par des pénitences, et par des confessions secrettes qu'ils se font les uns aux autres, ils mangent d'un certain pain qu'ils appellent le Sacrement de l'Eucharistie, où ils imaginent que leur Messie est réelement present, aussitôt que leur Prêtres ont prononcé certaines paroles. As-tu jamais rien vu de si fou?" The original Italian version of this passage was much more cautious, as noted in Guido Almansi, "L'Esploratore turco' e la genesi del romanzo epistolare pseudo-orientale," *Studi Secenteschi* 7 (1966): 35–65: 60n104. See also Roscioni, *Sulle tracce*, p. 171.

51. C. Ginzburg, "Straniamento," in *Occhiacci di legno: Nove riflessioni sulla distanza* (Milan: Feltrinelli, 1998), pp. 15–39.

52. A. Momigliano, "Il contributo di Gibbon al metodo storico," in *Sui fondamenti della storia antica*, pp. 294–311.

53. C. Ginzburg, *Rapporti di forza: Storia, retorica, prova* (Milan: Feltrinelli, 2000), pp. 55–56. Cf. G. C. Roscioni, *Sulle tracce* (1992 ed.), p. 164.

54. Madame du Deffand, who had been delighted by Gibbon's spirit, reacted tepidly to his book: "Je souscris à vos éloges sur la *Décadence de l'Empire*," she wrote to Horace Walpole, "je n'en ai lu que la moitié, il ne m'amuse ni m'intéresse; toutes les histoires universelles et les recherches des causes m'ennuient; j'ai épuisé tous les romans, les contes, les théâtres; il n'ya plus que les lettres, les vies particulières et les mémoires écrits par ceux qui font leur propre histoire qui m'amusent et m'inspirent quelque curiosité. La morale, la métaphysique me causent un ennui mortel. Que vous dirais-je? J'ai trop vécu," *Horace Walpole's Correspondence: Madame du Deffand and Wiart*, vol. 6, tome 4, pp. 469–470 (Madame du Deffand to Walpole, 23 August 1777).

55. Momigliano, "Il contributo di Gibbon."

56. Silvia Bordini, *Storia del panorama: La visione totale nella pittura del XIX secolo* (Rome: Officina, 1984). See also the section "panorama" in W. Benjamin, *Parigi capitale del XIX secolo*, ed. Rolf Tiedemann (Turin: Einaudi, 1986), pp. 679–689 (in English: "Paris, Capital of the 19th Century," *New Left Review* 1 [March–April 1968]).

57. See C. Ginzburg, "The Inquisitor as Anthropologist," in idem, *Clues, Myths and the Historical Method*, trans. John and Anne C. Tedeschi (Baltimore: Johns Hopkins University Press, 1989), pp. 156–164, 220–221.

CHAPTER 9. FOLLOWING THE TRACKS OF ISRAËL BERTUCCIO

Different versions of this paper were presented at various times during 2005: to the Archivio di Stato, Venice (January); to the Department of History at the University of Siena (April); and to the Department of History at the University of Pisa (November).

1. E. Hobsbawm, *Interesting Times: A Twentieth-Century Life* (London: Allen Lane, 2002), p. 288.

2. Ibid., p. 293.

3. Ibid., p. 294. The juxtaposition of analysis and description is taken from Lawrence Stone, "The Revival of Narrative: Reflections on a New Old History," *Past and Present* 85 (1979): 3–24.

4. *Interesting Times*, p. 428n12. The review, unsigned (as was then the practice in the *Times Literary Supplement*), was reprinted as a "Foreword" to the English translation of *I benandanti: The Night Battles: Witchcraft and Agrarian Cults in the Sixteenth and Seventeenth Centuries*, trans. John Tedeschi and Anne Tedeschi (Baltimore: Johns Hopkins University Press, 1983), pp. ix–x.

5. See chap. 15 below, "Witches and Shamans."

6. Hobsbawm, *Interesting Times*, p. 296.

7. See, for example, chap. 12, "Just One Witness," below in this book; C. Ginzburg, *Occhiacci di legno: Nove riflessioni sulla distanza* (Milan: Feltrinelli, 1998); idem, *History, Rhetoric and Proof* (London and Hanover, NH: University Press of New England, 1999).

8. Hobsbawm, *Interesting Times*, p. 294.

9. C. Ginzburg, "L'historien et l'avocat du diable," second installment in a conversation with L. Vidal and C. Illouz, *Genèses* 54 (March 2004), esp. pp. 117–121. Cf. also C. Ginzburg, "Germanic Mythology and Nazism: Thoughts on an Old Book by Georges Dumézil," in *Clues, Myths and the Historical Method*, trans. John Tedeschi and Anne C. Tedeschi (Baltimore and London: Johns Hopkins University Press, 1989), pp. 126–145, 214–218.

10. E. Hobsbawm, "Manifeste pour l'histoire," *Le Monde Diplomatique*, December 2004, p. 20. I should like to thank Eric Hobsbawm for permitting me to read the text of his talk to the British Academy and for responding to my queries about the differences between the two versions.

11. Stendhal, *The Red and the Black*, trans. Horace B. Samuel (New York: Barnes & Noble, 2005), p. 313. I discuss this technique below in chap. 10, "The Bitter Truth." See also Simona Crippa, "Au bal avec Stendhal," *L'Année Stendhalienne* 1 (2002): 190–206.

12. Stendhal, *The Red and the Black*, p. 313; *Le Rouge et le Noir*, in Yves Ansel and Philippe Berthier, eds., *Œuvres romanesques complètes* (Paris: Gallimard, 2005), 1:616: "Il se trouvait que, justement l'avant-veille, Julien avait vu *Marino Faliero*, tragédie de M. Casimir Delavigne. Israël Bertuccio n'a-t-il-pas plus de caractère que tous ces nobles vénitiens, se disait notre plébéien révolté." See also at p. 623: "son triste rôle de plébéien révolté."

13. C. Delavigne, *Marino Faliero*, in *Œuvres*, 4 vols. (Brussels: A. Wahlen, 1832), vol. 3.

14. Antoine-François Varner and Jean-François-Alfred Bayard, *Marino Faliero à Paris*, folie-à-propos, vaudeville en un acte (Paris: Théâtre du Vaudeville, 1829), p. 15.

15. Delavigne, *Marino Faliero*, p. 87: "Les travaux, eux seuls, donneront la richesse; / le talent le pouvoir; les vertus, la noblesse."

16. Ibid., p. 27.

17. Stendhal, *The Red and the Black*, p. 313; "Une conspiration anéantit tous les titres donnés par les caprices sociaux" (Stendhal, *Le Rouge et le Noir*, pp. 616–617).

18. C. Delavigne, *Marino Faliero* (Paris: Ladvocat, 1829), pp. 11–12 (the preface does not appear in the *Œuvres complètes* (cited above at n. 13). I have not been able to consult K. Kiesel, *Byron's und Delavigne's "Marino Faliero"* (Düsseldorf, 1870), or Tauba Schorr, *Über Casimir Delavigne*, Gießener Beiträge zur Romanischen Philologie 20 (Gießen, 1926).

19. Stendhal, *Courrier Anglais*. New Monthly Magazine, ed. Henri Martineau, 5 vols. (Paris: Le Divan, 1935–1936), 3:480ff. (translated back from the English text; the original French version is no longer extant). See also the derisive allusion to Delavigne in *Correspondance générale*, ed. Victor Del Litto, 6 vols. (Paris: Champion, 1999), 3:619.

20. Ibid., 3:455–459 (letter to Louise Swanton-Belloc, who included it in her book on Byron [1824]); *Souvenirs sur Lord Byron* (August 1829), published by Romain Colomb (*Journal Littéraire* [Paris 1870], 3:167–173, ed. du Divan, vol. 35); "Lord Byron en Italie: Récit d'un témoin oculaire (1816)," *Revue de Paris* (March 1830) (*Mélanges: II, Journalisme* [Paris 1972], ed. du Divan, vol. 46).

21. Stendhal, *Correspondance générale*, 3:106 (to Adolphe de Mareste, 14 April 1818). In 1830 the list of names differs a bit: Rossini, Napoleon, Byron (p. 754, in a letter to Sophie Duvancel). Another of Stendhal's triads: Correggio, Mozart, Napoleon.

22. Ibid., 3:323.

23. George Gordon Noel Byron, *Marino Faliero, Doge of Venice. An Historical Tragedy in Five Acts with Notes. The Prophecy of Dante, a Poem* (London: Murray, 1821), p. xx (the citations, unless so noted, are to this edition).

24. See Alan Richardson, "Byron and the Theater," in *The Cambridge Companion to Byron*, ed. Drummond Bone (Cambridge and New York: Cambridge University Press, 2004), pp. 133–150: 139–141.

25. Lord Byron, "Marino Faliero," in *The Complete Poetical Works*, ed. Jerome J. McGann, 7 vols. (Oxford: Clarendon, 1980–1993), 4:525–526.

26. Ibid., p. xx: "I forgot to mention that the desire of preserving, though still too remote, a nearer approach to unity than the irregularity, which is the reproach of the English theatrical compositions, permits, has induced me to represent the conspiracy as already formed, and the Doge acceding to it, whereas in fact it was of his own preparation and that of Israel Bertuccio."

27. Richard Landsdown, *Byron's Historical Dramas* (Oxford: Oxford University Press, 1992), pp. 102ff. See also the app., "Shakespearian Allusions in *Marino Faliero*" (pp. 237ff.).

28. *Macbeth*, act 2, sc. 2.

29. Lord Byron, *Marino Faliero*, act 3, sc. 2, p. 95.

30. Ibid., act 3, sc. 2, p. 93. See also Michael Simpson, *Closet Performances: Political Exhibition and Prohibition in the Dramas of Byron and Shelley* (Stanford, CA: Stanford University Press, 1998), pp. 172ff.

31. If I am not mistaken, in Delavigne's play the term *plébéien* occurs only once, in a soliloquy by Faliero: "Mais prince ou plébéien, que je règne ou conspire / Je ne puis échapper aux soupçons que j'inspire" (act 3, sc. 3).

32. On this point as well, see chap. 10, "The Bitter Truth."

33. [Philo-Milton], *A Vindication of the Paradise Lost from the Charge of Exculpating "Cain": A Mystery* (London: J. F. Dove, 1822).

34. Thomas L. Ashton, "The Censorship of Byron's *Marino Faliero*," *Huntington Library Quarterly* 36 (1972): 27–44. Cf. also Simpson, *Closet Performances*, pp. 172ff.

35. Lord Byron, *Marino Faliero*, pp. xx–xxi.

36. Ibid., pp. 175–184.

37. Ibid., p. 179.

38. *Rerum Italicarum Scriptores*, ed. L. A. Muratori, 25 vols. in 28 tomes (Mediolani: ex typographia Societatis Palatinae, 1723–1751), 22: coll. 628–635: 632.

39. M. Sanudo il Giovane, *Le vite dei dogi 1423–1474*, vol. 1, *1423–1457*, ed. Angela Caracciolo Aricò (Venice: La Malcontenta, 1999), introd.

40. See Venice, Biblioteca Correr, Marin Sanudo, "Vite dei dogi," MS. Cicogna 1105–1106 (3768–3767). The section on the Falier conspiracy is in MS. Cicogna 1105 (3768), fols. 178v–181v.

41. *Laurentii de Monacis Veneti Cretae Cancellarii Chronicon de rebus Venetis ab U. C. ad annum MCCCLIV sive ad conjurationem ducis Faledro . . . omnia ex mss. editisque codicibus eruit, recensuit, praefationibus illustravit Flaminius Cornelius senator Venetus* (Venetiis: ex typographa Remondiniana, 1758), p. 316.

42. *Add. MSS.* 8574. Cf. Paul Oskar Kristeller, *Iter Italicum* (Leiden: Brill, 1989), 4:69, which cites (with a typographical error on the date of the MS.) C. Foligno, "Codici di materia veneta nelle biblioteche inglesi," *Nuovo Archivio Veneto*, n.s. 10 (1905): 104n10. Filippo de Vivo (to whom I am most grateful) informs me that at fol. 158r the same personage appears as "Bertasium Isardo," "Bertucius," "Bertucius ergo Isardo." This last version is changed to "Isarelo" by a hand other than the copyist's.

43. Giovanni Pillinini, "Marino Falier e la crisi economica e politica della metà del '300 a Venezia," *Archivio Veneto*, ser. 5, vol. 84 (1968): 45–71. Frederic C. Lane (*Venice, a Maritime Republic* [Baltimore: Johns Hopkins University Press, 1973], pp. 181–183) is much more cautious.

44. *Laurentii de Monacis Veneti Cretae Cancellarii Chronicon de rebus Venetis*, p. 317.

45. Vittorio Lazzarini, *Marino Faliero* (Florence: Sansoni, 1963), p. 155.

46. Ibid., pp. 156–157.

47. Archivio di Stato, Venice (hereafter cited as ASV), *Grazie*, vol. 3, fol. 56 (cf. V. Lazzarini, *Marino Faliero*, p. 158; I have corrected "*navelero*," presumably a typographical slip).

48. Ibid., vol. 10, fol. 81 (cf. V. Lazzarini, *Marino Faliero*, p. 158).

49. Vittorio Lazzarini, "Filippo Calendario l'architetto della tradizione del palazzo ducale," in *Marino Faliero*, pp. 299–314. And see also Lionello Puppi, "Calendario, Filippo," *Dizionario Biografico degli Italiani* 16:658–660.

50. Venice, Biblioteca Correr, Marin Sanudo, "Vite dei dogi," MS. Cicogna 1105 (3768), fol. 179v.

51. V. Lazzarini, *Marino Faliero*, p. 300. The exchange had already occurred in a passage of the chronicle of Nicolò Trevisan, appropriated by Sanudo: "The plot had these chiefs: Bertuzi Isarello stonecutter of San Trovaso, Filippo Calandario, his son-in-law" (Cod. Marc. cl. VII it., 800, fol. 199v).

52. I have used the fifteenth-century copy housed in ASV, *Miscellanea Codici I. Storia veneta* 142 (originally *Miscell. Codd.* 728), fol. IV. On the chronicle, see Lazzarini, *Marino Faliero*, p. 98.

53. This is what emerges from the research of Lazzarini, *Marino Faliero*, pp. 159ff.

54. ASV, *Miscellanea Codici I. Storia veneta* 142 (originally *Miscell. Codd.* 728), fol. 5r.

55. *Cronaca pseudo-Zancaruola*, Biblioteca Marciana, VII it., 50 (9275), fol. cccxi r.

56. ASV, *Miscellanea Codici I, Storia veneta* 142 (originally *Miscell. Codd.* 728), fol. 2v.

57. C. Ginzburg, "Somiglianza di famiglia e alberi genealogici: Due metafore cognitive," in Clemens-Carl Härle, ed., *Ai limiti dell'immagine* (Macerata: Quodlibet, 2005), pp. 227–250.

58. R. Needham, "Polythetic Classification," in *Against the Tranquillity of Axioms* (Berkeley and Los Angeles: University of California Press, 1983), pp. 36–65.

59. See Chaohua Wang, ed., *One China, Many Paths* (London: Norton, 2003), pp. 254–255: A youth from the countryside (specifically from the county of Yancheng, in the province of Jiangsu) mentioned in his diary Julien Sorel as a model for anyone who aspired to have a career in a bureaucratic and oppressive society. The editor observes that the allusion probably refers not to Stendhal's novel but to the film by Chabrol (which circulated in China in the '80s), in which the part of Julien was played by Gérard Philipe.

CHAPTER 10. STENDHAL'S CHALLENGE TO HISTORIANS

Different versions of this paper have been presented at Harvard University, at the Siemens Stiftung in Munich, and to the Department of History at the University of Siena. I am grateful to the Siemens Stiftung and to its director, Heinrich Meier, for making it possible for me to spend a fruitful research leave there in 2000.

1. Erich Auerbach, *Mimesis: The Representation of Reality in Western Literature*, trans. Willard R. Trask (Princeton, NJ: Princeton University Press, 1974), chap. 18.

2. Hayden White, "Auerbach's Literary History: Figural Causation and Modernist Historicism," in *Figural Realism: Studies in the Mimesis Effect* (Baltimore and London: Johns Hopkins University Press, 1999), pp. 87–100. (I discuss this study in a forthcoming essay on Auerbach and Dante.)

3. We should note that in the epilogue Auerbach speaks of the realism of the Middle Ages, thereby underlining both the differences and the continuity with respect to modern realism (*Mimesis*, pp. 554–557).

4. C. Ginzburg, *Occhiacci di legno: Nove riflessioni sulla distanza* (Milan: Feltrinelli, 1998), pp. 171–193.

5. Auerbach, *Mimesis*, p. 52.

6. Ibid., pp. 462, 463.

7. Ibid., p. 463.

8. Ibid., pp. 473, 477.

9. Auerbach repeatedly mentions Friedrich Meinecke, *Die Entstehung des Historismus* (1936); see *Mimesis*, index.

10. Ibid., pp. 546–547.

11. Ibid., pp. 548ff.

12. Ibid., pp. 454ff. On the general theme, see Lucien Dällenbach, *Le récit spéculaire: Essai sur la mise en abîme* (Paris: Éditions du Seuil, 1977).

13. "Rome, 24 mai 1834. J'ai écrit dans ma jeunesse des biographies (Mozart, Michelangelo) qui sont une espèce d'histoire. Je m'en repens. Le *vrai* sur les plus grandes, comme sur les plus petites choses, me semble presque impossible à atteindre, au moins un vrai *un peu détaillé*. M. de Tracy me disait [cancelled: il n'ya plus de vérité que dans] on ne peut plus atteindre au *Vrai*, que dans le Roman. Je vois tous les jours davantage que partout ailleurs c'est une prétention" (an almost identical transcription can be read in Stendhal, *Œuvres romanesques complètes*, ed. Yves Ansel [Paris: Gallimard, 2005], p. 997, from which I have taken all the following quotations).

14. The Pléiade edition prepared by Henri Martineau contained only the second subtitle; and only the first appears in Stendhal, *The Red and the Black*, trans. Horace B. Samuel, with an introd. and notes by Bruce Robbins (New York: Barnes and Noble, 2005), p. xxix. Auerbach's *Mimesis* cites both subtitles, but without comment. According to Robert Alter (*A Lion for Love* [New York: Basic Books, 1979], p. 201n), the original subtitle was changed to "Chronique de 1830" because it seemed to allude to the barricades of July 1830.

15. Charles Baudelaire, *Conseils aux jeunes littérateurs* (1846), in *Œuvres complètes*, ed. Claude Pichois (Paris: Gallimard, 1976), 2:17.

16. Stendhal, *Œuvres romanesques complètes*, p. 578; *The Red and the Black*, p. 270 (slightly modified). Cf. Auerbach, *Mimesis*, p. 455.

17. Auerbach, *Mimesis*, pp. 455–456.

18. Stendhal, "Projet d'article sur *Le Rouge et le Noir*" (1832), in *Œuvres romanesques*, pp. 822–838; V. Salvagnoli, *Dei romanzi in Francia e del romanzo in particolare di M. Stendhal Le Rouge et le Noir* (1832), inedito con integrazioni autografe e postille di Stendhal, ed. Annalisa Bottacin (Florence: Polistampa, 1999). See also A. Jefferson, "Stendhal and the Uses of Reading: *Le Rouge et le Noir*," French Studies 37 (1983): 168–183: 175.

19. *Œuvres romanesques*, p. 824: "Rien de semblable aujourd'hui, tout est triste et guindé dans les villes de six à huit mille âmes. L'étranger y est aussi embarrassé de sa soirée qu'en Angleterre."

20. Pierre Victor, baron de Besenval, *Spleen*, trans. H. B. V., with an Introduction by Havelock Ellis (London: Chapman & Hall, 1928).

21. Stendhal, "Projet d'article," in *Œuvres romanesques*, p. 827: "La France *morale* est ignorée à l'étranger, voilà pourquoi avant d'en venir au roman de M. de S[tendhal] il a fallu dire que rien ne ressemble moins à la France gaie, amusante, un peu libertine, qui de 1715 à 1789 fut le modèle de l'Europe, que la France grave, morale, morose que nous ont léguée les jésuites, les congrégations et le gouvernement des Bourbons de 1814 à 1830. Comme rien n'est plus difficile en fait des romans que de peindre d'après nature, de ne pas *copier des livres*, personne encore avant M. de S[tendhal] ne s'était hasardé à faire le portrait de ces mœurs si peu aimables, mais qui malgré cela, vu l'esprit mouton de l'Europe, finiront par régner de Naples à Saint-Pétersbourg."

22. Ibid., p. 827: "En faisant le portrait de la société de 1829 (époque où le roman a été écrit). . . ."

23. *The Red and the Black*, p. [5]; *Œuvres romanesques*, p. 349: "Nous avons lieu de croire que les feuilles suivantes furent écrites en 1827."

24. Idem, *Œuvres intimes*, ed. Victor Del Litto (Paris: Gallimard, 1982), 2:129: "Je dicte la scène de la cathédrale de Bisontium [i.e., Besançon]." Cf. Del Litto's comment, p. 1079.

25. Michel Crouzet, *Le Rouge et le Noir: Essai sur le romanesque stendhalien* (Paris: Presses Universitaires de France, 1995), pp. 10–11. See the entry "Lablache, Louis," in *Nouvelle biographie française*. Cf. Y. Ansel in *Œuvres romanesques*, pp. 960–962.

26. Henri Martineau, introduction to Stendhal, *Romans et nouvelles* (Paris: Gallimard, 1956), 1:198.

27. Stendhal, *The Red and the Black*, p. 532; *Le Rouge et le Noir*, p. 807: "L'inconvénient du règne de l'opinion, qui d'ailleurs procure *la liberté*, c'est qu'elle se mêle de ce dont elle n'a que faire; par exemple: la vie privée. De là la tristesse de l'Amérique et de l'Angleterre." See *Correspondance*, ed. Victor Del Litto and Henri Martineau, 3 vols. (Paris: Gallimard, 1962–1968), 2:193–194 (letter to Daniello Berlinghieri).

28. For an enlightening discussion on this theme, see Franco Moretti, *Il romanzo di formazione* (1986) (Turin: Einaudi, 1999), chap. 2, "Waterloo Story," pp. 82–141.

29. See, for example, Stendhal, *Œuvres romanesques*, p. 1104 (in the chapter "Un siècle moral" of *Le Rouge et le Noir*).

30. Auerbach, *Mimesis*, p. 480.

31. Excellent observations in J. T. Booker, "Style direct libre: The Case of Stendhal," *Stanford French Review* (1985): 137–151.

32. Stendhal, *The Red and the Black*, p. 270 (slightly modified); Cf. Auerbach, *Mimesis*, p. 455.

33. V. Mylne, "The Punctuation of Dialogue in Eighteenth-Century French and English Fiction," *The Library* 1 (1979): 43–61. Against the so-called *ponctuation forte*, or abundant, see two writings which appeared the same year: A. Frey, "ancien prote [foreman] et correcteur d'imprimerie," *Principes de ponctuation fondés sur la nature du langage écrit* (Paris: De l'imprimerie de Plasson, 1824); and the *Traité raisonné de ponctuation* published in app. to F. Raymond, *Dictionnaire des termes appropriés aux arts et aux sciences, et des mots nouveaux que l'usage a consacrés . . .* (Paris, 1824). In the app., see esp. chap. 10, p. xxviii, apropos parentheses, quotation marks, and so forth: "Leur apposition dans le langage est presque abandonnée dans ce moment. Les auteurs en général évitent les parenthèses, le tiret et les guillemets, le plus possible."

34. Stendhal, *Le Rouge et le Noir*, pp. 569, 612.

35. Stendhal, *Scarlet and Black*, trans. Margaret R. B. Shaw (Harmondsworth: Penguin, 1953), pp. 257, 303.

36. Moretti, *Il romanzo di formazione*, p. 107: "Certain pages of Stendhal, broken and almost fractured by sudden passages from one point of view to another."

37. *The Red and the Black*, pp. 270, 298.

38. *The Red and the Black*, p. 309; *Le Rouge et le Noire*, p. 613: "Mathilde ne perdait pas une syllabe de leur conversation. L'ennui avait disparu." On what may have inspired Stendhal, see C. Liprandi, "Sur un épisode du *Rouge et Noire*: Le bal du duc de Retz," *Revue des Sciences Humaines* 76 (1954): 403–417.

39. *The Red and the Black*, p. 310; *Le Rouge et le Noir*, p. 614: "Il n'ya plus des passions véritables au XIXe siècle; c'est pour cela que l'on s'ennuie tant en France."

40. M. Crouzet, *Le Rouge et le Noir*, p. 11: "Les propos du bal de Retz et les pensées d'Altamira sont en parfaite consonance avec la Révolution, ils l'appellent et l'annoncent. Stendhal indique au lecteur qu'il l'avait bien dit, que son roman conduit aux barricades et les contient, même s'il n'en parle pas."

41. *The Red and the Black*, p. 303; *Le Rouge et le Noir*, p. 607: "Je ne vois que la condamnation à mort qui distingue un homme, pensa Mathilde, c'est la seule chose qui ne s'achète pas."

42. *Le Rouge et le Noire*, p. 644. A strikingly similar observation is made in A. Sonnenfeld, "Romantisme (ou ironie): Les épigraphes du *Rouge et Noire*," *Stendhal Club* 78 (January 1978): 143–154: 153.

43. *The Red and the Black*, p. 309; *Le Rouge et le Noir*, p. 613: "Mlle de la Mole, penchant la tête avec le plus vif intérêt, était si près de lui, que ses beaux cheveux touchaient presque son épaule."

44. Stendhal, *Romans*, ed. H. Martineau, 1:1432: "Dimanche ennuyeux, promenade au Corso with Mister Sten[dhal], et pour toute sa vie ainsi till the death. 15 mars 35" (only partially legible note scribbled on the Bucci copy of *Armance*: see *Œuvres romanesques*, p. 896).

45. J. Starobinski, *L'œil vivant* (Paris: Gallimard, 1961), chap. "Stendhal pseudonyme" (pp. 191–240); idem, "Leo Spitzer et la lecture stylistique," introd. to L. Spitzer, *Études de Style* (Paris: Gallimard, 1970), pp. 27–28.

46. See the remarks in Y. Ansel, *Œuvres romanesques*, pp. 1131–1133.

47. I owe this suggestion to Vyacheslav Ivanov.

48. Stendhal, *Romans*, ed. H. Martineau, 1:1401: "5 mai 1834. . . . A Marseille, en 1828, je crois, je fis trop court le manuscrit du *Rouge*. Quand j'ai voulu le faire imprimer à Lutèce, il m'a fallu faire de la substance au lieu d'effacer quelques pages et de corriger le style. De là, entre autres défauts, des phrases heurtées et l'absence de ces petits mots qui aident l'imagination du lecteur bénévole à se figurer les choses."

49. Ibid., 1:1458, 1483. The first annotation is no longer available. See Stendhal, *Œuvres romanesques*, p. 992.

50. Alter, *A Lion*, p. 165.

51. Stendhal, *Œuvres intimes. I. Journal*, pp. 301–302: "C'est un peintre qui voudrait s'illustrer dans le genre de l'Albane, qui aurait judicieusement commencé par l'étude de l'anatomie, et pour qui, come objet utile, elle serait devenue tellement agréable, qu'au lieu de peindre un joli sein, voulant enchanter les hommes, il peindrait à découvert et sanglants tous les muscles qui forment la poitrine d'une jolie femme, d'autant plus horrible, en leur sotte manie, qu'on s'attendait à une chose plus agréable. Ils procurent un nouveau dégoût par la vérité des objets qu'ils présentent. On ne ferait que les mépriser s'ils étaient faux, mais ils sont vrais, ils poursuivent l'imagination." See also the *Journal* entry for 13 December 1829, "Il faut avoir le courage des Carrache" (p. 108).

52. Stendhal, *Correspondance*, 2:858–859: Mérimée observed that Stendhal, given his relationship with Madame Azur, could not, unlike Swift, claim impotence as an alibi. Both Mérimée and Stendhal had been lovers of Madame Azur (Alberthe de Rubempré), who a little earlier in a Parisian drawing room had waxed eloquent about Stendhal's amorous prowess: see Alter, *A Lion*, pp. 183–184. Stendhal had mentioned Swift's impotence speaking of the plot of *Armance* in a letter to Mérimée dated 23 December 1826 (see *Romans et nouvelles*, 1:190–192).

53. Quoted in Muriel Augry-Merlino, *Le cosmopolitisme dans les textes courts de Stendhal et Mérimée* (Geneva and Paris: Slatkine, 1990), p. 102.

54. P. Mérimée, "H. B. (1850), in *Portraits historiques et littéraires*, ed. Pierre Jourda (Paris: Champion, 1928), p. 155: "Toute sa vie il fut dominé par son imagination, et ne fit rien que brusquement et d'enthousiasme. Cependant, il se piquait de n'agir jamais que conformément à la raison. 'Il faut en tout se guider par la LO-GIQUE,' disait-il

en mettant un intervalle entre la première syllabe et le reste du mot. Mais il souffrait impatiemment que la *logique* des autres ne fût pas la sienne."

55. Stendhal, *Vie d'Henry Brulard,* in *Œuvres intimes,* 2:858–859.

56. Ibid., 1:208; idem, *Journal littéraire,* in *Œuvres complètes,* 34:172. Cf. also pp. 166, 168.

57. P. Mérimée, "[Stendhal] Notes et souvenirs," in *Portraits,* p. 179.

58. Stendhal, *Correspondance,* 1:352 (to Pauline Beyle, 3 June 1807): "Je relis la *Logique* de Tracy avec un vif plaisir; je cherche à raisonner juste pour trouver une réponse exacte à cette question: 'Que désiré-je?'"

59. Idem, *Souvenirs d'égotisme,* ed. Beatrice Didier (Paris: Gallimard, 1983), p. 114: "On peut tout connaître, excepté soi-même."

60. Nicola Chiaromonte, "Fabrizio a Waterloo," in *Credere e non credere* (Bologna: Il Mulino, 1993), pp. 23–48: 30: "Stendhal not only does not believe in History with a capital H, but not even in the one he himself narrates." Actually, he believed in both, from which came the combination of scorn (in the final years, disgust) and joy which is his alone.

61. C. Ginzburg, *Rapporti di forza: Storia, retorica, prova* (Milan: Feltrinelli, 2000), p. 48.

CHAPTER II. ON THE FRENCH PREHISTORY OF THE *PROTOCOLS*

Slightly different versions of this essay have been presented to Darwin College, Cambridge, and to the Departments of History at the Universities of Siena and Cagliari. I am grateful to Gopal Balakrishnan, Michele Battini, Pier Cesare Bori, Cesare G. De Michelis, Andrea Ginzburg, Maria Luisa Catoni, Mikhail Gronas, and Sergei Kozlov for their help.

1. Jean-François Revel, ed. (Paris: Calmann-Levy, 1968). My quotations are taken from M. Joly, *Dialogue in Hell between Machiavelli and Montesquieu: Humanitarian Despotism and the Conditions of Modern Tyranny,* trans., ed., and with commentary by John S. Waggoner (Lanham, MD: Lexington Books, 2003).

2. For Joly's biography, see P. Charles, *Les Protocoles des sages de Sion* (1938), reprinted in *Les Protocoles des sages de Sion,* ed. Pierre-André Taguieff, 2 vols. (Paris: Berg International, 1992), 2:9–37: 25 (henceforth cited as Taguieff). Cf. also Joly, *The Dialogue in Hell,* pp. xvii ff. and idem, *Dialogo agli Inferi tra Machiavelli e Montesquieu,* ed. R. Repetti, trans. E. Nebiolo Repetti (Genoa, 1995), p. 12n4. In 1870 Joly stated that a second, enlarged edition of the *Dialogue,* on which he had worked during his confinement at Sainte-Pélagie, was in press. But there is no evidence that it ever appeared (*Maurice Joly: Son passé, son programme, par lui-même* [Paris: Lacroix, 1870], p. 10n2).

3. Ibid., p. 9: "Un soir que je me promenais sur la terrasse au bord de l'eau, près du Pont Royal, par un temps de boue dont je me souviens encore, le nom de Montesquieu me vint tout à coup à l'esprit comme personnifiant tout un côté des mes idées, que je voulais exprimer. Mais quel serait l'interlocuteur de Montesquieu? Une idée jaillit de mon cerveau: et pardieu c'est *Machiavel!*

"*Machiavel* qui représente la politique de la force à côté de Montesquieu qui représentera la politique du droit; et Machiavel, ce sera Napoléon III, qui peindra à lui-même son abominable politique."

4. Ferdinando Galiani, *Dialogue sur le commerce des bleds*, in *Opere* (*Illuministi italiani*, vol. 6), ed. Furio Diaz (Milan and Naples: Ricciardi, 1975), pp. 357–612.

5. *Satyre Menippée ou la vertu du Catholicon d'Espagne*, ed. C. Nodier, 2 vols. (Paris: Delangle, 1824).

6. After having finished the present essay, I discovered that this connection had already been proposed by Johannes Rentsch in *Lukian-Studien* (Plauen: Programm Plauen Gymnasium, 1895), p. 39 (I cite from Nicoletta Marcialis, *Caronte e Caterina: Dialoghi dei morti nella letteratura russa del XVIII secolo* [Rome: Bulzoni, 1989], p. 19). Rentsch mentioned the German translation of the *Dialogue aux Enfers entre Machiavel et Montesquieu*, which appeared anonymously.

7. Lucian, *Dialogues of the Dead*, 12.

8. Bernard le Bovier de Fontenelle, *Nouveaux dialogues des morts* (1683), new, enlarged ed. (London: Printed for Jacob Tonson, 1711), dedicated to Lucian: "J'ai suprimé Pluton, Caron, Cerbère et tout ce qui est usé dans les Enfers." On the contrast between ancients and moderns, see, for example, the dialogue between the physicians Erasistratus and Hervé (William Harvey).

9. J. Egilsrud, *Le "dialogue des morts" dans les litteratures française, allemande et anglaise (1644–1789)*, thesis (Paris: L'Entente Linotypiste, 1934); Frederick Keener, *English Dialogues of the Dead: A Critical History, an Anthology, and a Check-List* (New York: Columbia University, 1973); Marcialis, *Caronte e Caterina*. For a typical example, see [A.-A. Bruzen de la Martinière], *Entretiens des ombres aux Champs Elysées* (Amsterdam: H. Uytwerf, 1723), which includes a dialogue (the sixth) between Confucius and Machiavelli (2:111–232).

10. M. Joly, *Dialogue aux Enfers entre Machiavel et Montesquieu*, preceded by Michel Bounan's *L'État retors* (Paris: Éditions Allia, 1987; 3rd ed., 1999). In English, see *The Crafty State*, preface to Joly's *Dialogue in Hell between Machiavelli and Montesquieu* (Paris: Editions Allia, 1992). The epilogue has appeared as an autonomous text: M. Joly, *Le Plébiscite: Épilogue du Dialogue aux Enfers entre Machiavel et Montesquieu*, with a postscript by F. Leclercq (Paris, 1996).

11. Joly, *Dialogue in Hell*, pp. 27–28; *Dialogue*, p. 40 (end of the fourth dialogue): "Je ne vois de salut pour ces sociétés, véritables colosses aux pieds d'argile, que dans l'institution d'une centralisation à outrance, qui mette toute la force publique à la disposition de ceux qui gouvernent; dans une administration hiérarchique semblable à celle de l'empire romain, qui règle mécaniquement tous les mouvements des individus; dans un vaste système de législation qui reprenne en détail toutes les libertés qui ont été imprudemment données; dans un despotisme gigantesque, enfin, qui puisse frapper immédiatement et à toute heure, tout ce qui résiste, tout ce qui se plaint. Le Césarisme du Bas-Empire me paraît réaliser assez bien ce que je souhaite pour le bien-être des sociétés modernes. Grâce à ces vastes appareils qui fonctionnent dejá, m'a-t-on dit, en plus d'un pays de l'Europe, elles peuvent vivre en paix,

comme en Chine, comme au Japon, comme dans l'Inde. Il ne faut pas qu'un vulgaire préjugé nous fasse mépriser ces civilisations orientales, dont on apprend chaque jour à mieux apprécier les institutions. Le peuple chinois, par exemple, est très commerçant et très bien administré."

12. I take the quotation from Arnaldo Momigliano, "Per un riesame della storia dell'idea di cesarismo," in idem, *Sui fondamenti della storia antica* (Turin: Einaudi, 1984), pp. 378–388: 380n6. See also his "Contributi ad un dizionario storico: J. Burckhardt e la parola 'cesarismo,'" ibid., pp. 389–392. Momigliano does not mention Joly's *Dialogue aux Enfers*. The latter's intellectual debt to Romieu's *Ere des Césars* has been noted by Tami Sarfatti in "Reading Machiavelli in Mid-Nineteenth-Century France: Auguste Romieu, Maurice Joly and a Critique of Liberalism" (paper presented at a seminar which I organized at UCLA, Winter 2002). On the entire question, the fundamental treatment is Innocenzo Cervelli, "Cesarismo: Alcuni usi e significati della parola (secolo XIX)," *Annali dell'Istituto Storico Italo-Germanico di Trento* 22 (1996): 61–197 (esp. pp. 103ff. on Romieu; pp. 135–136n255, on Joly).

13. A. Romieu, *Le spectre rouge de 1852*, 2nd ed. (Paris: Ledoyen, 1851), pp. 5–6: "Je crois à des besoins sociaux, non à des droits naturels. Le mot DROIT n'a aucun sens pour mon esprit, parce que je n'en vois, nulle part, la traduction dans la nature. Il est d'invention humaine...."

14. Joly, *Dialogue in Hell*, pp. 10–11; *Dialogue*, p. 12 (first dialogue): "Tous les pouvoirs souverains ont eu la force pour origine, ou, ce qui est la même chose, la négation du droit.... Ce mot de droit lui-même, d'ailleurs, ne voyez-vous pas qu'il est d'un vague infini?"

15. For the eighteenth-century discussions, see Franco Venturi, "Despotismo orientale," *Rivista Storica Italiana* 72 (1960): 117–126.

16. A. de Tocqueville, *De la Démocratie en Amérique*, ed. François Furet (Paris: Garnier-Flammarion, 1981), 2:386: "J'ai toujours cru que cette sorte de servitude, réglée, douce et paisible, dont je viens de faire le tableau, pourrait se combiner mieux qu'on ne l'imagine avec quelques-unes des formes extérieures de la liberté, et qu'il ne lui serait pas impossible de s'établir à l'ombre même de la souveraineté du peuple." Cf. also C. Cassina, "Alexis de Tocqueville e il dispotismo 'di nuova specie,'" in Domenico Felice, ed., *Dispotismo: Genesi e sviluppi di un concetto politico-filosofico* (Naples: Liguori, 2002), 2:515–543.

17. Tocqueville, *De la Démocratie en Amérique*, 2:392.

18. Joly, *Dialogue in Hell*, p. 90; *Dialogue*, pp. 153–154 (end of the fifteenth dialogue): "Un des mes grands principes est d'opposer les semblables. De même que j'use la presse par la presse, j'userai la tribune par la tribune.... Les dix-neuf vingtièmes de la Chambre seraient des hommes à moi qui voteraient sur une consigne, tandis que je ferais mouvoir le fils d'une opposition factice et clandestinement embauchée."

19. Idem, *Dialogue in Hell*, p. 91; *Dialogue*, p. 155 (beginning of the sixteenth dialogue): "L'anéantissement des partis et la destruction des forces collectives."

20. Idem, *Dialogue in Hell*, pp. 69–70; *Dialogue*, pp. 112, 114 (twelfth dialogue): "... j'entrevois la possibilité de neutraliser la presse par la presse elle-même. Puisque c'est une si grande force que le journalisme, savez-vous ce que ferait mon gouvernement? Il se ferait journaliste, ce serait le journalisme incarné.... Comme le dieu Wishnou, ma presse aura cent bras, et ces bras donneront la main à toutes les nuances d'opinion quelconque sur la surface entière du pays. On sera de mon parti sans le savoir. Ceux qui croiront parler leur langue parleront la mienne, ceux qui croiront agiter leur parti agiteront le mien, ceux qui croiront marcher sous leur drapeau marcheront sous le mien." "Sont-ce là des conceptions réalisables ou des fantasmagories? Cela donne le vertige."

21. Joly, *Dialogue in Hell*, p. [5], "No one should ask whose hand wrote these pages. In a certain sense, a work like this is anonymous. It answers a call to conscience. Everyone hears this call. The ideas take form. The author withdraws to the background ...'; *Dialogue*, p. 4: "On ne demandera pas quelle est la main qui a tracé ces pages: une œuvre comme celle-ci est en quelque sorte impersonnelle. Elle répond à un appel de la conscience; tout le monde l'a conçue, elle est exécutée, l'auteur s'efface. ..."

22. *Maurice Joly: Son passé, son programme*, p. 9.

23. On universal suffrage as a new form of legitimacy, see Domenico Losurdo, *Democrazia o bonapartismo: Trionfo e decadenza del suffragio universale* (Turin: Bollati Boringhieri, 1993); and Albert O. Hirschman, *Shifting Involvements: Private Interest and Public Action* (Princeton, NJ: Princeton University Press, 1982), esp. pp. 112–120 (brought to my attention by Andrea Ginzburg).

24. Joly, *Dialogue in Hell*, p. 51; *Dialogue*, p. 80 (ninth dialogue): "Jamais les choses ne se sont passés autrement, j'en atteste l'histoire de tous les fondateurs d'empire, l'exemple des Sésostris, des Solon, des Lycurgue, des Charlemagne, des Frédéric II, des Pierre Ier.' 'C'est un chapitre d'un de vos disciples que vous allez me développer là.' 'Et de qui donc?' 'De Joseph de Maistre. Il y a là des considérations générales qui ne sont pas sans vérité, mai que je trouve sans application.'"

25. Joseph de Maistre, *Considerations on France*, trans. Richard A. Lebrun (Montreal and London: McGill–Queen's University Press, 1974), p. 95 (J. de Maistre, *Considérations sur la France*, ed. J. Toulard [Paris: Éditions Bernard Grasset, 1980], p. 63: "Une assemblée quelconque d'hommes ne peut constituer une nation; et même cette entreprise excède en folie ce que tous les *Bedlams* de l'univers peuvent enfanter de plus absurde et de plus extravagant").

26. Niccolò Machiavelli, "Discourses on the First Ten Books of Titus Livius," in *The Prince and the Discourses*, with an introd. by Max Lerner (New York: Modern Library, 1940), p. 138.

27. J. de Maistre, *Essai sur le principe générateur des constitutions politiques et des autres institutions humaines* (Paris: Société Typographique, 1814), p. vi.

28. Joly, *Dialogue*, pp. 142–143: "Un machiavélisme infernal s'emparant des préjugés et des passions populaires a propagé partout une confusion de principes qui rend toute entente impossible entre ceux qui parlent la même langue et qui ont les mêmes

intérêts." The passage is quoted also in Henri Rollin, *L'Apocalypse de notre temps: Les dessous de la propagande allemande d'après des documents inédits* (Paris: Gallimard, 1939) [1991], p. 235.

29. Joly, *Dialogue in Hell*, p. 34; *Dialogue*, p. 49 (sixth dialogue): "Un de plus vos illustres partisans."

30. H. Speier, "La verité aux enfers: Maurice Joly et le despotisme moderne," *Commentaires* 56 (1991–1992): 671–680: 673. See also F. Leclercq, "Maurice Joly, un suicidé de la démocratie," postscript to M. Joly, *Le Plébiscite: Epilogue du Dialogue aux Enfers entre Machiavel et Montesquieu*, pp. 107–108.

31. Peter Saurisse, "Portraits composites: La photographie des types physionomiques à la fin du XIXe siècle," *Histoire de l'Art* 37–38 (May 1997): 69–78; and C. Ginzburg, "Somiglianze di famiglia e alberi genealogici: Due metafore cognitive," in C.-C. Härle, ed., *Ai limiti dell'immagine* (Macerata, Italy: Quodlibet, 2005), pp. 227–250. Galton began working on the composite portraits in 1878, the year of Joly's death.

32. C. Ginzburg, *No Island Is an Island: Four Glances at English Literature in a World Perspective* (New York: Columbia University Press, 2000), p. 33.

33. For a listing of the French editions and translations, see M. Joly, *Dialogue aux Enfers* (Paris: Éditions Allia, 1999).

34. H. Barth, "Maurice Joly, der plebiszitäre Cäsarismus und die 'Protokolle der Weisen von Zion,'" *Neue Zürcher Zeitung* 31 March 1962; Werner Kaegi, "Burckhardt e gli inizi del cesarismo moderno," *Rivista Storica Italiana* 76 (1964): 150–171: 150–152.

35. "Un classique de la politique qui, avec un siècle d'avance, a mis a nu les procédés du despotisme moderne."

36. I shall cite only Norman Cohn, *Warrant for Genocide: The Myth of the Jewish World Conspiracy and the Protocols of the Elders of Zion* (London: Eyre & Spottiswoode, 1967); *Les Protocoles des Sages de Sion*, ed. P.-A. Taguieff; and Cesare G. De Michelis, *The Non-Existent Manuscript: A Study of the Protocols of the Sages of Zion*, trans. Richard Newhouse (Lincoln and London: University of Nebraska Press, 2004).

37. P. Charles, *Les Protocoles*; J. F. Moisan, "Les Protocoles des sages de Sion en Grande-Bretagne et aux USA," in Taguieff 2:163–216. See now Maurice Olender, *La chasse aux évidences: Sur quelques formes de racisme entre mythe et histoire* (Paris: Galaade, 2005): "La chasse aux 'évidences': Pierre Charles (S.J.) face aux *Protocoles des Sages de Sion.*"

38. Pierre Pierrard, *L'entre-deux-guerres: Les "Protocoles des sages de Sion" et la dénonciation du péril judéo-maçonnique* (taken from *Juifs et catholiques français: De Drumont à Jules Isaac [1886–1945]* [Paris: Fayard, 1970; enlarged ed., 1997]), in Taguieff 2:241; see also P.-A. Taguieff, in Taguieff 1:94.

39. P. Charles, "Les Protocoles," in Taguieff 2:11–37.

40. Joly, *Dialogue in Hell*, p. 70; *Dialogue*, p. 114 (twelfth dialogue); De Michelis, *Il manoscritto inesistente*, p. 264.

41. In the Italian translation of the *Protocols* published by De Michelis and appended to *Il manoscritto inesistente* (pp. 227–289), the passages taken from Joly's *Dialogue aux Enfers* are in italics.

42. De Michelis, *Il manoscritto inesistente,* p. 276.

43. According to Norman Cohn (cited from De Michelis, *Il manoscritto inesistente,* p. 17).

44. Ibid., pp. 58–60.

45. According to De Michelis (*Il manoscritto inesistente,* p. 40), "Discussing the 'rarity' of Joly's text is an empty exercise which ends up interesting especially the zealots"—namely, those who believe in the authenticity of the *Protocols.* But the instrumental use of a fact does not demonstrate its nonexistence.

46. Ibid., p. 53. The last French edition is dated 1868.

47. Ibid., p. 230 (and for the hypothesis of the excerpts, p. 56).

48. Ibid., p. 50 (Tarde); p. 52 (Chabry).

49. (Paris: Gallimard, 1939; new ed. Paris: Éditions Allia, 1991). See also De Michelis, *Il manoscritto inesistente,* p. 11.

50. R. Repetti, introduction to M. Joly, *Dialogo agli Inferi,* p. 19.

51. Édouard Drumont, *La France juive* (Paris: Marpon & Flammarion, 1885; 1886), 2:410–411; idem, *Le testament d'un antisémite* (Paris: E. Dentu, 1891), p. 285.

52. For examples of the Catholic anti-Semitic current, see l'abbé Emmanuel-Augustin Chabauty, honorary canon of Angoulême and Poitiers, *Les Juifs, nos Maîtres!, Documents et devellopements nouveaux de la question juive* (Paris, 1882); idem, *Lettre sur les prophéties modernes et concordance de toutes les prédictions jusqu'au règne d'Henri V inclusivement,* 2nd. corrected and expanded ed. (Poitiers, 1872); *Les prophéties modernes vengées, ou Défense de la concordance de toutes les prophéties* (Poitiers, 1874). On Chabauty, see Pierre Pierrard, *Juifs et catholiques français: d'Édouard Drumont à Jakob Kaplan [1886–1994]* (Paris: Cerf, 1997); C.C. de Saint-André [i.e., "l'abbé Chabotet" (!)]: manuscript addition in the catalogue of the Bibliothèque Nationale, *Francs-Maçons et Juifs: Sixième âge de l'Eglise d'après l'Apocalypse* (Paris, 1880); Jean Brisecou, *La grande conjuration organisée pour la ruine de la France,* preface by É. Drumont (Autun, France: Impr. de J. Coqueugniol, 1887). As an example of the Socialist anti-Semitic current, see Alphonse Toussenel, *Les juifs, rois de l'époque: Histoire de la féodalité financière,* 2 vols. (Paris: Librairie de l'École Sociétaire, 1845); reprinted in 1886 and praised in Drumont, *La France juive,* 1:341–342. By the same author, see also *Travail et fainéantise: Programme démocratique* (Paris: Au Bureau de Travail Affranchi, 1849).

53. Rollin, *L'Apocalypse de notre temps,* p. 260.

54. Auguste Rogeard, *Les propos de Labiénus,* 4th ed. (New York: H. De Mareil, 1865).

55. Rollin, *L'Apocalypse de notre temps,* p. 283 (the chapter is entitled "Drumont, professeur de plagiat").

56. É. Drumont, "La fin d'un soldat," *La libre parole* (3 September 1898): "Ce qu'il a fait n'est pas bien, mai c'est un enfantillage à côté de tous les moyens infâmes que les Juifs ont employés pour s'enrichir et devenir nos maîtres." Drumont compared Henry, who died in infamy, to Bismarck, author of the Ems telegram, who died in glory.

57. Gyp, "L'affaire chez les morts," *La libre parole* (26 February 1899): "On a beaucoup crié contre moi dans l'Histoire!... et pourtant il y'aurait une Sainte-Barthélemy Juive que j'en ne serais pas autrement surprise...."

58. Mention in the *Protocols* of the election of a president who had "some sort of Panama" in his past must refer to Émile Loubet, elected on 18 February 1899, and the scandal connected with the bankruptcy of the French company intending to build the Panama canal (De Michelis, *Il manoscritto inesistente*, p. 58); this should be taken as the earliest possible date for the compilation of the *Protocols*.

59. Joly, *Dialogue in Hell*, p. 27 ("Their mercantile morals rival those of the Jews whom they have taken for models"); *Dialogue*, p. 39 (fourth dialogue): "De la lassitude des idées et du choc des révolutions sont sorties des sociétés froides et désabusées qui sont arrivées à l'indifférence en politique comme en religion, qui n'ont plus d'autre stimulant que les jouissances matérielles, qui ne vivent plus que par l'intérêt, qui n'ont d'autre culte que l'or, dont les mœurs mercantiles le disputent à celles des juifs qu'ils ont pris pour modèles." See C. G. de Michelis, *Il manoscritto inesistente*, p. 251. Joly's passage is noted in Rollin, *L'Apocalypse de notre temps*, pp. 290–291.

60. C. G. De Michelis, "La definizione di regime," *La Repubblica* (2 February 2004), emphasizes the "structural similarities" between the "machiavellian-bonapartist model" described by Joly and the "regime" of Silvio Berlusconi.

61. M. Bounan, "L'État retors," introduction to M. Joly, *Dialogue aux Enfers entre Machiavel et Montesquieu* (Paris: Éditions Allia, 1991), pp. xvii–xviii.

62. Ibid., p. xii.

63. C. Ginzburg, *Ecstasies: Deciphering the Witches' Sabbath*, trans. Raymond Rosenthal (New York: Pantheon, 1991), pp. 12, 49–50.

CHAPTER 12. THE EXTERMINATION OF THE JEWS AND REALITY

An earlier version of this paper was presented at the conference "The Extermination of the Jews and the Limits of Representation," held at the University of California, Los Angeles, 25–29 April 1990. See now *Probing the Limits of Representation: Nazism and the Final Solution*, ed. Saul Friedlander (Cambridge, MA: Harvard University Press, 1992).

1. J. Schatzmiller, "Les Juifs de Provence pendant la Peste Noire," *Revue des Études Juives* 133 (1974): 457–480: 469–472.

2. *Storia notturna: Una decifrazione del sabba* (Torino: Einaudi, 1989), chap. 1; *Ecstasies: Deciphering the Witches' Sabbath*, trans. Raymond Rosenthal (New York: Pantheon, 1991), chap. 1.

3. Martin Bouquet, *Recueil des historiens des Gaules et de la France*, 24 vols. (Paris: Aux dépens des libraires associés, 1840), 20:629–630.

4. See Josephus, *The Jewish War*, trans. G. A. Williamson (Harmondsworth: Penguin Books, 1985). Cf. P. Vidal-Naquet, "Flavius Josèphe et Masada," in *Les Juifs, la mémoire, le présent* (Paris: Maspero, 1981), pp. 43ff, which perceptively analyzes the parallelism between the two passages.

5. Vidal-Naquet, "Flavius Josèphe," pp. 53ff.

6. See *The Latin Josephus*, ed. Franz Blatt (Aarhus: Universitetsforlaget, 1958), 1:15–16. Cf. also Guy N. Deutsch, *Iconographie et illustration de Flavius Josèphe au temps de Jean Fouquet* (Leiden: Brill, 1986), p. xi (map).

7. P. Schmitz, "Les lectures de table à l'abbaye de Saint-Denis à la fin du Moyen Age," *Revue Bénédictine* 42 (1930): 163–167; André Wilmart, "Le couvent et la bibliothèque de Cluny vers le milieu du XIe siècle," *Revue Mabillon* 11 (1921): 89–124: 93, 113.

8. D. Nebbiai-Dalla Guarda, *La bibliothèque de l'abbaye de Saint-Denis en France du IXe au XVIIIe siècle* (Paris: Editions du CNRS, 1985), regarding a request sent by Reichenau to Saint-Denis for a copy of Josephus's *Antiquitates Judaicae* (p. 61; see also p. 294).

9. B.N. Lat. 12511; cf. *The Latin Josephus*, p. 50.

10. *Hegesippi qui dicuntur historiarum libri V*, ed. Vincentius Ussani (Corpus Scriptorum Ecclesiasticorum Latinorum, vol. 66) (Vindobonae [Vienna]: Hölder-Pichler-Tempsky, 1932, 1960), preface by K. Mras (on the siege of Masada, cf. 5: 52–53, 407–417). The Bibliothèque Nationale in Paris possesses twelve manuscripts of "Hegesippus" written between the tenth and fifteenth centuries: cf. Deutsch, *Iconographie*, p. 15.

11. See the English translation: Pierre Vidal-Naquet, "A Paper Eichmann?" *Democracy* (April 1981): 67–95. Note the question mark, which is absent in the original French title.

12. Maria Daraki's proposal, mentioned in Vidal-Naquet, *Les Juifs*, p. 59n48, that in the first case the parallel should refer to the woman who denounced Flavius Josephus and his companions appears less persuasive to me.

13. Hendrik Van Vliet, *No Single Testimony*. Studia Theologica Rheno-Traiectina 4 (Utrecht: Rijkuniversiteit, 1958). The advantage of having more than one witness is underlined from a general (or logical) point of view in Vidal-Naquet, *Les Juifs*, p. 51.

14. Van Vliet, *No Single Testimony*, p. 11.

15. See, for example, Anne Libois, "À propos des modes de preuves et plus spécialement de la preuve par témoins dans la juridiction de Léau au XVe siècle," in *Hommage au Professeur Paul Bonenfant (1899–1965)* (Brussels: Universa, 1965), pp. 532–546: 539–542.

16. On this topic, see the rather hasty remarks in Paul Peeters, "Les aphorismes du droit dans la critique historique," *Académie Royale du Belgique, Bulletin de la Classe des Lettres* 32 (1946): 82ff. (see pp. 95–96 apropos the *testis unus, testis nullus*).

17. François Baudouin, *De institutione historiae universae et ejus cum jurisprudentia conjunctione, prolegomenon libri II*, cited in Donald R. Kelley, *Foundations of Modern Historical Scholarship* (New York and London: Columbia University Press, 1970), p. 116 (but the entire book is important).

18. I have used the 2nd, Liège 1770 edition. The importance of this brief treatise was perceptively underlined in Allen Johnson, *The Historian and Historical Evidence* (New York: Scribner's, 1926). I cite from the New York 1934 edition, p. 114. Johnson

dubbed it "the most significant book on method after Mabillon's *De re diplomatica*." Cf. Arnaldo Momigliano, *Ancient History and the Antiquarian*, in *Contributo alla storia degli studi classici* (Rome: Edizioni di Storia e letteratura, 1979), p. 81.

19. See R. Faurisson, *Mémoire en défense. Contre ceux qui m'accusent de falsifier l'histoire. La question des chambres à gaz*, preface by Noam Chomsky (Paris: La Vieille Taupe, 1980).

20. *Michel de Certeau*, ed. Luce Giard (Paris: Centre Georges Pompidou, 1987), pp. 71–72. From reading Vidal-Naquet, we learn that the participation of the two correspondents in the public discussion of the *thèse* by François Hartog, later published with the title *Le miroir d'Hérodote* (Paris: Gallimard, 1980), occasioned this exchange of letters. On some of the book's implications, see chap. 4.

21. What follows is based on Hayden White's published writings. His paper "Historical Employment and the Problem of Truth," appearing in the proceedings of the UCLA conference *Probing the Limits of Representation*, ed. Saul Friedlander (Cambridge, MA: Harvard University Press, 1992), pp. 37–53, is marked by a less rigid (but not a little contradictory) skepticism.

22. Carlo Antoni, *From Historicism to Sociology*, trans. Hayden White (Detroit: Wayne State University Press, 1959), with a preface by White, "On History and Historicism" (pp. xxv–xxvi). Cf. the review by Bruce Mazlish in *History and Theory* 1 (1960): 219–227.

23. Benedetto Croce, *Contributo alla critica di me stesso* (Bari: Laterza, 1926), pp. 32–33; R. G. Collingwood, *The Idea of History* (Oxford: Oxford University Press, 1956), pp. 91ff. (rev. ed., 1993).

24. Hayden V. White, *Metahistory: The Historical Imagination in Nineteenth-Century Europe* (Baltimore: Johns Hopkins University Press, 1973), pp. 281–288; Benedetto Croce, *Primi saggi* (Bari: Laterza, 1927), pp. 3–41.

25. White, *Metahistory*, p. 385.

26. Ibid., pp. 378, 434.

27. Ibid., p. 407.

28. Eugenio Colorni, *L'estetica di Benedetto Croce: Studio critico* (Milan: La Cultura, 1932).

29. The Croce–Gentile correspondence is highly revealing from this point of view: see Benedetto Croce, *Lettere a Giovanni Gentile, 1896–1924*, ed. Alda Croce, introd. by Gennaro Sasso (Milan: Mondadori, 1981).

30. See Benedetto Croce, *Logica come scienza del concetto puro* (Bari: Laterza, 1971), pp. 193–195. Cf. also Giovanni Gentile, *Frammenti di critica letteraria* (Lanciano: Carabba, 1921), pp. 379ff. (a review of Croce's *Il concetto della storia nelle sue relazioni col concetto dell'arte* [1897]). Gentile's influence on Croce's development during the crucial years 1897–1900 can be judged from Gentile's *Lettere a Benedetto Croce*, ed. Simona Giannantoni (Florence: Sansoni, 1972), vol. 1. Cf. also Giuseppe Galasso in the appendix to his edition of Croce's *Teoria e storia della storiografia* (Milan: Adelphi, 1989), pp. 409ff.

31. Here I am developing a number of astute observations by Piero Gobetti (see "Cattaneo" in Gobetti's *Scritti storici, letterari e filosofici* [Turin: Einaudi, 1969], p. 199 [originally published in *L'Ordine nuovo*, 1922]).

32. Giovanni Gentile, "The Transcending of Time in History," in Raymond Klibansky and H.J. Paton, eds., *Philosophy and History: Essays Presented to Ernst Cassirer* (Oxford: Oxford University Press, 1936), pp. 91–105: 95, 100. Thirty years earlier Antonio Labriola, in a letter to Croce, had described the Croce–Gentile relationship in curiously similar terms: see A. Labriola, *Lettere a Benedetto Croce, 1885–1904* (Naples: Nella sede dell'Istituto, 1975), p. 376 (2 January 1904): "I do not understand why Gentile, who inveighs in hieratic style against the wicked world, does not dedicate himself to the good deed (since he has the devil at home) of converting especially you." For Gentile's allusion to Croce, see the following note.

33. G. Gentile, "Il superamento del tempo nella storia," in *Memorie italiane e problemi della filosofia e della vita* (Rome, 1936), p. 308: "La metafisica storica (o storicismo) . . ."; the essay had appeared previously in *Rendiconti della R. Accademia Nazionale dei Lincei, classe di scienze morali*, ser. 6, vol. 11 (1935): 752–769. The words in parentheses ("that is, historicism") were omitted in the English translation which had appeared a few months earlier ("The Transcending of Time in History") (the editors' preface is dated "February 1936"). The missing words were added presumably after the publication of Croce's essay "Antistoricismo" (an Oxford lecture of 1930, but only published later in *Ultimi saggi* [Bari: Laterza, 1935], pp. 246–258). Gentile delivered his lecture at the Accademia dei Lincei on 17 November 1935 and returned the corrected proofs on 2 April 1936 (see *Rendiconti*, pp. 752, 769). For Croce's reaction to the essays collected in *Philosophy and History*, see *La storia come pensiero e come azione* (1938) (Bari: Laterza, 1943), pp. 319–327 (this section is lacking in the English translation by Sylvia Sprigge, *History as the Story of Liberty* [New York: Norton, 1941]); on p. 322 we find a hostile reference to Gentile ("a murky tendency to mystification . . ."). In the same volume, see also the pages on "Historiography as Liberation from History . . ." ("*History*," pp. 43–45; *La storia*, pp. 30–32: "We are products of the past and live immersed in the past, which all around presses upon us. . . ." Gentile, whose idealism was much more radical and consistent, had stated that the past (and time as well) are purely abstract notions, overcome in concrete spiritual life ("The Transcending of Time," pp. 95–97). The importance of this essay was noted in Cesare Garboli, *Scritti servili* (Turin: Einaudi, 1989), p. 205.

34. See G. Gentile, *Teoria generale dello spirito come atto puro* (1916), 2nd rev. and enlarged ed. (Pisa: Mariotti, 1918), pp. 50–52; *The Theory of the Mind as Pure Act* (London: Macmillan, 1922).

35. I do not mean to be suggesting the existence of a simple and unilinear causal connection. Undoubtedly, White's reaction to Italian neo-idealism passed through a specifically American filter. But even White's pragmatism, to which Perry Anderson alludes at the end of his contribution to the UCLA symposium (*Probing the*

Limits of Representation, p. 65), had undoubtedly been reinforced by the pragmatist current (mediated by Giovanni Vailati) which is discernible in Croce's work, particularly in his *Logica*.

36. See H. White, "Interpretation in History" (1972–1973), in *Tropics of Discourse* (Baltimore: Johns Hopkins University Press, 1978), p. 75.

37. Ibid., p. 2.

38. "Foucault Decoded" (1973), in ibid., p. 254.

39. Barthes appears only once in the index of names; but see also p. 24n2, where he is mentioned with other scholars working in the field of rhetoric, such as Kenneth Burke, Gérard Genette, Umberto Eco, and Tzvetan Todorov.

40. G. Gentile, "La filosofia della praxis," in *La filosofia di Marx: Studi critici* (Pisa: Spoerri, 1899), pp. 51–157; the book was dedicated to Croce. See now the ample introduction by Eugenio Garin to his edition of Gentile's *Scritti filosofici*, 2 vols. (Milan: Garzanti, 1991).

41. Gentile, "La filosofia della praxis," pp. 62–63.

42. For the first thesis, see Giancarlo Bergami, *Il giovane Gramsci e il marxismo* (Milan: Feltrinelli, 1977); for the second, Augusto Del Noce, *Il suicidio della rivoluzione* (Milan: Rusconi, 1978), pp. 121–198 ("Gentile e Gramsci").

43. See Salvatore Natoli, *Giovanni Gentile filosofo europeo* (Turin: Bollati Boringhieri, 1989), pp. 94ff. (somewhat superficial); a propos A. Gramsci, *Quaderni del carcere*, ed. Valentino Gerratana (Turin: Einaudi, 1975), 3:2038. On Gramsci's opinion on Futurism, see *Socialismo e fascismo: L'Ordine Nuovo, 1919–1922* (Turin: Einaudi, 1966), pp. 20–22.

44. B. Croce, "Antistoricismo," in *Ultimi saggi*, pp. 246–258.

45. White, *Tropics*, pp. 27–80.

46. Idem, *The Content of the Form* (Baltimore: Johns Hopkins University Press, 1987), p. 63.

47. Ibid., p. 227n12.

48. Gentile, "The Transcending of Time," p. 99.

49. See, for example, G. Gentile, "Caratteri religiosi della presente lotta politica," in *Che cosa è il fascismo: Discorsi e polemiche* (Florence: Vallecchi, 1924 [actually 1925]), pp. 143–151.

50. See, for example, the section entitled "La violenza fascista," in *Che cosa è il fascismo* (a lecture delivered in Florence, 8 March 1925), pp. 29–32.

51. "State and individual . . . are one and the same; and the art of governing is the art of reconciling and identifying these two terms so that the maximum of liberty agrees with the maximum of public order. . . . For always the maximum liberty agrees with the maximum of public force of the state. Which force? Distinctions in this field are dear to those who do not welcome this concept of force, which is nevertheless essential to the State, and hence to liberty. And they distinguish moral from material force: the force of law freely voted and accepted from the force of violence which is rigidly opposed to the will of the citizen. Ingenuous distinctions, if made in

good faith! Every force is a moral force, for it is always an expression of will; and whatever be the argument used—preaching or black-jacking—its efficacy can be none other than its ability finally to receive the inner support of a man and to persuade him to agree" (quoted from G. Gentile, *Making the Fascist State*, trans. H. W. Schneider [New York: Oxford University Press, 1928], p. 347). The speech, delivered in Palermo on 31 March 1924, first appeared in such journals as *La Nuova Politica Liberale* 2 (2 April 1924). When he reprinted it a year later, after the Matteotti crisis and its violent conclusion, Gentile, who had earned for himself the title of "the philosopher of the truncheon," inserted an embarrassed and arrogant note. In it he clarified that the force for which he had intended to recognize a moral significance was one alone, that belonging to the State, for which the truncheon of the Fascist squads had been the necessary instrument in a time of crisis: see Gentile, *Che cosa è il fascismo*, pp. 50–51. Gentile's reasoning was not especially original: see, for example, B. Mussolini, "Forza e consenso," *Gerarchia* (1923) (in *Opera omnia*, ed. Edoardo and Duilio Susmel [Florence: La Fenice, 1956], 19:195–196).

52. "The Politics of Historical Interpretation" (1982), in *The Content of the Form*, pp. 74–75.

53. Ibid., p. 77. The italics do not appear in the French text.

54. Ibid., p. 80. My italics.

55. Ibid., p. 227n12.

56. I should like to thank Stefano Levi Della Torre for some enlightening thoughts on this last point.

57. White, *Content of the Form*, p. 74.

58. See R. Serra, *Scritti letterari, morali e politici*, ed. Mario Isnenghi (Turin: Einaudi, 1974), pp. 278–288. Cesare Garboli (*Falbalas* [Milan: Garzanti, 1990], p. 150) has proposed a similar interpretation of Serra's essay.

59. See, for example (but not only), the celebrated *Triptych* (*Those who depart*, etc.), housed in the Metropolitan Museum of Art.

60. See R. Serra, *Epistolario*, ed. Luigi Ambrosini, Giuseppe De Robertis, and Alfredo Grilli (Florence: Le Monnier, 1953), pp. 454ff.

61. B. Croce, *Teoria e storia della storiografia* (Bari: Laterza, 1927), pp. 44–45.

62. Serra, *Epistolario*, p. 459 (11 November 1912).

63. Serra, *Scritti letterari*, p. 286.

64. Ibid., p. 287.

65. See Hayden White's passage quoted above (pp. 540–541), as well as "Historical Emplotment," in *Probing the Limits of Representation*.

66. J.-F. Lyotard, *The Différend: Phrases in Dispute*, trans. G. Van Den Abbeele (Minneapolis: University of Minnesota Press, 1988), pp. 55–57.

67. P. Levi, *Survival in Auschwitz*, trans. Stuart Woolf (New York: Collier Books, 1961), pp. 5–6.

68. E. Benveniste, *Indo-European Language and Society* (London: Faber, 1973 [1969], pp. 522ff. (The difference between *testis* and *superstes* is examined on p. 526.)

NOTES TO PAGES 180–184 ✦ 299

CHAPTER 13. THOUGHTS ON A BOOK BY SIEGFRIED KRACAUER

1. S. Kracauer, *History: The Last Things before the Last*, "completed after the Death of the Author by Paul Oskar Kristeller" (Princeton, NJ: Wiener, 1995), pp. viii–ix (henceforth cited in the notes as *History*).

2. I. Mülder-Bach, "History as Autobiography: The Last Things before the Last," *New German Critique* 54 (1991): 139–157: 139. Against this, see P. O. Kristeller, introduction to Kracauer, *History*, pp. v–x.

3. Kracauer, *History*, pp. 3–4.

4. Now in English as *The Mass Ornament: Weimar Essays*, trans., ed., and with an introd. by Thomas Y. Levin (Cambridge, MA: Harvard University Press, 1995), pp. 47–63.

5. Kracauer, *Mass Ornament*, pp. 49–50.

6. Ibid., p. 59.

7. On this point I disagree with Mülder-Bach, "History as Autobiography," p. 141.

8. S. Kracauer, *Theory of Film: The Redemption of Physical Reality* (Princeton, NJ: Princeton University Press, 1997), pp. 14–17, 20, 54ff.; *History*, pp. 82–84.

9. M. Proust, *Remembrance of Things Past. I. The Guermantes Way*, trans. C. K. Scott Moncrieff, 2 vols. (New York: Random House, 1934), pp. 814–815.

10. Erich Auerbach comments on the passage (but without mentioning Proust): *Mimesis: The Representation of Reality in Western Literature*, trans. Willard R. Trask (Princeton, NJ: Princeton University Press, 1974), p. 430; *Mimesis: Dargestellte Wirklichkeit in der abendländischen Literatur* (Tübingen and Basel, 1994), p. 399.

11. "Das Gesicht gilt dem Film nichts, wenn nicht der Totenkopf dahinter einbezogen ist. 'Danse macabre.' Zu welchem Ende? Das wird man sehen." See M. Hansen, "'With Skin and Hair': Kracauer's Theory of Film, Marseille 1940," *Critical Inquiry* 20 (1993): 437–469: 447. In Hansen's introduction (signed M. Bratu Hansen) to the new edition of Kracauer's *Theory of Film*, p. xxiv, the quoted passage is linked to the allegorical impulse derived from Benjamin's book on *Trauerspiel*.

12. S. Kracauer and Erwin Panofsky, *Briefwechsel, 1941–1966*, ed. Volker Breidecker (Berlin: Akademie Verlag, 1996), pp. 83–92: 83 ("Tentative Outline of a Book on Film Aesthetics").

13. In addition to Hansen, "'With Skin and Hair,'" see the evidence adduced by K. Michael, "Vor dem Café: Walter Benjamin und Siegfried Kracauer in Marseille," in Michael Opitz and Erdmut Wizisla, eds., *"Aber ein Sturm weht vom Paradiese her"*: *Texte zu Walter Benjamin* (Leipzig: Reclam, 1992), pp. 203–221.

14. M. Proust, *Die Herzogin von Guermantes*, trans. Walter Benjamin and Franz Hessel (Munich: Piper, 1930).

15. W. Benjamin, "Piccola storia della fotografia," in *L'opera d'arte nell'epoca della sua riproducibilità tecnica*, trans. E. Filippini (Turin: Einaudi, 1966), pp. 59–77: 63. The same expression recurs in the essay "L'opera d'arte nell'epoca della sua riproducibilità tecnica" (1936), ibid., pp. 41–42. See also Béla Balázs, "Physiognomie" (1923), in

Helmut H. Diedrichs et al., eds., *Schriften zum Film* (Budapest: Akadémiai Kiadó, 1982), pp. 205–208 (cited in M. Hansen, "Benjamin, Cinema and Experience: 'The Blue Flower in the Land of Technology,'" *New German Critique* 40 [1987]: 179–224: 208n48).

16. "Ahasuerus, or the riddle of time," in Kracauer, *History*, pp. 139–163.

17. V. Breidecker, "'Ferne Nähe': Kracauer, Panofsky and 'the Warburg Tradition,'" in Kracauer and Panofsky, *Briefwechsel*, pp. 129–226, esp. the section "Interpretation als Entfremdung" (pp. 165–176); but the entire paper is very important. See also my "Straniamento: Preistoria di un procedimento letterario," in *Occhiacci di legno: Nove riflessioni sulla distanza* (Milan: Feltrinelli, 1998), pp. 15–39.

18. Kracauer, *History*, p. 84. See the astute observations in Breidecker, "'Ferne Nähe,'" pp. 176ff. (section "Das Exil als Text"). Arnaldo Momigliano alludes to the great Greek historians as exiles in "La traduzione e lo storico classico," in *La storiografia greca* (Turin: Einaudi, 1982), pp. 42–63: 60 (originally published in *History and Theory* [1972]).

19. S. Kracauer, *Theory of Film*, pp. 16–17, where he comments on B. Newhall, "Photography and the Development of Kinetic Visualization," *Journal of the Warburg and Courtauld Institutes* (1944): 40–45. Cf., in general, D. N. Rodowick, "The Last Things before the Last: Kracauer and History," *New German Critique* 41 (1987): 109–139: 123; Breidecker, "'Ferne Nähe,'" pp. 178–179.

20. Hansen, "'With Skin and Hair,'" p. 447.

21. T. W. Adorno, "Der wunderliche Realist," in idem, *Noten zu Literatur* (Frankfurt a. M.: Suhrkamp, 1985). I have used the Italian version: "Uno strano realista: Su Siegfried Kracauer," in *Note per la letteratura 1961–1968* (Turin: Einaudi, 1979), pp. 68–88: 68.

22. E. Panofsky, "Style and Medium in the Motion Pictures," in *Three Essays on Style*, ed. Irving Lavin (Cambridge, MA: Harvard University Press, 1995), pp. 93–125: 108 (revised version of an essay first appearing in 1936).

23. T. Y. Levin, "Iconology at the Movies: Panofsky's Film Theory," in Irving Lavin, ed., *Meaning in the Visual Arts: Views from the Outside. A Centennial Commemoration of Erwin Panofsky (1892–1968)* (Princeton, NJ: Institute for Advanced Study, 1995), pp. 313–333: 319ff.

24. E. Panofsky, "Die Perspektive als 'symbolische Form,'" *Bibliothek Warburg. Vorträge 1924–1925* (1927): 258–330.

25. W. Benjamin, *Briefe an Siegfried Kracauer*, ed. Theodor W. Adorno Archiv (Marbach am Neckar: [Deutsche Schillergesellschaft], 1987), pp. 65–66 (cited in Breidecker, "Ferne Nähe," pp. 186–187).

26. E. Panofsky, *Renaissance and Renascences in Western Art* (Stockholm: Almquist & Wiksell, 1960), pp. 82ff. See also Breidecker, "'Ferne Nähe,'" p. 175.

27. S. Kracauer, *History*, pp. 56–57, 105, 123.

28. On the first, see the astute observations in Breidecker, "'Ferne Nähe,'" pp. 176–191.

29. S. Kracauer, *History*, p. 122.

30. C. Ginzburg, "Distanza e prospettiva: Due metafore," in *Occhiacci di legno*, pp. 171–193.

31. Sergei M. Eisenstein, "Dickens, Griffith and the Film Today," in idem, *Film Form: Essays in Film Theory and the Film Sense*, ed. and trans. Jay Leyda (Cleveland and New York: Meridian Books, 1963), pp. 195–255.

32. Idem, "Through Theater to Cinema," ibid., pp. 3–17: 12–13.

33. C. Ginzburg, *Rapporti di forza: Storia, retorica, prova* (Milan: Feltrinelli, 2000), pp. 109–126.

34. *Revue des Deux Mondes* (15 December 1869): 987–1004.

35. Saint-René Taillandier, *Histoire et philosophie religieuse: Études et fragments* (Paris, 1859); *Études littéraires* (Paris: Plon, 1881).

36. *Revue des Deux Mondes* (15 February 1863): 840–860. See also, by the same author, the article "La tentation de Saint-Antoine (Une sotie au dix-neuvième siècle)," ibid. (1 May 1874): 205–223.

37. *Revue des Deux Mondes* (15 February 1863): 860 (the italics are in the original text).

38. K. Witte, "'Light Sorrow': Siegfried Kracauer as Literary Critic," *New German Critique* 54 (1991): 77–94: 93–94 (apropos Hemingway's *In Our Time*); Kracauer to Panofsky, 8 November 1944 (Kracauer and Panofsky, *Briefwechsel*, p. 38).

39. M. Baxandall, *Painting and Experience in Fifteenth-Century Italy* (Oxford: Clarendon, 1972).

40. Jules Michelet, *Histoire de France*, 19 vols. (Paris: C. Marpon & E. Flammarion, 1879), 19: 360–361 (the preface is dated 1 October 1855). For a preliminary overview, see Jean Sgard, *Les trente récits de la Journée des Tuiles* (Grenoble: Presses Universitaires de Grenoble, 1988), esp. p. 93.

41. I have quoted and discussed it in *Rapporti di forza*, pp. 113–114.

42. S. Kracauer, *History*, p. 122.

43. On this point, see my *Rapporti di forza*. According to Peter Burke, Kracauer was the first to argue that the novels of Joyce, Proust, and Virginia Woolf offer to the historical narrative "a challenge and an opportunity." See Burke's "Aby Warburg as Historical Anthropologist," in Horst Bredekamp, Michael Diers, and Charlotte Schoell-Glass, eds., *Aby Warburg: Akten des internationalen Symposions, Hamburg 1990* (Weinheim: VCH, 1991), p. 237, quoted in Kracauer and Panofsky, *Briefwechsel*, p. 147n80. But Kracauer (*Theory of Film*, p. 219) was referring to Auerbach.

44. Kracauer, *Theory of Film*, p. 301.

45. S. Kracauer, "The Hotel Lobby," in *The Mass Ornament*, p. 178 (a chapter from Kracauer's *Der Detektiv-Roman: Ein philosophischer Traktat*, in idem, *Schriften* [Frankfurt a. M.: Suhrkamp, 1971], 1:103–204). According to T. Clark, the expression "disenchanted world" came from Schiller (*Farewell to an Idea* [New Haven, CT, and London: Yale University Press, 1999], p. 7). But Schiller probably knew the book by Balthasar Bekker with the same title.

46. Hansen, "With Skin and Hair."

47. Breidecker, "'Ferne Nähe,'" pp. 178–179.

48. W. Benjamin, "On the Concept of History," in idem, *Selected Writings. IV. 1938–1940*, trans. Edmund Jephcott et al., ed. Howard Eiland and Michael W. Jennings, 4 vols. (Cambridge, MA, and London: The Belknap Press of Harvard University Press, 1996–2003), p. 391 (slightly modified).

49. Kracauer and Panofsky, *Briefwechsel*, p. 91. Cf. also the epilogue of Kracauer, *History*, p. 219.

50. Ibid., p. 202.

51. See the conclusion of *Theory of Film*, pp. 300–311 (where much attention is paid to the closing pages of Auerbach's *Mimesis*).

CHAPTER 14. MICROHISTORY

I should like to thank Patrick Fridenson, with whom I discussed this article while I was writing it. Perry Anderson read it and critiqued it before it assumed a definitive form: my debt to him is once again very great.

1. Levi remembers the first discussions about the series that he had with Giulio Einaudi and me to have been in 1974, 1975, or 1976 (see "Il piccolo, il grande, il piccolo: Intervista a Giovanni Levi," *Meridiana*, September 1990, p. 229); but this is a lapse in memory.

2. Made possible by ORION, the program on which the UCLA Library computer catalogue is based (now YRL).

3. Kantorowicz, who is not named but is easily recognizable, makes a fleeting appearance in Stewart's account: see *The Year of the Oath: The Fight for Academic Freedom at the University of California* (Garden City: Doubleday, 1950), p. 90. See also E. H. Kantorowicz, *The Fundamental Issue: Documents and Marginal Notes on the University of California Loyalty Oath* (San Francisco: Parker Print Co., 1950), p. 1: "This is not intended to be the history of 'The Year of the Oath.' This subject has been admirably dealt with by Professor George R. Stewart."

4. See Madison S. Beeler, "George R. Stewart, Toponomyst," *Names* 24 (June 1976): 77–85 (the fascicle is entitled *Festschrift in Honor of Professor George R. Stewart*). Cf. also the interview "George R. Stewart on Names and Characters," ibid. 9 (1961): 51–57; and John Caldwell, *George R. Stewart* (Boise, ID: Boise State University, 1981).

5. See Stewart, "The Regional Approach to Literature," *College English* 9 (1948): 370–375.

6. Stewart, *Pickett's Charge: A Microhistory of the Final Attack on Gettysburg, July 3, 1863* (Boston: Houghton Mifflin, 1959; reprinted Dayton, 1983), pp. ix, 211–212.

7. Ibid., p. ix.

8. See Luis González y González, *Pueblo en vilo: Microhistoria de San José de Gracia* (Mexico: El Colegio de Mexico, 1968), p. 2: "La pequeñez, pero la pequeñez tipica" (the reference to Leuilliot is on p. 16); trans. John Upton as *San José de Gracia: Mexican Village in Transition* (Austin: University of Texas Press, 1974).

9. See Luis Aboites, *La revolución mexicana en Espita, 1910–1940: Microhistoria de la formación del Estado de la revolución* (Centro de Investigaciones y Estudios Superiores en Antropologia Social. Cuadernos de la Casa Chata 62) (Mexico, 1982).

10. L. González y González, "El arte de la microhistoria," in *Invitación a la microhistoria* (Mexico: Sepsetentas, 1973), pp. 12, 14.

11. Ibid., p. 13. The introduction has been reprinted, in part, under the title "Histoire et sociologie" in Braudel's *Écrits sur l'Histoire* (Paris: Flammarion, 1969), pp. 97–122 (now in English: F. Braudel, *On History*, trans. Sarah Matthews [Chicago: University of Chicago Press, 1980]).

12. See Braudel, *On History*, pp. 74–75; *Écrits sur l'Histoire*, pp. 112ff.: "Le fait divers (sinon l'événement, ce socio-drame) est répétition, régularité, multitude et rien ne dit, de façon absolue, que son niveau soit sans fertilité, ou valeur, scientifique. Il faudrait y regarder de près."

13. See the section entitled "Fait divers, fait d'histoire," with contributions by Maria Pia Di Bella, Michel Bée, Raffaella Comaschi, Lucette Valensi, and Michelle Perrot, in *Annales: E.S.C.*, 38 (1983): 821–919. In his introduction to these essays, Marc Ferro juxtaposes the analysis of the *fait divers* to works in microhistory as similar and inverse but complementary operations (p. 825). In the same issue Perrot, in "Fait divers et histoire au XIXe siècle" (see p. 917), referred to the passage by Braudel quoted above.

14. Still today the term cannot free itself from ironic connotations, as emerges, for example, from an allusion in Georges Charachidzé, *La Mémoire indo-européenne du Caucase* (Paris: Hachette, 1987), pp. 131–132 ("ce que j'avais voulu appeler, par jeu, micro-histoire . . .").

15. Although an excellent English version exists (R. Queneau, *The Blue Flowers*, trans. Barbara Wright [New York: Atheneum, 1967]), the present rendering is based directly on the French original: *Les fleurs bleues* (Paris: Gallimard, 1965), pp. 84–85:

"Que voulez-vous savoir au juste?"

"Ce que tu penses de l'histoire universelle en général et de l'histoire générale en particulier. J'écoute."

"Je suis bien fatigué, dit le chapelain."

"Tu te reposeras plus tard. Dis-mois, ce Concile de Bâle, est-ce de l'histoire universelle?"

"Oui-da. De l'histoire universelle en général."

"Et mes petits canons?"

"De l'histoire générale en particulier."

"Et le mariage des mes filles?"

"A peine de l'histoire événementielle. De la microhistoire, tout au plus."

"De la quoi? hurle le duc d'Auge. Quel diable de langage est-ce là? Serait-ce aujourd'hui ta Pentecôte ?"

"Veuillez m'excuser, messire. C'est, voyez-vous, la fatigue."

If I am not mistaken, the Braudelian texts cited apropos this passage in Ruggiero Romano, "Un modèle pour l'histoire," in Andrée Bergens, ed., *Raymond Queneau* (Paris: Éditions de l'Herne, 1975), p. 288, are relevant for *histoire événementielle*, not for *microhistoire*.

16. See L. Gonzales [sic], *Les barrières de la solitude: Histoire universelle de San José de Gracia, village mexicain*, trans. Anny Meyer (Paris: Plon, 1977).

17. The *Grande dizionario della lingua italiana*, ed. Salvatore Battaglia, 10 vols. (Turin: UTET, 1961–1978), 10:365, refers to this passage apropos the entry for "microstoria" (defined as "voce dotta"—that is, "learned entry"). The definition that follows— "particularly brief and succinct history, summary and essential account"—is definitely unsatisfactory (but see the *postscriptum* below).

18. Primo Levi, *The Periodic Table*, trans. Raymond Rosenthal (New York: Schocken Books, 1984), p. 224.

19. See Italo Calvino, *Il barone rampante* (Turin: Einaudi, 1957), now available in English as *The Baron in the Trees*, trans. Archibald Colquhoun (San Diego: Harcourt, Brace, Jovanovich, 1959). Cesare Cases did not miss the similarity in his introduction to Levi, *Opere*, 3 vols. (Turin: Einaudi, 1987–1990), 1: xvii. For his concern in regard to Levi, apprentice-writer, see Calvino, *I libri degli altri: Lettere, 1947–1981*, ed. Giovanni Tesio (Turin: Einaudi, 1991), pp. 382–383, as well as the letter (in a very different tone) on the revision of *Il sistema periodico* (p. 606). See also Severino Cesari, *Colloquio con Giulio Einaudi* (Rome: Theoria, 1991), p. 173.

20. See Queneau, *Piccola cosmogonia portatile*, trans. Sergio Solmi (Turin: Einaudi, 1982), followed by Calvino's "Piccola guida alla *Piccola cosmogonia*," p. 162. See also Levi, *L'altrui mestiere* (Turin: Einaudi, 1985), pp. 150–154 (trans. R. Rosenthal as *Other People's Trades* [New York: Summit Books, 1989]), and the declaration by Carlo Carena in Cesari, *Colloquio con Giulio Einaudi*, p. 172.

21. At any rate it was an unconscious echo: to the question "from what does the term 'microhistory' derive?" Giovanni Levi stated (29 December 1991) that he knew only that the term had been used by Queneau. The last part of Queneau's passage quoted above was used as the epigraph for Raul Merzario's *Il paese stretto: Strategie matrimoniali nella diocesi di Como nei secoli XVI–XVIII* (Turin: Einaudi, 1981), one of the first books published in the series Microstorie.

22. See Edoardo Grendi, "Micro-analisi e storia sociale," *Quaderni storici* 35 (1977): 506–520.

23. Richard Cobb, *Raymond Queneau* ("The Zaharoff Lecture for 1976") (Oxford: Clarendon, 1976).

24. R. Queneau, *Une histoire modèle* (Paris: Gallimard, 1966) (but written in 1942); idem, *Bâtons, chiffres et lettres*, enlarged ed. (Paris: Gallimard, 1965), pp. 170–172, an article that had appeared in the *Front National*, 5 January 1945.

25. See, instead, the fine introduction by Italo Calvino to Queneau's *Segni, cifre e lettere e altri saggi* (Turin: Einaudi, 1981), especially pp. xix–xx (a different and larger collection than the French edition of the same title).

26. See Cobb, *A Sense of Place* (London: Duckworth, 1975), about which see Grendi, "Lo storico e la didattica incosciente (Replica a una discussione)," *Quaderni Storici* 46 (1981): 338–346: 339–340.

27. Impatience with the pretenses of scientific historiography is more evident in a study by González y González which in its very title closely echoes Nietzsche's second *Untimely Meditation*. See González y González, "De la múltiple utilización de la historia," in Carlos Pereyra, ed., *Historia? para qué?* (Mexico: Siglo XXI Editores, 1990), pp. 55–74.

28. See Traian Stoianovich, *French Historical Method: The "Annales" Paradigm* (Ithaca, NY: Cornell University Press, 1976), with an introduction by F. Braudel, who calls the two preceding paradigms, respectively, "exemplar" and "developmental" (p. 25). On microhistory as a response to the crisis of the "great Marxist and functionalist systems," see G. Levi, "On Microhistory," in Peter Burke, ed., *New Perspectives on Historical Writing* (University Park: Pennsylvania State University Press, 1992), pp. 93–113: 93–94. See also Levi's *Inheriting Power: The Story of an Exorcist*, trans. Lydia G. Cochrane (Chicago: University of Chicago Press, 1988).

29. See *Mélanges en l'honneur de Fernand Braudel. II. Méthodologie de l'histoire et des sciences humaines* (Toulouse: Privat, 1973), pp. 105–125, 227–243. The text by Furet and Le Goff is divided in two parts that develop two communications "préparées en collaboration," entitled, respectively, "L'histoire et 'l'homme sauvage'" and "L'historien et l'homme quotidien." In the first piece Furet outlines a general picture; in the second Le Goff proposes a program of research with examples drawn from the sphere of medieval studies. Even if I distinguish between the two texts in my discussion, I am assuming basic agreement between their authors, as they have stated, except in cases where the opposite is indicated. On both Chaunu and Le Goff, one can read their self-portraits included in Pierre Nora, ed., *Essais d'ego-histoire* (Paris: Gallimard, 1987).

30. Chaunu, "Un nouveau champ pour l'histoire sérielle," p. 109. In French, the term *ethnologue* is more widely used than its synonym *anthropologue*.

31. Ibid., p. 231.

32. Ibid., p. 237.

33. Emmanuel Le Roy Ladurie, "L'historien et l'ordinateur" (1968), in idem, *Le territoire de l'historien* (Paris: Gallimard, 1973), p. 14; now in English as "The Historian and the Computer," in idem, *The Territory of the Historian*, trans. Ben Reynolds and Siân Reynolds (Chicago: University of Chicago Press, 1979); and idem, *Montaillou, village occitan de 1294 à 1314* (Paris: Gallimard, 1975; reprinted 1982); and in English as *Montaillou, the Promised Land of Error* (New York: Vintage Books, 1979).

34. See Furet, "L'histoire et 'l'homme sauvage,'" p. 232.

35. On this historiographical mutation, see, in a perspective partially diverse from the one advanced here, Jacques Revel, "L'histoire au ras du sol," introduction to G. Levi, *Le pouvoir au village: Histoire d'un exorciste dans le Piémont du septième siècle,*

trans. Monique Aymard (Paris: Gallimard, 1989), pp. i–xxxiii, more fully developed in J. Revel, "Micro-analyse et reconstitution du social," in *Ministère de la Recherche de la Technologie: Colloque "Anthropologie contemporaine et anthropologie historique,"* no. 2, pp. 24–37; text prepared for the Marseilles colloquium, 24–26 September 1992.

36. For a recapitulation, see *La nouvelle histoire,* ed. Jacques Le Goff, Roger Chartier, and Jacques Revel (Paris: Retz, 1978). See also the introductory essay by Peter Burke to *New Perspectives on Historical Writing,* pp. 1–23.

37. See Georges Duby, *Le dimanche de Bouvines, 27 juillet 1214* (Paris: Gallimard, 1985), pp. 7–8 (1st ed., 1973): "L'histoire ... qu'on devait dire, plus tard et abusivement, 'nouvelle' (je dis abusivement, car la plupart des interrogations que nous fûmes si fiers de forger, nos prédécesseurs, avant que ne s'appesantisse la chape du positivisme, les avaient formulées dans le second tiers du XIXe siècle)." See, in this regard, the extremely instructive book by Charles Rearick, *Beyond Enlightenment: Historians and Folklore in Nineteenth-Century France* (Bloomington: Indiana University Press, 1974).

38. See J. Le Goff, *Les mentalités: Une histoire ambigüe,* in J. Le Goff and P. Nora, eds., *Faire l'histoire,* 3 vols. (Paris: Gallimard, 1974), 3:76–94.

39. P. Ariès, "L'histoire des mentalités," in Le Goff, Chartier, and Revel, *La nouvelle histoire,* p. 411.

40. P. Ariès and Michel Winock, *Un historien du dimanche* (Paris: Seuil, 1980).

41. Alf Lüdtke, ed., *Alltagsgeschichte: Zur Rekonstruktion historischer Erfahrungen und Lebensweisen* (Frankfurt a. M.: Campus Verlag, 1989); Geoff Eley, "Labor History, Social History, Alltagsgeschichte: Experience, Culture, and the Politics of the Everyday—A New Direction for German Social History?" *Journal of Modern History,* 61 (1989): 297–343.

42. Furet, "L'histoire et 'l'homme sauvage,'" p. 230: 'Il n'ya rien d'étonnant à ce que, en même temps qu'elle [la grande histoire du XIX siècle] cherche désespérément à sauver son impérialisme comme porteuse de la 'modernisation,' elle retourne à l'ethnologie comme consciente de ses échecs."

43. Ibid., p. 233.

44. Ibid., p. 232.

45. I discussed this theme in my "Clues: Roots of an Evidential Paradigm," in *Clues, Myths, and the Historical Method,* trans. John Tedeschi and Anne C. Tedeschi (1979) (Baltimore: Johns Hopkins University Press, 1989), pp. 96–125.

46. Now available in English: *The Night Battles: Witchcraft and Agrarian Cults in the Sixteenth and Seventeenth Centuries,* trans. John Tedeschi and Anne Tedeschi (Baltimore: Johns Hopkins University Press, 1983), and *Ecstasies: Deciphering the Witches' Sabbath,* trans. Raymond Rosenthal (New York: Pantheon, 1991).

47. Now available in English: *The Cheese and the Worms: The Cosmos of a Sixteenth-Century Miller,* trans. John Tedeschi and Anne Tedeschi (Baltimore: Johns Hopkins University Press, 1980), p. xx. In the introduction to *The Night Battles* I had

already stressed, against the undifferentiated notion of "collective mentality," the importance of the development of specific beliefs on the part of single individuals.

48. See M. Vovelle, "Histoire sérielle ou 'case studies': vrai ou faux dilemme en histoire des mentalités," in *Histoire sociale, sensibilités collectives et mentalités. Mélanges Robert Mandrou* (Paris: Presses Universitaires de France, 1985), pp. 39–49.

49. R. Chartier, "Intellectual History or Sociocultural History? The French Trajectories," in Dominick La Capra and Steven L. Kaplan, eds., *Modern European Intellectual History: Reappraisals and New Perspectives* (Ithaca, NY: Cornell University Press, 1982), p. 32; the emphasis is mine.

50. Furet, "L'histoire et 'l'homme sauvage,'" p. 231.

51. This unstated identification is implied even in the famous essay by Lawrence Stone, "The Revival of Narrative: Reflections on a New History," *Past and Present* 85 (1979): 3–24; this did not advance the subsequent discussion.

52. Here I elaborate some observations formulated in my review of J. Le Goff, *Pour un autre Moyen Age*, in *Critique*, no. 395 (1980): 345–354.

53. Richard Cobb contemporaneously had become aware of the methodological implications of the *Exercices de style*: "apart from its brilliance both as parody and as conversation totally recaptured, [it] might also be described as an essay on the relative value and interpretation of conflicting or overlapping historical evidence" (*Raymond Queneau*, p. 7).

54. I am speaking of lacunae in a relative, not absolute, sense (historical evidence is always lacunar by definition). But new research questions create new lacunae.

55. On the silences of Menocchio, see *The Cheese and the Worms*, pp. 110–112. These concluding words allude to my "The Inquisitor as Anthropologist" in my *Clues, Myths and the Historical Method*, pp. 156–164, 220–221. The connection between "échelle d'analyse" and "écriture de l'histoire," identified as "questions majeures," is grasped with great perspicacity in the anonymous editorial "Histoire et sciences sociales: Un tournant critique?" *Annales: E.S.C.* 43 (1988): 292–293.

56. See Isaiah Berlin, "The Hedgehog and the Fox: An Essay on Tolstoy's View of History," (1953), in Henry Hardy and Aileen Kelly, eds., *Russian Thinkers* (London: Hogarth Press, 1978), pp. 22–81.

57. Tolstoy was perfectly aware of his indebtedness. See *Paul Boyer (1864–1949) chez Tolstoï: Entretiens à Iasnaïa Poliana* (Paris: Institut d'Études Slaves, 1950) (quoted also in Berlin, "The Hedgehog and the Fox," p. 56). Cf. Nicola Chiaromonte, *Credere o non credere* (Bologna: Il Mulino, 1993). I am grateful to Claudio Fogu for the reference.

58. Duby, *Le dimanche de Bouvines*.

59. Otto Benesch, *Der Maler Albrecht Altdorfer* (Vienna: Scholl, 1939): "Makrokosmos und Mikrokosmos werden eins" (p. 31). I realize that I had already broached this theme in speaking of a Brueghel landscape (*Dark Day*) and of the battle with which Roberto Rossellini's film *Paisà* concludes. See, respectively, my *Spurensicherungen: Über verborgene Geschichte, Kunst und soziales Gedächtnis*, trans. from the

Italian by Karl Friedrich Hauber (Berlin: Verlag Klaus Wagenbach, 1983), pp. 14–15; and "Di tutti i doni che porto a Kaisàre . . . Leggere il film scrivere la storia," *Storie e Storia* 5 (1983): 5–17. On the conclusion of *Paisà*, see also the anecdote reported by Federico Fellini, who had worked on the film as Rossellini's assistant director, in Fellini, *Comments on Films*, trans. Joseph Henry, ed. Giovanni Grazzini (1983) (Fresno: California State University Press, 1988), p. 66. On Altdorfer's *Battle between Alexander and Darius*, see also the essay, written from a point of view very different from the one sketched here, which opens Reinhart Koselleck's *Vergangene Zukunft: Zur Semantik geschichtlicher Zeiten* (Frankfurt a. M.: Suhrkamp, 1979).

60. Paul Oskar Kristeller, foreword, in Siegfried Kracauer, *History: The Last Things before the Last* (1969) (Princeton, NJ: Markus Wiener Publishers, 1995), p. xiv; emphasis added. See esp. chap. 5, "The Structure of the Historical Universe," pp. 104–138, which Kracauer left unfinished.

61. Ibid., p. 134.

62. In fact, they have not had much of an echo generally; but see the penetrating analysis by Martin Jay, who demonstrates convincingly that "in many ways, *History* is one of Kracauer's most compelling and original works, which deserves to be 're-deemed,' if one may borrow his own word, from an unmerited oblivion" ("The Extraterritorial Life of Siegfried Kracauer," *Salmagundi*, nos. 31–32 [1975–1976]: 87).

63. Jay, "The Extraterritorial Life," p. 62, on *Minima moralia*; p. 63, on Kracauer's diffidence toward the category of "totality"; and p. 50, on the connection, in Kracauer's thought, between "wholeness and death." See also, Jay, "Adorno and Kracauer: Notes on a Troubled Friendship," *Salmagundi*, no. 40 (Winter 1978): 42–66; and *Marxism and Totality: The Adventures of a Concept from Lukács to Habermas* (Berkeley and Los Angeles: University of California Press, 1984), pp. 245–246, passim. The young Adorno read Kant under Kracauer's guidance; see Remo Bodei, introduction, in Theodor W. Adorno, *Il gergo dell'autenticità [Jargon der Eigentlichkeit: Zur deutschen Ideologie]* (Turin: Bollati Boringhieri, 1989), p. vii. I have acknowledged my debt to *Minima moralia* in the introduction to *Clues, Myths, and the Historical Method*, p. ix. In the final page of *Dialettica negativa* (as Hans Medick has brought to my attention), Adorno ascribes a decisive function to "the micrological view."

64. Viktor Shlovskii [Sklovskij], *Materiali e leggi di trasformazione stilistica: Saggio su 'Guerra e Pace,'* trans. Monica Guerrini (Parma: Pratiche, 1978).

65. R. Serra, *Scritti letterari, morali e politici*, ed. Mario Isnenghi (Turin: Einaudi, 1974), pp. 278–288. Here I am returning to ideas I expressed in "Just One Witness" (chap. 12 in this volume).

66. R. Serra, *Epistolario*, ed. Luigi Ambrosini, Giuseppe De Robertis, and Alfredo Grilli (Florence: Le Monnier, 1934), pp. 453–454.

67. B. Croce, *History: Its Theory and Practice*, trans. Douglas Ainslie (1915) (New York: Russell & Russell, 1960), p. 55.

68. Serra, letter to Croce, 11 Nov. 1912, *Epistolario di Renato Serra*, p. 459. Serra's differences with Croce have been noted in Eugenio Garin, "Serra e Croce," in *Scritti*

in onore di Renato Serra: Per il cinquantenario della morte (Florence: Le Monnier, 1974), pp. 85–88.

69. Serra, *Scritti letterari,* pp. 286–287.

70. See chap. 4, "Proofs and Possibilities."

71. Calvino's piece, first published in the newspaper *Corriere della Sera* on 25 April 1974 (anniversary of the Liberation), can now be read in the collection *La strada di San Giovanni* (Milan: Mondadori, 1991), pp. 75–85 (trans. Tim Parks as *The Road to San Giovanni* [New York: Pantheon Books, 1993]). The printing of Isenghi's Einaudi edition was completed on 16 Feb. 1974.

72. F. R. Ankersmit, "Historiography and Postmodernism," *History and Theory* 28 (1989): 137–153 (esp. pp. 143, 149–150). See also the response in Perez Zagorin, "Historiography and Postmodernism: Reconsiderations," ibid. 29 (1990): 263–274; and Ankersmit's further rejoinder, "Reply to Professor Zagorin," pp. 275–296, where we read this characteristic statement (apropos such constructionist theoreticians of historiography as M. Oakeshott, L. Goldstein, and M. Stanford): "The past as the complex referent of the historical text as a whole has no role to play in historical debate. From the point of view of historical practice this referential past is epistemically a useless notion. . . . Texts are all we have and we can only compare texts with texts" (p. 281).

73. Namier is thought to have said: "Toynbee, I study the individual leaves, you the tree. The rest of the historians study the clusters of branches, and we both think *they* are wrong" (quoted in Kracauer, *History,* p. 110). But see also the passage in Tolstoy's diary quoted in Isaiah Berlin, "The Hedgehog and the Fox," p. 30. For a precocious formulation of Namier's program to study "individual leaves" (members of the House of Commons), see his "The Biography of Ordinary Men" (1928), in *Skyscrapers and Other Essays* (London: Macmillan, 1931), pp. 44–53.

74. By Levi, see "I pericoli del geertzismo," *Quaderni Storici* 58 (1985): 269–277; and "On Microhistory." See also, in the present volume, "Proofs and Possibilities" (chap. 4); "Description and Citation" (chap. 1); "Just One Witness" (chap. 12). See also my "Checking the Evidence: The Judge and the Historian," *Critical Inquiry* 18 (1991): 79–92; as well as "The Inquisitor as Anthropologist" (cited in full at n. 55).

75. Peter Burke emphasizes the cultural relativism of the "new history" in his introduction to *New Perspectives on Historical Writing,* pp. 3–4.

76. See, respectively, Ginzburg, *Indagini su Piero: Il Battesimo, il ciclo di Arezzo, la Flagellazione* (Turin: Einaudi, 1981; new ed., 1994) (trans. Martin Ryle and Kate Soper as *The Enigma of Piero della Francesca: The Baptism, the Arezzo Cycle, the Flagellation* [London: Verso, 1985]); Pietro Redondi, *Galileo eretico* (Turin: Einaudi, 1983) (trans. Raymond Rosenthal as *Galileo Heretic* [Princeton, NJ: Princeton University Press, 1987]); Franco Ramella, *Terra e telai: Sistemi di parentela e manifattura nel Biellese dell'Ottocento* (Turin: Einaudi, 1984); and Osvaldo Raggio, *Faide e parentele: Lo stato genovese visto dalla Fontanabuona* (Turin: Einaudi, 1990). Alberto M. Banti ("Storie e microstorie: l'histoire sociale contemporaine en Italie [1972–1989]," *Genèses* 3 [March 1991]: 134–147: 145) emphasizes the presence in Italian microhistory of two

tendencies, centered respectively on the analysis of social structure and of cultural implications. Banti assigns to my essay "Clues" some of the responsibility for the ultimate failure of the microhistorical paradigm (the true one, the first of the two just mentioned).

77. Grendi, "Micro-analisi e storia sociale," p. 512.

78. The subtitles of the two books are, respectively, *Carriera di un esorcista nel Piemonte del Seicento* and *Naissance d'un langage corporatif (Turin 17e–18e siècles)*. Some of the intellectual and political implications of this research could be clarified by a parallel reading of *Riprendere tempo*, the dialogue—it, too, published in 1982 in the series Microstorie, between Vittorio Foa and Pietro Marcenaro. The two are not historians, contrary to what Edward Muir states in the introduction to *Microhistory and the Lost Peoples of Europe* (Baltimore: Johns Hopkins University Press, 1991), p. xxii n7, even though Foa, politician and trade unionist, is also the author of a book of history: *La Gerusalemme rimandata: Domande di oggi agli inglesi del primo Novecento* (Turin: Rosenberg & Sellier, 1985); Pietro Marcenaro, after having worked as a laborer for a time, is once again a trade unionist.

79. Cf. Revel, "L'histoire au ras du sol," p. xxxii, and "Micro-analyse et reconstitution du social," pp. 34–35.

80. Martin Jay has underlined this difficulty, citing Kracauer, "Of Plots, Witnesses and Judgments," in S. Friedlander, ed., *Probing the Limits of Representation* (Cambridge, MA: Harvard University Press, 1992), p. 103. Gwyn Prins has called the "small scale" a "trap," observing, "It is not there that the propulsive forces of historians' explanatory theories can be found" ("Oral History," in P. Burke, ed., *New Perspectives in Historical Writing*, p. 134).

81. Levi, "On Microhistory," p. 111. It would be useful to have the version of the other scholars involved in this enterprise, starting with Edoardo Grendi (but see now "Ripensare la microstoria?" *Quaderni storici*, n.s., vol. 86 [1994]: 539–549).

CHAPTER 15. WITCHES AND SHAMANS

This is a revised version of a lecture read in Tokyo in 1992 on the occasion of the Japanese translation of a *Storia Notturna: Una decifrazione del sabba* (1989).

1. The source for the quip is Georges Dumézil; see Jacques Bonnet, ed., *Georges Dumézil* (Paris: Éditions Pandora, 1981), p. 25.

2. Bruno Latour and Steve Woolgar, *Laboratory Life: The Social Construction of Scientific Facts*, introd. by Jonas Salk (Princeton, NJ: Princeton University Press, 1986).

3. Natalia Ginzburg, "Inverno in Abruzzo" (1944), in *Le piccole virtù* (Turin: Einaudi, 1962), p. 18.

4. *Storia notturna: Una decifrazione del sabba* (Turin: Einaudi, 1989); trans. Raymond Rosenthali as *Ecstasies: Deciphering the Witches' Sabbath* (New York: Pantheon, 1991).

5. Franco Venturi, *Il populismo russo* (Turin: Einaudi, 1952), 2:1163.

6. C. Levi, "Ricordo di Leone Ginzburg," in *Le tracce della memoria,* ed. Maria Pagliara (Rome: Donzelli, 2002), pp. 101–103.

7. Keith Thomas, "The Relevance of Social Anthropology to the Historical Study of Witchcraft," in Mary Douglas, ed., *Witchcraft Confessions and Accusations* (London: Tavistock, 1970), p. 47.

8. The situation changed somewhat in the decades that followed.

9. The friend was Paolo Fossati.

10. Eric J. Hobsbawm, *Primitive Rebels: Studies in the Archaic Forms of Social Movement in the Nineteenth and Twentieth Centuries* (Manchester, UK: University Press, 1959); idem, "Per lo studio delle classi subalterne," *Società* 16 (1960): 436–449 (I allude to this essay in *The Cheese and the Worms,* trans. John Tedeschi and Anne Tedeschi [Baltimore: Johns Hopkins University Press, 1980], p. 130).

11. "Witchcraft and Popular Piety: Notes on a Modenese Trial of 1519" (1961), in my *Clues, Myths and the Historical Method,* trans. John Tedeschi and Anne C. Tedeschi (Baltimore: Johns Hopkins University Press, 1989), pp. 1–16, 165–170.

12. Morton Smith, *The Secret Gospel: The Discovery and Interpretation of the Secret Gospel According to Mark* (New York: Harper & Row, 1973), p. 96. Through a lapse, I failed to make the attribution for these words in C. Ginzburg and Adriano Prosperi, *Giochi di pazienza: Un seminario sul "Beneficio di Cristo"* (Turin: Einaudi, 1975), p. 183.

13. "Witchcraft and Popular Piety," p. 16.

14. See Roman Jakobson, *Autoritratto di un linguista,* trans. G. Banti and B. Bruno (Bologna: Il Mulino, 1987), p. 138 (translation of Jakobson's *Retrospects* [not seen]), who cites L. V. Scerba, although the reference should be to Nietzsche, preface to *Aurora.*

15. See the preface to *I benandanti: Ricerche sulla stregoneria e sui culti agrari tra Cinquecento e Seicento* (Turin: Einaudi, 1966). I quote from the English version, *The Night Battles: Witchcraft and Agrarian Cults in the Sixteenth and Seventeenth Centuries,* trans. John Tedeschi and Anne Tedeschi (Baltimore: Johns Hopkins University Press, 1983), p. xvii. I presented the anomaly in these terms ". . . the voices of these peasants reach us directly, without barriers, not by way, as usually happens, of fragmentary and indirect testimony, filtered through a different and inevitably distorting mentality." Recently, this observation was dispatched as ingenuous (Franco Nardon, *Benandanti e inquisitori nel Friuli del Seicento* [Trieste: Edizioni Università di Trieste; Montereale Valcellina: Centro Studi Storici Menocchio, 1999], pp. 36, 106; see also the preface by Andrea Del Col, p. 6). But the person who quoted this sentence to criticize it forgot to cite what immediately followed: "Such a statement may seem paradoxical, and this leads to the specific interest of the research." Between "the image underlying the interrogations of the judges and the actual testimony of the accused," there was, I explained, a "discrepancy," a "gap" which "permits us to reach a genuinely popular stratum of beliefs which was later deformed and then expunged by the superimposition of the schema of the educated classes" (*The Night Battles,* p. xviii).

16. For a striking example, see Keith Thomas, *Religion and the Decline of Magic* (New York: Charles Scribner's Sons, 1971), pp. 163–165; and the pungent comment in E. P. Thompson, "Anthropology and the Discipline of Historical Context," *Midland History* 3 (1972): 41–45.

17. Adriano Sofri, "Il segreto di Natalia," *L'Unità* (16 November 1992). Cf. *Storia notturna*, p. xxxvii; *Ecstasies*, p. 22.

18. C. Ginzburg, "Momigliano e De Martino," *Rivista Storica Italiana* 100 (1988): 400–413.

INDEX

Notes have not been indexed.

Romieu, Auguste, 154; *Le spectre rouge de 1852*, 154
Rostovzeff, Michael I., 69
Rostow, W. W., 199
Russia: Catherine of, 121; empire, 92; explorers from, 91; folklore, 65; formalists, 83–84; October revolution, 159; populism, 217; *Protocols of the Elders of Zion*, 5–6, 151, 159–64; Siberian shamans, 91–92, 94
"rustic style," 40–42, 43

Sade, Marquis de, *Français, encore un effort si vous voulez être républicains*, 112
Saint-Denis, convent, 166, 167
Sainte-Beuve, Charles-Augustin, 139
St. Peter dome, 117
saints: cult of martyrs' relics, 30; history of cult of, 30; stereotype, 32. *See also* Ambrose; Augustine; Jerome; John Chrysostom; Philip Neri; Stephen
Saint-Simon, 4; *Mémoires*, 3, 183–84
St. Stephen relics, 25–31; *De revelatione corporis sancti Stephani*, 29, 30; *Liber de miraculis sancti Stephani protomartyris*, 28, 29
Salius brothers, 81
Salomon, Bernard "le petit Salomon," 36, 37*fig*
Salter, Samuel, 123
Salvagnoli, Vincenzo, 141
Sanguinetti's "archhistory," 214
San José de Gracia, 194–95
Sanudo, Marin, *Vite dei dogi*, 132–33
Sarasin, Jean-François, 72–73, 75
Satyre Ménippée, 152
Saulnier, V.-L., 115
Savonarola, Christianity of, 14
Saxer, Victor, 30
Saxo Grammaticus, 76
Scaliger, Julius Caesar, 22
Scarpa, Domenico, 213, 214; *Le poesie e prose scelte*, 214
Schatzmiller, Joseph, 165
Scheffer, John, 92
Schilling, Georg, 187
Schmitt, Carl, 158
science: microhistory and, 214; scientific character of historiography, 65
Scythians: Anacharsis, 117, 118, 124–25; du Creux and, 89; Herodotus on, 65, 88, 93, 94, 124; Maximus of Tyre on, 90, 93;

Meuli on, 94; Potocki on, 94; shamanistic beliefs and practices diffused from Asia to Europe, 225–26; Voltaire on, 120
"searchlight device," 97, 101
Seguí Vidal, Gabriel, 27, 28
Seneca, 38
serial history, 200, 202, 203
Serlio, Sebastiano: Fontainebleau buildings, 42; *Libro di architettura*, 41; *Libro estraordinario*, 41–42, 43, 44*fig*
Serra, Renato, 177–78; "Partenza di un gruppo di soldati per la Libia," 177, 209–10
Severus of Minorca, Bishop, letter, 5, 26–28, 29, 32
Sextus Empiricus, 15, 16, 76, 77; *Adversus mathematicos*, 13–14, 76–77; grammarians, 76–77, 80; *Outlines of Pyrrhonism*, 14, 76
Shakespeare, William, 149; *Macbeth*, 131
shamans, 83, 90–95, 215, 224–25
Shaw, M. R. B., 144
shields of Achilles, *Iliad*, 11
Siberia, shamans, 91–92, 94
Sigonio, Carlo, 16
Silius Italicus, 77
Simmel, Georg, 208
Simon, Marcel, 30–31
Simonde de Sismondi, J. C. L., 117
Simonides, 11
Situationists, 163
skepticism, 7, 13, 14, 176–78; ancient, 76; antipositivist, 3–4; euphoric, 211; Greek, 13; positivist, 3; postmodern, 2–3, 212; unsustainable position, 5; White and, 176, 211
Sklovskij, Viktor, 83–84, 99, 101
slave trade, Voltaire and, 103, 108–9
Smith, Morton, 220
smoking, 84–90, 92–93
social customs, Voltaire on, 99
Socialists, Serra essay vs., 177
social movements ('60s), 127
Società journal, 220
sociology, 65, 180
Sofri, Adriano, 96, 113, 226
Solinus, *Polyhistor*, 88, 89, 90, 93
Spanish travelers, 38
Speroni, Sperone, 21; *Dialogo della Istoria*, 17, 18, 19–20; *Dialogo delle lingue*, 18–19; *Dialogo secondo Virgilio*, 17

TEXT
10.5/14 Jenson

DISPLAY
Jenson Pro, Benton Gothic Regular and Light

COMPOSITOR
Westchester Book Group

INDEXER
Barbara Roos

PRINTER AND BINDER
Thomson-Shore, Inc.